PATHS FOR CUBA

PITT LATIN AMERICAN SERIES
JOHN CHARLES CHASTEEN AND
CATHERINE M. CONAGHAN
EDITORS

PATHS· FOR— CUBA—

REFORMING COMMUNISM IN COMPARATIVE PERSPECTIVE

EDITED BY
SCOTT MORGENSTERN,
JORGE PÉREZ-LÓPEZ,
AND JEROME BRANCHE

UNIVERSITY OF PITTSBURGH PRESS

We dedicate this book to our colleague and co-author, Kevin Morrison, whose path ended too soon. He taught us not only through his scholarship, but also through his courage and humanity.

Published by the University of Pittsburgh Press, Pittsburgh, Pa., 15260
Copyright © 2018, University of Pittsburgh Press
Manufactured in the United States of America
Printed on acid-free paper
10 9 8 7 6 5 4 3 2 1

Cataloging-in-Publication data is available from the Library of Congress

ISBN 13: 978-0-8229-6549-7
ISBN 10: 0-8229-6549-6

Cover art: *Havana building restored and old*. Leah Simpson / Alamy Stock Photo
Cover design: Joel W. Coggins

CONTENTS

INTRODUCTION: Reforming Communism in Comparative Perspective
Jorge Pérez-López and Scott Morgenstern, with Jerome Branche   1

PART 1: ECONOMICS

1. **Models of Economic Reform and Cuba's "Updating" of Its Model**
   Scott Morgenstern and Jorge Pérez-López,
   with Carlos Alzugaray and Kevin Morrison   41

2. **Initial Conditions and Economic Development: The East Asian "Tigers" and Cuba**
   James W. McGuire   55

3. **Foreign Investment and Economic Growth in Cuba: Lessons from China**
   Jorge Pérez-López and Yu Xiao   85

4. **Resolving U.S. Property Expropriation Claims against Cuba**
   Matías F. Travieso-Díaz   117

PART 2: POLICY AND POLITICS

5. **Socialist Social Contracts and Accountability**
   Martin K. Dimitrov   135

6. **The Cuban Communist Party at the Cusp of Change**
   Larry Catá Backer   157

7. **The Prospects for Cuban Democracy in the Post-Transition Era**
   Aníbal Pérez-Liñán and Scott Mainwaring   192

8. **Cuban Social Security Reforms Compared with Latin America, China, and Vietnam**
   Carmelo Mesa-Lago   211

9. The Future of the Cuban Social Protection: Analysis from the Latin American Window
   Javier Vázquez-D'Elía   **244**

10. After the Fall: Postcommunist Dynamics in Central and Eastern Europe and Their Implications for Cuba
    Ronald H. Linden   **271**

PART 3: CITIZENS AND SOCIETY

11. The Living Lie and the Living Eye: Cuba's Reforms and the Racial Contract
    Alan West-Durán   **299**

12. From Domestic to Statist Violence: Debate and Representation in the Cuban Cultural Field
    Ana Belén Martín Sevillano   **321**

13. Somos Mucho Más (We Are Much More): An Analysis of Cuban Hip-Hop Artivism and Arts-Based Public Spheres
    Tanya Saunders   **342**

CONCLUSION: Comparative Lessons for Understanding Cuba's Path: Politics, Economics, and Society
Scott Morgenstern and Ronald H. Linden   **368**

Contributors   **385**

Index   **391**

PATHS FOR CUBA

JORGE PÉREZ-LÓPEZ AND SCOTT MORGENSTERN,
WITH JEROME BRANCHE

INTRODUCTION

REFORMING COMMUNISM IN COMPARATIVE PERSPECTIVE

Although Cuban officials avoid the word "reform," Cuba has been "updating" or "modernizing" its socioeconomic development model or on the brink of making significant changes for several decades. Cuba is a country of contrasts and contradictions that feed internal and external conflicts. The surprising December 17, 2014, announcement by President Barack Obama and President Raúl Castro about a new direction for U.S.–Cuban relations, followed by the formal reestablishment of diplomatic relations on July 1, 2015, and the reciprocal reopening of embassies in Washington and Havana in July and August 2015, respectively, confirmed Cuba's ongoing updating process. Recent political changes in the United States, however, have put into question the future of the direction of the bilateral relations and exposed, again, how dependent Cuban politics are on its giant neighbor. We will also set out in this volume how Cuban economic policies have been dependent on their benefactors; support by the Soviet Union and Venezuela sustained Cuba for many decades, and their respective decay (in the late 1980s and the 2010s) forced Cuba to consider changes. As we complete this manuscript, over a year since the Trump administration took office, and just as Raúl Castro stepped down from his presidential post, it is far from clear whether the momentum towards reform initiated around 2010 will continue, stall, or reverse. This suggests, overall, that reform is fragile and dependent on both domestic and international actors and contexts.

At roughly the time that Fidel Castro passed the presidential torch to his brother Raúl (2006), Venezuela's support of Cuba waned, and the island initiated a tentative yet important set of changes. Today Cubans can open small businesses, travel abroad, more easily access the internet, and purchase cell phones, microwave ovens, (prohibitively expensive) new cars, and even homes. Important steps aimed at influencing the external environment by attracting foreign investment were the creation of the Mariel Special Development Zone (ZED Mariel) in November 2013 and the approval of a new foreign investment law in March 2014, offering protections and incentives to foreign capital to participate in updating the Cuban economic model. The evolving relationship with the United States could accelerate many of these trends, in part by bringing more Americans and more American goods into Cuba. Of course these changes in economics and international relations also influence society, moving the needle on social issues such race, youth, and gender, which in turn is reflected in the arts.

Shortly before the historic December 2014 coordinated statements by Presidents Obama and Castro announcing the intention of the United States and Cuba to work toward normalization of relations, many of the authors in this book met at the University of Pittsburgh at a conference to examine Cuba's internal reforms and their external influences within a comparative framework. The goal of the conference was to draw on experiences from different parts of the world to explore Cuba's reform process and potential directions and challenges for future changes. This volume is the result of our discussions, supplemented with contributions from other scholars who were not in attendance but whose work spoke to issues that were relevant to the project.

Our goal in this volume is to move beyond studies that focus on a single reform theme, such as economic development. We have instead considered potential reforms in multiple issue areas, which we have grouped under the themes of economics, politics, and society. In so doing, we have crossed traditional lines, by including both social scientists and scholars from the humanities in order to consider reforms from diverse academic perspectives. While this has sacrificed some unity in methodology—some chapters use the comparative framework less explicitly than others—there are substantial gains from providing broader perspectives.

The overall goal of the book is to discuss and analyze concerns about reform in Cuba, and where possible to draw lessons from a comparative context. To be most useful, the comparisons require a detailed description of the Cuban case itself. This chapter, therefore, focuses specifically on Cuba, providing a general outline of the historical and ongoing—though generally hesitant—reforms on the island. Using a comparative framework, a thesis for this book is that reforms in Cuba and elsewhere take a nonlinear path without a predetermined end, because the directions are contingent on changing factors such as the international climate and relations, economic exigencies, social structures, historical precedent, and political maneuvering. At the end of this chapter we summarize the book's comparative chapters, which show the variety of winding paths and highlight the lack of a teleological result of reforms around the world. With an eye on how the countries analyzed relate to Cuba, the comparative chapters also examine the factors that have led the different countries along their particular circuitous (and not always successful) paths with respect to reform within the areas of economics, politics, and society. The comparative context is particularly important for the first two of these areas, where the authors address issues such as the efficacy and effectiveness of social security policy, investment policies, and the sustainability of democracy. The goal of these chapters is to offer lessons for reform both generally and for Cuba, and to outline potential directions based on policy options and sources of pressure on the system. The other chapters look inward, considering how Cuba's society must face challenges in terms of race and domestic violence.

CONTRADICTIONS AND THE NEED FOR REFORM

In spite of being an island nation of just 11 million people, Cuba has had a big-nation foreign policy impact. The Cuban model has been an inspiration—from both positive and negative perspectives—for social movements, political leaders, and cultural expressionists around the world. Leftist groups have drawn hope from Cuba's advances in public health and education, as well as the country's ability to survive in the face of U.S. animosity. Opponents of the regime, meanwhile, point to violations of human, civil, and political rights, as well as the stagnation of the economy and decay of infrastructure. The highly visible and eccentric transportation system provides a microcosmic view of the inconsistencies that abound in the island. Alongside luxury tourism buses and modern airports are the ubiquitous U.S. cars from the 1950s and Soviet Ladas from the 1980s, as well as nineteenth-century horse-drawn wagons, especially outside Havana.

There are many other contradictions. While many people live in buildings that are crumbling around them, and it is not uncommon for multigenerational families to live under the same roof because of the severe housing shortage and deterioration of the housing stock from lack of maintenance, those same inhabitants typically do not pay rent as they own their dwellings and also enjoy free universal health care and education. With the emergence of agricultural markets selling produce in convertible currency, citizens with access to such currency can obtain foodstuffs to supplement goods available through the rationing system. Personal hygiene items such as soap, toothpaste, toilet paper, and cleaning supplies are today much more available than they were just a few years ago, but are very costly, as attaining them usually requires convertible currency.

Another oddity in the economy is the growing private sector, financed and usually operated by international firms. These companies, many of which operate in the tourist sector, generate hard currency for the government, but the government continues to severely restrict private employment contracts. Further, the companies operate in spite of outstanding conflicts over the Cuban regime's nationalization of land and businesses after the revolution. Travieso-Díaz (chapter 4) discusses potential directions for resolving these disputes. Pérez-López and Xiao (chapter 3) point out that Cuba's needs are vast and "resources assigned to investment over the last decade [have] been abysmally low and insufficient to generate vigorous economic growth."

Cuba's policies of universal education and health care for its citizens are widely recognized as significant achievements. Cuba's literacy rates are among the highest in Latin America and the Caribbean, approaching 100 percent. Similarly, school life achievement (measured by the number of years of schooling, from primary to tertiary, that a child is expected to receive) is also very high, reflecting Cuba's compulsory education at the primary and secondary levels and generalized free education at all levels. Despite large cadres of teachers trained by Cuban higher education institutions and a falling enrollment—for demographic reasons—Cuba has recently faced difficulties in staffing schools because of the decision by many teaching professionals to abandon the field and enter more remunerative employment in low-skill tourism and other occupations that pay in convertible currency. To fill the teacher gap and properly staff schools, Cuba has resorted to offering financial incentives to retired teachers to induce them to return to the classroom.

Cuba's robust public health care system, emphasizing preventive care through the deployment of public health personnel at the neighborhood level (the so-called médico de familia program) and aggressive vaccinations, has virtually eliminated communicable diseases. The main causes of death for Cubans today are similar to those that kill citizens in developed countries: noncommunicable diseases such as cardiovascular diseases, cancer, and chronic lung diseases. Cuba also has one of the lowest infant mortality rates in the world and one of the highest doctor-to-patient ratios. With over a dozen medical schools, including the Escuela Latinoamericana de Medicina (ELAM), which trains students from many countries (including the United States), Cuba annually turns out a prodigious number of medical school graduates. Moreover, Cuba has made inroads in the area of biotechnology and developed some medications with potential for breaking into international markets. Yet the overall public health system has been deteriorating, with shortages of basic medicines and medical supplies. Moreover, there is a palpable shortage of doctors in many of Cuba's medical institutions, as a high share of medical graduates are performing services abroad on behalf of the Cuban government and others have chosen to leave the island to practice their career elsewhere.

Another area of contradiction is race relations. The revolution intended to end racism, but while blacks attend the same schools as whites, get the same medical attention, and lead important institutions, economic conditions are clearly affected by race. Within cities, blacks continue to be overrepresented in poor neighborhoods and whites in wealthier ones. This is in part attributable to heritage issues, as prior to the revolution whites lived in the wealthier neighborhoods and these dwellings have been passed on to their heirs. While there is no reliable information on this, consumption levels of black households are believed to be lower than those of white households given the importance of remittances, which are tied to historical emigration; fewer blacks in Cuba have relatives living abroad who can remit to those in the island.

The situation with regard to women has certain parallels with that of blacks. Early on, Cuba's leaders pledged to eliminate all forms of discrimination against women; to oversee the dismantling of such discrimination, in 1960 Cuba established the Federación de Mujeres Cubanas (FMC) under the leadership of a very visible leader, Raúl Castro's wife, Vilma Espín. The laudable objectives of the FMC included incorporating women into the labor force, providing equal opportunities for women in education, careers, and jobs, and attracting women into political activities and government administration. Cuba has been quite successful in eradicating discrimination in education, with women enrolling in higher education at rates equal to or higher than men, but less so in other areas, such as participation at the highest levels of government administration. While women's share of seats in the National Assembly and in provincial and local assemblies has been rising, the top echelon of the Cuban government is still controlled by (white) men. To some extent this reflects the prominent role that the generation of históricos have played in leadership positions, but it does not seem that women are well represented in the generations that will take over once the earlier generation departs.

Cuba has two domestic currencies, the Cuban or "national" peso (CUP) and the "convertible" peso (CUC). The Cuban peso can be converted to convertible pesos at the rate of 26 CUP = 1 CUC. Cuban citizens who work for the state and state pensioners, among others, are paid in CUP: the average monthly salary of employees of state and mixed enterprises in 2015 was 687 CUP (about $26.42, assuming parity between the CUC and the U.S. dollar), while the average monthly pension was roughly 270 pesos ($10.39) and the monthly social welfare payment about 199 pesos ($7.65). These income levels are grossly insufficient for Cubans to maintain a reasonable level of consumption, even if prices for the basket of goods available to all citizens through the rationing system (the *libreta de racionamiento*) are very low and denominated in CUP. Certain products, such as potatoes, peas, and cigarettes, have recently been removed from the rationing system; households have to acquire them in other markets where prices in Cuban pesos are higher or prices are denominated in CUC. Products such as cooking oil, fresh vegetables, and high-quality cuts of meat are available only for CUCs. The circulation of the two currencies gives rise to numerous oddities and distortions. For some goods, such as ice cream at Havana's iconic Coppelia ice cream shop, and services such as entrance fees to theaters and dance clubs, one price is charged in CUP for Cuban patrons and the same price in CUC for foreigners (e.g., 10 CUP for Cuban citizens and 10 CUC for tourists). The high purchasing power of CUCs makes them highly desirable and sends ordinary Cubans to chase tourists to get tips in CUC or to go into other lines of work that allow access to CUC.

The celebrated education and health systems are not without serious problems. A common refrain, especially during the economic emergency of the 1990s called the Special Period was "you can't eat education and health care." Today, citizens with a university education in philosophy, pedagogy, or even medicine drive cabs or work in the tourism sector, preferring to work in occupations outside their field of study to have access to hard currency. Although high priority has been placed on stimulating the agricultural sector and individuals can get some land from the state to operate a private farm, few want to become farmers, in part because that would mean very harsh labor conditions, including plowing fields with beasts of burden. Further, while the national health care system does provide preventive care, basic supplies such as aspirin are difficult to acquire.

Chapters in this volume by Mesa-Lago (8) and Vázquez-D'Elía (9) document the needs of the health and welfare systems in Cuba. In comparison with those in Eastern Europe and Latin America, the Cuban system has some strengths (namely coverage) but many weaknesses. Financial sustainability is questionable, especially as the population ages. To adjust, the Cuban government has increased the retirement age and reduced the tiny monthly stipends to levels that provide food for only seven to ten days. Dramatic cuts have also been made in health care; many rural hospitals have closed and the decline in care and availability of medicine has led to a noticeable worsening of health statistics (e.g., a sharp rise in infections in hospitals).

A final area where critics demand reform is in the area of democratic freedoms. The country has only one political party and leadership is tightly centralized and controlled. After the revolution Fidel Castro promised elections, but instead he consolidated power and used his control of the state to watch the citizenry rather than allowing the reverse. There have been few reforms in this area and the potential for successful transformation is dubious. Chapters by Dimitrov (5) Backer (6) Pérez-Liñán and Mainwaring (7) and Linden (10) make this point. Dimitrov, first, studies the odd inclusion of citizens' letters in *Granma,* the official organ of the Central Committee of the Partido Comunista de Cuba, that complain about government performance. This "proxy accountability" has some value especially with respect to local officials, but by implication there is need for more direct methods with greater scope and impact. Backer analyzes the Cuban Communist Party, which continues to monopolize the country's politics. Pérez-Liñán and Mainwaring show that for countries like Cuba that have had limited democratic experience there is also a low likelihood of building a sustainable democracy in the short term. In chapter 10, Linden casts doubt on the prospects for Cuba's democratic future by looking at Eastern Europe. Some countries have made the transition, but others, even with some favorable factors aiding their paths, have not. Cuba does exist within a "democratic neighborhood," but there are concerns about one particular neighbor, as well as internal and external leadership.

HAVE THE REFORMS STARTED AT LAST?

The newly opened Mariel port and the free trade zone, the new foreign investment law and the opening to the United States, all in the context of continuing poor economic performance and a fast-approaching (biological) end to the "historical" generation of leaders who fought Batista and have governed the country for more than five decades, are potential signs that the pressures have finally built to herald Cuba's long-expected age of reform. As Cuba engages in such a reform process, it will have as reference the paths followed by many other countries that have made full or partial political and/ or economic transitions: countries in Eastern Europe and Asia have moved away from socialism, while countries in Latin America have experimented with different reform models of the welfare state. They and other countries have many lessons to offer Cuba about reforms of socioeconomic and political institutions.

A great challenge for Cuba will be to examine these other experiences and apply the pertinent lessons in such a way that the country will be able to build on the positive aspects of its culture and system, avoiding some of the pitfalls that have befallen democratic and capitalist countries. Cuba might want to avoid duplicating the conditions that permitted the emergence of crony capitalists and oligarchs in the former socialist nations, who benefitted from bungled privatization processes and gained inordinately large economic and political clout, which acted as a brake on economic growth and development. Similarly, if the experiences of others in Latin America are examples, as Cuba rolls back controls and expands the freedoms of its citizens it will likely struggle to prevent international crime organizations and drug trafficking cartels from getting a foothold in the island. Today crime is lower and personal safety is much greater in Cuba than in nearly all of Latin America, and a great challenge for the future is to preserve those valuable traits.

Perhaps the question about reform for which there is most debate regards how Cuba will adapt its economic model. Vietnam, China, and the states of the former Soviet Union provide divergent examples of reforms of socialist systems that Cuba could follow, but chapter 1 of this volume (by Morgenstern and Pérez-López, based on contributions in the conference by Alzuguray and Morrison) calls attention to the idea that Cuba's history and culture will demand a unique path. Meanwhile, McGuire's chapter (2) uses the examples of South Korea and Taiwan to delve into the conditions for economic growth. An important finding of his research is that while Cuba has some traits necessary for growth, it also faces significant challenges.

In its more idealistic stages, the Cuban revolution tried to eliminate all elements of market mechanisms and to create a communist society and economy. During the ideological 1960s, the Cuban government nationalized essentially the entire productive sector of the economy, including manufacturing, commercial agriculture, wholesale commerce, and utilities. In 1968, as part of the so-called "Revolutionary Offensive," the Cuban state took over the retail trade sector, from cafeterias and fruit stands to beauty salons, and converted all owners and workers in these enterprises into state employees. In the early 1960s, Cuba abolished teaching of economics and accounting at universities, and Che Guevara went so far as to propose the eventual elimination of money in Cuba.

Despite efforts to exterminate market behavior, Cubans have displayed, and continue to display today, an innate commercial impulse. Goods obtained under the rationing system are regularly sold and bought between households. Black markets are also supplied with goods that are surreptitiously taken from workplaces by workers. Many individuals resell clothes and cell phones that they receive from relatives abroad or from international visitors. Still others charge tourists illegal fees for taxi rides or purchases. And they seek employment in jobs that will allow them to *"desviar"* (divert) state property for their own use and exchange. The opportunity to earn a few more pesos a month is highly attractive, and jobs that touch the tourist sector and can lead to tips in CUC, allowing workers to realize in a few days more than what their state job would pay in a month. Such incentives thus drain the professional ranks, as they act as a magnet for university graduates.

The emergence of a private sector in the island has been most evident since the issuance of the economic and social development guidelines adopted by the Sixth Congress of the Cuban Communist Party (Partido Comunista de Cuba, PCC) in April 2011. Among other actions, the guidelines dictated the reduction of state employment and elimination of some of the constraints on self-employment. Although self-employment had been authorized since the early 1990s (as will be discussed in more detail below, it was one of the emergency measures adopted to address the economic crisis of the 1990s, the so-called Special Period in Time of Peace), its growth had been choked by red tape and other restrictions. Many of the restrictions have now been lifted and certain retail enterprises formerly under state control (e.g., barbershops, cafeterias) have been turned over to their workers to be operated as cooperatives. These are indeed substantive steps, but limits remain on the types of private jobs that Cubans can pursue in private practice. Professionals are not allowed to practice their specializations: Cubans can become clowns or refillers of cigarette lighters in the private sector, but they cannot practice their professions as lawyers or doctors.

Looking externally, the government inaugurated in 2013 a high-tech port facility at Mariel, built by a Brazilian multinational construction company with financing from a Brazilian public institution. The Mariel megaport will be able to handle traffic by the very large container ships that will traverse the enlarged Panama Canal (and perhaps future Nicaraguan transoceanic canals, if they are built). Cuba sees Mariel becoming the premier logistical center in the Caribbean, receiving and redistributing cargoes throughout the region and to other continents. To try to capitalize on the business that the port is expected to generate, Cuba has also taken the step of creating a free trade zone in the area neighboring the port. Cuba anticipates that the combination of the container port and the free trade zone will attract foreign investors and create well-paying jobs for thousands of Cuban workers.

In the social area, there is also a debate about the past and recent reforms. How much have blacks advanced since the revolution? What is the role of women in the new Cuba? How much activism does the regime tolerate? The chapters by West-Durán (11), Martín Sevillano (12), and Saunders (13) speak to these questions. West-Durán's article highlights the state's timid or ignorant response to racial concerns. Martín Sevillano's chapter looks at the portrayal of domestic violence on state television, highlighting the state's recognition of the problem. At the same time, she does not portray the state actors (here the police) as resolving the problem. Saunders, finally, focuses on the mobilization and politicization of artists—"artivism"—on the island. The chapter discusses how the art activists "do not directly challenge the state, but [instead] impact on the state's monopoly on official revolutionary discourse." She also argues that the economic changes, especially during the Special Period, radicalized people and helped to awaken activist groups.

In discussing these reforms, it needs to be remembered that Cuba is a poor developing country, and its system is rife with tremendous social and economic problems and contradictions. One commentator at the conference even suggested that the level of development was so low and challenges were so great that Cuba would be "lucky to reach the level of development of Costa Rica within a generation." Others strongly disagreed, citing Cuba's rich tradition, which has produced many political and social achievements, and generated sufficient economic growth for the regime to survive for nearly sixty years. The challenges ahead and the optimism of the Cuban leadership about the future of its system are encapsulated in a Havana billboard: "New challenges, new victories."

CUBA'S FIRST PERIOD OF REFORM: 1959–1990

Cuba has been reforming or experimenting with its economic, social, and political system since the advent of its revolution in 1959. During its first years in power, the Castro regime adopted radical policies associated with state-run socialism. In nationalizing both domestic and foreign-owned companies, as well as taking control of private housing and agricultural land, the government embarked on a historic experiment. The experiment led to immediate roadblocks, some expected based on the theoretical problems

JORGE PÉREZ-LÓPEZ AND SCOTT MORGENSTERN, WITH JEROME BRANCHE of communist systems, and others arising from the practical application of domestic and international politics. The economic collapse that was widely predicted, after relations with the United States soured and that government imposed economic sanctions, was avoided by Cuba's forging new political and economic alliances and other exogenous factors that political and economic models were unable to predict.

On the economic policy side, revolutionary Cuba experimented with different industrial policies and forms of land tenure. Initially, the Cuban government sought economic diversification away from sugar and eagerly adopted state-led import substitution industrialization policies that were in vogue in Latin America at the time. The inflated economic development visions of the new regime generated classic statements by then Minister of Industries Guevara at the Special Meeting of the Inter-American Economic and Social Council of the Organization of American States in Punta del Este, Uruguay, on August 8, 1961. Guevara stated that within four years, Cuba would be the most highly industrialized country in Latin America relative to its population, achieving first place in the region with respect to per capita production of steel, cement, electricity, and—with the exception of Venezuela—oil refining. Cuba would also reach first place in the region with respect to production of tractors, rayon, shoes, textiles, and other industrial products.

Within two years, the expansive industrialization plans had been shelved and Cuba had returned to sugar specialization. Gone was the negative public discourse about the sugar industry and the ills of sugar monoculture. In fact, in the mid-1960s, Fidel Castro put all bets on the sugar industry, publicly committing Cuba to producing 10 million tons of sugar in 1970, a production level that would have been a historical record. The 1970 sugar crop wound up reaching slightly over 8 million tons, about 20 percent below the target, at a very high cost in terms of misallocation of resources, adverse impact on other agricultural endeavors, and undue wear and tear on sugar workers and mills. For the next two decades, sugar would be the engine of the Cuban economy, essentially the only commodity that Cuba exported consistently to the socialist-bloc nations.

Although the expressed objective of the agrarian reform law promulgated by Cuba's rebel army from the mountains of Oriente province in October 1958, a few months before overthrowing the Batista regime, was breaking up latifundia and distributing "land to the tiller," the policy objective changed shortly after the revolutionary takeover. The May 1959 First Agrarian Reform Law did distribute some land to individual (landless) peasants, but the bulk of the sugar farms nationalized in 1959–61 were organized into cooperatives and the rice farms and cattle ranches into state farms. A new round of nationalization of agricultural land, under the aegis of the Second Agrarian Reform of 1963, increased the state's share of agricultural land. It should be noted that these so-called agricultural cooperatives were so in name only, as they were organized by the state, had no financial autonomy, obtained all of their inputs from the state, were instructed by the state as to which crops to plant and where. Further, they were required to sell all—or most—of their output to the state at prices set by the state. State farms, inspired by Soviet collective farms (*kolkhozy*), were essentially government-owned latifundia where farmers were employees rather than independent producers. Cuba has experimented with different forms of cooperatives and land tenure, seeking a way to organize the agricultural sector to increase productivity given the ideological constraints on ownership.

In the area of cultural reform, Che Guevara's imprint was again a primary determining factor. Institutional reformulation of cultural production in the early years of the revolution, which saw the creation of such organizations as the Cuban Institute of Cinematographic Art and Industry (ICAIC), established in March 1959, and the Union of Cuban Artists and Writers (UNEAC), which came into being in August 1961, operated under the premise of a generalized usefulness of art for education and ideological uplift for the popular masses. It also saw artists themselves undertaking a leading role in this change; Guevara laid out his principles in the famous 1965 policy essay "Socialism and Man in Cuba." Culturally and cognitively, the prerequisite for this artistic infusion would be the massive Literacy Campaign that took place during 1961 and raised the general level of literacy islandwide some 30 points, bringing it to 96 percent of the population. The Literacy Campaign built schools, deployed educators and volunteers, and was of greatest benefit to Cuba's guajiros or white rural dwellers, and to the hitherto underserved black community.

One of the primary results of the cultural politics of literacy was the promotion of creative writing and the organization of literary competitions within the country. As might be imagined, the recent and current revolutionary process and the accompanying "ideological" positioning of the writers were primary considerations. Fidel Castro's famous 1961 dictum on freedom of artistic expression, in his "Words to the Intellectuals" address, that "everything" within the revolution was permissible, but that outside of it "nothing" was, would directly and indirectly guide not only the process of literary production, but also its reception and official recognition. This model had writers and artists, as intellectuals, in their public role as "teachers," ostensibly working to strengthen the revolutionary consciousness of the popular masses through their art (Sánchez Vásquez, p. 406). Accordingly, massive editions of books sometimes totaling 100,000 copies were published by state editorial houses and works that appropriately supported revolutionary premises received the most prestigious prizes. Indeed, the revolution's first decade saw Havana develop into a cultural mecca for Latin American and Caribbean progressive thought, as regional competitions in varying genres were organized by the Casa de las Américas, and that organization's prizes, whether for essay, novel, poetry, or other genres, became highly coveted distinctions. It is a point of historical record, in this regard, that the presence and support of current and future literary luminaries like Colombia's Gabriel García Márquez, Uruguay's Julio Cortázar, and Cuba's own Alejo Carpentier, helped usher in what became known as the "Boom" in Latin American writing.

The revolutionary orthodoxy and didacticism that was expected of the writers and artists had the perhaps foreseeable result that many of the more adventurous or imaginative artists fell afoul of accepted requirements and were either blacklisted or would not be published by the state-controlled publishing houses. The expressiveness sought by *Lunes de Revolución*, the weekly literary supplement to the daily newspaper *Revolución*, for example, under the directorship of the iconoclastic writer Guillermo Cabrera Infante, and the independent publishing group El Puente, an outlet for writers of purportedly suspicious sexuality and Black Power sympathizers, fell out of favor and quickly were closed down in 1961 and 1965, respectively. The government harassed homosexuals and in 1965 imprisoned important writers such as Virgilio Piñera, José Mario Rodríguez, and Ana María Simo at the newly established labor camps (Unidades Militares de Ayuda a la Producción, UMAP). The former El Puente associate, Afro-Cuban poet Nancy Morejón, would not appear in print for over a decade as what was known subsequently as the 1968–1973 "grey half-decade" or *quinquenio gris* of censorship, was imposed. A similar fate befell her former El Puente colleague Miguel Barnet, before he, like Morejón, was reincorporated into the official fold. One of the more noteworthy indications of the tensions arising from the struggle over artistic expression in the revolution's first decade concerns the so-called Padilla case in which Heberto Padilla's poetry collection *Fuera del juego* (1968) resulted in his arrest early in 1971, and to incarceration, humiliation, and a public confession, although the collection had received a major literary prize and been published by the UNEAC.

The Cuban government's dismantling of the private sector extended beyond the productive sector of the economy. In September 1961, the Cuban government nationalized all private schools and universities. A significant proportion of the nationalized schools and universities were owned and operated by the Catholic church. At the same time that it nationalized the private schools, the Cuban government expelled over 100 Spanish Catholic priests and brothers who were still in the island; since May 1961, several hundred Catholic nuns, priests, and brothers had voluntarily departed—most of them bound for Spain—after Fidel Castro announced the socialist nature of the revolution and the intention to launch investigations into the Catholic church's involvement in antirevolutionary actions. Also in 1961, the Cuban government nationalized all major private hospitals, so that by 1963, the entire health sector was under state control. The over 50 private social insurance funds serving different professional groups were gradually seized by the state and their administration unified under state control in 1963. In 1968, with the so-called "revolutionary offensive" that nationalized over 50,000 small businesses, primarily in the retail sector, the Cuban state's control over retail trade (estimated at 75 percent in 1963) rose to nearly 100 percent, as did control over industry (95 percent in 1963), construction (98 percent in 1963), and transportation (95 percent in 1963).

After a decade of experimentation and policy zigzagging, in the 1970s, Cuba strengthened its ties with the socialist bloc, adopted the Soviet economic development model, and launched a process of institutionalization of the revolution. By the 1980s, Cuba had become a full-fledged member of the socialist community and its economy was interlinked with that of the Soviet Union and the socialist countries through the Council for Mutual Economic Assistance (CMEA or COMECON) and other socialist-bloc institutions. Cuba's role was that of supplier of sugar to the Soviet Union and other socialist countries, receiving in exchange oil, other raw materials, and machinery and consumer goods from the Soviet Union and the socialist community. Implicit in these commercial relations were preferential prices the Soviet Union paid to Cuba for its sugar exports and financial assistance and subsidized exports (primarily of oil) from the Soviet Union to the island.

In February 1982, Cuba reversed its longstanding aversion to foreign investment, adopting a law that authorized the creation of joint ventures between Cuban entities and foreign interests for the specific purpose of engaging in profit-making activities that promoted Cuban development. This limited opening to foreign investment did not result in a significant amount of incoming capital but, together with a decision by the Cuban government to prioritize tourism development at the end of the 1980s and the creation of the government tourism enterprise Cubanacán in 1987, formed the basis for foreign tourism operators to enter the Cuban market. Spanish hotel chains were the first movers, in the late 1980s, establishing joint ventures to build and manage hotels suitable for international tourism. By the early 1990s, hospitality chains from other (mostly European) countries were heavily engaged in the Cuban tourism industry; by the end of the decade, tourism had surpassed the venerable sugar industry as the largest generator of hard-currency revenue.

The 1980s were a golden age for the economy of revolutionary Cuba. Fully integrated into the socialist economic community, recipient of development assistance from that community, and boosted by trade subsidies and seemingly unlimited credits from the Soviet Union, Cuba turned in a decade of strong and steady economic growth. Sugar was the main driver of the economy—the Soviet Union's demand for Cuban sugar was insatiable and sugar exports so beneficial that in the first half of the 1980s, Cuba built seven new sugar mills, the first net additions to sugar production capacity in the island since the 1920s. Oil imports from the Soviet Union, bartered for sugar under preferential terms, spared Cuba of the adverse impact of rising oil prices and even allowed Cuba to re-export some of the oil for hard currencies. In 1988, the last year for which these data are available, the Soviet Union and the EE-6 countries (Bulgaria, Czechoslovakia, the German Democratic Republic, Hungary, Poland, and Romania) absorbed 82 percent of Cuba's merchandise exports and provided 85 percent of Cuba's imports. Pérez-López (1991b) reported that through 1986, the Soviet Union alone had assisted Cuba in completing 360 development projects and an additional 289 projects were in progress.

In the political arena, Cuba has made fewer reforms than in other areas, and in fact some historical reforms have not moved toward decentralization or openness, as documented in Backer's contribution to this volume (chapter 6). In the 1970s, Cuba began to institutionalize the revolution. In December 1975, the Cuban Communist Party (PCC) held its first Party Congress, at which it elected its Secretariat and Political Bureau, and adopted several normative documents, principal among them a very detailed economic and social development plan for the period 1975–80. The latter replaced the ad hoc, short-term economic and social development plans that had been adopted since the early 1960s. The First Party Congress of the PCC elected Fidel Castro as first secretary and president. The following year, Cuba adopted by popular referendum a new (socialist) constitution; consistent with this foundational document, nationwide (but restricted) elections were held that same year to elect the members of the National Assembly of People's Power (Asamblea Nacional del Poder Popular, ANPP). Members of the ANPP are elected (though contests are not free and fair) every five years. Although in principle Cuba's main legislative body, to date the ANPP has not distinguished itself in acting independently of the Cuban political leadership and has gained a reputation as being largely a rubber-stamping institution.

To sum up, during the first three decades of revolutionary government, Cuba expanded its public educational system and developed an extensive public health and welfare system. Arguably, Cuba met the basic social needs of most of its citizens better than did other Latin American countries, with much better results in terms of infant mortality, life expectancy, literacy, and income distribution, although its economy struggled and Cuba lagged behind with respect to meeting citizens' economic needs. On the other side of the balance sheet, while the regime began in the 1960s to formalize its system with a series of institutions that have democratic traits—such as multiple levels of government with elected officials—elections have always been highly restricted and the party is intertwined with the government. Cuba's record with respect to human rights has been spotty, travel by citizens restricted, and repression of the opposition—through many means, including imprisonment—commonplace. Today there is somewhat more dissent than in the past, and government opponents are more likely to be hassled than jailed. Further, international travel has opened up (for those who have the means to do it, most often with funding from relatives living abroad), and some international media is surreptitiously available. Still, Cuban citizens lack basic civil rights.

SPECIAL PERIOD REFORMS

While the 1960s–1980s saw important economic policy innovations, Cuba's most significant period of economic reforms came in the early 1990s, prompted by a crisis of monumental proportion that was triggered by the fall of Cuba's Soviet patron. The disappearance of the socialist community of nations and the dissolution of the former Soviet Union dealt a severe economic blow to Cuba. In a matter of two to three years, Cuba's main economic partners transitioned away from socialism/communism and toward free markets, forcing a restructuring of the island's external economic relations and the search for new buyers for Cuba's exports and sources for its imports. It has been estimated that the island's exports fell by about 80 percent between 1990 and 1993, and imports by about 75 percent. Cuba also lost military and economic support from the former Soviet Union, which was valued at many billions of dollars. Overall economic activity, as measured by the gross domestic product (GDP), shrank by an estimated 35 percent during this period, one of the largest economic contractions on record anywhere.

The economic emergency that Cuba faced in the early 1990s was termed the Special Period in Time of Peace, to compare the situation to a war. The severity of the economic crisis, and the threat to regime survival, created an environment for policy innovation that otherwise would have been unthinkable. The situation was dire: there were generalized shortages of food, nutrition levels fell sharply, creating famine-like conditions, the cutbacks in imported oil meant that electricity blackouts lasted for eight hours or more per day in Havana (it was even worse in the rest of the country), many workplaces suspended work or closed operations because of shortages of raw materials and energy, and the public transportation system collapsed. In this scenario, the Cuban government implemented several important changes, principal among them the following (roughly in chronological order):

- Holding and use of foreign currencies: In the summer of 1993, Cuba decriminalized the holding and use of hard currency by Cuban citizens. The purpose of this action was twofold: 1) stem the booming hard-currency black market; and 2) stimulate hard-currency remittances to Cuban citizens by relatives and friends living abroad that would help in closing the balance of payments gap. To give concrete meaning to this so-called "dollarization" policy, the government created special stores at which individuals holding hard currencies could shop for items not available to Cubans holding pesos and liberalized travel to the island by relatives and friends of Cuban citizens. Later, the government created foreign-currency exchange houses (Casas de Cambio, CADECA) at which Cuban citizens could exchange hard currencies for pesos at rates close to those prevailing in the hard-currency black market and facilitated remittances by easing the procedures for receiving foreign funds and allowing private foreign companies to carry out some transactions.

- Self-employment: In September 1993, the Cuban government authorized self-employment in over 100 occupations, subject to some restrictions. The authorized occupations were almost exclusively in the services sector. Among the restrictions on self-employment were, for example, that professionals holding a university degree could not become self-employed; similarly, since education and public health services continued to be supplied by the state, physicians, dentists, teachers, professors, and researchers were excluded from self-employment. Candidates for self-employment had to request a license, could not hire others, had to pay fees and taxes to the government, and were restricted in how they sold the goods or services they produced. The list of occupations approved for self-employment was expanded in October 1993 and in June 1995, bringing the total number of authorized occupations to 140.

- Agricultural cooperatives: Also in September 1993, the Council of State approved breaking up large state farms into Basic Units of Cooperative Production (Unidades Básicas de Producción Cooperativa, UBPC). These UBPCs would have the use of the land they worked for an indefinite period of time, own the output they produced, be able to sell their output to the state through the state procurement system (*acopio*) or through other means, have their own bank accounts, and be able to elect their own management. The rationale for the policy change was that the shift from state farms to cooperatives would give workers greater incentives to increase production with the least expenditure of material resources.

- Tax code: In August 1994, the National Assembly approved a new and very broad tax code, to be implemented gradually beginning in October 1994. The system levied taxes on: the income of enterprises, including joint ventures with foreign investors, as well as on the value of assets owned; earned income; sales; consumption of products such as cigarettes, alcoholic beverages, electrodomestic appliances, and other luxury goods; public services such as electricity, water and sewer, telephone, telegrams, transportation, restaurants and lodging; real estate holdings; gasoline- or draft animal–powered transportation vehicles; transfer of property, including inheritances; public documents issued; payrolls; and use of natural resources. The law also foresaw employer contributions to social security, user fees on roads (tolls) and airport services, and charges for advertising of products or services.

- Agricultural markets: Complementing the creation of the UBPCs, in late September 1994, Cuba authorized the creation of agricultural markets—locations at which producers of selected agricultural products could sell a portion of their output at prices set by demand and supply. In most respects, the agricultural markets authorized in September 1994 are similar to the farmers' free markets (*mercados libres campesinos,* MLC) that were created in 1980 and scuttled in 1986 as part of a campaign to eliminate market-oriented mechanisms. In October 1994, the Cuban government announced that it would also allow the free sale of a wider range of consumer products through a network of artisan and manufactured products markets.

- Foreign investment facilitation: In September 1995, the National Assembly adopted a new foreign investment law that codified the de facto rules under which joint ventures had been operating and introduced some innovations to the legal framework for foreign investment. For example, pursuant to the new law, 100 percent foreign ownership of investments would be permitted, up from the 49 percent allowed by the earlier statute. The new law also simplified the process for screening foreign investment, explicitly allowing foreign investment in real estate, and authorized the establishment of export processing zones. In June 1996 the Council of State passed legislation creating export processing zones (*zonas francas y parques industriales*).

Though implementation of some of the policy measures was shallow—indicative of the lack of enthusiasm of the leadership toward them—the package of measures was sufficient to pull the economy out of the abyss. No significant measures were implemented after 1996, by which time the economy had stabilized. From that point forward, the reform process was essentially stopped and the decentralization measures that had been implemented reversed somewhat. The Special Period reforms were more formally reversed beginning in 2003 under the aegis of an ideological construct promoted by Fidel Castro called the "Battle of Ideas."

In addition to economic hardship, the Special Period brought changes to the arts, race, and class relations, in part due to the peculiar discipline that the situation demanded. The period is marked by a gradual relaxation of government vigilance over cultural production, and an emergence of more diffuse and decentralized creative practices as new periodicals appeared and diverse new nuclei of interests emerged as the internet, social media, and more and more contemporary American and global cultural flows made their presence felt.

As has been mentioned, remittances from the United States, mostly from white Cuban emigrés, grew rapidly, increasing the consumption capacity of households receiving remittances and supporting incipient small-scale entrepreneurship. This contributed to a noticeable widening of the social and racial gap between those receiving and not receiving remittances. In fact, the very ethos of scarcity and limited opportunities that had characterized the revolution throughout has been said to contribute to a resurgence of patterns of racism under a different guise in this period. Indeed, to the degree that the revolution might be associated with "reform" in terms of Cuba's colonially determined racial dynamic, it must be mentioned that in its articulation under orthodox Marxist thinking, class trumped race, and complaints from the aggrieved black constituency were usually met with the rationale that the dissolution of class divisions under socialism would bring with it an end to racist behaviors and attitudes, or alternatively, that the broader notion of national unity overrode the division that protests from Cuban blacks implied.

According to Roberto Zurbano, noted cultural commentator, there was little specific official attention paid to the topic of race after some overt references to it by Fidel Castro in 1959, and it was thereafter rendered almost taboo or confined to the discursive strictures mentioned above. Zurbano also notes its current resurgence even in the presence of an increased ventilation of the topic in journals, popular art forms, and academic discourse starting in the Special Period and continuing into the current century. He concludes that on account of its dogged presence in Cuba's living archive of phrases, gestures, and a multiplicity of exclusionary and discriminatory practices in the workplace, in academic settings, and in mass media, Cuba is experiencing a period of what he dubs an unsettling "neo-racism." On the question of a possible reform in this troublesome aspect of social life, Zurbano concludes that Cuba lacks the kind of "social debate, adequate tools with a racial policy and strategy that would destroy those racist structures that are not always political and economic, but also ideological and cultural, such as those that are continually reproducing themselves in education, mass media and in legislation." (Zurbano 2015, 26).

Critical to Cuba's economic recovery after the crisis of the 1990s was the coming into power of Hugo Chávez in Venezuela in 1999 and the economic support oil-rich Venezuela has provided to Cuba. Particularly since 2001, Venezuela provided Cuba with an economic lifeline in the form of guaranteed volumes of oil imports at preferential prices, markets for Cuban exports, investments in development projects, and credits to help Cuba plug up balance of payments imbalances. By 2010, Venezuela had become Cuba's largest trading partner, accounting for 40 percent of Cuba's goods trade. A critical element of the Cuba–Venezuela economic relationship has been the very large number of Cuban professionals (physicians, other health professionals, teachers, sports instructors, and coaches) who work in Venezuela and whose salaries are captured by the Cuban government and used to finance the island's huge trade deficits.

Another important development, resulting from the combination of U.S. commercial policies and natural forces, was the emergence and surge in U.S. agricultural exports to Cuba. In 2000, farm interests in the United States were successful in amending the U.S. embargo to create an exception for agricultural products. The Trade Sanctions Reform and Export Expansion Act (TSRA) of 2000 authorized sales of U.S. agricultural commodities to Cuba provided: 1) the exported commodities did not include any form of U.S. government assistance, credits, or guarantees; and 2) sales were made in cash in advance or financed through third-country banks; the legislation also denied Cuba access to all forms of U.S. private sector credit.

U.S. sales of agricultural commodities to Cuba under the TSRA were not significant in 2000 and 2001, but the situation changed drastically in 2002. Over a 12-month period—from November 2001 through September 2002—

Cuba was battered by three hurricanes, Michelle (November 2001), Isidore (early September 2002) and Lili (late September 2002), which wreaked havoc with Cuba's agricultural sector. Cuba had to turn to imports to meet food consumption needs, and U.S. agricultural businesses were there to provide the desired commodities, profiting handsomely from sales to Cuba. U.S. sales of agricultural commodities to Cuba reached nearly $1.8 billion in 2008. The concentrated efforts of U.S. agricultural exporters to trade with Cuba, and their success in creating an exception of the U.S. embargo to allow such transactions, may be a harbinger of what could be expected in the future in a new scenario of U.S.–Cuba relations.

The economic crisis of the 1990s led Cuba to make political-institutional reforms as well. In 1992, Cuba amended the 1976 Constitution to recognize property rights for joint ventures with foreign investors and to declare itself a secular state, thereby providing an opening for religious practice by the citizenry. Nevertheless, the 1992 Constitution did not affect the political centralism of the regime nor did it loosen restrictions on dissent.

RAUL'S REFORMS (AND LACK THEREOF)

Cuba began to implement a new round of economic reforms—although at a crawling pace—after Raúl Castro assumed Cuba's top leadership position, temporarily in 2006 and permanently in 2008. Many of these reform measures revived earlier efforts that were either abandoned or withered on the vine. There were also, however, several reforms that tackled some important issues that heretofore had been ignored by Cuba's leadership.

In February 2011, the PCC held its Sixth Congress, the first coming together of the party in more than a decade (the Fifth Party Congress was held in 1997). In preparation for the Sixth Congress, in November 2010 the PCC circulated a comprehensive set of 291 draft economic and social development guidelines (*lineamientos*) seeking public discussion and comment. According to PCC officials, the draft guidelines were discussed at thousands of meetings held at workplaces, schools, neighborhoods, and at the community level throughout the island. Ultimately, the PCC Congress adopted 313 agreements, of which 92 percent addressed economic issues and 8 percent social issues. The subject matters covered by the guidelines included the economic development model, macroeconomic policies, external economic policies, investment policies, social policies, tourism policies, construction policies, and transportation policies.

To a large extent, reform measures adopted by Raúl Castro's government implemented the policy agreements reached by the Sixth Party Congress. Raúl's reform measures included a mix of what Mesa-Lago and Pérez-López

(2013) have categorized as administrative measures, nonstructural changes, and structural reforms.

- Administrative measures are governmental actions aimed at improving efficiency and reducing costs, such as reorganization of government structures and campaigns against corruption or labor indiscipline.

- Nonstructural changes are bolder and more creative measures, but of secondary order; they include, for example, one-off actions such as allowing citizens access to hotels and restaurants formerly accessible only to tourists, payment of arrears to farmers, sale of certain goods (e.g., household electric appliances) to the population, authorization for citizens to operate taxicabs, and so on.

- Administrative measures and nonstructural changes can be implemented in a relatively short time period and tend to achieve fairly immediate measurable impacts. Structural reforms, in contrast, alter the economic model or development strategy; they are more complex and more time consuming to implement. Finally, their impact may not be noticeable for some time after implementation. These different initiatives tend to be conflated by analysts, thereby missing some important differences among them with respect to breadth, impact, and timing.

Among the principal structural reforms that Cuba has implemented since 2008 are the following:

- Dismissal of state workers and stimulation of private sector jobs: These reforms built on earlier measures that allowed self-employment, but took them to a higher level, as they foresaw a reduction of about 1 million redundant jobs from the state payroll and their absorption by the private sector. New regulations raised the number of occupations that could be practiced by self-employed persons to 178, 21 more than previously approved; permitted entrepreneurs to hire up to five non-family members in about half of the occupations; permitted the possibility of self-employed workers selling goods and services to state enterprises; and made available some financing to self-employed workers. The state also permitted some state employees working in certain state enterprises to leave state employment and join the private sector in the form of cooperatives in services occupations, such as workers in barbershops, beauty salons, shops for repairing small electrical appliances or shoes, and small cafeterias.

- Distribution of state idle lands to individuals and cooperatives in usufruct: Another impactful reform has been the distribution of idle state lands in usufruct to individuals and cooperatives. The granting of land to individuals was a significant change in land tenure, as for the previous five decades the Cuban state had deemed collective holding of land as a "superior" form of organization. Pursuant to the new rules issued in 2008: 1) landless individuals could obtain up to 13.42 hectares and existing landholders could bring their total holding up to 40.26 hectares for their use for 10 years, renewable for an additional 10 years; and 2) existing state farms, cooperatives, and other legal entities could apply for the usufruct of unlimited amounts of idle lands for 25 years, renewable for another 25 years. Although there are significant restrictions on the distributed land—the usufruct for individuals and other legal entities is time-limited, the usufruct is not transferable to another party, there are some restrictions on what structures can be built on the land, and it is not clear how farmers who make improvements to their land (e.g., clearing the land from marabú and other invasive plants) would be paid for such improvements at the end of usufruct period—nevertheless the distribution of land is having some positive impact on certain crops amenable to production in small farms. The growing ability of private farmers to sell their products in free agricultural markets has increased the amount of fresh agricultural products that are available to Cuban consumers.

- Migration reform: Another important measure implemented in November 2012 was a major overhaul of the migration system. Since the start of the Cuban revolution through 2011, Cuban citizens did not have the right to travel abroad and had to secure permits (the so-called "white card") from the Cuban government to do so as well as an invitation letter from relatives or friends abroad. Travelers had to return within a certain time period or lose their citizenship plus all their assets. The new regulations eliminated the exit permit and invitation letter requirements and extended the time Cuban citizens could remain abroad. The new regulations also reduced the overall cost of traveling abroad by Cuban citizens.

- Tax reform: Enacted at the start of 2013, the new tax code—which superseded the 1994 code—was intended to be consistent with the country's new economic and social scenario, shifting the burden of taxation from indirect taxes (sales taxes, turnover taxes) toward direct taxes on income, profits, and assets held. The new tax system reinforces other policies, providing preferential tax treatment to priority sectors such as private agriculture and self-employment.

- Sales/purchases (exchanges) of homes and automobiles: The Urban Reform Law of 1960 confiscated most of the country's housing stock, banned real estate transactions, and gave tenants the right to own properties they rented after 20 years. Freezing of the real estate market—individuals who wanted to move from one location to another had to create fictitious scenarios and go through the very inefficient mechanism of arranging a swap (*permuta*)—coupled with the lack of construction materials, meant that maintenance of homes was disregarded. The lifting of restrictions on home sales has stimulated home repair and maintenance, and has given renters the possibility of leveraging their home ownership into the possibility of purchasing other goods or services. A similar situation holds for automobile sales.

- Foreign investment: As mentioned earlier, Cuba issued a comprehensive foreign investment law in 1995 as part of the reform measures associated with the Special Period. The Guidelines adopted by the Cuban Communist Party in 2011 recognized an important role for foreign investment in the nation's development and promised a series of measures to facilitate foreign investment. The first such measure was embodied in a law decree passed in 2013 that created the ZED Mariel and offered a range of incentives to companies that invested in the zone. This was followed in 2014 by a comprehensive foreign investment law (replacing the earlier 1995 law) that expanded the suite of incentives offered to potential foreign investors. In this regard, the Cuban government has undertaken an aggressive public relations campaign promoting foreign investment in the island and identifying specific projects that are suitable for foreign investment.

Notably absent in this list of reforms are changes to the political system. Backer (chapter 6) argues that in Cuba, the state and party structure are "symbolic" and that the power is still highly centralized. Comparing it to the reform process in China, he goes so far as to say that "the concept of socialist modernization, key to the scientific development of [Chinese Communist Party] CCP political lines, is noticeably absent from PCC discussion." The example of China suggests that economic openings do not necessarily engender political reforms. But if there were a political opening, there are diverse potential directions. First, Mexico and countries of the former Soviet Union suggest that parties that ruled during authoritarian periods can also participate successfully in a democracy. In addition to Backer's chapter, Dimitrov's (chapter 5) contribution in this volume suggests an alternative direction for the Cuban state and the PCC. Dimitrov argues that the state is concerned with accountability, but it is unclear whether the state's responses to citizen grievances is simply symbolic. Another concern is about the irrationality and incompleteness of reforms. This issue is evident in several of our chapters (e.g., Mesa-Lago and Pérez-López and Xiao), and Edward Malesky raised it with reference to Vietnam at our conference. There he explained that while some relatively simple reforms can dramatically increase economic activity, state involvement in key sectors has continued to distort incentives and thus prevent sustained growth.

Also absent from the reform agenda have been initiatives with regard to social relations. The revolution had immediate and direct impacts on Afro-Cubans, formally ending discrimination. On the informal level, however, racism continues and some careful analysts (e.g., de la Fuente 2011) go so far as to argue that the revolution has not improved the lot of Afro-Cubans. Still, there are notable changes, at least for some. While some blacks have risen to important positions in medicine, government, business, and other areas, it is the case that blacks live predominantly in poor neighborhoods, and whites in the wealthier areas. New policies that will increase remittances will only exacerbate these divisions, because more whites have relatives living abroad. Given that the government does not officially recognize racism, it has not developed policies to improve opportunities for average Afro-Cubans. West-Durán's chapter in this volume (11) discusses some implications of this view, focusing on citizenship, civil society, and identity. He also considers the "philosophical notions of equality under Cuba's economic model."

While political and social reforms have been slow to arrive, there are signs of some changes in terms of citizen–government relations and perhaps moves toward reforming the role of women in society. Martín Sevillano's chapter (12) in this volume suggests that there is a growing awareness about the role of women within the household, and that the government, at least through the police, has a role to play in effecting a positive change. The problem is severe, but the fact that such issues are portrayed in state-controlled television is an important indicator that the state recognizes the problem.

The pace of reforms has slowed since 2014. Raúl is fond of saying that Cuba's "updating" of its economic model (i.e., reform process) is proceeding *sin prisa, pero sin pausa,* slow but steadily, but the lack of significant structural reforms since then is quite noticeable. Reforms still to be made that have been discussed by Cuban academics and by Cuban government officials include the thorny monetary reunification, a deep enterprise reform, elimination of the rationing system, elimination of the agricultural *acopio* system, and broad-based price liberalization. These are all difficult but critically important issues that Cuba's leadership has to address.

The Seventh Congress of the PCC, held in April 2016, was deeply disappointing for reform advocates. First, an assessment of the implementation of the guidelines approved by the Sixth Congress conducted in January 2016 found that only 21 percent of the 313 agreements had been implemented, with 77 percent still in progress. Second, unlike previous congresses, the preparatory work did not include extensive documentation and public consultation. The two core documents presented at the Congress, "Conceptualización del Modelo Económico y Social Cubano de Desarrollo Socialista" (Conceptualization of the Cuban Socioeconomic Socialist Model) and "Plan Nacional de Desarrollo Económico y Social hasta 2030: Propuesta de Visión de la Nación, Ejes y Sectores Estratégicos" (National Socioeconomic Development Plan to 2030: Proposal for a National Vision, Axes, and Strategic Sectors) were discussed and approved in principle. However, in an unusual move, the time period for national discussion of the two documents was extended until the end of September, suggesting either that the documents had not been properly vetted or that there is a sufficiently large number of persons not willing to play a rubber-stamping role with party documents. Third, in terms of the number of the reforms, while the Seventh Congress approved 268 guidelines, 31 were unchanged from the previous set, 193 reworked earlier guidelines, and only 44 were new. It remains to be seen how newly designated President Miguel Díaz-Canel will approach the scope and pace of the badly needed economic reform process.

A significant recent development was the negotiation that led to large concessions from Cuba to its foreign creditors. In that 2015 process, Cuba and the group of creditor nations known as the Paris Club agreed on $15 billion as the total amount that Cuba owed to this group of nations, which includes Russia; it is worth recalling that Cuba's debt to the former Soviet Union alone in the mid-1990s was estimated at about $35 billion (there was a dispute about the exchange rate between the ruble and the dollar) and therefore the $15 billion debt amount incorporates a substantial concession on the part of Russia. Prior to that, Cuba achieved significant foreign debt concessions from China (47.2 percent), Mexico (70 percent), and Russia (90 percent), and from Japanese commercial banks (80 percent). The combination of individual debt renegotiation pacts and the Paris Club agreement provided a boost to Cuba's international creditworthiness and provided Cuba the ability to turn to international markets for financing. Nevertheless, revolutionary expropriations of property are unresolved and remain an obstacle to normalization of economic relations with the United States (see chapter 4, by Travieso-Díaz), and more generally, Cuba's future access to international credit markets and membership in international financial institutions.

Deeply disappointing to Cuba was the lack of success of deep-water exploratory drilling for oil conducted in the Gulf of Mexico, in areas leased to international oil companies within Cuba's Exclusive Economic Zone. Between January and November 2012, the state-of-the-art semisubmersible rig Scarabeo 9 drilled three offshore exploratory deep-water wells for international oil companies Repsol (Spain), Petronas (Malaysia), Gazpromneft (Russia), and PDVSA (Venezuela), which turned out either to be dry or not to contain oil in commercial quantity and quality and extractable at competitive costs. Cuban leaders had hoped for a significant oil find that would permit Cuba to generate international interest in oil exploration and provide badly needed foreign exchange. While oil exploration is likely to continue in the future, the hope that oil would transform Cuba's economy appears not very likely, at least in the short run.

In addition to seeking to reduce its foreign debt—and open up opportunities to tap international financial markets—Cuba has been trying to diversify its commercial relationships and develop new economic allies. Brazil has emerged as an important commercial partner, source of investments, and provider of technology. As mentioned earlier, an example of Brazilian presence in Cuba is the Mariel megaport, built by a Brazilian multinational construction company with financing from a Brazilian export credit agency. Brazil is also an important market for Cuban physicians, who have been locating in that country since 2003 as part of the Más Médicos Program intended to bring health services to underserved areas in Brazil. According to Brazilian sources, in mid-2015 the Más Médicos Program employed 18,240 physicians, of which 11,487 (63 percent) were Cuban. Also important are Cuba's developing alliances in Asia. China is now Cuba's second-largest trading partner (after Venezuela) and the largest importer of Cuban sugar, taking about 400,000 tons of Cuban sugar per annum. The Chinese are second (after Brazil) in the construction and furnishing of equipment for the Mariel port and are building infrastructure and oil refineries; supporting oil exploration; and building hospitals throughout the island. Singapore company PSA International has been chosen as the port's operator.

While China and Brazil have become important partners, Spain and Canada have had a substantial presence in Cuba for a longer period and continue to be important in Cuba's external sector. Spanish hospitality companies dominate the international tourism sector, managing a significant share of the hotels devoted to international tourism. Spanish medium-size investors are also quite active in the island, accounting for a large share of a form of foreign investment called "international economic associations," which are medium-size enterprises that produce goods that substitute for imports. Canada is the largest source of tourists and of investment in nickel mining and oil exploration and extraction.

One of Cuba's main worries since at least 2014 has been the economic and political stability of Venezuela's government, and the continuing ability of that country to lend economic support to the island. Venezuela, whose oil exports revenues account for about 95 percent of export earnings, has been buffeted by declining oil world prices and by serious mismanagement of the economy. The victory by the opposition in the December 2015 election for the National Assembly dealt a heavy blow to the government of President Nicolás Maduro. Cuban leaders, who already had lived through a very difficult adjustment upon the collapse of the former Soviet patron, have reason to be concerned about history repeating itself. In July 2016, President Raúl Castro informed the National Assembly that Cuba's economy was being adversely affected by Venezuela's financial problems as a result of the fall in the world price of oil. Added to this was a drop of 40 percent in crude oil imports from Venezuela in the first half of 2016 compared to the same period in 2015. Analysts disagree on whether this export shortfall is temporary, caused by a short-term disruption in Venezuelan oil supplies, or if it portends a shift to lower levels of Venezuelan oil exports to Cuba. In 2018, Venezuela faced an economic collapse, with hyperinflation and generalized shortages of consumer and investment goods.

During the first few years of Raúl's reforms, the economy grew at a rate of 2–3 percent per annum. Cuban officials reported that economic growth was 1.3 percent in 2014, but GDP growth rose to a higher 4.0 percent in 2015; for 2016, a growth rate of 4 percent was again anticipated. However, a looming liquidity crisis brought about by low prices of Cuba's export commodities compounded by Venezuela's woes led Cuban officials in late December 2015 to cut the expected 2016 growth rate to 2 percent. In July 2016, President Raúl Castro indicated that the growth rate in the first half of 2016 was actually 1 percent, and a new set of emergency austerity measures would be required. At the close of 2016, Cuban authorities reported that the economy had actually contracted by 0.9 percent in that year. The reduction in Venezuelan oil supplies in the first half of 2016 and the broad range of austerity measures announced by the Cuban government to address the crisis have raised the specter of a new Special Period. Although Cuban officials deemed the reduction in Venezuelan oil supplies to be temporary phenomenon, caused by short-term disruption in oil production, it nevertheless exposed the vulnerability of the Cuban economy to oil supplies and was a vivid reminder for the population of the hardships associated with the Special Period. Economic growth for 2017 has been estimated at 1–2 percent.

REFORMS AND THE POTENTIAL END OF U.S. ECONOMIC SANCTIONS

The announcements by Presidents Obama and Castro in December 2014, of the intention of the two countries to reestablish diplomatic relations raised the stakes for the Cuban reform process. If and when the U.S. economic sanctions are lifted, will the Cuban economy be in a condition to take advantage of access to the U.S. market, closed for over five decades, for the benefit of the island's economy?

What is commonly known as the "U.S. embargo" (although the Cuban government insists on calling it the "U.S. blockade") is actually a web of regulations, executive orders and actions, and legislation issued over decades that govern specific aspects of U.S. relations with Cuba in areas as disparate as trade, capital flows, credit, air transportation, communications, maritime transportation, and so on. Many of these U.S. policies controversially have extraterritorial reach, limiting commercial and financial relations between third countries and Cuba. The nature of the instrument determines which entity within the U.S. government would have the authority to lift it and the process for doing so. For example, regulations issued by the executive branch or independent agencies presumably could be modified or even eliminated following procedures embodied in the U.S. Administrative Procedure Act (APA). The APA, which was enacted in 1946 and reformed several times, sets out processes that agencies might follow for issuing or modifying regulations, including requirement for economic (cost-benefit) analysis, notice period, opportunity for public comment, and so on. Executive orders and actions are directives by the president that may be binding on the executive branch; they can be modified or eliminated by another order or action from the president who issued the directive or a successor. Meanwhile, restrictions that were put in place through legislation—or were "codified," i.e., made part of U.S. legislation—can only be modified or eliminated by legislative action, which in the United States means passage of a bill by both houses of Congress and signature by the president. Clearly, restrictions of a legislative nature face the highest and most complicated path for modification or elimination.

Together with President Obama's December 2014, statement, the White House issued a fact sheet of administration actions that would be taken immediately in support of the new policy. The changes announced would be implemented via amendments to regulations of the Departments of the Treasury and Commerce. Specifically, the announced policies would 1) facilitate an expansion of travel to Cuba under general licenses for the 12 existing categories of travel to Cuba authorized by law, 2) facilitate remittances to Cuba by U.S. persons, so that remittance levels will be raised from $500 to $2,000 per quarter for general remittances to Cuban nationals (except to certain officials of the government or the Communist Party); 3) authorize expanded commercial sales/exports from the United States of certain goods and services to empower the nascent Cuban private sector; 4) authorize American citizens to import up to $400 worth of goods from Cuba; 5) facilitate authorized financial transactions between the United States and Cuba, including the use of credit cards; 6) initiate new efforts to increase Cubans' access to communications and their ability to communicate freely; and 7) update the application of Cuba sanctions in third countries with a view to facilitating trade. This latter policy may allow U.S. companies to trade with Cuba via foreign subsidiaries, thus cutting a large hole in the embargo, even if Congress refuses to end that policy. In addition, the U.S. State Department announced that the United States would pursue discussions with the Cuban and Mexican governments to discuss the unresolved maritime boundary in the Gulf of Mexico. Finally, the U.S. removed Cuba from the list of countries designated as state sponsors of terrorism, and lifted objections to Cuba's participation in the 2015 Panama Summit of the Americas.

The United States and Cuba also launched an intense process of discussion and negotiation over numerous aspects of the relationship. The two countries established a Bilateral Commission, whose first meeting was held in Havana in September 2015, to tackle issues key to full normalization. A press release issued by the U.S. Department of State after the September session stated that the issues the commission would be discussing through the end of 2015 included human rights, combating trafficking in persons, claims by U.S. citizens (from Cuban government expropriations), migration, counternarcotics, regulatory issues, environmental cooperation, telecommunications and the internet, and direct mail. Indicative of the long process ahead to reach agreement on bilateral issues, Cuba's Ministry of Foreign Relations issued its own press release of the meeting, putting the items for discussion in three buckets: 1) establishment of cooperation mechanisms in new mutually beneficial areas such as environmental protection, prevention of natural disasters, health, civil aviation, and law application and enforcement, including trafficking in persons and drugs and transnational crime; 2) dialogue on bilateral and multilateral issues on which the two countries have different conceptions, such as trafficking in persons and human rights on the bilateral agenda and climate change and epidemics, pandemics and other threats to global health on the multilateral agenda; 3) pending bilateral issues, such as compensation from the United States to the Cuban people for the human and economic damage inflicted by different U.S. administrations over 50 years and compensation for U.S. properties nationalized by the Cuban government as well as protection of trademarks and patents. The Cuban Ministry of Foreign Relations stated that "lifting of the blockade is fundamental at the current time and is essential for the normalization of bilateral relations. In addition, it restated that for normal relations to exist, it would be necessary to return to Cuba the territory illegally occupied by Guantanamo Naval Base, the suspension of illegal radio and TV broadcasting to Cuba, and the elimination of programs intended to destabilize and subvert Cuban constitutional order." To be sure, these are public positions and much can happen in a negotiations setting, but two years hence it is clear that resolution of these complex issues is not imminent.

Taking steps to normalize diplomatic and economic relations between the two countries continued in 2015 and 2016. The U.S. Treasury and Commerce Departments announced several tranches of measures to eliminate U.S. restrictions on travel, remittances, and financial and trade relations. The Bilateral Commission held additional meetings in November 2015 and May, September, and December 2016 to discuss a very broad bilateral agenda. Progress was made with respect to numerous topics, among them:

- In December 2015, the United States and Cuba signed an agreement restoring direct mail service between the two nations; initially, direct mail service would be established through a pilot program with the intention of full reestablishment as soon as possible. Direct mail service had been suspended for more than five decades, requiring routing of mail through third countries.

- Also in December 2015, the two countries agreed to restore regularly scheduled commercial airline flights, with 20 daily flights to Havana already approved, with the possibility of additional flights to other Cuban cities to be considered in the future. The formal agreement was signed in February 2016 and first direct commercial flight left Fort Lauderdale on August 31, 2016, and landed in Santa Clara.

- In March 2016, the U.S. and Cuba signed a Memorandum of Understanding on agricultural cooperation whereby the U.S. Department of Agriculture would allow industry-funded research and promotion programs and marketing order organizations to conduct authorized research and information activities in Cuba.

- In June 2016, the U.S. Department of Health and Human Services and Cuba's Ministry of Health signed a Memorandum of Understanding to establish a strategy to collaborate in the field of health through scientific, academic, technical and research-based projects and exchanges, addressing priorities such as communicable diseases, including Zika and dengue, noncommunicable diseases, public health management, exchanges of health professionals, and aging.

- In late October 2016, the U.S. Food and Drug Administration approved the first clinical trial to test a Cuban drug in the United States, a lung cancer vaccine developed by Cuba's biotechnology industry. The test will be conducted at the Roswell Park Cancer Institute in Buffalo, New York, and will probably take at least three years to complete.

Significant in its symbolism was President Obama's visit to Cuba, which took place on March 21–22, 2016, and was the first time a sitting U.S. president visited the island since Calvin Coolidge in 1918. While on the island, Obama made a very powerful speech that was transmitted to the Cuban people in which he restated his conviction that it was time for the U.S. and Cuba to bury the differences of the past and have normal diplomatic and economic relations. President Obama also met with Cuban entrepreneurs and civil society activists and dissidents.

It is important to keep in mind that elements of the U.S. embargo of significant interest to Cuba—such as unfettered merchandise trade between the two countries, access to trade credits from U.S. private and government institutions, and flow of U.S. tourists to the island—are governed by legislation and are not subject to modification by the President. These all-important changes will need to wait until there is a U.S. Congress that is amenable to modifying/lifting some or all of the restrictions and a president who would be willing to enact a law incorporating such changes. Resolution—or at least meaningful progress—on the extensive bilateral agenda referenced above will be essential for creating a congressional climate that would be open to dismantling the embargo.

Notwithstanding the long and tortuous path ahead for the elimination of the embargo, the possibility of normal commercial relations between the United States and Cuba has created a great deal of expectations within the U.S. and international business communities who see potential economic opportunities. Generally speaking, the areas that have piqued the interest of foreign businesses included tourism, oil exploration and production (particularly Cuban import of advanced oil drilling and enhanced production technologies), nickel mining and processing, agriculture and processing of agricultural products, and biotechnology. Interest on the part of consumer goods industries is moderate, as the relatively low purchasing power of the population might limit this market, particularly for high-end goods. A handful of U.S. companies have made inroads into the Cuban market:

- In February 2015, video streaming company Netflix announced that it would make its subscription service available in Cuba at a monthly fee of $7.99. Significant because it was the first U.S. company to enter the Cuban market, the move by Netflix was largely symbolic, as few Cuban households can afford the monthly fee and moreover, the service must be paid in U.S. dollars and Cuban citizens are not able to make transactions in U.S. dollars.

- Airbnb, the internet peer-to-peer short-term hospitality company, began to offer accommodations in Cuba for licensed U.S. travelers effective April 2015. In essence, Airbnb internationalized the practice of lodging in *casas particulares*, one of the forms of private employment that was legal under Cuban legislation. In 2016, Airbnb expanded its services in Cuba to include travelers from third countries.

- Financial company MasterCard unblocked the use of its credit cards in Cuba effective March 2015. Like the move by Netflix, this was mostly a symbolic action, as very few outlets had the technology to use credit cards and they were not accepted by ATMs. In November 2015, Stonegate Bank and Mastercard began to issue a debit card that can be used in the island. In June 2016, Cuban ATMs began to accept U.S.-issued Mastercards.

- In February 2016, the U.S. press reported that Cleber LLC, a manufacturer of tractors headquartered in Alabama, has been approved by the U.S. and Cuban governments to set up a factory to manufacture tractors in the Mariel Special Development Zone, the first U.S. investment in the island in more than 50 years. (The Cuban government subsequently voided the deal, arguing that the proposed investment did not involve new technology and did not offer growth opportunities for Cuba.) Just prior to President Obama's visit to Cuba, Starwood Hotels and Resorts announced a deal with Cuban authorities to manage three hotels in Havana.

The reestablished relations with the United States brought Cuba some tangible improvements, but their regime seemed unwilling to push for further reform. While the Trump administration has not reverted back to the status quo ante, the hardened rhetoric suggests that the United States will be a less willing partner for reform. The new Cuban leader, Miguel Díaz-Canel, has not yet signaled that how Cuba will confront challenges of currency unification, privatization of state enterprises, elimination of restrictions on self-employment, permanence with respect to land tenure arrangements, and so on. The present United States administration has certainly created new pressures for Cuba to make these types of changes, but as we discuss in the next chapter, modifications would threaten the legacy of the Cuban revolution. The open question, then, is how Díaz-Canel will balance pent-up pressures for social and economic reform, which come from both domestic and international sources, with a desire from other actors to hold on to at least some of the legacy of the island's long-running experiment with a socialist model. Other countries have also faced similar predicaments, and the rest of the volume therefore puts the challenges facing Cuba into a comparative framework.

ROADMAP FOR THE BOOK

The book addresses multiple areas of reform, using authors from a variety of backgrounds. We begin with four papers that focus on economic policies, each using different comparative cases to generate their lessons for Cuba. The first of these, by Morgenstern and Pérez-López (but based on work with Morrison and Alzugaray) considers the applicability of standard capitalist models to the Cuban context. Next, McGuire considers conditions and policies that contribute to economic growth and compares the Cuban situation to that of Taiwan and South Korea. To discuss foreign direct investment, which is crucial to growth, Pérez-López and Xiao use China as a model. The fourth paper in this part of the book deals with resolution of property rights disputes between Cuba and the United States. Here Travieso-Díaz relies on the experiences of Central and Eastern Europe to develop the theme.

Part 2 looks at social policies and political parties. Dimitrov begins his innovative and empirical discussion of the "socialist social contract" using examples from the Soviet Union and China. Next, Backer compares the Cuban Communist Party to those of other parts of the world (including some parties that are now defunct). Cuba is an outlier, he explains, in terms of its continued centralized rule. He notes, however, that the death of Fidel could allow party reform. Next, Pérez-Liñán and Mainwaring consider how a country's democratic history predicts its future; from the comparative context, they find that Cuba's limited experience with democracy lowers its chances of future success. The following two chapters consider social welfare programs. Mesa-Lago compares the Cuban system to those in other parts of Latin America as well as China and Vietnam. Although Cuba's system compares favorably in terms of coverage, it is inadequate in the support it offers its populace. Mesa-Lago concludes with a series of recommendations, which include reallocation of resources (e.g., toward elder care and away from infant mortality) and reform of the tax structure to increase the system's financial stability. Vázquez D'Elía builds from Mesa-Lago's analysis by looking at changes in Latin American pension and health systems. His explanatory focus emphasizes both societal and economic changes and the role of changing political power. Political and economic reforms in Cuba will inevitably give power to new actors, thus changing the system. Foreign firms, for example, could provide separate systems for their employees. The final chapter of the part, by Linden, uses the fall of the ex-Soviet states to put democratic reforms into context. These examples provide warnings, since only some have succeeded democratically. The form of the transition (upheaval versus negotiation) plus the role of external factors (admission into the European Union for Eastern Europe) played central roles in determining the success of transition in these countries. The parallels to the Cuban case are clear.

The third part of the book moves the focus from government and economic structures to societal concerns. The chapters are less comparative in nature, but round out our book by emphasizing the needs for reforms within the broader society. The first of the chapters, by West-Durán, focuses on race, emphasizing how economic reforms increase pressures to confront the issue. The discussion also touches on how Cuban society views race within a context of suspicion of paradigms emanating from the United States or Europe. In the next chapter, Martín Sevillano explores domestic violence. The need for reform in both society and governmental institutions is clear. She notes, for example, that "domestic violence as a concept is absent in Cuban law, and . . . therefore there are no particular legal procedures to address it." Another aspect of the discussion is aggression of the police and security forces against dissidents, as well as the role of police in dealing with domestic violence. Domestic violence generally, including the role of the police, is depicted within the popular soap opera *Bajo el Mismo Sol* (Under the Same Sun) on which the chapter is based. In the last chapter, Saunders emphasizes how repression and hardship on the island helped spur a grassroots movement—"artivism"— to campaign for political change.

Perhaps a primary lesson that the totality of the chapters provides is that the idea of "reform" touches all aspects of government, economics, and society. The comparisons help to outline the many issues that Cuba is facing and they provide important lessons (e.g., about the inadequacy of half measures). They also serve as a reminder that reforms are not always successful.

In the book's conclusion, Morgenstern and Linden reflect on reform in Cuba after the death of Fidel, the opening of relations with the United States, and the election of Donald Trump. In reviewing the discussions about social issues in Cuba and the comparative lessons about the reform process that result from the collective writings of the volume's authors, the authors emphasize, as noted at the outset of this essay, the unique domestic and internal context that put the direction of reform into question. With regard to economics, they discuss the strengths and weaknesses of the current system, but also the opportunities and threats facing Cuba. They note that the volume's authors are not sanguine about political change, as there have been fewer openings than in other reforming regimes, or as compared to the updating of the economic model. Borrowing from Linden's chapter, they also remind us that because democracy has not always brought hoped-for advances, support for reform can quickly dissipate. Reform processes, therefore, are not linear.

BIBLIOGRAPHY

Alvarez, José. *Cuba's Agricultural Sector.* Gainesville: University Press of Florida, 2004.

Cuba. Ministerio de Relaciones Exteriores. Comunicado de prensa de la delegación cubana a la primera reunión de la Comisión Bilateral Cuba-EE.UU. September 11, 2015. http://cubaeeuu.cubaminrex.cu/article/comunicado-de-prensa-de-la-dele gacion-cubana-la-primera-reunion-de-la-comision-bilateral.

de la Fuente, Alejandro. "Race and Income Inequality in Contemporary Cuba." *NACLA Report on the Americas* 44, no. 4 (July/August 2011): 30–33, 43.

de la Torre, Augusto, and Alain Ize. "Exchange Rate Unification: The Cuban Case." In Richard E. Feinberg and Ted Piccone, eds., *Cuba's Economic Change in Comparative Perspective.* Washington, DC: Brookings Institution, 2014.

Domínguez, Jorge I. *Cuba: Order and Revolution.* Cambridge: Belknap Press of Harvard University Press, 1978.

Espina Prieto, Rodrigo, and Pablo Rodríguez Ruiz. "Race and Inequality in Cuba Today." *Socialism and Democracy* 24, no. 1 (2010): 161–77.

Mallen, Patricia Mey. "China and Cuba: Skip the Ideology, Let's Talk about Money." *International Business Times,* April 24, 2014.

Mesa-Lago, Carmelo. *Institutional Changes of Cuba's Economic-Social Reforms: State and Market Roles, Progress, Hurdles, Comparisons, Monitoring and Effects.* Washington, DC: Brookings Institution, 2014.

Mesa-Lago, Carmelo. *Normalización de relaciones entre EEUU y Cuba: Causas, prioridades, progresos, obstáculos, efectos y peligros.* Documento de Trabajo No. 6/2015. Madrid: Real Instituto Elcano, May 8, 2015.

Mesa-Lago, Carmelo, and Fernando Gil. "Soviet Economic Relations with Cuba." In Eusebio Mujal-León, ed., *The USSR and Latin America.* Boston: Unwin Hyman, 1989.

Mesa-Lago, Carmelo, and Jorge Pérez-López. *Cuba Under Raúl Castro: Assessing the Reforms.* Boulder: Lynne Rienner Publishers, 2013.

Morales, Emilio. "Cuba-US Thaw Leads to Debt Renegotiation with Paris Club." *Café Fuerte,* June 11, 2015.

Nova González, Armando. *El modelo agrícola y los lineamientos de la política económica y social en Cuba.* Havana: Editorial de Ciencias Sociales, 2013.

Pérez-López, Jorge F. *The Economics of Cuban Sugar.* Pittsburgh: University of Pittsburgh Press, 1991a.

Pérez-López, Jorge F. "Swimming Against the Tide: Implications for Cuba of Soviet and Eastern European Reforms in Foreign Economic Relations." *Journal of Interamerican Studies and World Affairs* 33, no. 2, Summer 1991b.

"Programa Más Médicos cumple dos años en funciones." *Cuba Debate,* August 4, 2015.

Sánchez Vásquez, Adolfo. "La libertad del arte y la revolución." In Adolfo Sánchez Vásquez, ed,. *Estética y Marxismo.* Mexico City: Ediciones Era, 1970.

Spadoni, Paolo, and Sagebien, Julia. "Will They Still Love Us Tomorrow? Canada-Cuba Business Relations and the End of the U.S. Embargo." *Thunderbird International Business Review* 55, no. 1, January/February 2013. http://thecubaneconomy .com/wp-content/uploads/2014/12/SagebienSpadoni-TIBR.pdf.

U.S. Department of State. *Fact Sheet: Charting a New Course on Cuba.* December 17, 2004. https://www.whitehouse.gov/the-press-office/2014/12/17/fact-sheet-charting -new-course-cuba.

U.S. Department of State. *Media Note. United States and Cuba Hold Inaugural Bilateral Commission in Havana,* September 11, 2015. http://www.state.gov/r/pa/prs /ps/2015/09/246844.htm.

Zurbano, Roberto. "Racismo vs. socialismo en Cuba: un conflicto fuera de lugar (apuntes sobre/contra el colonialism interno)." *Meridional. Revista Chilena de Estudios Latinoamericanos* 4 (2015): 11–40.

—PART 1—
ECONOMICS

SCOTT MORGENSTERN AND JORGE PÉREZ-LÓPEZ
WITH CARLOS ALZUGARAY AND KEVIN MORRISON

1

MODELS OF ECONOMIC REFORM AND CUBA'S "UPDATING" OF ITS MODEL

Over the past five decades, Cuba has achieved significant advances in the areas of health and education, but has lagged with respect to economic growth. Perhaps the most significant challenge facing Raúl Castro's administration in the short and medium terms is how to promote vigorous and sustained economic growth. The consensus within and outside the island is that economic policy reforms are essential to kindle economic performance.[1]

This paper begins with a discussion of broad economic reform strategies that have been adopted by developed and developing countries over the past three decades, with special emphasis on the set policy reforms that has come to be called the "Washington Consensus," which dominated thinking in the economic development discipline for most of the 1980s and 1990s. The market-oriented reforms embodied in the Washington Consensus were deemed to bring broad benefits to society and thus had the characteristics of public goods. This package of market-oriented reforms was supported by many academicians and economic development practitioners and embraced by the World Bank and other key institutions in the development field, raising their profile and acceptability. As Morrison (2011) describes in his review of world trends in economic reforms, by now some of the glitter of the Washington Consensus has worn off, giving rise to a healthy reconsideration of development strategies and rejecting facile, one-size-fits-all approaches to economic reform.

How does that analysis translate to Cuba? The second part of the paper focuses on the Cuban leadership's analysis of economic reform priorities and economic policy choices. The emphasis here is that context and culture matter in choosing a model and Cuba's cautious moves reflect a pervasive lack of a reform mentality, which Raúl Castro is trying to change. Cuba's long and strong tradition of demonization and elimination of the market—emphasizing, for example, moral vs. economic incentives and egalitarianism vs. efficiency—circumscribes reform options for the Cuban leadership. They are clearly not ready to adopt Washington Consensus–type reforms, but the global market and internal pressures for economic growth are forcing dramatic experiments. Our expectation, then, is that there will be pockets of reform; in some areas Cuban policy makers will open the economy, but in others they will seek to preserve their heritage. Over time these parts may merge together, but for a time a dual strategy, which seems consistent with the slow steps they have been taking, could provide them with an opportunity to learn from other development models as well as build on their own economic successes and cultural legacies.

ECONOMIC POLICY REFORMS, THE WASHINGTON CONSENSUS

In 1989, as the economics profession was grappling with a global debt crisis that afflicted many developing countries and was seeking ways to invigorate economic growth, U.S. economist John Williamson wrote a paper for the Washington-based Institute for International Economics (IIE) in which he identified and discussed ten policy instruments "about whose proper deployment [to address overwhelming debt burdens] Washington can muster a reasonable degree of consensus."[2] By "Washington" Williamson meant the United States government (and its agencies, such as the Treasury Department and the U.S. Agency for International Development) as well as international financial institutions (IFIs), that is, the International Monetary Fund (IMF), the World Bank(WB), and multilateral regional development banks. The ten policy instruments identified by Williamson (1990, 2–3) were:

1. Fiscal discipline: Reducing large fiscal deficits to avoid balance of payments crises and high inflation that hit mainly the poor.

SCOTT MORGENSTERN AND JORGE PÉREZ-LÓPEZ

2. Reordering public expenditure priorities: Switching expenditure in a pro-growth and pro-poor way, from subsidies from areas that did not merit them to basic health, education, and infrastructure.

3. Tax reform: Aim was a tax system that would combine a broad tax base with moderate marginal tax rates.

4. Liberalizing interest rates: Removing controls on interest rates.

5. A competitive exchange rate: Avoiding overvalued or undervalued exchange rates.

6. Trade liberalization: Removal or reduction of tariff and nontariff barriers to trade.

7. Liberalization of inward foreign direct investment: Removal or reduction of barriers to foreign direct investment.

8. Privatization: Sale or transfer of state-owned resources to the private sector.

9. Deregulation: Easing barriers to entry and exit into markets.

10. Property rights: Providing the informal sector with the ability to gain property rights at acceptable cost.

In an important survey of economic policy reform, Rodrik (1996, 9) stressed the concurrence of views on economic reforms implicit in the Washington Consensus: "What is remarkable about current fashions on economic development policy (as applied to both developing and transitional economies), however, is the extent of convergence that has developed on the broad outlines of what constitutes an appropriate economic strategy. This strategy emphasizes fiscal rectitude, competitive exchange rates, free trade, privatization, undistorted market prices, and limited intervention (save for encouraging exports, education, and infrastructure)." The common assumption of proponents was that the set of market-oriented reforms would ultimately make all, or nearly all, of the citizenry better off.

Twenty-five years after Williamson's seminal paper, it is fair to say the intellectual attraction of the Washington Consensus has ebbed. Williamson has defended his construct, clarifying that he only attempted to identify economic policy areas and did not prescribe specific implementation steps. Moreover, he has stated that it was not his intention to set forth a one-size-fits-all approach to economic policy reform, and it was well understood in his presentation that national circumstances would govern the potential application of each of the policy prescriptions.

Despite these pronouncements, many in Latin America would argue that the international economic community did see the Washington Consensus as a prescription. Through the 1980s and 1990s, loans and restructuring packages from the international financial institutions required privatization, reduction of state payrolls, increased interest rates, and elimination of trade barriers. Clearly these policies had some positive impacts: some inefficient state enterprises were sold, bloated government budgets were trimmed, and governments introduced more accountability in their economic models. The neoliberal reforms, however, did not result in anticipated growth and in many instances sharpened distributional disparities. In a continent of poor people, more belt-tightening had its limits. Further, privatization was handled badly, resulting in state property going to political cronies and limiting revenue to the state from the sales. The implementation of neoliberal schemes and austerity policies also led to severe protests and riots, as seen in Venezuela, Bolivia, and Argentina. The dissatisfaction with policy reforms by certain groups who felt that the reform imposed costs on them rallied them to use the political process to block their implementation.

POLICY REFORM AFTER THE WASHINGTON CONSENSUS

The disappointing results of the implementation of the Washington Consensus brought about a reconsideration of economic reforms in promoting growth and addressing the challenges of poverty and wide differences in living standards across countries. In April 2006, the World Bank established a Commission on Growth and Development that brought together 21 leading practitioners from government, business, and the policy-making arenas, mostly from the developing world, "to take stock of the state of theoretical and empirical knowledge on economic growth with a view to drawing implications for policy for the current and next generation of policy-makers."[3] The rationale for the establishment of the Commission was:

1. The sense that poverty cannot be reduced in isolation of economic growth, and that that link has been missing in the minds and strategies of many;

2. Growing evidence that the economic and social forces underlying rapid and sustained growth are much less well understood than generally thought—economic advice to developing countries has been given with more confidence than justified by the state of knowledge;

3. Realization that the accumulation of highly relevant (both successful and unsuccessful) growth experiences over the past 20 years provides a unique source of learning; and

SCOTT MORGENSTERN AND JORGE PÉREZ-LÓPEZ

4. Growing awareness that, except for China, India, and other rapidly growing economies in East Asia, developing countries need to accelerate their rates of growth significantly for their incomes to catch up with income levels in industrialized countries, and for the world to achieve a better balance in the distribution of wealth and opportunity.

The final report of the Commission (2008) represents a milestone in thinking about pro-growth policy reforms. The Commission identified some of the distinctive characteristics of high-growth economies that could be emulated by other countries but does not provide a formula for policy makers to apply, as no generic formula exits. Each country's specific characteristics and historical experiences, the Commission concluded, must be reflected in its growth strategy.

Drawing on the report of the Commission, Morrison (2011) notes that countries should take an "experimental" direction in devising a reform strategy because there is no "generic" direction for growth. What special conditions are there for Cuba, assuming we accept the proposition that there is no "generic" agreed-upon best direction for reform?

CUBA'S "UPDATING" OF THE ECONOMIC MODEL

Cuba has, of course, much company in working to reform its economic policies. Most in Latin America have done this within the context of leftist politics, though as popularized by Castañeda (2006), some Latin American leaders have emphasized "populist" solutions, while others have leaned more toward solutions emphasized by the Washington Consensus. As mentioned by John Beverley—a participant in the conference that was the basis of this current volume—Castañeda (2006) and Reid (2008) harshly criticize the populists. Needless to say, those on the other side—especially Venezuela and Bolivia—have ended up with much more antagonistic relations with the United States. Cuba has fallen even further afield in terms of both opposition to neoliberal economic policy reforms and political relations with the United States. There was an odd parallel, however, in that Cuba implemented austerity measures during its Special Period in Time of Peace of the 1990s that were quite similar to those demanded by the IMF and the World Bank as part of their structural adjustment programs. Still, as the ideological vanguard of anti-Americanism, Cuban leaders would have a strong political and cultural reason to resist reforms that had a taint of bending to American-led policy prescription.

This cultural taint of the term "reform" has yielded several neologisms. Since the international lending institutions and the Washington Consensus appropriated the term "reform" to connote market-oriented changes, the former Soviet Union referred to its economic policy changes as "perestroika" (restructuring), the Chinese as "modernization," and the Vietnamese as "renovation." Thus, instead of "reforming" their economy, Cubans are "updating their economic model."

After five decades of implementing and promoting the virtues of a socialist economic model, it is difficult for the Cuban leadership and the Cuban people to change course and abandon the socialist ways. Adding to the policy immobilism, Cubans live by the proverb "better the devil you know than the saint you don't." Perhaps for these reasons, "updating" of the Cuban model has proceeded very slowly, but there are some notable changes as outlined in other chapters in this volume. This slow pace, which includes areas of experimentation overlaid within a continuation of socialism and economic centralism, fits at least three logics.

First, the resistance to change represents a recognition that change based on neoliberalism has not brought the promised results to the countries that have adopted it. In addition to examples of lackluster growth in earlier decades throughout Latin America, the region is continually plagued by income inequality and poverty. If this were not enough to bring caution to Cuban reformers, they must add the legacy that their economy has been conditioned by the longstanding U.S. embargo. Rightly or wrongly, the Castro regime instilled the idea in the Cuban population that the U.S. embargo was the primary reason for the island's poor economic performance. Cuba's political and economic allies have reinforced this view. Venezuela's support, which has been vital, has reinforced an anti-American stand.

Second, socialism has been shown to maintain power in the hands of the leadership, and thus the unwillingness to reform represents a political maneuver by the leadership to maintain power. This is one of the attractions for the Cuban leadership of the Vietnamese or Chinese models, which have reformed their economy but preserved political order. This dovetails with what Alzugaray believes is a sincere movement to save the legacy of the "historic" generation. The historic generation knows that its members are passing away and they want to leave behind to their children and grandchildren something better than what is happening in Cuba today. Therefore, Cuba is following the Vietnamese or Chinese general path, namely to reform the economy in order to preserve political order.

Cuba has in common with these socialist countries that its reforms have been "top down." They have not come from below, but actually imposed from the top. It is within the party and government structure that reforms happen. However, in the longer term it is impossible to pretend that reforming the economy can be accomplished without affecting the political order.

Thus, future Cuban leaders must consider the effect of changes not only on their powers but also on the likelihood of economic success.

While there is recognition in Cuba of Chinese and Vietnamese successes in policy reform and some academics and think tanks feel that Cuba should do something similar, Alzugaray argues that at the same time there is a cultural tendency—which is actually quite old and entrenched—that Cuba is exceptional. While politicians and many others think that the United States is exceptional, so do their counterparts in Cuba. The thinking that "Cuba has to do this differently" has been in place for a long time and continues to be so today.

Thinking about Cuban reforms requires considering a biological variable—in the next few years, there will be a political succession in Cuba whether political actors want it or not. If we accept that Fidel and Raúl Castro have had unique concerns with centralizing power and maintaining the centralized socialist system, then reform will naturally occur once those octogenarians pass the leadership torch. The experience of multiple past and current leaders in Latin America and other parts of the world suggests that future Cuban leaders may also see political advantages in the current centralized model. A key question may be whether future leaders will have the ability to mobilize the citizenry in their support. Cuban citizens have begun to criticize policies and make demands on their government. This has led to notable policy changes and reversals, such as opening possibilities for private employment, new opportunities for obtaining loans to set up small businesses and construct a high-tech port and free trade zone in Mariel. An open question is whether future leaders will marshal support in favor of what they have accomplished or face threating pressure for further changes.

Third, the Cubans have a particular concern with nationalism and preserving the legacy of the historic generation that was involved in the revolution. While it would be cynical to assume that the Cuban leadership is unconcerned with growth, it also seems reasonable to argue that the generation that fought in the revolution and built an anti-American political and economic system would be particularly focused on the successes of the revolution, whether mythical or actual. The "historic" generation is passing away, but it is unclear whether the next generation of leaders will still privilege this legacy as they devise the economic future.

The legitimacy of the Cuban political system, and thus its economic model, is based on five premises. First, Cuba has a strong nationalistic sentiment, based on more than a half century of conflict with the United States. Second, the Castros based their leadership on charisma. It is not clear that representative democracy is a strong value in the island. Third, at the same time, the Cubans have built some semblance of popular representation, because the government has consulted with people through different referenda. This third factor is reinforced by the fourth, the peculiarities of Cuban historical evolution: its Spanish heritage and revolution against Spain in the nineteenth century, American domination in the early 1900s, the socialist revolution ending in 1959, and so forth. Fifth, the revolution delivered public goods in its initial phase and it has maintained at least two: public health and education.

THE HISTORICAL LEGACY AND THE PACE OF REFORMS

These cultural and political factors explain the slow and irregular pace of reforms. While there are also many examples of experimenting with reforms under Fidel, there have been clear and dramatic changes under Raúl, in spite of his statement that he did "not want to improvise because in the past there was a lot of improvisation."

The reforms under Raúl through the end of 2012 are outlined in detail by Mesa-Lago and Pérez-López (2013); more recent changes are included in other chapters of this book. In what follows we illustrate the reforms focusing on three broad policies: the special development zone and shipping port at Mariel, employment policies, and rules to promote private agriculture. In addition to describing these policies briefly, we also bring out their incomplete nature and some inconsistencies in application that are hindering results.

Mariel Special Development Zone

The Economic and Social Development Guidelines approved by the Sixth Congress of the Cuban Communist Party in 2011 foresaw the establishment of special development zones (*zonas especiales de desarrollo*, ZED) with the objective of increasing exports, promoting import substitution, attracting high-technology investment, and promoting employment. The first ZED was established at Mariel, west of Havana, in 2013. Concurrently, the port of Mariel was also the location of a major infrastructure development project in the form of a shipping container megaport whose construction, estimated at a cost of $1 billion, was financed by Brazilian export promotion agencies. Illustrating the multinational nature of the project, the bulk of the Mariel port loading equipment originates from China and a Singaporean company will manage the facilities.

This is a clear example of Cuba's reforms implemented without full confidence, since it combines a dramatic change with severe restrictions. On the dramatic side, Cuban economist Omar Everleny Pérez Villanueva has stated that businesses that locate in the ZED will be able to operate for 50 years, own 100 percent of assets, operate tax-free for a decade, and be exempt from paying tariffs on imported equipment and raw materials (Johnson 2015). Businesses located in the ZED are expected to generate some 8,000 direct and indirect jobs for Cuban citizens, who will earn good salaries and be better able to support their families. If successful, it seems that the model would put great pressure on the government to open up other areas of the economy.

These important reforms with their potentially game-changing impacts are hamstrung in terms of their reach and impact by some national polices and others directed specifically at the free trade zone. At the national level, a limiting factor is the dual currency system, which distorts economic signals. Also at the national level, businessmen and workers in the zone will see the inconsistencies between economic freedoms in that area compared to severe limitations elsewhere. Activities in the zone will be affected by policies with respect to at least two areas. First, the free trade zone is limited by the employment system. Foreign firms will be allowed to set up manufacturing facilities and other businesses, but they must hire workers though an agency of the Cuban government. Thus workers will continue to earn the paltry government wages, while working alongside foreigners earning many times what they are earning. Second, the free trade zone has high hurdles that companies will have to jump in order to build businesses in the zone, including a complex, time-consuming, and uncertain application process.

Employment Policies

For most of the revolutionary period, the Cuban state was the overwhelming employer in the country, with the private sector limited to some agricultural and transportation activities. In 1993, in the depth of the economic crisis brought about by the end of the economic relationship between Cuba and the former Soviet Union, the Cuban government authorized self-employment by Cuban citizens in 157 specific occupations, among them production of food items (which led to the creation of small private restaurants, *paladares*), operation of private taxis, as well as a host of menial occupations (such as party clown, cigarette lighter refiller, etc.). Workers seeking to become self-employed had to register with the authorities, seek a license, and pay taxes in accordance with a special schedule for self-employed workers. Self-employed workers were allowed to hire family members in their activities, but not workers without a familial tie.

Shortly after ascending to Cuba's top leadership position in 2006, Raúl Castro announced the intention to reduce the size of the state payroll, indicating that up to 20 percent of state employees (around 1 million workers) were redundant and would be removed from their positions. The intention was that the retrenched workers would be absorbed by the private sector. After the Sixth Party Congress in 2011, the scope of self-employment was slightly expanded, with an additional 21 occupations authorized, bringing the total of authorized occupations to 178. Self-employed workers were also authorized to hire up to five nonfamily workers in about half the occupations. However, professionals are still not allowed to practice the trade for which they were trained, which means that accountants, physicians, architects, engineers, teachers, and other professionals must continue as employees of the state sector. (Many professionals, unable to practice their profession as self-employed, leave white-collar state jobs and join the tourism sector in menial jobs as they are able to increase their income through tips. It has been observed that Cuba has the most highly educated taxi drivers and tourism labor force in the world.) Rather than designating the occupations that are allowable under self-employment, a stronger and more positive action by the Cuban government would be to allow all occupations to be suitable for self-employment and strategically create a *short* list of occupations not allowed for self-employment at this time.

A very significant constraint on the expansion of the private sector is the lack of markets for intermediary goods, i.e., outlets where self-employed workers could legally purchase the inputs to ply their trade, for example, beef, rice, chicken, eggs for *paladares*; spare parts and tools for automobile mechanics; fabric, leather, buttons, and other sewing notions for dressmakers and tailors. Recently, the Cuban government has facilitated the sale to individuals of construction materials as a way to improve housing maintenance, but for most private sector workers, the black market and other illegal transactions provide a significant portion of their inputs and raw materials.

Promoting Private Agriculture

One of the most significant Cuban reforms to date is Decree Law no. 259 of 2008, which provided for the distribution of idle state lands in usufruct to private farmers not possessing land and to cooperatives. The logic of this reform measure was impeccable: on the one hand, it removed from the state inventory lands that were not being productively used and often had deteriorated (e.g., they had been infested by the invasive shrub *marabú*, which renders the land unusable) and on the other provided an incentive for private farmers and cooperatives to produce higher volumes and variety of agricultural products that would contribute to reducing the huge food import bill.

Despite the strong logic of the agricultural reform measure, the legislation that was approved by the Cuban government placed significant restrictions on the distribution of land that limited the measure's beneficial impact.

SCOTT MORGENSTERN AND JORGE PÉREZ-LÓPEZ

Thus, as originally proclaimed, the maximum amount of land that could be distributed to individuals pursuant to the reform measure was too small to permit crop rotation and other good agricultural practices; disallowed the construction of houses or other structures on the land (which meant that farmers who worked the land could not build even a tool shed and had to live elsewhere and possibly travel daily a long distance from and to their homes); limited the possession in usufruct to 10 years, although it could be renewed for a similar length of time (the criteria for renewal were not set out, however); and did not make any financial or credit provision to assist workers in clearing the land from *marabú* and otherwise preparing the land for cultivation. Subsequently, some of the above restrictions have been relaxed, but nevertheless the full impact of the distribution of land is being hampered.

LOOKING TO THE FUTURE

Raúl has rejected expediting economic reforms, which Cuban officials associated with the despised "shock treatment" they claim devastated the economies of the former Soviet Union and Eastern Europe, and stated that the pace of Cuba's reforms will be "*sin prisa, pero sin pausa*" (Castro 2013).[4] This suggests a lack of urgency, which was summed up by a former Spanish Ambassador to Cuba who expressed to one of the authors,[5] "Cuban leaders seem to think that time doesn't exist." International observers express a sense that Cuba faces enormous challenges and that time is running out on the "updating of the model."

There is no clear model for Cuba to follow, however. Given the negative consequences of neoliberal policies in much of Latin America and the resulting breakdown (or at least softening) of the Washington "consensus," plus the ideological hesitation that they would surely feel about adopting U.S.-led neoliberal policies, Cuba must find a new model. Several countries, including Cuba's ideological brethren Bolivia and Venezuela as well as the dominant player in the region, Brazil have developed a model centered on more state-centered capitalism. The model is not without its problems, but it has allowed the state to maintain control of important sectors and earn significant income with which it can support its highly valued social programs. Market oriented critics, of course, question the viability of this approach, as they argue that state enterprises are inefficient, wasteful, and have been unable to attract needed foreign capital to expand productive capacity. The simple response is that private enterprise has not always supported positive and equitable growth in Latin America, either.

Beyond the broad categories of economic plans, Cuba must deal with specific challenges. It faces pressures to simultaneously reform government enterprises, generate alternative employment, and unify the currency. Further, reforming the state would imply devolving decision-making power to the managers, which would be a new responsibility for a group of cadres who are used to following directives. The basic premise of the reform process—that economic change will bring benefits to all citizens that will ensure the stability of the system—is not happening. There is an increasing consciousness that political reform should accompany economic reform but there is no consensus yet on this point. The definition of what the new economic model will look like, on which it will be difficult to reach consensus, will carry with it the acceptance of the new mentality. There is increasing pressure from citizens to improve their standard of living, which has been demonstrated each time that a reform is reversed or modified or that the necessities of citizens are ignored by bureaucrats.

The Seventh Party Congress, held in April, 2016, was an opportunity for the country to revise its path, given the new opening to the United States. The Congress, however, largely reaffirmed the past, and offered few important changes. It confirmed, for example, that Raúl would step down from his government posts in 2018, but he will remain party secretary until 2021. This continuity is somewhat surprising, given the results of the efforts to "update the model," which has and will continue to lead to an inevitable assessment by the population of in terms of tangible improvements in their standard of living. The announced retirement of Raúl Castro does provide another opportunity for reform, since for the first time in six decades the new top leader will not likely be part of the "historicals" cohort and may not have the Castro surname. And, of course, there are the international issues, which are critical to the Cuban economy. Looming large is the future of economic support from Venezuela whose economy has been in free-fall and its political situation highly unstable.

Management of the new relationship with the United States announced by President Obama but now controlled by the Trump administration is, of course, critical. The economic and political opening at first brought both the prospect of an erosion or even elimination of the U.S. trade embargo, but also political challenges for the leadership. So far the Trump administration has been boisterous about clamping down on trade and political openings to Cuba, but while President Trump decreed some new restrictions on travel and the ability of U.S. companies to do business in Cuba, there have not been many material changes. U.S. public opinion and many from the business sector generally favor openness to the island, but pressure has not risen to a level to raise Cuba on Trump's priority list. The most important forces that could bring reform, then, are likely the passing of the Castro regime with the historicals, the continuing crisis in Venezuela, and the domestic pressures that have arisen from those hoping for improved living conditions. For six decades the regime has withstood the latter two types of pressures, but it remains to be seen whether a change in leadership will continue to avoid serious "updating."

NOTES

This chapter has been prepared by Scott Morgenstern and Jorge Pérez-López relying heavily on transcripts of presentations made at the conference by Kevin Morrison, "The Washington Consensus and the New Political Economy of Economic Reform," and Carlos Alzuguray, titled respectively: "The 'Updating of the Economic Model' in Cuba: An Initial Comparative Perspective of Its Domestic and Foreign Political Contexts and Implications." Morrison's presentation at the conference drew from Morrison (2011). The paper has been reviewed by Alzugaray and Morrison and their comments incorporated into the final draft.

1. For a discussion of the economic situation in Cuba through 2012 that underlies the current economic reforms see Mesa-Lago and Pérez-López (2013).

2. The historical background on the Washington Consensus is from Williamson (2004, 2). The classic exposition of the Washington consensus is Williamson's (1990).

3. The information on the formation of the Commission has been extracted from the World Bank website, http://web.worldbank.org/WBSITE/EXTERNAL/EXT ABOUTUS/ORGANIZATION/EXTPREMNET/0,contentMDK:23225570~page PK:64159605~piPK:64157667~theSitePK:489961,00.html.

4. Roughly translated as "without haste, but steadily."

5. In a conversation with Carlos Alzugaray.

BIBLIOGRAPHY

Castañeda, Jorge. "Latin America's Left Turn," *Foreign Affairs* 85 (2006): 28–43.

Castro, Raúl. "En Cuba no permitiremos terapias de choque," *Cuba Debate*, December 21, 2013.
http://www.cubadebate.cu/especiales/2013/12/21/presidente-raul-castro-comparece -en-asamblea-nacional-del-poder-popular-fotos/#.VjD7gitUETE.

Commission on Growth and Development. The Growth Report: Strategies for Sustained Growth and Inclusive Development. Washington, DC: World Bank, 2008.

Johnson, Tim. "U.S.-Cuba Diplomatic Thaw Puts Mariel Port Back in Spotlight." *The Miami Herald,* January 21, 2015.

Mesa-Lago, Carmelo, and Jorge Pérez-López. *Cuba Under Raúl Castro: Assessing the Reforms.* Boulder: Lynne Rienner Publishers, 2013.

Morrison, Kevin M. "When Public Goods Go Bad: The Implications of the End of the Washington Consensus for the Study of Economic Reform." *Comparative Politics* 44 (October 2011).

Reid, Michael. *Forgotten Continent: The Battle for Latin America's Soul.* New Haven: Yale University Press, 2008.

Rodrik, Dani. "Understanding Economic Policy Reform." *Journal of Economic Literature*, 34 (March 1996).

Williamson, John. *Latin American Adjustment: How Much Has Happened?* Washington, DC: Institute for International Economics, 1990.

Williamson, John. "Short History of the Washington Consensus." Paper commissioned by Fundación CIDOB for the conference "From the Washington Consensus towards a New Global Governance," 2. Barcelona, September 24–25, 2004. http://www.iie.com/publications/papers/williamson0904-2.pdf.

INITIAL CONDITIONS AND ECONOMIC DEVELOPMENT

THE EAST ASIAN "TIGERS" AND CUBA

To indicate some of the main challenges facing and opportunities available to Cuban policy makers over the next few decades, the initial conditions for economic development in Cuba in 2018 are compared to those in South Korea and Taiwan in 1960. In these Asian economies, such initial conditions contributed (along with good policy choices) to a half century of rapid economic growth, accompanied by low income inequality. The comparison suggests that Cuba is in some ways well positioned to make rapid and shared economic progress over the next fifty years, as South Korea and Taiwan have done over the previous fifty, provided that economic reforms broaden and deepen and that the United States lifts its trade embargo.

A review of the largely qualitative literature on the role of initial conditions in contributing to rapid economic growth in South Korea and Taiwan suggests that Cuban policy makers in 2018, like South Korean and Taiwanese policy makers in 1960, will be able to take advantage of a small domestic market (which encourages exports), low wages (which make exports more competitive), a healthy and well-educated population (which increases human capital and productivity), low initial GDP per capita (which is associated with faster growth), and weakly organized labor and business interests (which raises the state's steering capacity). The literature review also suggests that Cuban policy makers will encounter circumstances that pose challenges to long-term economic development, including the volatility of foreign exchange earnings from tourism, remittances, and nickel, widening income inequalities and racial disparities, a fall in the working-age share of the population, and modest state capacity.

Which initial conditions—those that encourage or those that discourage rapid economic growth—are likely to exercise the greatest influence in Cuba over the next twenty to fifty years? There is no better way to answer this question than to observe which initial conditions have done the most to influence economic growth in the past, preferably across a large set of countries over a long period of time. In 2010 the Economist Intelligence Unit (EIU) used a statistical model to forecast GDP per capita growth from 2010 to 2030 in a set of eighty-six countries, including Cuba and eleven other Latin American countries. The model included many, although not all, of the initial conditions identified in this study's review of the qualitative literature on South Korean and Taiwanese development. The EIU model predicted that the Cuban economy would grow by 172 percent from 2010 to 2030—in the top third of all countries, and second among the twelve Latin American countries for which forecasts were generated (Morris 2011: 22–27; EIU 2017).

The EIU model thus suggests that the initial conditions that Cuban policy makers will face in coming years are likely, on balance, to promote rather than inhibit rapid economic growth. This chapter's concluding section compares the initial conditions included in the EIU model to the initial conditions identified in this study's review of the qualitative literature on South Korean and Taiwanese development. It finds that the EIU model neglected several initial conditions that scholars believe to have been important to South Korean and Taiwanese development, but that most of these omitted factors are actually favorable for long-term economic growth. Hence, the present study finds that the EIU's conclusions would hold, and possibly be even more optimistic, if a more comprehensive set of growth-affecting initial conditions were taken into account.

POLICIES, INITIAL CONDITIONS, AND DEVELOPMENT PERFORMANCE IN EAST ASIA

In 1960, GDP per capita was $2,061 in Taiwan (about the level in Paraguay) and $1,610 in South Korea (about the level in Gambia). By 2010 GDP per capita had soared to $32,865 in Taiwan (about the level in Belgium) and $28,702 in South Korea (about the level in Italy). In the half century from 1960 to 2010

GDP per capita grew at an annual rate of 5.9 percent in South Korea and 5.7 percent in Taiwan. Among 106 societies with GDP per capita figures for both years, these rates of GDP per capita growth ranked fourth and fifth in the world, behind Botswana (6.2 percent), China (6.3 percent), and Equatorial Guinea (6.5 percent) (calculated from Feenstra, Inklaar, and Timmer 2013; all figures in 2005 U.S. dollars at purchasing power parity).

The development achievements of South Korea and Taiwan went beyond rapid GDP per capita growth. The Gini index of income inequality was low and stable in both places. In South Korea it fell from an already low 34.4 in 1965 to 31.0 in 2010, and in Taiwan it fell from 32.1 in 1964 to 31.8 in 2010 (UNU-WIDER 2014). From 1960 to 2010 infant mortality fell 96 percent in South Korea (from 79 to 3.5 per 1,000 live births) and 92 percent in Taiwan (from 54 to 4.2 per 1,000), compared to 88 percent in Cuba (from 39 to 5.4 per 1,000) and 76 percent in the United States (from 26 to 6.3 per 1,000). Among 104 societies with data for both 1960 and 2010 South Korea ranked 2nd, Taiwan 8th, Cuba 29th, and the United States 65th on percent decline of infant mortality from 1960 to 2010 (World Bank 2014 except Cuba 1960: McGuire and Frankel 2005: 90; Taiwan 1960: Mirzaee 1979: 233; and Taiwan 2010: Taiwan. DGBAS 2013: 111).

Policy explanations for rapid shared growth in South Korea and Taiwan stress market friendliness or industrial policy. The market-friendly explanation holds that South Korea and Taiwan grew rapidly and equitably after 1960 because policy makers maintained a small public sector and kept the economy open to trade and foreign capital (Balassa 1988; Hughes, ed. 1988; Paldam 2003). The industrial policy explanation stresses policy maker decisions to override market forces, "getting relative prices 'wrong'" (Amsden 1989: ch. 6), as well as the state's autonomy from interest group pressure, which made it easier for policy makers to implement these decisions (Evans 1995; Gereffi and Wyman eds. 1990; Haggard 1990; Wade 1990).

The governments of South Korea and Taiwan avoided persistent budget deficits, negative real interest rates, and overvalued currencies (Wade 1990: 52–61). Cautious macroeconomic management is one thing, however, and a free-market approach to development is another. From 1960 to 1990 the governments of South Korea and Taiwan consumed as much, relied as heavily on state firms, and spent almost as much as the governments of Argentina, Brazil, and Mexico (Jenkins 1991: 48–50). Moreover, the governments of South Korea and Taiwan restricted cross-border flows of goods, capital, and labor; redistributed land; initiated effective family planning; invested in primary and secondary schooling; subsidized labor-intensive manufactured exports;

and enacted effective disease control and primary health care programs (Mc-Guire 2016).

The South Korean and Taiwanese governments, as compared to their counterparts in Argentina, Brazil, and Mexico, were thus more successful, not less involved, in promoting economic growth. Development policies were not the whole story, however. Shaping and constraining those policies in South Korea and Taiwan, as well as influencing development in ways not mediated by policies, were shared growth-friendly initial conditions. Rodrik (1994: 14) singled out high educational attainment and low income and wealth inequality. Other writers have expanded the list to natural resource exports, colonial legacy, and other factors by comparing the East Asian cases to nations in Africa (Temple 1998), Latin America (McGuire 2016), and Southeast Asia (Booth 1999; Doner, Ritchie, and Slater 2005).

"Initial" conditions are not completely exogenous policy determinants. Such conditions come to be the way they are in part because of the results of previous policies, interacting with their own sets of initial conditions (turtles all the way down . . .). The more exogenous the factor, the more it should count as a true initial condition, rather than merely as an intervening mechanism or a policy consequence. Temple (1998: 310) suggests that "it is useful to think of initial conditions as ranged along a spectrum. At one end of the spectrum are factors that are plausibly exogenous (geography, ethnic diversity). At the other end are the results of previous policies (education, health care). Somewhere in the middle are variables that are influenced by policy, but are likely to change only slowly (social arrangements, income distribution)."

In the analyses cited above the hypothesized initial conditions most influentially mentioned as leading to rapid shared growth in South Korea and Taiwan include, at the mostly exogenous end of the spectrum, 1) a Japanese colonial legacy; 2) ethnic homogeneity; 3) a Confucian (or Sinic) cultural heritage; and 4) favorable international conditions for rapid shared growth, whose most pertinent aspects were 4a) a military threat from a powerful neighbor and 4b) few low-wage manufactured export competitors. Partly exogenous initial conditions include 5) a dearth of exportable mineral or petroleum resources; 6) low initial income inequality; 7) being on the threshold of a rapid rise in the ratio of working-age to nonworking–age people; 8) high state capacity; 9) a small internal market; 10) weakly organized landowners, industrialists, and urban workers; and 11) low initial GDP per capita. At the mostly endogenous end of the spectrum—strongly shaped by previous policies—are 12) high educational attainment and health status and 13) low wages (table 2.1). Imagining contemporary Cuba as embarking in the medium term

TABLE 2.1. Hypothesized Growth-Promoting Initial Conditions: South Korea and Taiwan 1960 vs. Cuba 2015

	S. Korean & Taiwan 1960	Cuba 2015	Exogeneity	Plausibility
8 conditions not shared:				
Japanese colony/legacy	Yes	No	High	High
Ethnic homogeneity	Yes	No	High	Low
Sinic	Yes	No	High	Moderate
Favorable int'l context	Yes	No	High	High
Scarce natural resources	Yes	No	Moderate	Moderate
Low income inequality	Yes	No	Moderate	High
Favorable age	Yes	No	Moderate	High
High state capacity	Yes	No	Moderate	High
5 conditions shared:				
Small market	Yes	Yes	High	Moderate
Weak social classes	Yes	Yes	Moderate	High
Low affluence	Yes	Yes	Low	High
Good health/education	Yes	Yes	Low	High
Low wages	Yes	Yes	Low	Moderate

on deepening economic and perhaps political reforms, where does it stand on these thirteen initial conditions, and what implications does its sharing (or not) of these conditions have for its economic development prospects?

INITIAL CONDITIONS IN SOUTH KOREA AND TAIWAN IN 1960 AND IN CUBA IN 2018

South Korea and Taiwan in 1960 had growth-promoting initial conditions that Cuba in 2018 lacks: a Japanese colonial legacy, a Sinic or Confucian culture, ethnic homogeneity, an existential military threat from a powerful neighbor, few low-wage manufactured export competitors, a dearth of mineral and petroleum resources, low income inequality, a rising ratio of workers to nonworkers, and high state capacity. On the other hand, South Korea and Taiwan in 1960 also had several hypothesized growth-promoting initial conditions that Cuba in 2018 shares: small domestic markets, weakly organized economic interests, a low level of initial affluence, low wages, and a high level of educational attainment and health status (see figure 2.1). The former conditions challenge Cuban policy makers; the latter provide opportunities.

Colonial Legacy

Japan colonized Taiwan from 1895 to 1945 and Korea from 1910 to 1945. Japanese colonialism contributed to rapid and shared economic growth in each society in part by weakening landed classes. In Taiwan, the Japanese in 1905 required many absentee landlords to cede their holdings to tenants in return for government bonds (Gold 1986: 36–38). In Korea, by contrast, the Japanese conducted a land-use survey that led to tax hikes and stricter definitions of property rights that pushed marginal farmers off the land. However, Japanese displaced Koreans as owners of many holdings, and Koreans who retained large properties were later compromised by their association with Japanese colonialism. The Korean landed class was thus fairly weak when colonial rule ended in 1945, facilitating subsequent land reform and raising the state's autonomy from the dominant social classes (Cumings 1981: 41–48).

The Japanese also created effective bureaucracies that penetrated throughout the colonial territories (Kohli 2004: 32–61). The strong, centralized bureaucracies that are often credited with a central role in the economic "miracles" of South Korea and Taiwan are in part legacies of the Japanese colonial state (Cumings 1987; Kohli 1994). Using these bureaucracies, the Japanese improved education, health care, water provision, and sanitation, enhancing welfare and productivity and building a foundation for subsequent economic growth (McGuire 2010: 181–227). In addition, the Japanese, unlike other colonizing powers, created extensive infrastructure and industry in their colonies. They modernized agriculture; improved ports, roads, and railways; constructed hydroelectric facilities; and built steel, aluminum, and chemical factories (Cumings 1987: 55–56). Colonial rule was harsh in East Asia, as elsewhere, but the Japanese colonial legacy was unusually conducive to subsequent economic development.

The Japanese in Korea and Taiwan weakened hitherto powerful landed classes; the Spanish in Cuba allowed land concentration by domestic sugar planters and later by U.S. business interests. The Japanese controlled diseases and expanded schooling; the Spanish spread epidemics and neglected education (Fitchen 1974). The Japanese built aluminum smelters and hydroelectric dams; the Spanish built sugar mills and cigar factories. A reforming Cuba will have to contend, however, not only with the Spanish colonial heritage (1512–1898), but also with sixty years of U.S. domination, weak governance, and intermittent dictatorship (1898–1958) followed by nearly sixty years of revolutionary rule (1959–2018). Of these three legacies the colonial heritage is probably least significant. The revolutionary legacy is by far the most important, but the years from 1898 to 1958 should not be underestimated in understanding Cuba's level of human development today, notably in the area of mortality decline (McGuire and Frankel 2005).

Ethnic Homogeneity

South Korea is among the world's most ethnically homogeneous countries (Fearon and Laitin 2003; Roeder 2001). About 2 percent of the Taiwanese population is of aboriginal descent; the remaining 98 percent is Han Chinese, although an important subethnic distinction exists between the 85 percent of Taiwanese whose ancestors arrived centuries ago and the 15 percent whose parents or grandparents arrived in the late 1940s during the Kuomintang's retreat toward the end of the Chinese Civil War (1945–1949). Cuba is ethnically homogeneous according to language-based indices of linguistic fractionalization, but ethnically heterogeneous according to self-identified race-based indices (Roeder 2001). These conflicting assessments underscore that ethnic and racial identities are hard to conceptualize and measure, but there can be little doubt that South Korea and Taiwan are more ethnically homogeneous than Cuba.

Some scholars have argued that ethnic homogeneity boosted economic growth in South Korea and Taiwan (Kim and Park 2003: 46). Other have made the corollary conjecture that ethnic heterogeneity slows economic growth, by increasing rent-seeking (Easterly and Levine 1997: 1206) or the risk of civil war (Collier and Hoeffler 1998: 567–70; Temple 1998: 338–39). Ethnic heterogeneity could also slow growth through ethnic discrimination, which (like gender bias) wastes talent. On the other hand, Norton (2000: 330–31) concluded that countries with *moderate* ethnic heterogeneity have the highest growth prospects, because "a diverse ethnic mix . . . brings about variety in abilities, experiences, and cultures that may be productive and may lead to innovation and creativity" (Alesina and La Ferrara 2005: 762).

The flexibility of ethnic identities and the challenges of measuring ethnic diversity make it risky to put much faith in the hypothesis that ethnic heterogeneity slows economic growth. The empirical evidence also casts doubt on the corollary proposition that ethnic homogeneity is good for economic growth. After all, South Korea and Taiwan, despite ethnic homogeneity, were extremely poor in 1960. Cuban policy makers, however, will have to acknowledge, confront, and rectify racial inequalities that originated long before the revolution but have been exacerbated in recent years by the inflow of U.S. dollars, mainly through remittances, to a high proportion of Cuban whites but a low proportion of Cuban blacks (Blue 2007; de la Fuente 2001).

Culture

Sinic culture, which originated in mainland China but continues to prevail in South Korea and Taiwan, is often said to encourage economic growth. According to Lawrence Harrison (1992: 112), "the Confucian emphasis on education, merit, hard work, and discipline, combined with the achievement-motivating tradition of ancestor-worship and the Tao emphasis on frugality, constitutes a potent, albeit largely latent, formula for growth comparable in its potential to Weber's view of Calvinism." A problem with the cultural-values approach is that it is tricky to use something that changes very slowly, like ethnic homogeneity or Sinic culture, to explain a sudden burst of economic growth. South Korea and Taiwan grew rapidly after 1960, but their performance during the previous 2,000 years, when Sinic culture was presumably even more deeply entrenched, was less impressive. The disdain for commerce characteristic of Confucianism seems especially disadvantageous to economic growth. The high value that Confucianism places on harmony and hierarchy could contribute to growth-promoting political stability, but could also reduce innovation. Likewise, strong family ties could contribute to the aggregation of capital, but excessive filial piety could inhibit individual initiative.

Harrison (1992: 113) argues that external factors, like an oppressive mandarin, colonial, or Leninist bureaucracy, long suppressed the growth-promoting traits of Sinic culture, and that upon their removal those traits begin to flourish. It would be remarkable, however, if so blunt a change as the removal of bureaucratic suffocation neutralized precisely those aspects of Sinic culture inimical to economic development and activated precisely the traits propitious for it. Cultural values shape the design and impact of policy, but do not make or break the prospects for development. Cubans respond to incentives in much the same way as people anywhere else, although distinctive features of Cuban culture should not be neglected in policy design.

Favorable International Context

The international context changed significantly between 1960 and 2018. On the geopolitical front, for several decades after World War II South Korea and Taiwan confronted a military threat from a powerful neighbor. This military threat, although providing a ready excuse for authoritarian rule, also contributed to rapid and equitable economic growth. Communist triumphs in China and northern Korea produced a countersurge of nationalism that mobilized citizens for development. The communist victories also produced an outflow of migrants bringing with them capital and entrepreneurship. The perceived threat of communism encouraged the United States government to provide massive foreign aid in the 1950s. In South Korea, the U.S. occupation in 1947, pressure from the Truman administration, and the North Korean invasion in 1950 combined to encourage and facilitate land redistribution (Cumings 1990: 472, 677–80). In Taiwan, the Kuomintang implemented the 1949–1953 land reform because, as outsiders, they needed domestic allies; and because they wanted to avoid repeating their experience in mainland China, where land reform in communist-occupied areas had won peasant support for the Red Army. Also, the rise of East Asian communism gave South Korean and Taiwan governments a pretext to repress unions, keeping wages low and facilitating the export of labor-intensive manufactured goods beginning in the early 1960s.

Taiwan and South Korea began to produce labor-intensive manufactured goods at an unusually propitious time: the 1960s, a period of rapid world economic growth, few low-wage manufactured export competitors, and fairly easy (but not unrestricted) access to markets in the United States, whose political leaders sought to strengthen economies thought to be threatened by communism. By the late 1970s world economic growth was slowing, new competitors had entered the export market, and the U.S. public was becoming more concerned with import competition than with the Cold War. Also, just because exporting labor-intensive manufactures benefited early adopters does not mean it will help subsequent emulators. More countries exporting labor-intensive manufactures mean fewer benefits for each successive adopter, in part because the rising supply will put downward pressure on prices (Broad and Cavanagh 1988). Thanks to high educational levels South Korea and Taiwan were able to meet this challenge by moving up through the product cycle, shifting production to higher value-added goods like ships, cars, and semiconductors (South Korea) and steel, electronics, and petrochemicals (Taiwan).

Cuba, it is to be hoped, will have to sacrifice in decades to come any economic growth "advantages" conferred by a military threat from a powerful neighbor. Such a threat existed in the 1960s and 1970s (and was realized in 1961 at the Bay of Pigs), but not in 2018. The world, moreover, is bristling with exporters of cheap, labor-intensive manufactured goods, so it would be unwise for Cuban policy makers to put all their eggs in that particular basket. The average monthly salary in Cuba in 2010 was $18 per month (Mesa-Lago and Pérez-López 2013: 133), which is certainly competitive with the lowest salaries on the planet, but it represents an enormous distortion in a country classified by the World Bank as "upper middle-income" that cannot survive even minimal economic rationalization. Cheap, labor-intensive manufactured exports might be a component of a development strategy in contemporary Cuba, provided the United States lifts the trade embargo, but recreating aspects of historical time that contributed to the development of South Korea and Taiwan is both undesirable and infeasible.

Petroleum and Mineral Resources

A rich hydrocarbon or hard-rock mineral resource endowment has been found to be associated with slower economic growth; likewise, a poor hydrocarbon or hard-rock mineral resource endowment has been found to be associated with faster economic growth (Sachs and Warner 1995). South Korea and Taiwan seem to confirm this association: with meager hydrocarbon and hard-rock mineral endowments, they experienced rapid as well as shared economic growth. Evidence of any kind that a resource curse exists should worry policy makers in Cuba, which is richly endowed with nickel and some petroleum resources. The resource curse seems, however, to be less universally damning than some once believed. A review of four mechanisms by which the resource curse is hypothesized to have worked its effects shows that some conjectured resource curse processes can be ameliorated by good policies, while others may be exploited for side benefits.

The first and most famous resource curse mechanism is the Dutch Disease. In 1959, a rise in Dutch natural gas exports led to an inflow of foreign exchange that drove up the value of the guilder and priced Dutch manufactured exports out of other markets. An inflow of foreign currency from the export of natural resources, if exchanged for the domestic currency, will drive up the price of the domestic currency, reducing demand from foreign buyers of the natural resource–exporting country's other exports (including manufactured and agricultural goods), as well as from foreign investors and foreign tourists. Overvaluation makes a country's exports less competitive in foreign markets, and from the producer's point of view, it makes exporting less profitable relative to selling on the domestic market, because export earnings arrive in (cheap) foreign currency, whereas most expenses (for labor, services, etc.) are paid in (expensive) local currency (Davis 1995: 1768; *Economist* 1995: 88). A related phenomenon is the "unbalanced productive structure," by which natural resource exporters suffer from higher equilibrium exchange rates than countries without many such exports (Diamand 1986; Mahon 1992).

An inflow of dollars can cause the Dutch Disease, however, only if the dollars are sold for pesos. To avoid such sales, governments can "sterilize" dollar inflows by spending them on imports, by paying off dollar-denominated debt, by investing them abroad, or by tucking them away in a stabilization fund that takes in dollars in good times and releases them in hard times (Sugawara 2014). Indonesia in the 1970s sterilized much of its oil windfall by buying imports priced in foreign currencies and by building up its foreign reserves while refraining from expanding the domestic money supply (Prawiro 1998: 114–24). By the late 1980s, thanks in part to these policies, Indonesia, defying the resource curse, had become a major exporter of light manufactured goods. The Dutch Disease cannot be ignored; it is an aspect of the environment in which policy makers in petroleum and mineral-exporting countries must operate. The Indonesian case shows, however, that good policies can do much to reduce its impact.

A second problem with exporting commodities—agricultural, as well as petroleum and mineral—is that commodities experience more price volatility than manufactures. If demand for nickel or sugar surges, prices will rise because the increase in supply lags. If demand subsequently falls, production, having recently responded to high demand, will be in oversupply. Volatility is particularly great with agricultural exports, which are vulnerable to the weather; and especially with perishables (seafood, flowers), which cannot be stockpiled when prices are low and then released from inventory when prices are high. Fuel, mineral, and agricultural price volatility is bad for economic growth insofar as it complicates investment decisions for businesses and economic planning for governments, but good insofar as price volatility creates incentives for governments, businesses, and households to save for a rainy day. Hence, although price fluctuations are wider for commodities than for manufactured goods, this price volatility could contribute to, as well as impede, economic growth.

A third challenge faced by resource-rich countries is that their policy makers are often tempted to make poor investment decisions. When commodity prices are high, more windfall often comes in than can be invested wisely. When prices are low, policy makers are often tempted to borrow abroad against anticipated future windfalls, especially if they expect to be leaving office soon. Accordingly, a rich natural resource endowment can encourage bad investments and a high foreign debt. Easy wealth from natural resource exports may also cause policy makers to indulge in "myopic sloth," leading to paralysis when decisions need to be made, or in "shortsighted euphoria," leading to bad investment decisions when paralysis would have been better (Ross 2001). Moreover, the sudden availability of investment capital as a result of a resource boom often tempts governments (especially those with short incumbencies) to invest in white elephant projects that confer prestige or electoral benefits but may be unsustainable or take a long time to mature. The next government has to continue investing in these white elephants even after the income from the resource boom is long gone (Torvik 2009: 253).

A fourth mechanism by which the resource curse can slow economic growth is by encouraging a suboptimal sequence of industrial development. Foreign exchange from commodity exports can be used to transit directly from light to heavy import substitution, without going through an intervening foreign exchange–earning stage of light manufactured exports (Auty 1994: 16). This sequence of industrialization is suboptimal for economic growth, not least because heavy import substitution is itself import-intensive, and thus encourages foreign borrowing. Moreover, by allowing higher wages, earnings from commodity exports make manufactures more expensive, discouraging labor-intensive exports. Mahon (1992) argues that relatively high wages may have made Latin America "too rich to prosper." Natural resource exports can also encourage protectionism if governments raise tariffs and other restrictions to counter the import surge produced by currency overvaluation (Sachs and Warner 1995).

The ability to export natural resources is not as "exogenous" (with respect to the consequences of previous policies) as it might seem at first thought. In addition to existing, natural resources must be discovered and exploited. In the conventional view, dependence on natural resource exports leads to bad policies and institutions, which lead in turn to slow economic growth. It is equally plausible, however, that countries with bad policies and institutions have both slow economic growth and a large share of commodities in their export profiles, because they can't export much else (Brunnschweiler and Bulte 2008). This could be one reason why nickel today is one of Cuba's main merchandise exports. Being an oil or mineral exporter creates challenges for a country's economic development, but does not doom the country to poor economic performance. Whether nickel and (possibly) petroleum become a curse or a blessing to the Cuban economy will depend on whether policy makers recognize the challenges posed by natural resource exports and take appropriate action to meet them.

Income Inequality

As noted earlier, the Gini index of income inequality in the mid-1960s was 34.4 in South Korea and 32.1 in Taiwan. These low levels of *income* inequality were attributable first and foremost to low *land* inequality, thanks to thoroughgoing land reform in each society in the late 1940s and early 1950s (Campos and Root 1996: 51–56; Rodrik 1994: 18). Low initial income inequality encourages economic growth in a variety of ways: by expanding the domestic market (Murphy, Schleifer, and Vishny 1989), by reducing social and political instability (Alesina and Perotti 1996), and by relieving pressure on policy makers to enact market-distorting income-redistributive policies (Persson and Tabellini 1994). Booth (1999) and Rodrik (1994) each identify low income inequality as an initial condition that contributed to economic growth in post-1960 South Korea and Taiwan, and Temple (1998) identifies high income inequality as an impediment to economic growth in Sub-Saharan Africa during the 1960s, 1970s, and 1980s.

In revolutionary Cuba, land reform and property redistribution in 1959 caused the Gini index to fall from 55–57 in the 1950s to 32 in 1962, 25 in 1978, and 22 in 1986 (Brundenius 2009: 40). From that point on, however, inequality began to rise. Contributing to the increase during the post-1989 "Special Period" were a rise in foreign currency remittances, the introduction of limited private and cooperative economic activity, a 1994 tax reform that increased the treasury's reliance on regressive indirect taxes, and the implantation of a dual exchange rate system in which convertible pesos (CUC) were worth about twenty-four times as much as the nonconvertible pesos (CUP) in which most Cubans were paid. As a result of these changes, "the Gini income inequality coefficient, estimated by foreign researchers based only on CUP, rose 64 percent between 1989 and 1999 (from 0.250 to 0.407); if CUC earnings and remittances were included, the coefficient would be even higher" (Mesa-Lago and Pérez-López 2013: 134).

It could be argued that high income inequality matters less to well-being in Cuba than in capitalist countries because the state in Cuba provides basic goods and services that would, in a capitalist society, require out-of-pocket outlays. Even if that were the case, however—food rations have been cut significantly in recent years (Mesa-Lago and Pérez-López 2013: 130)—high income inequality could still impede economic growth by shrinking the internal market, creating political instability, or encouraging market-distorting income-redistributive policies. In 1960, South Korea and Taiwan reaped the diverse economic growth advantages of a low initial level of income inequality. In decades to come, Cuba will not have these advantages.

Demography

The age distribution of the population deserves close scrutiny in explanations for GDP per capita growth. A society receives a demographic dividend when a baby boom generation enters the labor force just as fertility (and thus the number of children) starts to decline, but before population aging raises significantly the number of retirees. As the baby boomers enter the workforce, the dependency ratio initially falls (there are fewer children but not yet many more elderly), savings initially rise (more people are contributing to rather than withdrawing from pension funds), women start to work outside the home (thanks to falling fertility), and parents invest more in each child's education (because they have fewer children) (Bloom, Canning, and Sevilla 2003: 39–42). Rapid fertility decline can thus contribute to faster GDP per capita growth not only by making the number of inhabitants—the denominator of the GDP per capita quotient—smaller than it would otherwise be, but also, for a number of decades, by reducing the dependency ratio by reducing the number of children. As working baby boomers start to retire, however, the dependency ratio rises again.

In South Korea the ratio of the working-age (15–64) to nonworking-age population rose from 124:100 in 1960 to 266:100 in 2010 (calculated from World Bank 2014). Similarly, in Taiwan, the ratio rose from 109:100 in 1960 to 279:100 in 2010 (calculated from Taiwan. CEPD 2012: 29). The rising ratio of workers to nonworkers boosted economic growth, especially from 1960 to 1990. "Estimates indicate that as much as one-third of the 'miracle' economic growth in East Asia between 1965 and 1990 can be accounted for by changes in age structure associated with the region's rapid demographic transition" (Bloom 2011: 566).

Cuba in 2018 has exhausted its demographic dividend (as have South Korea and Taiwan). In Cuba the ratio of working-age (15–64) to nonworking-age inhabitants rose from 152:100 in 1960 to 236:100 in 2010 (calculated from World Bank 2014). By 2020, however, the ratio is projected to fall to 228:100. From that point on it is predicted to fall to 174:100 in 2030, 126:100 in 2040, 119:100 in 2050, and 105:100 in 2060 (calculated from United Nations Population Division 2014). Moreover, the nonworkers in 2060 will be much more expensive to support, in real terms, than the nonworkers in 1960, because they will comprise mostly elderly people requiring usually expensive medical care rather than children requiring usually inexpensive medical care. Recent government efforts to encourage Cuban parents to have more children, even if successful, will only raise the dependency ratio in the short run. It is difficult to see how the projected rapid decline in the ratio of the working-age to nonworking-age population could be anything but a significant drag on economic growth in Cuba over the next 50 years.

State Capacity

The state was highly capable in both South Korea and Taiwan in 1960, in part because of state-building under Japanese colonialism (Kohli 1994: 1270; Ho 1987: 246–47). Over the period from 1970 to 1990 South Korea and Taiwan scored second and third among thirty-five developing countries rated by experts on a "Weberianness Scale," which involved the experts answering specific questions about whether a particular state practices meritocratic recruitment and offers a predictable career ladder (Evans and Rauch 1999: 755). South Korea and Taiwan have not been free of corruption, but it has been mostly "limited to the very top echelons of the bureaucracy, whereas in many other developing countries it runs all the way down to the lowest ranks" (Rodrik 1994: 46). Hence the distortions that corruption imposes in South Korea and Taiwan are restricted to a few transactions rather than spread across many, where they compound one another (Rodrik 1994: 47).

The World Bank in each year from 1996 to 2013 has used experts to measure the perceived "quality of government" in about 200 countries. Of the six dimensions so analyzed, the three most pertinent to state capacity as usually defined are control of corruption, government effectiveness, and rule of law. Cuba fares quite well on control of corruption; in 2013 it ranked above the median (62nd percentile) among the 214 countries rated, and fourth-best among twenty Latin American countries. Although its percentile rank had been even higher in 1996 (70), its percentile rank in 2013 (62) remained almost as high as those of South Korea (70) or Taiwan (73). Cuba fared less well on government effectiveness, defined as "perceptions of the quality of public services, the quality of the civil service and the degree of its independence from political pressures, the quality of policy formulation and implementation, and the credibility of the government's commitment to such policies" (Kaufmann, Kraay, and Mastruzzi 2011: 223). On government effectiveness Cuba in 2013 had a percentile rank of only 40, placing it twelfth among 20 Latin American countries. Although higher than its rank of 18 in 1996, Cuba's percentile rank of 40 in 2013 remained well below those of South Korea (82) and Taiwan (84). On rule of law, including "the quality of contract enforcement, property rights, the police, and the courts," Cuba in 2013 had a percentile rank of 32, up from 17 in 1996 but only 10th among 20 Latin American countries and well below the percentile ranks of South Korea (79) and Taiwan (84).

Relative to contemporary states, then, South Korea and Taiwan in 1960 ranked higher on state capacity than Cuba ranked in 2013. Cuban policy makers in recent years have done well in preventing and treating HIV/AIDS (Anderson 2009), preparing people for hurricanes (Moore, Chandra, and Feeney 2013), and promoting energy conservation (Käkönen, Kaisti, and Luukkanen 2014). On the other side of the ledger the provision of health care, the flagship achievement of the revolution, has lagged in some respects (Kath 2010). On the whole, however, relative to other countries, state capacity in Cuba in 2013 was at best moderate, rather than high as in South Korea and Taiwan in 1960. In coming years the challenge of building effective state institutions will be at least as important to Cuban economic development as the task of making wise policy choices.

The Cohesion and Organization of Economic Interests

State autonomy depends not only on features of the state bureaucracy, but also on the pliability of economic interests. The less cohesive and organized such interests, the higher the state's steering capacity. Governments in South Korea and Taiwan from 1945 to 1960 faced unusually weak landowning, industrialist, and working classes. In each society, as previously noted, the Japanese colonial regime directly or indirectly weakened landowners. Had landowners been stronger they might have resisted more effectively the land reforms the South Korean and Taiwanese governments launched in the late 1940s and early 1950s. These land reforms made a powerful contribution to the subsequent achievement of rapid and widely shared economic growth. In South Korea in the 1950s the Rhee government coddled certain industrialists (Cheng 1990: 147–51), but shortly after the May 1961 coup "those who had profited from import substitution were marched through the streets, carrying sandwich signs with slogans like 'I was a parasite on the people'" (Cumings 1987: 69). With industrialists so discredited, it was easier for the Park government to engineer a shift toward manufactured exports (e.g., by ending currency overvaluation)—another policy crucial to shared growth. Taiwan never developed a class of import-substitution industrialists because the Kuomintang kept most former Japanese firms under state control (Cheng 1990: 150).

When South Korea switched around 1960 from encouraging light import substitution to promoting light manufactured exports, less than 1 percent of its labor force belonged to unions. Eight percent of the Taiwanese labor force was unionized in 1958, but Taiwanese unions had rules restricting strikes, forbidding collective bargaining, requiring new unions to have government approval, and granting membership to managers (Deyo 1989: 70–73, 115–18). The weakness of organized workers in South Korea and Taiwan in the early 1960s helped South Korean and Taiwanese policy makers encourage a shift from import substitution to export promotion. Paradoxically, then, weak labor unions in South Korea and Taiwan facilitated a development strategy that led in the long run to higher wages and more secure employment.

Cuba in 2018 has no autonomous unions or organized economic interests. Like Taiwanese unions in the early 1960s, Cuban unions include managers as well as workers (Radfar 2016: 5). The Cuban Workers' Central (CTC) endorsed the government's 2008 decision to raise the retirement age by five years, and backed the government's 2010 proposal to reduce the number of state sector workers by half a million (Prieto Samsónov and Díaz Torres 2014: 31 n. 19). The layoffs were delayed, but there is no sign that pressure from the CTC contributed to the postponement (Mesa-Lago 2013: 35–36). Business interests, properly so called, do not exist in Cuba, although the Cuban military and individuals connected to the Castros control the powerful CIMEX and GAESA conglomerates that control a good part of Cuba's finance, international and retail trade, tourism, and real estate. The future of these conglomerates is hard to predict, but it seems safe to say that, if market reforms progress, they will end up looking more like the conglomerates controlled by Russian oligarchs—highly vulnerable to central government pressure—than like the South Korean *chaebol*, which initially depended on the state for subsidized loans but eventually became more autonomous. Accordingly, even if state capacity in Cuba is not high, society's capacity is even lower, making the Cuban state in 2018 at least as autonomous as the South Korea and Taiwanese states were in 1960. Too much state autonomy can deprive state officials of information and allies for policy implementation (Evans 1995), but too little forces the state to "dance to the tune of the dynamics of civil society," as happened in Argentina from 1955 to 1976 (O'Donnell 1978: 25). The weakness of economic interests in contemporary Cuba should therefore be counted as an initial condition that the island shares with South Korea and Taiwan and that is, on balance, conducive to shared growth.

Market Size

In 1960 South Korea had 25 million inhabitants; Taiwan had 10 million. Almost all of these people were poor, so domestic demand for manufactured goods was too weak to sustain an industrialization strategy based on capital-intensive heavy import substitution, as happened in the larger Latin American countries. A large domestic market does not *preclude* the alternative strategy of light manufactured exports (Japan and China are cases in point), but a small domestic market makes less attractive the single-minded pursuit of premature heavy import substitution, which turned out to be counterproductive in Argentina and elsewhere.

The export of labor-intensive manufactures is more conducive than heavy import substitution to rapid and sustained economic growth. Labor-intensive export-oriented industrialization permits economies of scale by expanding the market to foreign as well as domestic buyers. It also forces industry to keep costs low and quality consistent in order to remain internationally competitive; it requires producers to anticipate and respond to changes in technology and international market conditions; it makes more efficient use of factor endowments (abundant labor and scarce land and capital); it spreads jobs and income, promoting growth by reducing inequality; and it generates rather than consumes foreign exchange, minimizing a bottleneck that led to unsustainable foreign borrowing in many Latin American countries.

Cuban policy makers interested in promoting industry will have strong incentives to invest in manufacturing for export, just as South Korean and Taiwanese policy makers did around 1960. With a population of only about 11 million in 2018, a modest level of GDP per capita (about the same, relative to other countries, as that of South Korea and Taiwan in 1960), and a moderate to high level of income inequality, Cuba's domestic market is too small to provide the economies of scale required for the production of capital goods, intermediate goods, or certain expensive consumer durables. The expansion of nontraditional exports will require, however, a lifting of the U.S. trade embargo, legalization of a much wider range of small and medium-sized private enterprises, unification of exchange rates, currency devaluation, and reduction of confiscatory taxes. Promising merchandise export sectors include pharmaceuticals, nickel, fruits and vegetables, cigars, and alcoholic beverages. For the medium-term future, though, Cuba's major sources of foreign exchange are likely to continue to be the export of health and education services, remittances from family members abroad, and foreign tourism (Ritter 2014).

Low GDP per Capita, High Human Capital, and Low Wages

Cuba in 2018 shares with South Korea and Taiwan in 1960 a low initial level of GDP per capita, a high initial level of educational attainment and health status, and extremely low wages. Each of these initial conditions is conducive to economic growth.

The principle of diminishing marginal returns to capital implies that, as technology diffuses internationally, poorer countries, with their initially low capital-to-labor ratios, will have faster growth of economic output than richer countries, with their initially high capital-to-labor ratios. As Robert Barro (1991) showed, however, countries that started out in 1960 with low GDP per capita grew, unexpectedly, slightly more *slowly* on average from 1960 to 1985 than countries with initially high GDP per capita. To explain this unexpected finding, Barro conjectured that some poorer countries lacked human capital sufficient to take full advantage of international technological diffusion. To test this hypothesis, he put initial school enrollment alongside initial GDP per capita on the right-hand side of a multiple regression model predicting GDP per capita growth. When initial school enrollment was added to the regression, the coefficient of initial GDP per capita became negative (as would be expected based on the principle of diminishing marginal returns to capital) and statistically and substantively significant. Once initial human capital was taken into account, an extra $1,000 of GDP per capita in 1960 slowed growth by an impressive 0.75 percent a year from 1960 to 1985 (Barro 1991: 414).

South Korea and Taiwan in 1960 benefited from the diminishing marginal returns principle. Cuba in 2018 should benefit from it as well. All three economies started out (in 1960 and 2018 respectively) with lower-than-average levels of GDP per capita combined with very high human capital. In 1960, among 141 countries and territories, South Korea and Taiwan were in the 36th and 41st percentiles respectively on GDP per capita, well below the median. By the same measure, Cuba in 2008 (the most recent year for which data are available) was also in the 41st percentile on GDP per capita, this time among 158 countries (Bolt and van Zanden 2013). Conversely, South Korea and Taiwan in 1960, like Cuba in 2010, had much better-educated and healthier populations than their respective levels of GDP per capita predicted (see figure 2.1).

High human capital in Taiwan and South Korea can be traced in part to Japanese colonial investment in basic education, health services, disease control, sanitation, and safe water provision (McGuire 2010: 181–227). After colonial rule ended in 1945 many South Korean and Taiwanese men acquired literacy through military service (Cumings 1987: 60). In South Korea in the late 1940s, the leftist People's Enlightenment Movement organized a literacy campaign that reportedly raised literacy from 23 to 71 percent of adults before being halted by the U.S. Army Military Government, which regarded it as subversive (Seth 2002: 45–46, 91). This unheralded South Korean literacy campaign may have been even more effective than the famous Cuban literacy campaign of 1961 (Fagen 1969: 32–68), which reportedly raised adult literacy, defined rather generously as the attainment of a first-grade level (UNESCO stipulates a fourth-grade level), from 74 to 97 percent of the adult population (Bengelsdorf 1994: 86).

High levels of educational attainment and health status in Cuba in 2018 can be traced in part to the education and health care policies of the revolution (Carnoy 2007; Díaz Briquets 1983; Feinsilver 1993). Relatively good educational and health status, however, already characterized prerevolutionary Cuba (see figure 2.1). In 1960 Cuba's infant mortality rate was 39 per 1,000 live births, much lower than Taiwan's (54 per 1,000) or South Korea's (79 per 1,000), and not much higher than the United States's (26 per 1,000). Despite slow economic growth, high income inequality, and corrupt, personalistic, and patronage-ridden governance, Cuba from 1900 to 1959 had the great-

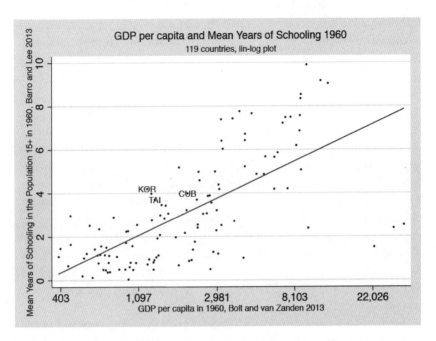

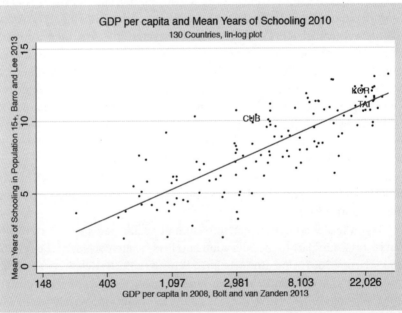

Figure 2.1. GDP per capita, Mean Years of Schooling, and Infant Mortality in Cuba, South Korea, and Taiwan, 1960 and 2008–2010.

est percent decline of infant mortality of any country in Latin America for which data are available. The accessibility of Cuba's *pre*-1959 health care system to a large fraction of the poor, as well as features of the island's history, geography, labor movement, and political system, help to explain Cuba's low infant mortality rate in 1959 (McGuire and Frankel 2005).

Cuba in 2018 shares with South Korea and Taiwan in 1960 not only low GDP per capita and high educational attainment and health status, but also low wages. In 1962 the average hourly manufacturing wage was $.10 in South Korea and Taiwan, compared to $.19 in Brazil, $.27 in Argentina, and $.38 in Mexico. Low wages formed a permissive condition for East Asia's turn to light manufactured exports (Mahon 1992: 253–56). As in South Korea and Taiwan in 1960, low wages prevail in contemporary Cuba. In 2010 the average salary in Cuba was about $18 per month (Mesa-Lago and Pérez-López 2013: 133). By comparison, the average monthly wage for manufacturing workers in 2010 was $212 in the Philippines and $814 in Brazil (ILO 2013: 11; monthly wage is the hourly wage multiplied by 35 hours per week and 4.3 weeks per month). For a time, Cuba will be highly competitive as an exporter of labor-intensive manufactured goods. In seizing this opportunity, it will be important to guard against squandering the country's human capital advantage, which is already threatened by the sharp decline since the early 1990s in vocational enrollment and in the share of university students studying the natural sciences and mathematics (Mesa-Lago and Pérez-López 2013: 143).

CONCLUSION

Large-N analyses ("N" means number of observations) permit a more rigorous evaluation of the correlates of outcome variation than is possible using individual case studies or small-N qualitative comparisons alone. Case studies and small-N comparisons have their own virtues, however, among which is the ability to identify, through "process-tracing," causal mechanisms behind the empirical associations detected in a large-N analysis. Another virtue of case studies and small-N analyses is to help to identify variables that may have been omitted from a large-N analysis and to check for reverse causation. Optimally, case studies, small-N, and large-N analyses can be effectively combined into multi-method research (Seawright 2016).

To this end it is well worth examining a study carried out in 2010 by the Economist Intelligence Unit (EIU). The EIU's time-series cross-sectional regression analysis estimated the impact of initial conditions on GDP per capita growth across a set of 86 countries, each observed over three decades (1970s, 1980s, or 1990s) such that there were 258 data points (Morris 2013; EIU 2017). The model included nine independent variables, almost all of which are initial conditions similar to those identified above: 1) the share of the population of working age, 2) the quality of state institutions, 3) initial GDP per worker, 4) initial educational attainment and health status, 5) colonial legacy, 6) evolution of the terms of trade, 7) geography (climate, remoteness, and the degree of primary export orientation), 8) the level of development of information and communications technology, and 9) a set of policy variables (fiscal balance, trade openness, amount of government regulation). The model projected that Cuban GDP per capita at purchasing power parity would grow by 178 percent from 2010 to 2030, second-highest among the 12 Latin American countries for which forecasts were generated.

Variables 1–4 in the EIU analysis closely resemble four of the hypothesized growth-promoting initial conditions depicted in table 2.1: a favorable age distribution, high state capacity, a low level of initial affluence, and good health status and educational attainment. Variables 5–7 correspond partly but not fully to such conditions. A colonial legacy, variable (5), is viewed by the EIU as invariably growth-inhibiting. The present study finds that a Japanese colonial legacy is growth-promoting, but that a Spanish colonial legacy is growth-inhibiting. However, the present study as well as Morris (2013: 157), who reviews the implications of the EIU growth forecast for Cuba, agree that "after more than one hundred years of independence from Spain, and having survived the rupture of two post-colonial dependent relationships . . . the influence of Cuba's colonial legacy [has] receded." On variable (6) the EIU reduces the "external economic environment" to the evolution of the country's terms of trade; the present study regards the "international context" as including geopolitical factors, the state of the world economy, and the share of countries heavily involved in the export of labor-intensive manufactured goods. For the EIU "geography," variable (7), involves not only tropical location and remoteness from major centers of world trade and finance, but also the "degree of primary export orientation"—which is closely related to the abundance or scarcity of natural resources, one of the variables highlighted in the qualitative literature on economic development in South Korea and Taiwan. EIU variable (8), the level of information and communications technology, is assumed in the present study to be closely related to the level of initial affluence. EIU variable (9) involves policies, whereas the present study distinguishes between policies and initial conditions (while recognizing that today's initial conditions resulted in part from yesterday's policies).

The EIU model is an imperfect test of the hypotheses produced by this study's review of the qualitative literature on initial conditions and economic development in South Korea and Taiwan. To the extent that the EIU model's predictors overlap with those identified in the review of the qualitative literature, however, the EIU's findings suggest that initial conditions may be, on balance, favorable to long-term economic growth in Cuba. Reinforcing this conjecture, the EIU model included a set of policy variables measuring market orientation, on which Cuba presumably scored quite poorly. Had the model *not* included these policy variables alongside the variables measuring initial conditions, the EIU model's forecast for Cuban economic growth from 2010 to 2030 might well have been even more optimistic.

As noted earlier, a virtue of case studies and small-scale qualitative comparisons is to help to identify variables that may have been omitted from a large-N analysis. The EIU model omitted several variables that play an important role in the literature on economic development in South Korea and Taiwan, and such omissions could have biased its predictions. Two such variables are ethnic homogeneity and the presence of a Sinic/Confucian culture. As noted earlier, however, scholars may have overstated the impact of each of these variables, so the omission may well be justified. Probably more significant is that the EIU model omits income inequality, wage levels, market size, and the strength and autonomy of labor and business organizations.

The current level of income inequality in Cuba is unknown, but it is almost certainly much higher than the levels of income inequality in South Korea and Taiwan in 1960. Omission of income inequality from the EIU model implies that the EIU's forecast of Cuban GDP per capita growth from 2010 to 2030 may be overly optimistic, because income inequality in Cuba today is moderate to high compared to all other countries, and because higher income inequality has been associated with slower economic growth. The EIU model's omission of the other three factors, conversely, suggests that its forecast of Cuban GDP per capita growth may be too pessimistic. Cuba in 2018, like South Korea and Taiwan in 1960, has low wages and small markets, each of which encourages exports. It also has weakly organized labor and business interests, increasing the state's steering capacity. Had the EIU model factored in each of the initial conditions identified in the preceding review while excluding the policy variables, its forecast of GDP per capita growth in Cuba from 2010 to 2030 might have been even higher.

This comparison of South Korea and Taiwan in 1960 to Cuba in 2018 suggests that some of the major economic challenges facing Cuba in the years to come will include building state capacity, managing nickel and petroleum resources, mitigating growth-inhibiting demographic trends, reducing income and race inequalities, and maintaining and expanding achievements in health care and educational attainment. To meet such challenges, Cuba has a healthy and well-educated population, low wages and small markets (which encourage exports), low GDP per capita (which tends to be associated, provided human capital is adequate, with faster economic growth), and weakly organized economic interests. If the government uses these resources wisely, Cuba could have the potential to become a Caribbean "jaguar" in part through the export of pharmaceuticals and other technology-intensive products (Kirk 2012: 86).

Among the policies that contributed to rapid shared growth in South Korea and Taiwan were land reform, investment in basic education, promotion of manufactured exports, and cautious macroeconomic management. Such policies may well be desirable in a wide range of circumstances, but what is desirable is not always feasible. Without the initial conditions depicted in figure 2.1, it is unlikely that South Korean and Taiwanese policy makers would have been willing or able to implement the policies that they did. Initial conditions comprise historical legacies and social-structural factors that contemporary actors do not control. Not only do initial conditions shape and constrain economic policies; they also influence development in ways not mediated by policies. A low initial GDP per capita combined with high initial education and a rising share of workers in the population, for example, puts upward pressure on economic growth regardless of policy choice, although poor policy choices can squander such advantages.

To claim that a certain set of initial conditions favored rapid shared growth in one context is not to assert that the same set of initial conditions is necessary for rapid shared growth in another context. Policy makers should tailor their decisions to the specific initial conditions that they face. Social science research can identify initial conditions that shaped and constrained development policies and outcomes, but political leaders and the public are responsible for proposing, designing, approving, and implementing policies that take advantage of the favorable initial conditions while meeting the challenges posed by the unfavorable ones.

BIBLIOGRAPHY

Alesina, Alberto, and Eliana La Ferrara. "Ethnic Diversity and Economic Performance." *Journal of Economic Literature* 43, no. 3 (September 2005): 762–800.

Alesina, Alberto, and Roberto Perotti. "Income Distribution, Political Instability, and Investment." *European Economic Review* 40, no. 6 (June 1996): 1203–28.

Amsden, Alice H. *Asia's Next Giant: South Korea and Late Industrialization.* Oxford: Oxford University Press, 1989.

Anderson, Tim. "HIV/AIDS in Cuba: Lessons and Challenges." *Revista Panamericana de Salud Pública* 2009, 26, no. 1: 78–86.

Auty, Richard M. "Industrial Policy Reform in Six Large Newly Industrializing Countries: The Resource Curse Thesis." *World Development* 22, no. 1 (January 1994): 11–26.

Balassa, Bela. "The Lessons of East Asian Development: An Overview." *Economic Development and Cultural Change* 36, no. 3 (1988): 273–90.

Barro, Robert. "Economic Growth in a Cross Section of Countries." *Quarterly Journal of Economics* 106, no. 2 (May 1991): 407–43.

Barro, Robert, and Jong-Wha Lee. "A New Data Set of Educational Attainment in the World, 1950–2010." *Journal of Development Economics* 104 (September 2013), 184–98. Associated data accessed November 3, 2016, http://www.barrolee.com /data/yrsch.htm.

Bengelsdorf, Carolee. *The Problem of Democracy in Cuba*. New York: Oxford University Press, 1994.

Bloom, David E. "7 Billion and Counting." *Science* 333, no. 562 (July 29, 2011): 562–69.

Bloom, David E., David Canning, and Jaypee Sevilla. *The Demographic Dividend: A New Perspective on the Economic Consequences of Population Change*. Santa Monica: RAND Corporation, 2003.

Blue, Sarah A. "The Erosion of Racial Equality in the Context of Cuba's Dual Economy." *Latin American Politics and Society* 49, no. 3 (Fall 2007): 35–68.

Bolt, Jutta, and Jan Luiten van Zanden. "The First Update of the Maddison Project: Re-Estimating Growth Before 1820." Maddison Project Working Paper WP-4 (January). 2013. Accessed October 30, 2014. http://www.ggdc.net/maddison/maddison -project/data.htm.

Booth, Anne. "Initial Conditions and Miraculous Growth: Why Is South East Asia Different from Taiwan and South Korea?" *World Development* 27, no. 2 (February 1999): 301–21.

Broad, Robin, and John Cavanagh. "No More NICs." *Foreign Policy* 72 (Autumn 1988): 81–103.

Brundenius, Claes. "Revolutionary Cuba at 50: Growth with Equity Revisited." *Latin American Perspectives* 36, no. 2 (March 2009): 31–48.

Brunnschweiler, C. N., and E. H. Bulte. "Linking Natural Resources to Slow Growth and More Conflict." *Science* 320 (May 2, 2008): 616–17.

Campos, José E., and Hilton Root. *The Key to the Asian Miracle*. Washington, DC: Brookings Institution Press, 1996.

Carnoy, Martin. *Cuba's Academic Advantage*. Stanford: Stanford University Press, 2007.

Cheng, Tun-jen. "Political Regimes and Development Strategies: South Korea and Taiwan." In *Manufacturing Miracles: Paths of Industrialization in East Asia and Latin America*. Edited by Gary Gereffi and Donald L. Wyman. Princeton: Princeton University Press, 1990.

Collier, Paul, and Anke Hoeffler. "On Economic Causes of Civil War." *Oxford Economic Papers* 50, no. 4 (October 1998): 563–73.

Cumings, Bruce. *The Origins of the Korean War*. Vol. I: *Liberation and the Emergence of Separate Regimes, 1945–1947*. Princeton: Princeton University Press, 1981.

Cumings, Bruce. "The Origins and Development of the Northeast Asian Political Economy: Industrial Sectors, Product Cycles, and Political Consequences." In *The Political Economy of the New Asian Industrialism*. Edited by F. C. Deyo. Ithaca: Cornell University Press, 1987.

Cumings, Bruce. *The Origins of the Korean War*. Vol. II: *The Roaring of the Cataract, 1947–1950*. Princeton: Princeton University Press, 1990.

Davis, Graham. "Learning to Love the Dutch Disease: Evidence from the Mineral Economies." *World Development* 23, no. 10 (October 1995): 1765–79.

de la Fuente, Alejandro. "Recreating Racism: Race and Discrimination in Cuba's Special Period." *Socialism and Democracy* 2001, 15, no. 1: 65–91.

Deyo, Frederick C. *Beneath the Miracle*. Berkeley: University of California Press, 1989.

Diamand, Marcelo. "Overcoming Argentina's Stop-and-Go Economic Cycles." In *Latin American Political Economy: Financial Crisis and Political Change*. Edited by Jonathan Hartlyn and Samuel A. Morley. Boulder: Westview Press, 1986.

Díaz-Briquets, Sergio. *The Health Revolution in Cuba*. Austin: University of Texas Press, 1983.

Doner, Richard F., Bryan K. Ritchie, and Dan Slater. "Systemic Vulnerability and the Origins of Developmental States: Northeast and Southeast Asia in Comparative Perspective." *International Organization* 59, no. 2 (April 2005): 327–61.

Easterly, William, and Ross Levine. "Africa's Growth Tragedy: Policies and Ethnic Divisions." *The Quarterly Journal of Economics* 112, no. 4 (November 1997): 1203–50.

Economist. "Ungenerous Endowments: The Natural Resources Myth." December 23, 1995: 87–89.

EIU [Economist Intelligence Unit]. "Data Tool: Long-Term Forecasts." Accessed January 7, 2017. http://graphics.eiu.com/data_services/contentguide/longterm.htm.

Evans, Peter. *Embedded Autonomy: States and Industrial Transformation*. Princeton: Princeton University Press, 1995.

Evans, Peter, and James E. Rauch. "Bureaucracy and Growth: A Cross-National Analysis of the Effects of 'Weberian' State Structures on Economic Growth." *American Sociological Review* 64, no. 5 (October 1999): 748–65.

Fagen, Richard R. *The Transformation of Political Culture in Cuba*. Stanford: Stanford University Press, 1969.

Fearon, James D., and David D. Laitin. "Ethnicity, Insurgency, and Civil War." *American Political Science Review* 97, no. 1 (February 2003): 75–90.

Feenstra, Robert C., Robert Inklaar, and Marcel P. Timmer. *Penn World Table 8.0*. 2013. Accessed October 15, 2014. http://www.rug.nl/research/ggdc/data/pwt/v80/pwt80.xlsx.

Feinsilver, Julie. *Healing the Masses: Cuban Health Politics at Home and Abroad*. Berkeley: University of California Press, 1993.

Fitchen, Edward D. "Primary Education in Colonial Cuba: Spanish Tool for Retaining 'La Isla Siempre Leal?'" *Caribbean Studies* 14, no. 1 (April 1974): 105–20.

Gereffi, Gary, and Donald L. Wyman, eds. *Manufacturing Miracles: Paths of Industrialization in East Asia and Latin America*. Princeton: Princeton University Press, 1990.

Gold, Thomas B. *State and Society in the Taiwan Miracle*. Armonk: M. E. Sharpe, 1986.

Haggard, Stephan. *Pathways from the Periphery: The Politics of Growth in the Newly Industrializing Countries*. Ithaca: Cornell University Press, 1990.

Harrison, Lawrence E. *Who Prospers? How Cultural Values Shape Economic and Political Success*. New York: Basic Books, 1992.

Ho, Samuel P. S. "Economics, Economic Bureaucracy, and Taiwan's Economic Development." *Pacific Affairs* 60, no. 2 (Summer 1987): 226–47.

Hughes, Helen, ed. *Achieving Industrialization in East Asia*. New York: Cambridge University Press, 1988.

ILO [International Labour Office]. *Global Wage Report 2012/13: Wages and Equitable Growth*. Geneva: International Labour Office, 2013.

Jenkins, Rhys. "Learning from the Gang: Are There Lessons for Latin America from East Asia?" *Bulletin of Latin American Research* 1991, 10, no. 1: 37–54.

Käkönen, Mira, Hanna Kaisti, and Jyrki Luukkanen. "Energy Revolution in Cuba: Pioneering for the Future?" Working Paper, Finland Futures Research Centre, University of Turku, 2014. Accessed October 26, 2014. http://www.utu.fi/fi/yksikot/ffrc/julkaisut/e-tutu/Documents/eBook_4-2014.pdf.

Kath, Elizabeth. *Social Relations and the Cuban Health Miracle*. New Brunswick: Transaction Publishers, 2010.

Kaufmann, Daniel, Aart Kraay, and Massimo Mastruzzi. "The Worldwide Governance Indicators: Methodology and Analytical Issues." *Hague Journal on the Rule of Law* 3, no. 2 (September 2011): 220–46.

Kim, Andrew Eungi, and Gil-sung Park. "Nationalism, Confucianism, Work Ethic and Industrialization in South Korea." *Journal of Contemporary Asia* 2003, 33, no. 1: 37–49.

Kirk, John M. "Cuban Medical Internationalism Under Raúl Castro." *Bulletin of Latin American Research* 31, no. 1 (March 2012): 77–90.

Kohli, Atul. "Where Do High Growth Political Economies Come From? The Japanese Lineage of Korea's 'Developmental State.'" *World Development* 22, no. 9 (September 1994): 1269–93.

Kohli, Atul. *State-Directed Development: Political Power and Industrialization in the Global Periphery*. New York: Cambridge University Press, 2004.

Mahon, James. "Was Latin America Too Rich to Prosper?" *Journal of Development Studies* 28, no. 2 (January 1992): 241–63.

McGuire, James W. *Wealth, Health, and Democracy in East Asia and Latin America.* New York: Cambridge University Press, 2010.

McGuire, James W. "The Politics of Development in Latin America and East Asia." In *Oxford Handbook of Politics of Development.* Edited by Carol Lancaster and Nicolas van de Walle. New York: Oxford University Press, 2016. DOI: 10.1093/oxfordhb/9780199845156.013.23.

McGuire, James W., and Laura B. Frankel. "Mortality Decline in Cuba, 1900–1959: Patterns, Comparisons, and Causes." *Latin American Research Review* 40, no. 2 (June 2005): 84–116.

Mesa-Lago, Carmelo. *The Economy of Socialist Cuba: A Two-Decade Appraisal.* Albuquerque: University of New Mexico Press, 1981.

Mesa-Lago, Carmelo. "Social Protection Systems in Latin America and the Caribbean: Cuba." Project Document, February. Santiago, Chile: Economic Commission for Latin America, 2013.

Mesa-Lago, Carmelo, and Jorge F. Pérez-López. *Cuba under Raúl Castro: Assessing the Reforms.* Boulder: Lynne Rienner Publishers, 2013.

Mirzaee, Mohammad. "Trends and Determinants of Mortality in Taiwan, 1895–1975." Ph.D. diss., University of Pennsylvania, 1979.

Moore, Melinda, Anita Chandra, and Kevin C. Feeney. "Building Community Resilience: What Can the United States Learn from Experiences in Other Countries?" *Disaster Medicine and Public Health Preparedness* 7, no. 3 (June 2013): 292–301.

Morris, Emily. "Forecasting Cuba's Economy: Two Years, Five Years, and Twenty Years." In Mauricio A. Font and Carlos Riobó, eds., *Handbook of Contemporary Cuba*, 137–64. Boulder: Paradigm Publishers.

Murphy, Kevin M., Andrei Shleifer, and Robert Vishny. "Income Distribution, Market Size, and Industrialization." *The Quarterly Journal of Economics* 104, no. 3 (August 1989): 537–64.

Norton, Seth W. "The Cost of Diversity: Endogenous Property Rights and Growth." *Constitutional Political Economy* 11, no. 4 (December 2000): 319–37.

O'Donnell, Guillermo. "State and Alliances in Argentina, 1955–1976." *Journal of Development Studies* 15, no. 1 (October 1978): 3–33.

Paldam, Martin. "Economic Freedom and the Success of the Asian Tigers: An Essay on Controversy." *European Journal of Political Economy* 19, no. 3 (September 2003): 453–77.

Persson, Torsten, and Guido Tabellini. "Is Inequality Harmful for Growth?" *American Economic Review* 84, no. 3 (June 1994): 600–21.

Prawiro, Radius. *Indonesia's Struggle for Economic Development: Pragmatism in Action.* New York: Oxford University Press, 1998.

Prieto Samsónov, Dmitri, and Isbel Díaz Torres. "Las reformas cubanas: imaginarios, contestaciones, y miradas críticas." *OSAL: Observatorio Social de América Latina* 14, no. 36 (December 2014): 17–46.

Radfar, Gabriela. "Una mirada crítica a la legislación laboral en Cuba: Del 'Periodo Especial' y la 'Batalla de Ideas' a la 'Actualización del Modelo.'" CLALS Working Paper No. 12 (April). Washington, DC: Center for Latin American and Latino Studies, American University, 2016.

Ritter, Archibald. "Does Cuba Have an Industrial Future?" Presentation, 2014 Annual Meeting of the Association for the Study of the Cuban Economy, Miami, July 31–August 2. Accessed October 31, 2014. http://thecubaneconomy.com/wp-content/uploads/2014/09/Presentation-2014.pptx.

Rodrik, Dani. "King Kong Meets Godzilla: The World Bank and the East Asian Miracle." In Albert Fishlow et al., eds., *Miracle or Design? Lessons from the East Asian Experience*, 13–53. Washington, DC: Overseas Development Council, 1994.

Roeder, Philip G. "Ethnolinguistic Fractionalization (ELF) Indices, 1961 and 1985," 2001. Accessed May 31, 2009, http://weber.ucsd.edu/~proeder/elf.htm.

Ross, Michael L. "Extractive Sectors and the Poor." October. New York: Oxfam America, 2001. Accessed May 26, 2003. http://www.oxfamamerica.org/static/oa3/files/extractive-sectors-and-the-poor.pdf.

Sachs, Jeffrey D., and Andrew M. Warner. "Natural Resource Abundance and Economic Growth." National Bureau of Economic Research Working Paper No. 5398 (December). Cambridge: NBER, 1995.

Seawright, Jason. *Multi-Method Social Science: Combining Qualitative and Quantitative Tools.* New York: Cambridge University Press, 2016.

Seth, Michael J. *Education Fever: Society, Politics, and the Pursuit of Schooling in South Korea.* Honolulu: University of Hawai'i Press, 2002.

Sugawara, Naotaka. "From Volatility to Stability in Expenditure: Stabilization Funds in Resource-Rich Countries." IMF WP/14/43. Washington, DC: International Monetary Fund, 2014.

Taiwan. CEPD [Council for Economic Planning and Development]. *Taiwan Statistical Data Book 2012.* Taipei: Council for Economic Planning and Development, 2012.

Taiwan. DGBAS [Directorate-General of Budget, Accounting and Statistics]. *Statistical Yearbook of the Republic of China.* Taipei: Republic of China, Executive Yuan, Directorate-General of Budget, Accounting and Statistics, 2013.

Temple, Jonathan. "Initial Conditions, Social Capital and Growth in Africa." *Journal of African Economies* 7, no. 3 (October 1998): 309–47.

Torvik, Ragnar. "Why Do Some Resource-Abundant Countries Succeed While Others Do Not? *Oxford Review of Economic Policy* 25, no. 2 (Summer 2009): 241–56.

United Nations Population Division. *World Population Prospects: The 2012 Revision.* New York: Population Division of the Department of Economic and Social Affairs of the United Nations Secretariat, 2014. Accessed November 1, 2014. http://esa.un.org/unpd/wpp/index.htm.

UNU-WIDER [United Nations University—World Institute for Development Economics Research]. "World Income Inequality Database (WIID3.0b)," 2014. Accessed October 30, 2014. http://www.wider.unu.edu/research/WIID3-0B/en_GB/database/.

Wade, Robert. *Governing the Market: Economic Theory and the Role of Government in East Asian Industrialization.* Princeton: Princeton University Press, 1990.

World Bank. *World Development Indicators online,* 2014. Accessed April 24, 2014. databank.worldbank.org.

JORGE PÉREZ-LÓPEZ AND YU XIAO

FOREIGN INVESTMENT AND ECONOMIC GROWTH IN CUBA

LESSONS FROM CHINA

One of the policy initiatives to spur economic growth being actively pursued by Cuba's authorities is the attraction of foreign investment. China has been very successful in attracting foreign investment since the 1980s. Although the differences between Cuba and China with respect to size, structure of the economy, patterns of external relations, geographic location, and culture, among others, are quite significant and have been well documented, the two countries share similarities in their political and economic institutions. Both are single-party regimes ruled by communist parties. Both adopted Soviet economic and political institutions prior to their reform periods, starting in the 1990s for Cuba and in the 1980s for China. Both countries were led for very long periods of time by larger-than-life revolutionary figures, Fidel Castro and Mao Zedong, both of whom were succeeded by appointed leaders with historical ties to the revolution who have accelerated the reform process.

The objective of this chapter is to analyze Cuba's efforts to attract investment and promote economic growth, focusing on lessons that can be learned from China's experience. The chapter first briefly discusses Cuba's domestic investment gap and the key role assigned to foreign direct investment (FDI) in filling this gap. It then compares the reforms of China and Cuba with respect to promoting FDI. This is followed by identification of challenges for attracting FDI in Cuba and lessons from the Chinese experience that may be relevant to Cuba.

The chapter concludes that in order to promote economic growth, it is imperative for Cuba to attract foreign investment, as China has done. The keys to China's success in attracting foreign investment have been policy stability and a commitment to market-oriented reform. In contrast, Cuba's reforms have been episodic and shallow. To succeed in attracting foreign investment, Cuba must move steadfastly forward with its opening-up reforms, creating a stable environment where foreign investors can feel confident that they will be able to operate their businesses and remit their profits without government interference.

CUBA'S INVESTMENT QUAGMIRE

As Pavel Vidal has pointed out,[1] one of the principal reasons for the slowdown in Cuban economic growth in recent years has been the failure of investment plans to meet anticipated targets. Vidal examined the period 2009–2013 and concluded that realized investment levels were approximately 20 percent below planned for each year. The underperformance of investment meant that a group of investment projects on which Cuba was banking for current and future growth—refineries and petrochemical plants, offshore oil prospecting, luxury real estate developments with golf courses, expansion of productive capacity in nickel and light manufacturing, infrastructure projects—failed either to materialize altogether or to keep pace with plans. Not only has Cuba fallen short in executing planned investments, but the amount of resources assigned to investment over the past decade has been abysmally low and insufficient to generate vigorous economic growth.

Economists often use the ratio of investment or gross capital formation to gross domestic product (GDP) as an indicator of future growth of an economy. The higher this ratio, all things being the same, the stronger—economists posit—will be the future growth performance of an economy. Cuba's gross capital formation to GDP ratio (in percentage terms) in 2014 was 12.9 percent and averaged 13.0 percent over the five-year period 2009–2013.[2] In comparison, the gross fixed capital formation to GDP ratio for Latin American and Caribbean nations averaged 20.5 percent in 2014, and from 19.3 percent to 21.3 percent over the period 2009–2013.[3] Two of the fastest-growing economies in Latin America in the first half of the 2010s—Colombia and Peru—had gross fixed capital formation to GDP ratios approximating 25

JORGE PÉREZ-LÓPEZ AND YU XIAO

percent, with this ratio peaking in Colombia at 26.3 percent in 2014 and Peru at 25.9 percent in 2012. By comparison, Cuba's gross fixed capital formation to GDP ratio, as reported by ECLAC, peaked at 10.0 percent in 2006 and fell to 8.6 percent and 8.8 percent in 2010 and 2011, respectively. Cuba's gross fixed capital formation to GDP ratio was below the worst-performing Caribbean and Central American nations—Dominican Republic, El Salvador, and Guatemala—and significantly below Costa Rica, Honduras, Nicaragua, and Panama.

To expand the comparisons, the so-called BRICS countries—Brazil, Russia, India, China, and South Africa—are large, fast-growing emerging economies that are seeking to play a larger role in the global economy and world affairs. Their gross capital formation to GDP ratios in 2014 were: Brazil 20.1 percent; India 31.6 percent; China 46.2 percent; Russia 20.3 percent; and South Africa 20.4 percent.[4] Finally, Vietnam's gross capital formation to GDP ratio in 2014 was 26.8 percent.[5]

Cuba's Minister of Foreign Trade and Foreign Investment Rodrigo Malmierca stated in early 2014 that Cuba needs to attract between $2 billion and $2.5 billion in foreign investment annually in order for the economy to grow at the 7 percent per annum rate that planners have set as a target for the next few years. "If the economy does not grow at levels around 7%," said Malmierca, "we are not going to be able to develop."[6] Likewise, Vice President of the Council of Ministers Marino Murillo told the National Assembly in March 2014, in the lead up to consideration by that body of the new foreign investment law, that Cuba required around $2.5 billion per annum in foreign investment in order to "stimulate development that would result in prosperity and sustainability of Cuba's socialist socioeconomic model."[7] Murillo went on to say that "it was essential to *seduce* foreign capital in order to raise the rate of growth, which has averaged 1.8 percent during the past decade, nearly half of the average rate of growth of Latin America."[8]

Writing in 2006, Cuban economist Omar Everleny Pérez Villanueva observed that robust economic growth capable of supporting economic recovery in Cuba would require achieving capital accumulation rates of about 25 percent of GDP, roughly the ratio recorded between 1975 and 1989.[9] Former Minister of the Economy and Planning José Luis Rodríguez similarly observed that gross capital formation fell from 26.9 percent of GDP in 1989 to 5.2 percent in 1994—1994 was probably the trough of the economic crisis that ensued from the breakdown of relations with the Soviet Union and the socialist bloc—and recovered only to about 8 percent in 2013.[10]

Referring to the current situation, Cuban economist Juan Triana has posited that the island needs $3 billion in foreign investment annually "in order to reach an adequate productive phase."[11] Elsewhere, Triana has argued that Cuba needs to increase its gross capital formation by about 15 percentage points—from about 7–8 percent to 22–23 percent—in order to be able to generate a growth rate of about 4 percent per annum.[12]

Given Cuba's urgent needs to attract foreign investment, it is critical to understand what specific measures Cuba could adopt to achieve its goals. In the following, we compare China and Cuba's reform experience and draw lessons from China's strategies and policies of attracting foreign investment that might contribute to Cuba's efforts.

REFORMS TO ATTRACT FOREIGN INVESTMENT: CHINA AND CUBA

In a stylized socialist centrally planned economy, the state owns the means of production and economic decisions are made centrally according to a prede-termined plan. The private sector, to the extent the model allows for it, would be small and insulated from the rest of the economy. The model also assumes that the state holds a monopoly over all international trade and international transactions. Strictly speaking, foreign investment—which is incompatible with the core principles of socialist centrally planned economies—would not exist in these economies. Despite this theoretical incompatibility, in the 1970s and 1980s, faced with serious economic challenges, socialist economies be-gan to experiment with ways and means to introduce foreign investment in their economies in order to promote diversification, introduce new technol-ogies, and boost economic growth. In what follows we focus on three aspects of the measures to attract FDI in China and Cuba: 1) the legal framework; 2) the creation of some form of special zones or enclaves for FDI to settle; and 3) the opportunity for the diaspora to participate in investment proj-ects. Overall we argue that while China put in place the necessary reforms to attract investment, Cuba has yet to do so fully. China also capitalized on its diaspora as a source of investment resources, which Cuba has not done to date. An open question, then, is whether the Cuban leaders will make the necessary changes to attract diaspora investment.

EXPERIENCE OF CHINA

China adopted the reform and opening-up policies in 1978, corresponding with the rise of Deng Xiaoping as the paramount leader. From 1978 to 2001, although there were periods when conservative forces at the central govern-ment level challenged the reform process, the general trend was to continue the opening-up policies. We end our analysis with 2001 because China joined the World Trade Organization (WTO) in that year; since then, its trade and investment policies have had to comply with WTO rules. The period prior to

JORGE PÉREZ-LÓPEZ AND YU XIAO

China's accession to the WTO is more relevant for comparison with Cuba's efforts to attract FDI.

LEGAL FRAMEWORK FOR FOREIGN INVESTMENT

Four major laws and associated provisions provide the legal framework of China's reform and opening-up policies: 1) the 1979 Law on Joint Ventures; 2) the 1982 Constitution; 3) 1986 Provisions to Encourage Foreign Investment; and 4) the 1992 Amendments to the Joint Venture Law. In addition to discussing these legal instruments, we also briefly highlight the political pushback after 1989 and how Deng Xiaoping propelled forward the reform and opening-up policies despite political resistance.

1) 1979 Law on Joint Ventures

After the Third Plenary Session of the Eleventh Central Committee of the Communist Party of China (CPC) in December 1978, Deng Xiaoping became China's paramount leader. The National People's Congress (NPC) passed the Law on Chinese–Foreign Joint Ventures in 1979. This law not only granted foreign investment a legal status in China, but its flexibility in regulating foreign investment created a relatively liberal legal environment to encourage a broader opening of the Chinese economy.

- The law did not set an upper limit of foreign ownership of joint ventures although it did set a lower limit of 25 percent for foreign ownership (Article 4). It should be noted that in practice certain industries did have upper limits for foreign ownership, which were not specified in the 1979 Law.

- The Chinese state guaranteed foreign partners' ability to remit profits abroad through the Bank of China, when the contract period ended or should the contract be canceled (Article 10).

- The law encouraged joint ventures that use world-class technologies by providing corporate tax exemption or reduction (Article 7).

- The law encouraged joint ventures to reinvest their profits in China by refunding part of the corporate taxes paid (Article 7).

- Joint ventures were permitted to employ foreign employees. Foreign employees could repatriate their income through the Bank of China after paying the personal income tax (Article 11).

- The law permitted joint ventures to hire Chinese workers directly and provided that the hiring and firing of employees of joint ventures would follow the contract drawn up by the parties of the joint ventures (Article 6).

- Foreign parties of the joint ventures could invest in advanced technology and equipment that suited China's needs. Projects that did not qualify as embodying advanced technology and equipment or might incur losses would require that the foreign party compensate the State (Article 5).

- The most obvious constraint was that the law required that the chairman of the board of directors of the joint venture be a representative from the Chinese partner. There could be one or two vice chairmen, and a representative of the foreign party might hold one of these posts (Article 6).

In addition to the constraints mentioned above, Chen et al. (1995) also point out financial disincentives embodied in the 1979 Law on Joint Ventures, as China required that "each foreign venture maintain its foreign exchange balance, making it difficult for foreign investors to repatriate any profits not earned in hard currency. Compounding this was the nonconvertibility of the Chinese currency, which meant that foreign-invested enterprises generally had to export to cover their foreign exchange expenses."[13] As is discussed below, over time China relaxed some of these restrictions and therefore made its economy more attractive to foreign investors.

2) 1982 Constitution

In December 1982, the Fifth NPC adopted a new State Constitution, replacing the charter that had been adopted in March 1978, before Deng became the paramount leader. The 1978 Constitution emphasized the importance of self-reliance in China's economic development (Article 11). The 1982 Constitution, in contrast, reflected the reform and opening-up policies and recognized the rights of legal foreign enterprises that operate in China (Article 18). Thus, this change to the Constitution created a constitutional basis for legislation that would follow to regulate FDI.

3) 1986 Provisions to Encourage Foreign Investment

Despite the passage of the 1979 Law on Joint Ventures and the 1982 Constitution, in the early 1980s foreign investors still had many concerns about China's business environment. To deepen the reform, in October 1986 the State Council promulgated the Provisions to Encourage Foreign Investment. These new regulations not only provided more fiscal incentives to foreign investors but also granted more autonomy to foreign enterprises, particularly "export enterprises" and "technologically advanced enterprises." For instance, the provisions required subnational governments and other bureaucracies to support the autonomy of foreign enterprises in managing their businesses. In terms of employment policy, foreign enterprises were given independence to hire and fire senior managers. They could also employ technical personnel, managers, and workers from other entities, which were encouraged to permit such personnel transfers (Article 15). Despite these positive steps, the provisions were considered to fall short with respect to management of foreign exchange shortages and dispute resolution issues.[14]

4) 1990 Amendments to the Joint Venture Law

In 1990, the Seventh NPC passed a series of Amendments to the 1979 Law on Joint Ventures that continued to further the creation of a more hospitable environment for foreign investment. Four major amendments reduced constraints and increased freedom for joint venture enterprises to operate:[15]

- Added the provision that "The State shall not nationalize or requisition any equity joint venture. Under special circumstances, when public interests require, equity joint ventures may be requisitioned by following legal procedures and appropriate compensation shall be made." (Article 3)

- Lifted the requirement that the Chinese side hold the office of chairman of each joint venture, although it is still required that the other side hold the office of vice-chairman (vice-chairmen). (Article 6)

- Similarly lifted the requirement that joint-venture enterprises operate through an account with either the Bank of China or a bank approved by the Bank of China. Pursuant to the 1990 Amendments, joint-venture enterprises may "open a foreign exchange account with a bank or any other financial institution which is permitted by the State agency for foreign exchange control to handle foreign exchange transactions." (Article 8)

- While the 1979 Law required all joint-venture enterprises to specify the duration of the joint venture contract, the 1990 Amendments allow joint ventures economic activities not to specify the duration of the contract. (Article 12)

The student demonstration in Tiananmen Square in 1989 temporarily weakened the liberal forces in the central government. Despite passage of the 1990 Amendments to the Joint Venture Law, the media began to question the reform and opening-up policies. Conservative leaders in the central government stated that allowing foreign investment and foreign ownership weakened the socialist regime. It is against this backdrop that in January 1992,

Deng Xiaoping traveled to four southern cities, Wuchang, Shenzhen, Zhuhai, and Shanghai, which had benefited from the reform and opening-up policies and supported its continuation and expansion. This tour is famously known as "the Southern Tour." Through his speeches in these cities, Deng sent a signal to the country that he strongly supported continuing the reform and opening-up policies despite the 1989 events. Local governments, including Guangdong and Fujian provinces, "launched campaigns to support continued FDI liberalization," which also gained support from local government beyond South China.[16] Deng was able to counterbalance the conservative forces at the center with support from the local governments.

In October 1992, the CPC held its Fourteenth National Congress. President Jiang Zemin stated, "on behalf of the Thirteenth CPC Central Committee, delivered a report titled *Accelerating the Reform, the Opening to the Outside World and the Drive for Modernization, So As to Achieve Greater Successes in Building Socialism with Chinese Characteristics*."[17] One of the major tasks for future development identified in the report was opening more places and industries to the outside world.

Deng's Southern Tour and the Fourteenth National Congress in 1992 established that China, as a socialist country, was determined to provide a stable environment for foreign investment.

Development of the Special Economic Zones (SEZs)

In addition to establishing a legal framework conducive to FDI, China also created special economic zones (SEZs) to attract foreign investment. China is a large country with heterogeneous regions. The opening to foreign investment started in earnest in SEZs in the coastal regions and gradually expanded to other locations. In 1980, four SEZs on China's southeast coast were established at Shenzhen, Zhuhai, Xiamen, and Shantou. These cities were selected because of 1) their vicinity to Hong Kong, Macao and Taiwan; 2) the great number of Chinese emigrants from these regions; and 3) the regions' history of foreign trade. In April 1988, Hainan Island became a province and China's fifth and largest SEZ.[18]

The main goals of the SEZs were to attract FDI, to earn foreign exchange through export, and to introduce advanced technology and modern management knowledge to China. To achieve these goals, the SEZs provided preferential treatment to foreign-owned enterprises with respect to taxes, foreign exchange, and land use policies. Preferential tax policies included lower tax rates on enterprise income, tax holiday periods, carryover of losses, and tax rebates for reinvestment. With regard to land use policies, foreign enterprises could obtain land use rights for their project construction through land leasing, with SEZs often giving very favorable conditions for land use to foreign enterprises. Moreover, foreign enterprises could transfer land use rights to other enterprises, or use land use rights as mortgage.[19]

In addition to preferential tax and land use policies, the SEZs also invested in infrastructure development and reformed the economic institutions to favor FDI. For example, Shenzhen, one of the earliest SEZs, developed several ports and industrial zones and reformed policies, among others, regarding the wage system (1979), employment system (1980), price system (1982), enterprise system (1983), cadre and personnel system (1982), and management of state-owned enterprises (1986) to make itself more attractive to investors.[20] It also opened up the financial sector by introducing foreign owned banks and established regional joint-equity banks, such as the China Merchants Bank (1987) and the Shenzhen Development Bank (1987). In 1988, Shenzhen, as a city, gained provincial-level economic management authority.[21]

DIASPORA INVESTMENT

From the very beginning of the reform and opening-up policies, China's central leadership realized the importance of attracting diaspora investment. In January 1979, Deng commented that although diaspora FDI carried some capitalist characteristics, unlike FDI from totally unrelated sources, diaspora investors wanted to protect their socialist homeland and wanted it to develop. Thus, China should allow diaspora investors to open factories.[22]

As mentioned earlier, attracting investment from the Chinese diaspora was one of the rationales for the establishment of the SEZs. In 1991, Deng Xiaoping recollected that the selection of the four SEZs was based on their locations and diaspora connections. Shenzhen was close to Hong Kong, Zhuhai was close to Macao, and Shantou and Xiamen were chosen because their emigrants were doing businesses in foreign countries.[23]

The State Council has promulgated specific provisions to regulate diaspora investment. In April 1985, it issued *Interim Provisions of the State Council on Investment Preferences for Overseas Chinese*, which granted preferential treatment to diaspora investment. The preferential policies included three years of exemption from enterprise income tax, lower enterprise income tax rates after the tax exemption period, tax rebates for reinvestment in China, and lower tariffs for importing advanced equipment.[24] The Interim Provisions were abolished in August 1990 and replaced by *Provisions of the State Council Concerning the Encouragement of Investments by Overseas Chinese and Compatriots from Hong Kong and Macao*. The 1990 Provisions also contained preferential treatment towards diaspora investment, but the policies were not as generous as the 1985 Interim Provisions.

At the beginning of the 1980s, "China was full of daunting problems that discouraged foreign investors."[25] Diaspora entrepreneurs were the early movers (entrants). Their personal connection with local governments and the central leadership provided them with more stable incentives to invest in China. When uncertainties over domestic economic reforms arose and Western investors became cautious, diaspora investment remained robust.[26] As of 2004, the total number of foreign-invested enterprises in China exceeded 490,000, of which around 70 percent were created by diaspora Chinese and compatriots from Hong Kong and Macao. The cumulative value of foreign investment actually realized exceeded $500 billion, with overseas Chinese and compatriots from Hong Kong, Macao, and Taiwan accounting for more than 60 percent.[27]

FDI Performance

Figure 3.1 shows FDI trends in three out of the four earliest Chinese SEZs based on the statistical yearbooks of each SEZ.[28] FDI in the three zones started from very low levels and developed as follows:

- It experienced the fastest growth in Shenzhen, from a little more than $15 million in 1979 to $715 million in 1992, and to $3,602 million in 2001, four times higher than the amount of foreign investment in 1992.[29]

- It also grew rapidly in Zhuhai from 1979 onward, although the growth was less dramatic than in Shenzhen. As of 1990, Zhuhai had "introduced 40,000 sets of foreign machinery and equipment, among which there were more than 80 production lines worth over $100,000, 133 advanced technology projects, and more than 4,000 contracts."[30] Thus, FDI increased from $4.2 million in 1979 to $199.9 million in 1992, and to $885.3 million in 2001.

- In Shantou, FDI increased from $4.9 million in 1980 to $239 million in 1992 and to $962 million in 1998 and subsequently declined to $182 million in 2001, lower than the level in 1992. One reason for Shantou's relative poor performance in attracting FDI compared to the other two SEZs was its lack of soft infrastructure development; according to Li, the bureaucratic reforms in Shantou have been slow and government is not run as efficiently and transparently as the market requires.[31]

According to China's *Statistical Yearbook*, over the period 1979 to 1983, FDI in China amounted to $14.4 billion. The yearly FDI average in this period was $2.9 billion. It increased from $2.7 billion in 1984 to $11.6 billion in 1991, expanding at an average annual rate of around 23 percent. FDI increased even more rapidly after 1992 from $19.2 billion to $64 billion in 1997, with the av-

JORGE PÉREZ-LÓPEZ AND YU XIAO

Figure 3.1. Foreign Investment Actually Realized in Shenzhen, Zhuhai, and Shantou (1979–2001). Source: *Shenzhen Statistical Yearbook 2010, Zhuhai Statistical Yearbook 2009,* and *Shantou Statistical Yearbook 2006.*

erage annual growth rate at around 27 percent. From 1997 to 2000, the stock of FDI remained at above $50 billion. In 2014, the stock of FDI in China was estimated at around $120 billion.[32]

The FDI growth trajectories in both individual SEZs and the country as a whole show that 1992 marks the inflection point when FDI transitioned from a slow growth to a much more rapid one. As discussed earlier, 1992 is the year when Deng Xiaoping made the Southern Tour and of the Fourteenth National Congress of the CPC. Both events demonstrated the strong commitment of the central leadership to continue opening up the country and deepening market reforms. They also led to specific FDI liberalization measures that caused FDI to grow at faster rates. Thus, in politically centralized countries, such as China and Cuba, the political will of the central leadership has a strong impact on their economic policies in general and their ability to attract FDI in particular.

Experience of Cuba

After nationalizing all foreign property in the early 1960s and shunning foreign investment during the 1960s and 1970s, in 1982 Cuba cracked open the door to foreign investment by allowing the formation of joint ventures between Cuban enterprises and foreign investors. In the mid-1990s, Cuba created a more robust legal framework for foreign investment via a foreign investment statute, supplemented by a host of bilateral investment treaties

(BITs) intended to offer guarantees to foreign investors and create a more welcoming environment toward foreign investment. In 2013, Cuba created a special development zone in the port of Mariel (ZED Mariel, or ZEDM, short for *Zona Especial de Desarrollo Mariel*) intended to attract foreign investment and in 2014 revised its general foreign investment statute.

LEGAL FRAMEWORK FOR FOREIGN INVESTMENT

1) 1982 Joint Venture Law

In February 1982, three years after China adopted the Law on Joint Ventures, Cuba's Council of State approved Law-Decree No. 50, a statute that authorized the creation of joint ventures in the island between Cuban entities and foreign interests for the specific purpose of engaging in profit-making activities promoting Cuba's economic development.[33] Compared to the Chinese statute, Cuba's joint venture law placed more requirements and limitations on prospective foreign investors. Some of the features and limitations of Law-Decree No. 50 were:

- Similar to China's statute, the Cuban state "guaranteed" foreign partners the unrestricted ability to remit abroad, in hard currency, profits or dividends of joint ventures or proceeds from liquidation of a joint venture.

- Also similar to China's statute, the Cuban law offered incentives to joint ventures in the form of duty exemptions for imports of raw materials and machinery and equipment, and reductions in taxes and levies.

- Unlike China's statute, which did not set upper limit of foreign ownership of joint ventures, the 1982 Cuban law stated that foreign partners were limited to minority ownership, i.e., 49 percent ownership of the value of assets of the joint venture.

- Unlike in China, joint ventures established pursuant to Law-Decree No. 50 were required to employ only Cuban citizens, except for managerial and some technical positions, which both partners agreed could be filled only by foreign citizens.

- More stringently than in China, Cuba's statute did not permit joint ventures to employ workers directly; an entity of the Cuban government hired workers for joint ventures and the entity in turn contracted with joint ventures to supply manpower for a monthly fee in hard currency that covered workers' wages and benefits. Moreover, joint venture workers were paid by the entity

JORGE PÉREZ-LÓPEZ AND YU XIAO

in local currency in accordance with national wage scales established by the appropriate government agency.

The requirement that joint ventures employ and pay workers through a government entity created for this purpose, and the further requirement that joint ventures pay the entity for the workers in hard currency (U.S. dollars), while the workers drew their salary in Cuban pesos, created significant distortions. In particular, this system resulted in the Cuban state confiscating over 95 percent of workers' pay.[34] This confiscatory scheme, first incorporated in the 1982 joint venture law, has remained in place with respect to subsequent foreign investment legislation, including the 1995 and 2014 Foreign Investment Laws (although as is discussed below, it has been relaxed somewhat with respect to workers in the ZED Mariel).

2) 1982 Constitutional Amendments and BITs

In July 1982, shortly after the enactment of Law-Decree No. 50, Cuba's National Assembly of People's Power passed three amendments to the constitution recognizing private property aimed at providing assurances to foreign investors that they could invest safely in the island: (1) the state recognized the ownership of property by joint ventures and other corporations established pursuant to domestic law; (2) exclusive socialist ownership of the means of production was limited to "fundamental" means of production; and (3) a constitutional basis was created for the transfer of state property to the private sector.

Cuba has also buttressed its legal structure to attract foreign investment through the negotiation of bilateral investment treaties (BITs) with a wide range of commercial partners. Cuban BITs generally provided national treatment and most-favored-nation treatment for foreign investors; guarantees of free transfers, in convertible currency, of investments and their returns; limitation that expropriation of investment of the parties would be exclusively for reasons of public utility, in accord with domestic law, on a nondiscriminatory basis, and pursuant to compensation; preference for settlement of state-to-state disputes through diplomacy and, where this is not possible, through arbitration following a mechanism set out in the BITs; and preference for settlement of investor-state disputes through consultations, with the possibility of either party referring the dispute for resolution to the United Nations Commission on International Trade Law (UNCITRAL) or the International Chamber of Commerce (ICC).[35] As of the time of this writing, Cuba had signed BITs with some 60 countries, including with most of its significant trade/investment partners.

3) 1995 Foreign Investment Law

Although symbolically important as an indicator of opening to foreign investment, the 1982 joint venture law had very limited success in attracting investment flows. Further changes to the legal framework for foreign investment were instituted in 1995 with the adoption by Cuba's National Assembly of a comprehensive foreign investment law, Law No. 77.[36] Pursuant to the new statute, foreign investments in the island could take three forms: (a) joint ventures formed between one or more Cuban entities and one or more foreign partners; (b) international economic association contracts concluded between Cuban entities and foreign partners, typically for a specified purpose, principally of two types: (i) cooperated production contracts for the production either of goods or of services; and (ii) management contracts whereby a domestic entity contracts with a foreign company to manage one or more production lines or an entire facility in Cuba; and (c) wholly foreign-owned companies.

The 1995 Foreign Investment Law broke new ground in certain areas. It:

- Allowed for the possibility of investments that are 100 percent owned by foreigners.

- Provided legal protections against expropriation and established rules for compensation in instances of expropriation for reasons of public utility or social interest.

- Simplified the administrative approval process for foreign investments.

- Expanded the scope of economic sectors open to foreign investment, exempting health and education services and national defense, but now including some forms of real estate.

- Gave joint ventures or wholly foreign-owned enterprises the right, consistent with domestic legislation, to export and import directly to meet their needs.

The requirement that Cuban government entities act as the employer of all employees of foreign-invested companies promulgated for joint ventures by the 1982 joint venture law continued to apply to foreign-invested companies pursuant to Law No. 77.

4) 2011 Party Guidelines

In April 2011, the Partido Comunista de Cuba (PCC) held its Sixth Congress, at which it adopted a set of guidelines intended to direct the country's economic and social development for the next five years. The guidelines continued to put forth the Cuban government's view that the role of foreign investment is to complement domestic investment and that the aim of foreign investment is to fulfill the economic needs of the country's short, medium, and long-term economic and social development plans. The guidelines also called for streamlining the foreign investment approval process, while setting stringent requirements for new investments to satisfy objectives such as access to advanced technologies, modern management techniques, diversification of export markets, import substitution, sufficiency of capital investment, and employment generation. Finally, consistent with the emphasis on increasing economic discipline, the guidelines called for more concreteness in commitments made by foreign investors and more "rigorous" enforcement of such commitments as well as of regulations. The guidelines also called for establishing time limits for an approved investment to commence operations and for a procedure to terminate projects that fail to meet such time limits.

5) 2014 Foreign Investment Law

In March 2014, Cuba adopted a long-awaited new foreign investment law, Law No. 118/2014, that codified the principles embodied in the 2011 Party Guidelines.[37] Although there were high expectations that the new law would break new ground by reducing red tape regarding investment projects, doing away with restrictions on investment in certain sectors of the economy, ending the discriminatory treatment of Cuban workers, and explicitly allow diaspora Cubans to invest in the island, the new law disappointed. As an astute observer of Cuba's legal framework titled an article on the topic in his blog, the foreign investment law is "'new' indeed, but barely."[38]

Law No. 118 went beyond its predecessor law in some respects, for example, by offering more generous incentives to investors (e.g., exemption from taxes on dividends; no income tax for the first eight years of operation, and 15 percent tax rate thereafter; permitting foreign investment in all areas of the economy except for health, education, and the armed forces; and allowing investments in real estate). However, Law No. 118 continues to require approval of investment projects on a case-by-case basis; prohibits foreign investors from association with Cuban entities unless they are approved by the Cuban government; and maintains the requirement that all employees of foreign-invested companies be employed by a Cuban hiring entity.

Development of SEZs

Emulating China's policy of designating certain geographic areas where foreign investment would concentrate, Cuba's 1995 Foreign Investment Law created a special set of incentives for investments in duty-free zones and industrial parks in areas designated by the Executive Committee of the Council of Ministers. In the late 1990s, the Council of Ministers designated two areas, Wajay and Berroa, in the vicinity of the city of Havana and the nearby port of Mariel for the establishment of export processing zones and industrial parks. By and large, this effort was unsuccessful as it failed to attract meaningful levels of foreign investment and the enterprises that settled in the designated areas were mainly warehouses and distribution facilities that did not meet the requirements of the desired foreign investment.

One of the economic and social development guidelines adopted by the PCC in April 2011 called for the creation of ZEDs "to increase exports, import substitution, high technology projects and local development and to contribute new forms of employment."[39] The first such zone was created in the port of Mariel by Law-Decree No. 313 of September 2013. The ZED Mariel offers an array of incentives to investors[40]:

- fifty-year contracts for investments, compared with then-current twenty-five years for foreign investments, with the possibility of extension;

- ten-year exemption (holiday) on taxes on profits, with the possibility of extension based on national interest determination; profit tax capped at 12 percent for the life of the investment;

- exemption from employment (labor force) tax; however, subject to social security contribution capped at 14 percent of wages;

- exemption from sales or services taxes for local transactions for the first year; subsequently capped at 1 percent; and

- exemption from territorial contribution taxes, although subject to 0.5 percent tax on income earmarked for a zone maintenance and development (infrastructure) fund.

The ZEDM law also created a special labor regime. As in the case of other forms of foreign investments in Cuba, enterprises established in the ZEDM cannot employ Cuban workers directly and instead have to rely on a state employment entity as intermediary. The operational aspects of the labor regime for the ZEDM differ from those set out in the joint venture law and the 1995 foreign investment law:

- The investor and the designated Cuban entity are required to enter into a labor supply agreement that specifies, among other things, the number and skill set of workers to be employed, the pay workers will earn, and length of time of employment.

JORGE PÉREZ-LÓPEZ AND YU XIAO

- The pay that the Cuban entity receives for the services of workers is agreed between the designated Cuban entity and the investor; the amount is established in CUP or U.S. dollars. However, the designated Cuban entity pays local employees in Cuban pesos.

- Special rules apply for the separation of workers, either by decision of the operator or by the worker's choice. The investor may "return" (*devolver*) a Cuban worker to the designated Cuban entity if the investor deems that the worker's performance does not meet job "exigencies."

In the first half of May 2014, the Cuban government defined certain key parameters to establish the compensation of ZEDM workers:[41]

- the Ministry of Finance and Prices set the personal tax rate for workers in the ZEDM at 5 percent;[42]

- the ZEDM decided that workers would receive 80 percent of the payment negotiated between the operator and the Cuban hiring entity;[43] and

- the Ministry of Labor and Social Security set the coefficient for adjusting the salary of Cuban workers at "10," meaning that the rate of exchange between the Cuban peso (CUP) and the Convertible Cuban Peso (CUC) to determine the amount paid to workers would be 10:1.[44]

For a job for which the investor and the Cuban hiring entity have agreed would be remunerated at the rate of $1,000 or 1,000 CUC per month, applying the 80 percent–20 percent split between the worker and the hiring entity, the worker would receive $800 or 800 CUC and the hiring entity $200 or 200 CUC. With a coefficient (exchange rate) of 10, this would mean that the Cuban worker would realize 8,000 CUP per month; the personal tax on an income of 8,000 CUP (5 percent) would be 400 CUP, for a net salary of 7,600 CUP. That is, out of the amount paid by the investor ($1,000 or 1,000 CUC, equivalent to 24,000 CUP at the current CUP/CUC exchange rate), the worker would receive 7,600 CUP or about 32 percent. Compared to the previous arrangements, ZEDM workers will realize a considerably higher percentage of the amount paid for their services by foreign companies, but the degree of state confiscation of worker salary is still very high at about 68 percent.[45]

DIASPORA INVESTMENT

Unlike China, attracting investment from its sizable and economically well-endowed diaspora has not been a priority of Cuba. While precise statistics on the magnitude of the Cuban diaspora are not available, it is clear that it is quite sizable. From 1959 through 2012, nearly 1.3 million Cubans left the island and settled in the United States; over the same time period, some 300,000 Cuban citizens moved to Spain, Puerto Rico, Venezuela, Mexico, and other Latin American and Caribbean countries, as well as to Canada and several European nations such as Germany, Italy, and France. It has been estimated that around 2013, at least 16 percent of the Cuban-origin population resided outside of the island, principally in the United States.[46] It is also clear that the diaspora is quite well off financially; there are numerous studies of the adaptation of Cubans to the countries to which they have migrated and their economic success stories.[47] Although there are no recent estimates of the economic endowment of the Cuban diaspora, circa 2000 it was estimated that the income and assets of the Cuban American community was between $40 and $50 billion.[48]

Not only has Cuba not actively sought investment from its diaspora (whether located in the United States or elsewhere) but it has also prohibited Cuban citizens from investing, for example, in association with a foreign investor. Finally, it should be noted that U.S. embargo policies dovetail with Cuban policies to prevent the diaspora residing in the United States from playing a role in Cuban FDI.[49]

FDI Performance

Official information on Cuban foreign investment flows and stocks are very scarce. For 1993–2001 only, Cuba published partial official statistics on the balance of payments. These data show that annual foreign investment flows fluctuated significantly, from $563 million in 1994 to under $5 million in 1995. Over the time span 1993–2001, cumulative foreign investment was $2.018 billion, or an average flow of $224 million per annum (figure 3.2). Focusing on 1996–2001, a time period after the passage of the 1995 foreign investment law, the average incoming foreign investment was $233 million per annum.

In the late 1990s–early 2000s, Cuba became more selective in the approval of private foreign investors. Since 2004 incoming foreign investment was dominated by projects with Venezuela and to a lesser extent China; investments from other countries were discrete and focused on natural resources or oligopolistic sectors.[50] In a press interview in 2007, the then-minister of foreign investment reported that investment (presumably investment flows) reached a "record high" level of $981 million in 2006, 22 percent higher than the year before (meaning that investment in 2005 was of the order of $765 million).[51] No other information on the magnitude of investment flows is available.

JORGE PÉREZ-LÓPEZ AND YU XIAO

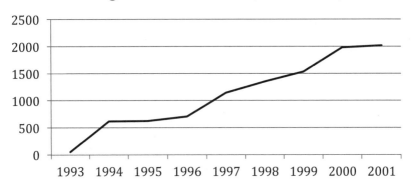

Foreign Direct Investment (Million USD)

Former minister of the economy and planning José Luis Rodríguez has stated that foreign investment *commitments*—similar to what is referred to as investment intentions or announcements—amounted to $5.2 billion between 1995 and 2002, as the creation of a multitude of foreign-invested enterprises was announced; however, the number of foreign-invested enterprises subsequently declined probably as a result of expiration of their term of operation, economic results that fell short of expectations, or failure on the part of the foreign partner to meet obligations. As of 2010, Rodríguez stated, committed foreign investment had declined to $4.2 billion.[52] Meanwhile, economist Pérez Villanueva has estimated that cumulative committed foreign investment through 2012 amounted to $5 billion.[53]

More recently, the Cuban government has launched an aggressive campaign to attract foreign investors, extolling the benefits embodied in the legislation creating the ZED Mariel and the new foreign investment law. In early November 2014, Cuba's minister of foreign trade and foreign investment made public a lengthy document titled *Cartera de Oportunidades de Inversión Extranjera*, which contains a wish list of projects for which the Cuban government seeks foreign participation.[54] In all, 246 investment projects were listed, for a total investment value of $8.7 billion, distributed across economic sectors and between the ZED Mariel and the rest of the country as shown in table 3.1. Only about 10 percent of the investment opportunities (25 out of 246) are specific to the ZED Mariel, with 90 percent located in the rest of the island and therefore subject to the provisions of the foreign investment law.

In terms of economic sectors, Cuba's list of investment priorities are: 1) oil

TABLE 3.1. Investment Opportunities Proposed by the Cuban Government

Sector	Location		Total
	ZED Mariel	Rest of country	
Processed foods	5	32	37
Sugar industry		4	4
Wholesale commerce		1	1
Biotechnology/medicines	13		13
Construction		6	6
Renewable energy	1	13	14
Industry	6	10	16
Mining		10	10
Oil		86	86
Transportation		3	3
Tourism		56	56
Total	25	221	246

Source: Ministerio del Comercio Exterior y la Inversión Extranjera, *Cuba: Cartera de Oportunidades de Inversión Extranjera* (2014).

(86 projects); 2) tourism (56); 3) processed foods (37); 4) renewable energy (14); and 5) biotechnology/medicines (13).

FDI Expansion in Cuba: Lessons from China

Notwithstanding the government campaign to attract FDI, foreign investors seeking to locate in Cuba face a number of important challenges. A very small convenience sample survey of 15 commercial officers of European Union embassies in Cuba conducted by Cuban researchers in early 2012 revealed the following positive and negative factors regarding investment in the island (scale is 1 to 3, with 3 being most significant and 1 least significant): Positive factors—personal security (2.7); potential for expansion (1.7); quality of the workforce (1.5); political stability (1.5); and low level of competition from other firms (1.0). Negative factors—labor regulations (1.9); financial system (1.5); macro stability (1.1); bureaucratic approval system for new enterprises (1.1); costs of establishment (1.0); legal framework (1.0); property rights guarantees (0.8); requirement of association with the state (0.8); import restrictions (0.7); and internal distribution system (0.7).[55]

Below we discuss several of these challenges and China's experiences in addressing them in its own efforts to attract FDI.

JORGE PÉREZ-LÓPEZ AND YU XIAO

BUREAUCRATIC APPROVAL PROCESS

One of the constraints in Cuba's policies to attract FDI has been a heavy-handed and lengthy approval process that adds time and cost to the decision-making process. The case-by-case nature of the approval process means that bureaucrats have substantial discretion at numerous points in the process and opens up the possibility for an investment opportunity to be derailed. Over time, Cuba has relaxed some of the red tape regarding investment approvals (e.g., by raising the monetary threshold for FDI projects that require the equivalent of a cabinet-level approval decision, limiting the sectors of the economy that are closed to foreign investment) but nevertheless the case-by-case approval requirements are time consuming and costly for foreign investors and introduce a great deal of subjectivity in the process.

In China, the approval is also case-by-case, but the authority is decentralized to lower levels of government. In the early 1980s, the approval authority was centralized in the national government but in 1985, provincial governments were authorized to approve certain projects under the conditions that these projects did not involve additional outlays on the part of the state and the amounts of investment did not exceed certain levels. The investment thresholds are different across different regions.[56] In 1988, the State Council expanded provincial governments' approval authority and raised the investment threshold for different provinces. For the coastal regions and SEZs, the threshold was $30 million, and for the inland provinces, the threshold was $10 million. Provincial governments also decentralized the approval authority to lower levels of government, based on their own conditions.[57] In 2010, the Ministry of Commerce further decentralized the approval authority by raising the investment threshold and eliminating the different treatment on inland and coastal provinces.[58]

In this aspect, Cuba and China are similar, since both countries require case-by-case approval, creating obstacles for attracting FDI. Over time, China eased and decentralized the approval authority, which helped to alleviate the problem. It may be unrealistic to expect Cuba in the short term to abandon the case-by-case approval process. A more pragmatic way to move in this direction would be to decentralize the decision making and let the provincial and municipal governments make approval decisions. Doing so can shorten the process as well as lead to better decisions, because the decision makers would have knowledge of local conditions and are likely to make better decisions than the central government.

INVESTMENT CLIMATE

One of the key determinants of FDI location is the investment climate, "the set of location-specific factors shaping the opportunities and incentives for firms to invest productively, create jobs, and expand."[59] The investment climate is shaped by numerous variables: rule of law, transparency, quality of government policy making, macroeconomic stability, openness to international trade, stability, perception of investment risks. Cuba consistently ranks near the bottom in international measures of property rights, ease of doing business, transparency, rule of law, quality of governance and so on, and similarly it is considered a high credit risk environment. For example, Cuba was ranked 177 (out of 178 countries) and considered in the "repressed" category in the 2016 Heritage Foundation–Wall Street Journal Index of Economic Freedom, based on four dimensions: 1) rule of law; 2) limited government; 3) regulatory efficacy; and 4) open markets. China, by comparison, while not a paragon of economic freedom, was ranked over 30 slots higher at 144, and grouped in the "mostly unfree" category.[60]

Importantly, an area in which China scores particularly well in the above index is trade liberalization. Prior to Deng's reform and opening-up policies, China's foreign trade was strictly controlled by the Ministry of Foreign Trade (MFT), which "was the leading body responsible for China's international commerce. . . . Under its direct supervision, state-owned foreign trade corporations (FTC) handled all of China's imports (including technology) and exports. The FTCs were organized along product lines with head offices in Beijing and branch offices in selected provinces and cities. . . . It (FTC) imported goods on request from end-users for a service fee as well as goods for domestic commercial channels which were settled at predetermined prices."[61] However, in 1979 China's government decentralized the existing trade structure to make it more flexible and responsive and to bring Chinese producers and end-users into closer contact with their foreign trading partners.[62] To a large extent, Cuba's current foreign trade regime—under which only a limited number of state entities can engage in foreign trade—is quite similar to that of pre-reform China.

INABILITY TO HIRE WORKERS DIRECTLY

As discussed above, foreign-invested companies operating in Cuba are not permitted to hire their own employees. Instead, these companies must use an intermediary employment agency owned and operated by the Cuban government to manage their labor resources. The intermediary employment agency carries out, among other human resources management activities,

JORGE PÉREZ-LÓPEZ AND YU XIAO

recruitment, interviewing, selection, salary negotiations, discipline, griev-ances procedures, and firing/termination. While some foreign investors are comfortable with outsourcing their personnel management to a Cuban gov-ernment agency, many react negatively to this overall impediment to man-age their human resources which they consider as an important asset. These government interventions in the employment relationship are likely to be troublesome to multinational corporations that have advanced corporate so-cial responsibility programs.

Implicit in this labor regime is a very detrimental factor for Cuban work-ers, namely that while the employment agency—on behalf of the Cuban government—receives compensation for the labor resources in convertible currencies (U.S. dollars or CUC) the Cuban workers are paid in domestic currency (CUP), which means that their earnings in convertible currency are a fraction of what the foreign investor paid the Cuban government. As has been mentioned earlier, until recently the Cuban government was con-fiscating over 90 percent of the earnings of Cuban workers, a share that has been reduced to about 60 percent for workers in the ZEDM. In the 2014 Foreign Investment Law the Cuban government recognized 12 employment agencies (focused on different sectors of the economy), a significant improve-ment over the single agency prior to the new law, and has introduced some flexibility in the negotiation of worker salaries, but the inability to manage human resources is still a significant factor in Cuba's ability to attract FDI.

Like Cuba, in the early reform period China also had constraints on the hiring process and wage setting in joint ventures. But the constraints were less stringent than Cuba's. According to the 1980 Provisions of the People's Republic of China for Labor Management in Chinese-Foreign Joint Ventures, the staff and workers of a joint venture could be recommended by the local department in charge of the venture or the local labor management depart-ment, or they could be recruited by the joint venture itself with consent of the labor management department. In practice, "when a joint venture recruits its employees, it has to apply to the local labor department for a quota for the recruitment of workers, stating the number of people to be recruited and the qualifications, on the basis of which the labor department tells the joint ven-ture where and from whom it may select its workforce."[63] Although this pro-cess was cumbersome for foreign investors, it was less so than in Cuba, where direct hiring of workers by foreign-invested enterprises has been—and still is—prohibited. In China, "a joint venture may dismiss staff and workers who become superfluous . . . but the venture must give them compensation in accordance with provisions of the labor contract." A joint venture could discharge workers and staff for violation of rules and regulations, but the sanction of discharge must be reported to the department in charge of the venture and the labor management department for approval.[64] In terms of wage-setting, "the wage levels of the staff and workers of joint ventures shall be fixed at 120 to 150 percent of the real wages of the staff and workers of state enterprises in the locality in the same line of business."[65]

COMMITMENT TO REFORMS

Cuba undertook a fairly robust set of economic reforms during the early 1990s, in the context of a deep economic crisis associated with the breakup of the Socialist community and dissolution of the former Soviet Union called the "Special Period in Time of Peace."[66] Measures adopted included (more or less in chronological order beginning in mid-1993): 1) legalization of the holding and use of foreign currency; 2) legalization of self-employment; 3) breakup of state farms and creation of quasi-cooperatives; 4) modification of the tax code; 5) creation of agricultural markets; 6) reforms to the banking system; and 7) passage of a comprehensive foreign investment law. The combination of macroeconomic stabilization actions and implementation of the aforementioned measures resulted in the return of positive economic growth at the same time strengthening the hand of opponents of further reforms and liberalization. Thus, from the late 1990s onward, Cuba's reform process was paralyzed and reversed in several respects, as Cuba pursued the ideologically laden "Battle of Ideas."

The beginning of a new cycle of reforms, which is still ongoing, can be traced to 2007–2008, roughly the time period when Raúl Castro consolidated his role as Cuba's leader. Mesa-Lago and Pérez-López (2013) assessed reforms through 2012 of what is officially called *actualización* (updating) of the Cuban economic model (to stress that the reforms are within socialism and are not intended to create markets) and concluded that administrative and nonstructural reforms, which include reorganization of government functions and removal of restrictions on restrictions on consumer behavior, had begun to have some positive effects, while the more complex structural reforms were progressing very slowly and often lacked depth.[67] Since then, additional reforms include privatization of petty state enterprises in retail commerce (beauty parlors, cafeterias, appliance repair shops) by converting them into cooperatives, limited decentralization of management of state enterprises, the aforementioned new foreign investment law, and a number of measures to provide greater access of Cubans to the internet. To date, however, Cuba has not tackled the creation of a private industrial sector, the government continues to hold a monopoly over foreign trade, and—despite much discussion and numerous hints about impending changes—Cuba has

JORGE PÉREZ-LÓPEZ AND YU XIAO

not tackled the elimination of monetary duality, a pernicious problem that creates distortions throughout the economy.

In contrast with the zigzagging of economic reforms in Cuba, which tend to create uncertainty among foreign investors, China has not wavered in its pursuit of the reforms launched in 1978. Particularly through establishing legal frameworks and SEZs as well as working to attract diaspora investment, China significantly increased its FDI since the 1980s. Although there were periods when investment uncertainties were relatively high, such as the years after the 1989 crisis, the leadership's resolve to deepen market reform served to strengthen investors' confidence and foster continuous FDI inflows.

Pérez Villanueva (2012), in a study of foreign investment policies and performance in China and Vietnam and implications for Cuba, makes two important points regarding the interplay between reforms and attraction of foreign investment that are quite relevant to Cuba's current efforts to promote foreign investment:

1. Foreign investment began to flow in significant amounts into China and Vietnam after domestic investment had developed. That is, foreign investors were willing to take the risks associated with investing in China and Vietnam only after domestic growth had taken off. The attraction of foreign investment was part of a gradual reform strategy, which began with the reform and opening-up policies and eventually enveloped the economy as a whole.

2. The experiences of China and Vietnam show that all of the country's institutions must be aligned with the objective of attracting foreign investment, facilitating—rather than obstructing—the flow of such resources. To the extent that some institutions or ministries do not buy into the imperative of attracting investment, suboptimal results will obtain. Particularly in the case of infrastructure projects, which have very long capital investment recovery periods, certainty of the planning horizon and stability are critical. It is essential that there be a national consensus on the wisdom of the policies.[68]

In sum, China's experience suggests that policy stability and a clear commitment to reform are critical for Cuba to attract foreign investment. While Cuba has made some important reforms, the lack of a clear direction and half-hearted nature of the policy "updating" does not bode well for great increases in investment in the near future.

CONCLUSION

In this chapter, we have explained that in order to promote economic growth, it is imperative for Cuba to attract foreign investment. However, so far Cuba has not experienced much success in achieving its goals. In contrast, China has been extremely successful in attracting foreign investment since it adopted its reform and opening-up policies in 1978 under the leadership of Deng Xiaoping. Foreign investment has been one of the pillars of China's rapid economic growth over the last three decades that has drastically changed the face of the nation and the economic situation of the Chinese people. By comparing different aspects of economic reform measures in Cuba and China, we find that the Chinese central leadership has been more committed to economic reforms than its Cuban counterpart, leading to a more hospitable environment for foreign investment in China. These include laws that are friendlier toward foreign investors, more decentralized bureaucratic approval process, a more liberal trade regime, and more flexible labor policies. Moreover, we also find that China's success in attracting FDI to a large extent has depended on its success in attracting diaspora investment, which Cuba has not done to date.

Thus, we argue that the key to China's success in attracting foreign investment has been policy stability and a commitment to market-oriented reform. This has not been the case in Cuba, whose reforms have been episodic and shallow. To succeed in attracting foreign investment, it is necessary for Cuba to be committed to opening-up reforms.

Finally, the hostile relationship between Cuba and the United States prior to 2014 made it challenging for Cuba to attract investment from the United States, both from U.S. investors and from the Cuban diaspora in the United States, which has a substantial capacity to invest in the island. It remains to be seen whether, in a new era of improved diplomatic relations with the United States—which are under tension since President Trump took power—Cuba will take the necessary policy steps to capitalize on foreign investment from that country and from its diaspora. From the experience of China's reforms, this opportunity can be promising for Cuba's economic growth.

NOTES

1. Pavel Vidal, "Foreign Investment Law and GDP Growth in Cuba," *Economic Trend Report, Cuba Standard* (2014).

2. Official Cuban statistics from Oficina Nacional de Estadística e Información, *Anuario Estadistico de Cuba 2014.*

3. These gross capital formation to GDP ratios are based on information supplied by national governments to the Economic Commission for Latin America and the Caribbean (ECLAC) and originate from ECLAC, *Economic Survey of Latin America and the Caribbean, 2015*, Table A.6.

JORGE PÉREZ-LÓPEZ AND YU XIAO

4. World Bank, World Development Indicators Database, http://databank.world bank.org/data/reports.aspx?source=world-development-indicators

5. See note 4.

6. Cited by Daniel Trotta, "Cuba approves law aimed at attracting foreign investment," Reuters (March 29, 2014).

7. Rafael Arzuaga, "Asamblea Nacional de Cuba aprueba nueva Ley de Inversión Extranjera," *Cuba Debate* (March 29, 2014).

8. See note 7. Emphasis added.

9. Omar Everleny Pérez Villanueva, "La situación actual de la economía cubana y sus retos," in Pérez Villanueva, comp., *Reflexiones sobre economía cubana* (Havana: Editorial de Ciencias Sociales, 2006), p. 15. See also José Antonio Alonso and Juan Triana Cordoví, "Nuevas bases para el crecimiento," in José Antonio Alonso and Pavel Vidal, editors, *¿Quo Vadis, Cuba? La incierta senda de las reformas* (Madrid: Libros de la Catarata, 2013), 53.

10. José Luis Rodríguez, "Cuba, la necesidad de nuevas inversiones y el capital extranjero," *Cuba Contemporanea* (March 18, 2014). http://cubacontemporanea.com /noticias/cuba-la-necesidad-de-nuevas-inversiones-y-el-capital-extranjero.

11. Cited by Carlos Batista, "Cuba se abre a la inversión extranjera con megapuerto de Mariel," *El Nuevo Herald* (January 25, 2014). Roughly speaking, an increase in investment of $3 billion would have brought Cuba's gross capital formation ratio in 2012 to about 20 percent of GDP.

12. "Inversión extranjera y desarrollo social," Catalejo, *El Blog de Temas* (March 26, 2014). Panel discussion moderated by Rafael Hernández with the participation of several experts, including Elvira Castro, Richard Feinberg, Roberto Pérez, Saira Pons, Fabio Grobart, and Juan Triana.

13. Chung Chen, Lawrence Chang, and Yimin Zhang, "The Role of Foreign Direct Investment in China's Post-1978 Economic Development," *World Development* 23, no. 4 (1995): 692.

14. Carolyn P. Casey, "The 1986 Provisions to Encourage Foreign Investment in China: Further Evolution in Chinese Investment Laws," *American University International Law Review* 2, no. 2 (1987): 579–614.

15. "中华人民共和国中外合资经营企业法 (People's Republic of China Law on Joint Ventures)," 中华人民共和国对外经济法律法规汇编 (People's Republic of China Compilation of Laws and Regulations on Foreign Economy). http://www .people.com.cn/zixun/flfgk/item/dwjjf/falv/2/2-1-01.html. Accessed September 21, 2015.

16. Min Ye, *Diasporas and Foreign Direct Investment in China and India* (New York: Cambridge University Press, 2014), 65–66.

17. "The 14th National Congress," News of the Communist Party of China. http:// english.cpc.people.com.cn/206972/206981/8188380.html, accessed November 23, 2015.

18. Chen, Chang, and Zhang, "The Role of Foreign Direct Investment," p. 692.

19. Junwei Cao, "对外资优惠政策的再认识" (Reconsideration of Preferential Treatment towards Foreign Investment), *Quarterly Journal of Shanghai Academy of Social Sciences* 2 (2000): 46–54.

20. Jian Zhong, "深圳经济特区改革开放的历史进程与经验启示" (The Historical Course of the Economic Reform and Opening-up to the Outside World of the Shenzhen Special Economic Zone), *Journal of Shenzhen University (Humanities & Social Sciences)* 25, no. 4 (2008): 17–18.

21. See note 20.

22. Guixiang Ren, "改革开放以来中国华侨投资政策及华侨投资研究" (China's Policy for Overseas Chinese Investment and Studies on Investment from the Overseas Chinese since the Initiation of Reform and Opening-up), *CPC History Studies* 1 (2008): p. 40.

23. Deng Xiaoping mentioned these reasons during his Southern Tour in 1992. See Wenshou Chen, "中国改革开放以来引资政策研究" (A Study of Foreign Investment Policy since China's Reform and Opening-up), 2011. http://qwgzyj.gqb.gov .cn/yjytt/160/1771.shtml, accessed December 15, 2015.

24. State Council, "国务院发布关于华侨投资优惠的暂行规定的通知" (Interim Provisions of the State Council on Investment Preferences for Overseas Chinese), 1985. http://www.gov.cn/zhengce/content/2012–09/21/content_5383.htm, accessed February 23, 2016.

25. Min Ye, *Diasporas and Foreign Direct Investment*, 54.

26. Min Ye, *Diasporas and Foreign Direct Investment*, 60.

27. Haifeng Li, "迎接全国华商组织的蓬勃发展" (Welcoming the Robust Development of Chinese Entrepreneurs Organization Nationwide), *Overseas Chinese Affairs Studies* 1 (2005). http://qwgzyj.gqb.gov.cn/jyjl/122/151.shtml, accessed February 23, 2016.

28. Xiamen is not included because data were not publicly available over this period.

29. Shenzhen Government, *Shenzhen Statistics Yearbook 2010*. http://www.sztj .gov.cn/xxgk/tjsj/tjnj/201012/t20101224_1620341.htm, accessed December 15, 2015.

30. Hongquan Chen and Jian Zhong, "珠海改革开放的历史回顾、主要成就与 经验教训" (The Historical Review, Main Achievements and Lessons of Zhuhai's Economic Reform and Opening-up), *2008 China Special Economic Zones Forum* (2008): 65-66. http://ir.lib.szu.edu.cn:8080/handle/244041/2228, accessed December 14, 2015.

31. Xiang Li, "关于汕头经济发展问题的实证考察" (An Empirical Examination of the Problems of Shantou's Economic Development), *Shantou University Journal (Humanities and Social Sciences Bimonthly)* 20, no. 3 (2004): 87.

32. National Bureau of Statistics of China, *China Statistical Yearbook* (2015). http:// www.stats.gov.cn/tjsj/ndsj/2001c/q1713c.htm, accessed February 26, 2016.

33. "Decreto-Ley No. 50—Sobre asociaciones económicas entre entidades cubanas y extranjeras," *Gaceta Oficial* (February 15, 1982). This section draws from Jorge F. Pérez-López, "Islands of Capitalism in an Ocean of Socialism: Joint Ventures in Cuba's Development Strategy," in Pérez-López, ed., *Cuba at a Crossroads: Politics and Economics After the Fourth Party Congress* (Gainesville: University Press of Florida, 1994).

34. With the exchange rate between the Cuban peso (CUP)/the convertible peso (CUC)/and the U.S. dollar being approximately 25CUP=1CUC=US$1, for any given CUC or dollar salary, the Cuban worker receives 1/25 or about 4 percent of the amount. Thus the Cuban state retains (confiscates) about 95 percent of the salary.

35. Jorge F. Pérez-López and Matías F. Travieso-Díaz, "The Contribution of BITs to Cuba's Foreign Investment Program," *Cuba in Transition*, vol. 10 (Washington, DC: Association for the Study of the Cuban Economy, 2000). The six BITs examined were those with Italy, Spain, Colombia, Chile, the United Kingdom, and Portugal.

36. "Ley No. 77—Ley de las inversiones extranjeras," *Gaceta Oficial* (September 6, 1995).

37. "Ley de la Inversión Extranjera, Ley No. 118/2014," *Gaceta Oficial* (April 16, 2014).

38. José M. Pallí, "Cuba's Foreign Investment Law: 'New' Indeed, But Barely," Cubargie Joe blog, March 18, 2014. http://cubargiejoe.com/cubas-foreign-investment-law-new-indeed-but-barely/

39. This section draws from Jorge F. Pérez-López, "Investment Incentives of the ZED Mariel: Will Foreign Investors Take the Bait?" *Cuba in Transition*, vol. 24 (Washington, DC: Association for the Study of the Cuban Economy, 2014.

40. The incentives below are specific to investments in the ZEDM and are over and above those applicable to all other investments pursuant to the foreign investment law. See "Aprueban un reglamento para las empresas que operarán en el puerto del Mariel," *Diario de Cuba* (April 2, 2013); Marc Frank, "Cuba Bids to Lure Foreign Investment with New Port and Trade Zone," Reuters (September 23, 2013); and Arch Ritter, "The Tax Regimen for the Mariel Export Processing Zone: More Tax Discrimination of Micro-enterprises and Citizens?" (September 23, 2013), The Cuban Economy/La Economia Cubana blog, http://thecubaneconomy.com/articles/2013/09/3802/.

41. "Queda definido impuesto para personal de Zona Especial Mariel," *Cuba Debate* (May 8, 2014).

42. Ministerio de Finanzas y Precios, Resolución No. 139/2014, *Gaceta Oficial* (May 7, 2014).

43. "Régimen de contratación en Zona Especial de Mariel beneficia a trabajadores," *Cuba Debate* (April 14, 2014).

44. "Régimen de contratación en Zona Especial de Mariel" op. cit.; "Cuba anuncia reglas salariales para empleados de la Zona Franca del Mariel," *El Nuevo Herald* (May 10, 2014); and Ministerio de Trabajo y Seguridad Social, Resolución No. 14/2014, *Gaceta Oficial* (May 7, 2014).

45. Pérez posits that this is probably one the highest personal income tax rates in the world. See Lorenzo L. Pérez, "Cuba: Assessment of the New Tax Law of 2012," *Cuba in Transition,* vol. 24 (Washington, DC: Association for the Study of the Cuban Economy, 2014), 395.

46. These statistics are from Jorge Duany, "Del exilio histórico a la diáspora contemporánea," in Duany, editor, *Un pueblo disperso: Dimensiones sociales y culturales de la diáspora cubana* (Valencia, Spain: Editorial Advana Vieja, 2014), 13. This share is probably higher today, as Cuban emigration has mushroomed recently, in anticipation of changes in very favorable U.S. immigration policies vis-à-vis Cuban arrivals that are currently in place but are facing pressure for elimination as the process of reestablishment of relations between the United States and Cuba. See also *La Diáspora Cubana en el Siglo XXI* (Miami: Florida International University, 2011).

47. See, e.g., the essays in Sam Verdeja and Guillermo Martinez, *Cubans: An Epic Journey* (Miami: Facts About Cuban Exiles, 2011).

48. Sergio Díaz-Briquets and Jorge Pérez-López, *The Role of the Cuban-American Community in the Cuban Transition* (Coral Gables: Institute for Cuban and Cuban-American Studies, University of Miami, 2003), 1. See also Pérez-López, "The Diaspora as a Commercial Network for Cuban Reconstruction," *Cuba in Transition,* vol. 17 (Washington, DC: Association for the Study of the Cuban Economy, 2007). http://www.ascecuba.org/c/wp-content/uploads/2014/09/v17-perezlopez.pdf

49. Thus, regulations issued by the Office of Foreign Assets Control (OFAC) of the U.S. Department of the Treasury, set forth that "persons subject to U.S. jurisdiction are prohibited from doing business or investing in Cuba unless licensed by OFAC"

50. See Jorge F. Pérez-López, "The Rise and Fall of Private Foreign Investment in Cuba," *Cuban Affairs* 3, no. 1 (2008). Investments from market-oriented countries during this period included a cement factory with Spanish capital, the expansion of a nickel production plant with Canadian capital, and the announced modernization of a container port facility with capital from the United Arab Emirates (this latter project did not go forward).

51. "Cuba: inversión reorganizada y con récord de ingresos," Associated Press, Havana (June 27, 2007).

52. José Luis Rodríguez, "Cuba: una revaloración indispensable de la inversión extranjera directa (I)," *Cuba Contemporánea* (February 3, 2014). http://www.cuba contemporanea.com/noticias/cuba-una-revaloracion-indispensable-de-la-inversion -extranjera-directa-i

53. Omar Everleny Pérez Villanueva, "La inversión extranjera directa en Cuba: necesidad de su relanzamiento," Centro de Estudios de la Economía Cubana (2014).

54. "Presentó Cuba su cartera de negocios para la inversión extranjera," *Cuba Debate* (3 November 2015). The portfolio of investment opportunities had been approved by the Council of Ministers at a meeting presided by Raúl Castro held at the end of October. See "Inversión extranjera, envejecimiento poblacional y otros temas en reunión del Consejo de Ministros," *Cuba Debate* (October 26, 2014).

55. See Pavel Vidal Alejandro, Omar Everleny Pérez Villanueva, and Saira Pons Pérez, *La inversión extranjera y de la Unión Europea en Cuba*. Centro de Estudios de la Economía Cubana y Unión Europea, March 16, 2012.

56. Baotai Chu, *Foreign Investment in China: A Question and Answer Guide* (Hong Kong: China International Economic Consultants Inc. and University Publisher and Printer, 1987), 187.

57. Mei Li, "当代中国外资审批机构中存在的问题及立法思考" (Problems with the Foreign Investment Approval Institutions and Thoughts on its Legislation in Contemporary China), *Journal of Guangzhou Economic Management College* (2005), pp. 39–40.

58. See the government website, http://wzs.mofcom.gov.cn/article/n/201006/201 00606965621.shtml, accessed April 14, 2016.

59. Warrick Smith and Mary Hallward-Driemeier, "Understanding the Investment Climate," *Finance and Development* (March 2005): 40.

60. Heritage Foundation-Wall Street Journal Index of Economic Freedom, 2016. http://www.heritage.org/index/.

61. Samuel P. S. Ho and Ralph W. Huenemann, *China's Open Door Policy: The Quest for Foreign Technology and Capital* (Vancouver: University of British Columbia Press, 1984), 34.

62. Ho and Huenemann, *China's Open Door Policy,* 35

63. Chu, *Foreign Investment in China,* 180.

64. See Articles 3, 4 and 5 in the *Provisions of the People's Republic of China for Labor Management in Chinese-Foreign Joint Ventures,* 1980. http://www.chinatoday.com/law/A04.HTM, accessed April 14, 2016.

65. *Provisions of the People's Republic of China,* Article 8.

66. Between 1989 and 1993, Cuba's GDP contracted by nearly 35 percent, gross domestic investment fell from 26.7 percent to an abysmally low 5.4 percent of GDP, the fiscal deficit grew from 7.3 percent to 33.5 percent of GDP, merchandise exports and imports declined by 78.9 percent and 75.6 percent, respectively, and the hard currency external debt grew by nearly 42 percent. See Pérez-López, "The Cuban Economy in an Unending Special Period," *Cuba in Transition,* vol. 12 (Washington, DC: Association for the Study of the Cuban Economy, 2002).

67. Carmelo Mesa-Lago and Jorge Pérez-López, *Cuba Under Raúl Castro: Assessing the Reforms* (Boulder: Lynne Rienner Publishers, 2013), pp. 250–53.

68. Omar Everleny Pérez Villanueva, "Foreign Direct Investment in China, Vietnam and Cuba," in Jorge I. Domínguez, et al., eds., *Cuban Economic and Social Development: Policy Reforms and Challenges in the 21st Century* (Cambridge: Harvard University Press, 2012), 224.

MATÍAS F. TRAVIESO-DÍAZ

RESOLVING U.S. PROPERTY EXPROPRIATION CLAIMS AGAINST CUBA

One of the most important bilateral issues that need to be addressed by the United States and the Cuban government in order to achieve normal commercial relations is the resolution of outstanding claims of U.S. nationals[1] for the uncompensated expropriation of their assets in the early years of the Cuban revolution.[2] The expropriation of U.S. assets in Cuba was one of the leading causes of the deterioration in relations between the two countries in the early 1960s and the imposition of the U.S. embargo on trade with Cuba, which remains in place to this date.[3] U.S. laws require resolution of U.S. nationals' expropriation claims before the embargo on trade with Cuba is lifted; also, apart from any legal requirements, resolution of U.S. nationals' expropriation claims has been since the days of President Kennedy's administration one of the stated U.S. conditions for the normalization of relations between the United States and Cuba.[4]

The resolution of outstanding property claims is also a precondition to major foreign capital flow into Cuba. As long as property titles remain unsettled, foreigners will perceive investing in Cuba as a risky proposition. Countries in Central and Eastern Europe that delayed the implementation of schemes to settle expropriation claims experienced a great deal of uncertainty over property rights. This uncertainty discouraged potential investors and delayed privatization efforts.[5]

Thus, while it appears inevitable that the claims resolution process will have some impact on Cuba's economic transition, the rapid development of a claims resolution plan would help minimize this impact.

This chapter addresses and comments on several potential claim resolution alternatives that could be implemented to address U.S. citizens' expropriation claims against Cuba. Where appropriate, the paper draws on experiences in Central and Eastern European countries in dealing with their own claims issues. However, it does not offer a specific proposal on how the outstanding property claims of U.S. nationals should be handled.[6] The viability of any proposed program will ultimately be determined by the circumstances under which a settlement of outstanding claims is undertaken, including the economic and political conditions in which Cuba finds itself when it deals with the issue.

HISTORICAL SUMMARY

Cuba seized the properties of U.S. and other foreign nationals on the island starting in 1959, with the bulk of the expropriations taking place in the second half of 1960.[7] The process started in 1959 with the takeover of agricultural and cattle ranches under the Agrarian Reform Law;[8] reached a critical stage in July 1960 with the promulgation of Law 851, which authorized the expropriation of the property of U.S. nationals;[9] was carried out through several resolutions in the second half of 1960, again directed mainly against properties owned by U.S. nationals, although those of other foreign nationals were also taken;[10] and continued through 1963, when the last U.S. companies still in private hands were expropriated.[11] The laws issued by the Cuban government to implement the expropriations of the holdings of U.S. nationals contained undertakings by the state to provide compensation to the owners.[12] Nevertheless, in almost all cases, no compensation was ever paid.

The expropriation claims by nationals of other countries were considerably smaller than those of U.S. and Cuban nationals, and for the most part have been settled through agreements between Cuba and the respective countries (Spain, France, Switzerland, United Kingdom, and Canada).[13] Claims have been settled at a fraction of the assessed value of the expropriated assets.[14]

It is instructive to examine the precedent of the settlement agreements that Cuba has negotiated with other countries for the expropriation of the assets of their nationals. According to a Cuban summary, those agreements have five important facts in common: 1) they were negotiated over long

MATÍAS F. TRAVIESO-DÍAZ

periods of time; 2) all the agreements were lump sum, country-to-country settlements that did not take into account either individually or collectively the amounts claimed by the nationals for the loss of their properties; 3) the payments were made in installments, rather than all at once; 4) the payment was in either the currency of the country advancing the claims or, as was the case with Spain and Switzerland, in trade goods as well as currency; and 5) all agreements were negotiated between Cuba and the state representing the claimants, without claimant participation.[15]

THE U.S. CLAIMS CERTIFICATION PROGRAM

In 1964, the U.S. Congress amended the International Claims Settlement Act to establish a Cuban Claims Program, under which the Foreign Claims Settlement Commission of the United States (FCSC) was given authority to determine the validity and amount of claims by U.S. nationals against the government of Cuba for the taking of their property since January 1, 1959.[16] The Cuban Claims Program of the FCSC was active between 1966 and 1972. During that time, it received 8,816 claims by U.S. corporations (1,146) and individual citizens (7,670).[17] It certified 5,911 of those claims, with an aggregate amount of $1.8 billion;[18] denied 1,195 claims, with an aggregate amount of $1.5 billion; and dismissed without consideration (or saw withdrawn) 1,710 other claims.[19] It should be noted that the value of the certified Cuban claims exceeds the combined certified amounts of all other claims validated by the FCSC for expropriations of U.S. nationals' assets by other countries (including the Soviet Union, China, East Germany, Poland, Czechoslovakia, Hungary, Vietnam, and others).[20] Although the Cuban Claims Act did not expressly authorize the inclusion of interest in the amount allowed, the FCSC concluded that interest should be added in a certifiable loss "in conformity with principles of international law, justice and equity, and should be computed from the date of loss to the date of any future settlement." The FCSC determined that simple interest at a 6 percent rate should be included as part of the value of the claims it certified. Applying such interest rate on the outstanding $1.8 billion principal yields a present value, as of September 2015, of approximately $8 billion.

ALTERNATIVE APPROACHES FOR DEALING WITH U.S. NATIONALS' CLAIMS

Any proposal for the resolution of the U.S. nationals' expropriation claims against Cuba must recognize the objectives that a claims resolution program needs to achieve, the fundamental differences between the various types of property subject to claims, and the practical limitations that will be encountered by the Cuban government as it seeks to provide remedies to both U.S.

and domestic expropriation victims. The interaction between these factors adds a significant degree of complexity to the problem.

There are also fundamental differences among the property interests covered by the claims, which suggests that certain remedies may be better suited for some types of property than for others. For example, restitution of residential property may be extremely difficult, both from the legal and political standpoints;[21] monetary compensation may be an inadequate remedy where the property is unique, such as in the case of beach-front real estate in a resort area.

Cuba will also be confronted with political, as well as financial, limitations to its ability to provide certain remedies. A settlement that involves huge financial obligations over a long period of time may be resisted politically by, among others, the generations that have come of age in the island after the expropriations were carried out.[22]

Alternative 1: Government-to-Government Negotiations

The president of the United States has wide, but not plenary, power to settle claims against foreign governments for the uncompensated taking of property belonging to U.S. citizens.[23] The U.S. Department of State, under authority delegated by the president, acts on behalf of U.S. claimants in the negotiation of their claims with an expropriating foreign country.[24] Under the "doctrine of espousal," the negotiations conducted by the Department of State are binding on the claimants, and the settlement that is reached constitutes their sole remedy.[25]

In most agreements negotiated in the past, the United States and the expropriating country have arrived at a settlement involving payment by the expropriating country to the United States of an amount that is a fraction of the total estimated value of the confiscated assets.[26] The settlement proceeds are then distributed among the claimants in proportion to their losses. In most cases, the settlement does not include accrued interest, although a 1992 settlement with Germany over East Germany's expropriations of the assets of U.S. nationals did include the payment of simple interest at the approximate annual rate of 3 percent from the time the U.S. properties were taken.[27]

Under standard practice, U.S. claimants may not "opt out" of the settlement reached by the U.S. government. Dissatisfied claimants are barred from pursuing their claims before U.S. courts or in the settling country.[28]

This traditional settlement agreement would not appear, in itself, to be adequate to satisfy the needs of the parties in the Cuban situation. The amount of the outstanding certified claims by U.S. nationals is so large that it would likely outstrip Cuba's ability to pay a significant portion of the principal, let

MATÍAS F. TRAVIESO-DÍAZ

alone interest. Thus, a traditional settlement involving the payment of a large sum of money, even if payment is spread out over time, would be likely to place Cuba in difficult financial straits. Such a settlement could also have adverse political repercussions.[29]

Alternative 2: Methods Not Involving Government-to-Government Negotiations

Whether as part of a government-to-government settlement or independently of it, U.S. claimants could be authorized to obtain relief directly from Cuba for their expropriation claims. This relief could be the result of private, individual negotiations with the Cuban government or through participation by the U.S. claimants in Cuba's formal claim resolution program.

A direct settlement between a U.S. claimant and Cuba, if successful, should satisfy the claimant in that it would represent the best resolution that he was able to obtain through bargaining with Cuba. Such a settlement attempt, however, might not be successful. Therefore, if the direct negotiations alternative were authorized, the United States and Cuba would have to agree on a mechanism for assuring that those claimants who waived the right to be represented by the U.S. government in the negotiations with Cuba received a fair and equitable treatment by Cuba, and that if such negotiations failed the claimant would not be left without a remedy.

One way of protecting the rights of the U.S. claimants who choose to negotiate directly with Cuba could be for the Cuban government to agree to submit to binding international arbitration any claim that it was unable to settle with a U.S. national. Historically, however, arbitration of disputes between private citizens and states has resulted in inconsistent decisions on key issues.[30] This lack of uniformity and predictability in the outcomes underscores the need to establish clearly and in advance the legal regime that would govern the arbitration of disputes between U.S. citizens and the Cuban government.

Predictability of applicable rules could be achieved if the United States and Cuba agreed in advance to a procedure analogous to that used by the Iran–U.S. Claims Tribunal ("Tribunal") set up in 1981 to resolve the expropriation claims of U.S. nationals against Iran.[31] One important aspect of the Tribunal's framework is the adoption of the United Nations Commission on International Trade Law's ("UNCITRAL") Arbitration Rules, which are designed to address international commercial arbitration.[32] This choice of rules allowed supervisory jurisdiction to the legal system of the Netherlands where the Tribunal was seated.[33] The nationals themselves thus both file the claims and present them, and also decide whether to withdraw or accept any settlement offer.

The main area of potential divergence between the Tribunal and a counterpart tribunal set up to adjudicate disputes between a U.S. claimant and Cuba would be that, in the case of Iran, significant assets of that country were, after the 1979 Iranian revolution, frozen in the United States and were made available to satisfy arbitration awards in favor of private claimants. No such funds exist in the case of Cuba, so provisions would have to be made to have Cuba set up an independent source of funds available to satisfy tribunal awards—else a victory by a U.S. claimant in arbitration could prove pyrrhic because no funds might be available from which to satisfy the award.

Alternative 3: Participation in Cuba's Claim Resolution Program

Assuming that it was not feasible to have direct negotiations between U.S. claimants and Cuba, another alternative could be to allow U.S. nationals to participate in Cuba's domestic claims resolution program (such a program does not exist at this time, but Cuba could establish it in the future). Under such a program, there could be several alternative forms of compensation that could be made available to U.S. claimants (as well as to Cuban claimants). These alternative remedies include restitution, issuance of state obligations, and other forms of compensation.

1) RESTITUTION

Direct restitution of the actual property that was confiscated would be the solution that many U.S. corporate claimants might prefer, assuming such a choice was available under Cuba's claims resolution program.[34] Some types of expropriated property, e.g., large industrial installations, may lend themselves readily to direct restitution since the identity of the former owners is likely to be uncontested and the extent of the ownership rights may be relatively easy to establish.[35]

Restitution, however, may in many instances prove difficult to implement even for readily identifiable property because the ability to grant restitution of the actual property seized by the Cuban government may be negated by a variety of circumstances. For instance, the property may have been destroyed or substantially deteriorated; it may have been subject to transformation, merger, subdivision, improvement, or other substantial changes; it may have been devoted to a use that may not be easily reversed or that may have substantial public utility; or its character may be such that the state decides for policy reasons not to return to its former owners. In such cases, some form of compensation would need to be given to satisfy the claimant.

In addition, since the 1990s, Cuba (through state-owned enterprises) has entered into a number of joint ventures and other arrangements with foreign,

MATÍAS F. TRAVIESO-DÍAZ

non-U.S. investors. Many of these endeavors involve property that was expropriated from U.S. and Cuban nationals. In deciding whether to provide direct restitution of those properties to the U.S. claimants, the Cuban government will have to balance the rights and interests of the former owners against those of third parties who have invested in Cuba. Also, the rights of any other lessors, occupants, or other users of the property would have to be taken into account in deciding whether direct restitution should occur.

There may be instances in which direct restitution will be impractical, but both Cuba and the U.S. claimant will still wish to apply a restitution type of remedy. Such circumstances may dictate restitution of substitute property (that is, the transfer to the claimant of other property, equivalent in value to the one confiscated). Where restitution of substitute property is proposed, it will be necessary to set rules on, among other things, how the equivalence of the properties is to be established. Substitutional restitution may be appropriate, for example, in cases where the confiscated property is farmland that has been conveyed to cooperatives or divided among small farmers. Rather than dispossessing the current occupants, Cuba may offer to convey to the U.S. claimants agricultural or other lands in state hands that may be equivalent to those expropriated.

2) ISSUANCE OF STATE OBLIGATIONS

A number of Eastern European countries have used state-issued instruments, which will be generally referred to here as "vouchers," to provide full or partial compensation to expropriation claimants.[36] The vouchers could not be redeemed for cash, but could be used, among other things, as collateral for loans; to pay (fully or in part) for property sold by the state, including shares in privatized enterprises; to purchase real estate put up for sale by the state; to be exchanged for annuities; or as investment instruments.[37]

A voucher system provides a potential way of resolving many of the U.S. nationals' expropriation claims in Cuba, particularly those of the former owners of small and medium enterprises who may not be interested in recovering the properties they once owned because of the obsolescence or physical deterioration of the facilities.[38] The system recognizes the limits of the country's ability to pay compensation claims, and avoids the dislocation costs and disputes associated with direct restitution systems. As with restitution remedies, an issue that would need to be resolved at the outset would be the level of compensation to be offered in proportion to the loss.

The system has potentially great flexibility, for the vouchers could be used for a variety of purposes, some of which may be more attractive than others to individual claimants. Also, in addition to vouchers, other state-issued instruments could be used as means of compensating U.S. claimants. These include annuities, bonds, promissory notes, stock certificates in privatized enterprises, and other debt or equity instruments.

There are several potential drawbacks to a system of vouchers or other state-issued instruments.[39] The instruments will fluctuate in value, and are likely to depreciate if Cuba's economy stagnates.[40] In addition, to the extent the instruments are used as income-generating devices (e.g., for the collection of annuities) the rate of return is likely to be very low.[41] Also, the basic underpinning of a voucher system is confidence in the state's ability to make good on its commitments. Therefore, the security, transferability, and marketability of the compensation instruments is a serious concern that the Cuban government will need to overcome in order for the remedy to have acceptability with the claimants.

3) OTHER COMPENSATION MECHANISMS

Other remedies that might be utilized in Cuba, and have not yet been tried elsewhere, could consist of economic incentives to invest in the country. These remedies could include, for example, giving credits on taxes and duties to the extent of all or part of the claim amount; granting the ability to exchange the claim for other investment opportunities, such as management contracts, beneficial interests in state-owned enterprises, or preferences in government contracting; and conferring other benefits. Each claimant might be interested in a different "package," so ad hoc, case-by-case negotiations would need to be conducted, at least to resolve the most significant claims.

While allowing a large degree of creativity in the development of claims resolution arrangements suitable for individual claimants, the ability to create ad hoc resolutions could potentially complicate the claims process to the point of making it unwieldy. An even more significant risk is that a perception could easily develop that there is a lack of transparency in the process, since comparing the economic benefit of one "deal" to another might be difficult and open to a variety of interpretations. Thus, extreme care will have to be exercised if this alternative is utilized.

CONCLUSIONS

There will come a time when the United States and Cuba will set out to negotiate a settlement of the expropriation claims of U.S. nationals against Cuba. The date of such an event is uncertain, although it seems closer than at any time in the past half century given the reestablishment of diplomatic relations between the two countries effective July 1, 2015. Despite the limited economic reforms that Cuba has implemented under Raúl Castro since 2010, it

MATÍAS F. TRAVIESO-DÍAZ

is most likely that the claims negotiations will be held while Cuba is besieged by a depressed economy.

The conditions under which the settlement will be negotiated will greatly restrict the remedies that Cuba will be able to offer the U.S. claimants. Certainly, the traditional way of settling expropriation claims—i.e., Cuba's payment of a lump sum of money to the U.S. government to be distributed pro-rata among all claimants—will not be adequate, given Cuba's inability to pay a significant portion of the amounts it owes. Lump-sum compensation should be given to the U.S. nationals to the extent funds are available, but should be substituted with (for those claimants wishing to opt out of the lump-sum settlement) a variety of other remedies to be negotiated by the claimants with Cuba, including restitution of the expropriated assets, compensation through state-issued instruments, and other means. While the eventual solution reached in each case is likely to grant only partial recovery to the claimants, the results in most cases would probably be more beneficial to the claimants than a lump-sum distribution.

The types of remedies available to U.S. nationals opting to participate in a parallel Cuban domestic claims program—when and if such a program develops—would of necessity have to be few in number, relatively straightforward in execution, and demand little in the way of up-front cash outlays by the state. The results of a domestic Cuban process are likely to leave many dissatisfied. Therefore, both the Cuban government and the claimants should be prepared to exhibit flexibility in working toward as fair and reasonable a resolution of the claims as can be achieved under those constrained circumstances.

The U.S. government will need to make a number of important policy decisions to prepare itself to discuss with Cuba the potential resolution of the claims issue. For example, it will need to decide whether to espouse the expropriation claims of those who were Cuban nationals at the time their assets were confiscated by Cuba, but who have since become U.S. citizens. These claims are not part of the claims certified by the FCSC and their inclusion in the program is prohibited by U.S. law,[42] but nevertheless these individuals will make a case before the U.S. government that their claims also should be pursued. The latter will also need to decide whether to organize its settlement approach around the traditional "espousal" principle and preclude claimants from engaging in separate negotiations with Cuba or whether it will adopt a more flexible approach that allows claimants to choose to be represented by the U.S. government or pursue other avenues to obtain redress.

Another important issue will be whether/how to consider the compensation claims of the Cuban government against the U.S. government for the "human and economic damages inflicted on the Cuban people by policies followed by several U.S. governments over more than fifty years"; a press release issued by Cuba's Foreign Affairs Ministry regarding the September 11, 2015 meeting of the Bilateral Commission states that the issue above is one that is of interest to Cuba[43] (the U.S. Department of State press release does not refer to this issue). A report on the embargo/blockade prepared by the Cuban government in July 2014 states that the U.S. actions had caused damages to Cuba estimated at $116.9 billion.[44]

It is risky, almost to the point of foolhardiness, to attempt to predict how the U.S. national expropriation claims against Cuba will ultimately be resolved. Nonetheless, given that the issue remains a major stumbling block to the full normalization of relations between the United States and Cuba, it appears inevitable that something will have to be done soon to address it. To this writer, the most likely outcome is one in which all parties will give up something. Cuba will agree to a partial payment of the certified amounts, without interest. The larger certified claimants, almost all of which are corporations (or their successors in interest) will recognize that there is more to be gained by establishing a business presence in Cuba and will negotiate with Cuba to exchange claims for trade and investment concessions. The United States will forego invoking its traditional espousal role and will instead seek to serve as umpire to make sure its citizens are treated fairly. Cuba's political claims to compensation for the effects of the trade embargo will be quietly put to rest.

That only leaves as an unknown what role will be played by Cuban expatriates living in the United States. The Cuban community in the United States is no longer monolithic (as it was probably 40 or 50 years ago) and is no longer composed mainly of dedicated opponents of the Castro regime. Time, changing demographics, and the influx of economically driven Cuban immigrants have robbed the more militant exiles of much of the political clout they once commanded. Indeed, many Cuban exiles are now entrepreneurs desirous of participating in the economic reconstruction of the island. For that reason, one can anticipate that the reaction of the Cuban "exile" community to a deal between the United States and Cuba to resolve the claims issue will be mixed: many of the older exiles will denounce the agreements that are reached, or will try to get their own expropriation claims addressed. Others, including some with outstanding claims now barred by U.S. law, will seek to join American claimants in trying to negotiate deals with the Cuban government. And perhaps that is as it should be: Cuba is going to need all the help it can get, from whatever the source, to overcome the effects of almost 60 years of mismanagement.

MATÍAS F. TRAVIESO-DÍAZ

NOTES

1. The term "U.S. nationals" means, in the claims context, those natural persons who were citizens of the United States at the time their properties in Cuba were seized by the Cuban government, or those corporations or other entities organized under the laws of the United States and 50 percent or more of whose stock or other beneficial interest was owned by natural persons who were citizens of the United States at the time the entities' properties in Cuba were taken. See 22 U.S.C. § 1643a(1).

2. Equally important may be the resolution of claims by Cuban nationals, whether on the island or abroad. These claims are not addressed in this chapter.

3. The trade embargo was officially imposed by President Kennedy in February 1962. See Proclamation 3447, 27 Fed. Reg. 1085 (1962), 3 C.F.R., 1059–63 Comp., at 157. Previously, authorization had been suspended for most industrial export licenses to Cuba. 43 Dept. State Bull. 715 (1960). President Eisenhower had also reduced the quota of Cuban sugar in the U.S. market to zero (Proclamation No. 3383, effective December 21, 1960, 25 Fed. Reg. 13131). Additional trade restrictions were imposed by other laws enacted in the 1960–1962 period. Therefore, by the time President Kennedy proclaimed a total trade embargo, trade between the U.S. and Cuba was already essentially cut off. For a Cuban perspective on the history of the embargo, see http://www.cubagob.cu/.

4. At a press conference during the reopening of the U.S. Embassy in Havana, a U.S. Department of State official stated that resolution of claims is "a priority for the Department of State and for the Cuban Government." Background Briefing on Cuba (July 17, 2015), www.state.gov/r/pa/prs/ps/2015/07/245049.htm. A brief note issued by the U.S. Department of State after the inaugural session of the Bilateral Commission indicated that claims were among the issues to be addressed between the two countries through the end of 2015. U.S. Department of State Media Note (September 11, 2015), www.state.gov/r/pa/prs/ps/2015/09/246844.htm.

5. Cheryl W. Gray et al., "Evolving Legal Frameworks for Private Sector Development in Central and Eastern Europe" (World Bank Discussion Paper No. 209) (1993), 4. While it appears inevitable that the claims resolution process will have some impact on Cuba's economic transition, the rapid development of a claims resolution plan would help minimize this impact.

6. But see Matías F. Travieso-Díaz, "Resolving U.S. Expropriation Claims Against Cuba: A Very Modest Proposal," *Law and Business Review of the Americas* 22 (Fall 2016): 3, which discusses one potential approach for addressing the claims issue. In the Conclusions section of this chapter, the author ventures to present an educated guess as to how the expropriation issue will ultimately play out.

7. For a detailed description of the process by which Cuba expropriated the assets of U.S. nationals, see Michael W. Gordon, *Cuban Nationalization: The Demise of Foreign Property Rights in Cuba* (Buffalo: William S. Hein, 1976), 69–108.

8. Ley de Reforma Agraria, *Gaceta Oficial,* June 3, 1959.

9. Law 851 of Nationalization of July 6, 1960, published in *Gaceta Oficial,* July 7, 1960.

10. Resolution No. 1, August 6, 1960, *Gaceta Oficial,* August 6, 1960; Resolution No. 2, September 17, 1960, *Gaceta Oficial,* September 17, 1960; Laws 890 and 891 of October 13, 1960, *Gaceta Oficial,* October 13, 1960; Resolution No. 3, October 24, 1960. For a listing of laws, decrees, and resolutions by means of which Cuba's expropriations of the assets of U.S. nationals were implemented, see Foreign Claims Settlement Commission, "Final Report of the Cuban Claims Program" (1972), 78–79 (hereafter 1972 FCSC Report).

11. Gordon, *Cuban Nationalization,* 105–06.

12. Law 851 of July 6, 1960, which authorized the nationalization of the properties of U.S. nationals, provided for payment for those expropriations by means of 30-year bonds yielding 2 percent interest, to be financed from the profits Cuba realized from sales of sugar in the U.S. market in excess of 3 million tons at no less than 5.75 cents per pound. The mechanism set up by this law was illusory because the U.S. had already virtually eliminated Cuba's sugar quota, see Proclamation No. 3355, 25 Fed. Reg. 6414 (1960) (reducing Cuba's sugar quota in the U.S. market by 95 percent). Nonetheless, the inclusion of this compensation scheme in the law constituted an explicit acknowledgment by Cuba of its obligation to indemnify the U.S. property owners for their losses.

13. Cuba has entered into settlement agreements with five foreign countries for the expropriation of the assets of their respective nationals in Cuba: France, on March 16, 1967; Switzerland, March 2, 1967; United Kingdom, October 18, 1978; Canada, November 7, 1980; and Spain, January 26, 1988. See http://www.cubavsbloqueo.cu/. See also Michael W. Gordon, "The Settlement of Claims for Expropriated Foreign Private Property Between Cuba and Foreign Nations Other Than the United States," *Lawyer of the Americas* 5, no. 3 (October 1973): 457–70.

14. The Spanish claims, for example, were valued at $350 million but were ultimately settled for about $40 million. Even this limited amount was not paid until 1994, six years after the claims were settled and three decades after the claims accrued. "Cuba to Compensate Spaniards for Property Seizures," Reuters Textline, February 15, 1994, available in LEXIS, World Library, Txtlne File.

15. See http://www.cubavsbloqueo.cu/.

16. 22 U.S.C. $1643 et seq. (1988) (amended in 1994).

17. 1972 FCSC Report, Exhibit 15.

18. 1972 FCSC Report, Exhibit 15.

19. 1972 FCSC Report, Exhibit 15. It should be noted that in 2005, pursuant to a request from then Secretary of State Condoleezza Rice, the FCSC conducted a Second Cuban Claims Program, whose purpose was to effect the adjudication and cer-

tification by the FCSC of claims for uncompensated taking of United States nationals' property by the Cuban government that arose after May 1, 1967, and were not adjudicated in the original Cuban Claims Program. The FCSC received a total of five new claims, denied three of them, and certified the other two claims in the total principal amounts of $51,128,926.95 and $16,000.00, respectively. See U.S. Department of Justice, Foreign Claims Settlement Commission, Completed Programs—Cuba, http://www.justice.gov/fcsc/claims-against-cuba.

20. Foreign Claims Settlement Commission 1994 Annual Report 146 (1994).

21. See Juan C. Consuegra-Barquin, "Cuba's Residential Property Ownership Dilemma: A Human Rights Issue Under International Law," *Rutgers Law Review* 46 (Winter 1994): 873, 897–98 (discussing the difficulties that a Cuban transition government will face in seeking to provide remedies for residential property expropriations.)

22. See Emilio Cueto, "Property Claims of Cuban Nationals," presented at the Shaw, Pittman, Potts, and Trowbridge Workshop on "Resolution of Property Claims in Cuba's Transition," Washington, DC, 9–12 (January 1995) (on file with author).

23. Dames & Moore v. Regan, 453 U.S. 654, 688, 101 S. Ct. 2972, 69 L. Ed. 918 (1981); Shanghai Power Co. v. United States, *supra*, 4 Cl. Ct., 244–45. The president's authority is limited by the rarely exercised power of Congress to enact legislation requiring that a settlement seen as unfavorable be renegotiated. Dames & Moore v. Regan, *supra*, 453 U.S. at 688–89 and n.13.

24. See Dames & Moore v. Regan, *supra*, 453 U.S. at 680 and n.9, for a listing of ten settlement agreements reached by the U.S. Department of State with foreign countries between 1952 and 1981.

25. Dames & Moore v. Regan, *supra*, 453 U.S. at 679–80; Asociacion de Reclamantes v. United States, 735 F.2d 1517, 1523 (D.C. Cir. 1984); Richard B. Lillich and Burns H. Weston, *International Claims: Their Settlement by Lump Sum Agreements, 1975–1995 (*Procedural Aspects of International Law Institute 1999), 6.

26. For example, the U.S. settled its nationals' claims against the People's Republic of China for $80.5 million, which was about 40 percent of the $197 million certified by the FCSC. Shanghai Power Co. v. United States, *supra*, 4 Cl. Ct. at 239; XVIII I.L.M. 551 (May 1979).

27. Letter from Ronald J. Bettauer, Assistant Legal Adviser for International Claims and Investment Disputes, U.S. Department of State, to claimants (May 29, 1992); Agreement Between the Government of the United States of America and the Government of the Federal Republic of Germany Concerning the Settlement of Certain Property Claims, May 13, 1992, TIAS 11959.

28. See Shanghai Power Co. v. United States, *supra*.

29. See Cueto, "Property Claims of Cuban Nationals," 9–12, 34–36.

30. In Saudi Arabia v. Arabian American Oil Co. (ARAMCO), reprinted in 27 ILR 117 (1958), for example, the arbitration tribunal refused to apply the law of Swit-

zerland (where the tribunal was located), even though Saudi Arabia had agreed to having the seat of the tribunal in Switzerland. By contrast, the arbitrator in Saphire International Petroleum v. National Iranian Oil Co., reprinted in 35 ILR 136 (1963), decided that the legal system of the place of arbitration would govern the arbitration. Likewise, inconsistent results on this issue were achieved in three other arbitrations between Libya and the nationals of foreign states that arose out of the nationalization of Libyan oil in the early 1970s.

31. See Patrick M. Norton, "A Law of the Future or a Law of the Past? Modern Tribunals and the International Law of Expropriation," *American Journal of International Law* 85 (1991), 474, 482–86.

32. See United Nations United Nations Commission on International Trade Law Arbitration Rules (1976) ("UNCITRAL rules"). http://www.jus.uio.no/lm/un.arbitration .rules.1976.

33. Article VI of the Claims Settlement Declaration allows the Tribunal to be located in The Hague "or any other place agreed by Iran and the United States." Whether the Netherlands was the most advantageous place for the Tribunal was debated internally within the United States government. See, e.g., Symposium on the Settlement with Iran, 13 Law. Am. 1, 46 (1981).

34. Restitution has been used as the remedy of choice for expropriations in many countries in Central and Eastern Europe, including Germany, Czechoslovakia, the Baltic republics, Bulgaria, and Romania. On the other hand, Hungary, Russia, and all other former republics of the USSR (with the exception of the Baltic republics) have expressly refused to grant restitution of property expropriated during the communist era. Frances H. Foster, "Post-Soviet Approaches to Restitution: Lessons for Cuba," in JoAnn Klein, ed., *Cuba in Transition: Options for Addressing the Challenge of Expropriated Properties* (Gainesville: Levin College of Law, University of Florida, 1994), 93.

The former Czechoslovakia is a good example of the restitution approach. Czechoslovakia implemented an aggressive, across-the-board restitution program, under which it enacted a series of restitution laws that distinguished between "small" property (such as small businesses and apartment buildings), "large" property, and agricultural lands and forests, with each type of property being subject to somewhat different procedures and remedies. The restitution of "small" property was governed by the Small Federal Restitution Law, which provided for direct restitution to original owners. Gray et al., "Evolving Legal Frameworks," 49. The Large Federal Restitution Law governed the restitution of "large" property (industries and associated real estate), and again provided for the return of the property to its former owners, except in situations where the property was in use by natural persons or foreign entities, in which case restitution was barred and compensation had to be paid instead. Anna Gelpern, "The Laws and Politics of Reprivatization in East-Central Europe: A Com-

MATÍAS F. TRAVIESO-DÍAZ

parison," *University of Pennsylvania Journal of International Business Law* 14 (1993): 315, 337–38.

Likewise, for agricultural land and forests, the Federal Land Law provided presumptive restitution of lands to the original owners. Where neither the land originally expropriated nor a substantially similar parcel in the locality was available, financial compensation was provided as an alternative remedy. Gelpern, "The Laws and Politics of Reprivatization," 341.

35. The top 20 certified U.S. claimants are all corporations. Their combined certified claims add up to $1.3 billion (not counting interest), over 70 percent of the total claims certified. Most of the corporations owned sugar mills and other large industrial installations that would be identifiable.

36. Hungary used compensation vouchers as the sole means of indemnifying expropriation claimants. Katherine Simonetti et al., "Compensation and Resolution of Property Claims in Hungary," in Klein, ed., *Cuba in Transition*, 61, 69. The means of compensation are interest-bearing transferable securities or "vouchers" known as Compensation Coupons, issued by a Compensation Office charged with the administration of the claims program. Simonetti et al., "Compensation and Resolution of Property Claims in Hungary."

Compensation is given on a sliding scale with regard to the assessed value of the lost property. Gray et al., "Evolving Legal Frameworks for Private Sector Development," 70. The vouchers are traded as securities, and pay interest at 75 percent of the basic interest rate set by the central bank.

37. Gray et al., "Evolving Legal Frameworks for Private Sector Development," 69–72. In Hungary, vouchers could be used also to purchase farmland in auctions held by the state; however, only former owners of land could their vouchers for that purpose. Gray et al., "Evolving Legal Frameworks for Private Sector Development."

38. A Cuban economist has included the issuance of vouchers as an option for providing compensation to U.S. corporate claimants. Pedro Monreal, "Las Reclamaciones del Sector Privado de los Estados Unidos Contra Cuba: Una Perspectiva Académica," paper presented at the Shaw, Pittman, Potts, and Trowbridge Workshop on "Resolution of Property Claims in Cuba's Transition," 5. The alternative proposed by this economist would require the claimant to invest in Cuba an amount equal to the value of the coupons it received.

39. See Cueto, "Property Claims of Cuban Nationals," 26–28 for a brief discussion of some of the valuation and financing issues that will surface if Cuba seeks to implement a voucher compensation scheme.

40. This was experienced, for example, in the Czech and Slovak republics. Heather V. Weibel, "Avenues for Investment in the Former Czechoslovakia: Privatization and the Historical Development of the New Commercial Code," *The Delaware Journal of International Corporate Law* 18 (1993): 889, 920.

41. The experience in Hungary has been that vouchers used to collect annuities have yielded very disappointing results. Simonetti et al., "Compensation and Resolution of Property Claims in Hungary," 78.

42. See Section 304 of the Cuban Liberty and Democratic Solidarity (Libertad) Act of 1996 ("Helms–Burton Law"), 22 U.S.C. § 6082 (5).

43. "Comunicado de Prensa de la Delegación Cubana a la Primera Reunión de la Comisión Bilateral Cuba-EE.UU." (September 11, 2015), http://cubaeeuu.cubaminrex .cu/article/comunicado-de-prensa-de-la-delegacion-cubana-la-primera-reunion-de -la-comision-bilateral.

44. *Report by Cuba on Resolution 68/8 of the United Nations General Assembly entitled "Necessity of ending the economic, commercial and financial blockade imposed by the United States of America against Cuba* (July 2014), p. 37, http://www.cuba vsbloqueo.cu/sites/default/files/informe_de_cuba_2014i.pdf.

PART 2

POLICY AND POLITICS

SOCIALIST SOCIAL CONTRACTS AND ACCOUNTABILITY

On March 14, 2008, *Granma* started publication of a new section titled *Cartas a la Dirección*, which printed letters to the editor containing complaints, criticisms, and suggestions. The section rapidly grew in popularity. During the first year of its existence, about 10,000 citizens sent in letters by email or by post. To accommodate the explosion in reader interest, *Granma* increased the size of the section from one to two printed pages. By *Granma*'s own assessment, this section is the most closely read portion of the Friday paper.[1] At this point, the section has appeared in more than 440 installments and stands as one of the most visible symbols of Raúl's reform policies, in particular his emphasis on openness to criticism (*apertura a la discusión y la crítica*).

Granma's attention to citizen letters raises several interrelated questions that have broader relevance beyond the specific case of Cuba. First, why would the flagship newspaper in a communist regime solicit citizen letters? Second, why would citizens be willing to send in such letters? And third, why would some of these letters be printed? The answers to these questions can shed light on a central problem in communist governance: how those in power gain an understanding of popular opinion. The political science literature has highlighted the existence of this information problem,[2] but has not reached conclusive answers about the channels that can be used to alleviate it.[3] In Cuba, as in other communist regimes, the analysis of citizen complaints serves as an important avenue for mitigating the shortage of information on popular opinion.

Although regime insiders value the information that is revealed through the analysis of complaints, citizens may be unwilling to complain either because they fear retaliation or because they do not believe that their letters will have any impact. This essay argues that by printing critical letters the editorial staff of *Granma* signals that those who write will not be punished for expressing their views. Furthermore, the newspaper makes complaining meaningful by printing responses to letters that specify what measures have been taken to redress the grievances identified in the letters and to punish those who are responsible for them. In addition to this signal of accountability, *Granma* encourages citizen complaints by authorizing the publication of letters about problems like bureaucratism, shortages, or poor customer service. Such letters allow for the collective letting off of steam as a result of the horizontal transmission of information revealing how widespread these popular grievances are. However, this openness to input is limited: only letters about the issues covered under the social contract are printed. Although this serves the ultimate goal of signaling to citizens that the social contract is enforceable and thus secures their quiescence in exchange for the provision of goods, services, and the protection of property rights, it also limits the scope of the permissible transmission of information to the leadership to the realm of social welfare (assuming that citizens interpret printed letters as delineating the scope of the complaints that the party-state is willing to receive). As such, printing letters in the state newspaper ultimately constrains the ability of the regime to comprehensively assess public opinion through the analysis of citizen complaints.

This paper proceeds as follows. First, the theoretical claims laid out above are developed in more detail. Next, a brief historical overview of letters to the editor published in *Granma* prior to the initiation of Raúl's reforms is provided, contrasting the letters found in *Granma* today with those that appear in other Cuban print media. The following section compares letters to the editor published in 2008 with those published in 2014 in an effort to assess the extent to which the content of these letters reveals changes in openness to criticism, in the degree of accountability, and in the ease of dissemination of information about widespread popular grievances. The decline in letters praising the party is used as a metric for openness to criticism; the increase in response letters as a measure for accountability; and the increase in critical letters (focusing on bureaucratism, shortages, and poor service quality) as an indicator of the horizontal dissemination of information about shared grievances. The conclusion reflects on the applications of the argument in other single-party states. Overall, this chapter argues, somewhat counterintuitively, that the regime may be able to maximize popular support by further delaying bold reforms that would lead to the rapid dismantling of the remnants of the socialist social contract.

Before proceeding, a brief description of the data on which this paper is based and its limitations is in order. I rely primarily on a dataset I constructed by compiling and coding all letters that appeared in *Cartas a la Dirección* between March 2008 and April 2015 (a total of 2,212 letters, 458 responses, and 78 postscripts [*coletillas*]), supplemented by a corpus of letters published in *Granma* prior to 2008 and by letters from other Cuban print media. These data do not allow us to address the question of how representative published letters are of the letters received by print media in Cuba. Although we know that *Granma* publishes less than 0.5 percent of the letters it receives,[4] no data is available on the process of selection involved in deciding which letters should be printed. Nevertheless, analysis of these printed letters allows us to study a subject that has not yet received systematic scholarly attention: the political logic of publishing letters to the editor in contemporary Cuba.

READERS' LETTERS, SOCIAL CONTRACTS, AND ACCOUNTABILITY IN COMMUNIST REGIMES

The typical letter to the editor in a single-party communist state is a complaint that articulates some type of grievance and demands redress from the authorities. The most puzzling aspect of complaints in dictatorships is that they occur at all. In a communist society, citizens have powerful *disincentives* to complain. We can illustrate this by a simple three-actor game. The actors in this game are the citizens, the central government, and the local government. These three actors have divergent preferences with regard to complaints. The central government is interested in a steady flow of complaints because analysis of the complaints allows it to ascertain the preferences of the population. In contrast, the local government is interested in suppressing complaints because they typically contain information about malfeasance or inaction by local government employees when faced with citizen requests for provision of goods, services, or protection of legal rights. Citizens would like to complain, but they are inclined not to do so because of fear of retaliation by the local government. Given these disincentives, it is surprising that citizens of communist societies complain with such great frequency. This raises the question of why citizens find it worthwhile to complain despite the possibility of retaliation.[5]

What makes lodging complaints possible is trust. Because rational citizens do not trust the integrity of the local government, their trust resides with higher levels of government, and ultimately with the central government. Opinion poll data indicate that, in contrast to democracies, low trust in the local government and high trust in the central government can be found across dictatorships as diverse as current-day China, the Soviet Union under Gorbachev, and Russia under Putin.[6] One indicator of how seriously communist regimes took the distinction between trust in the central and local governments comes from Stoian Mikhailov, the head of the Propaganda and Agitation Department of the Central Committee of the Bulgarian Communist Party between 1973 and 1988. In an article on the mechanisms for letting off steam, Mikhailov opined: "When the residents of a village are unhappy because of the shortcomings and corruption of their mayor, they should know that his shortcomings and corruption are not a consequence of central policy but rather represent his personal qualities. . . . The residents of the village should be given explanations about the specific shortcomings and corruption . . . dissatisfaction with the shortcomings of the mayor should not be directed against the party as a ruling power and against the government as a central leading organ."[7]

However, the central government cannot take citizen trust for granted. Rather, it has to work actively to build and maintain it. In a communist dictatorship, the central government can build trust through a system of *proxy accountability*. In such a system, the central government acts as the proxy of citizens, holding local officials accountable on their behalf. If local officials fail to respond to citizen complaints, higher levels of government can instruct lower levels of government to resolve the problems referred to in the complaint. In more egregious cases, higher levels of government may also punish unresponsive local officials by unleashing corruption investigations or by deducting points from their annual performance reviews.[8] In the end, local officials are more likely to respond to citizen complaints when higher levels of government are involved. This essay argues that as long as the public trusts the central government to intervene on its behalf (or *Granma* in the case of Cuba, as *Granma* represents the party-state), it will continue to provide information through citizen complaints. Thus, proxy accountability undergirds the effective operation of the complaints system. How does proxy accountability differ from a more familiar type of vertical accountability, which involves citizens holding officials accountable through the ballot box? To answer this question, we first need to agree on what we mean by accountability. This essay argues that accountability rests on two pillars: responsiveness and sanctioning.[9] Responsiveness refers to the require-

MARTIN K. DIMITROV

ment that officials provide an explanation or a justification for their behavior, as for example why they have authorized the construction of a heavily polluting chemical plant in dangerous proximity to people's homes. Sanctioning refers to the ability of citizens to punish officials for being unresponsive or corrupt. Typically, responsiveness and sanctioning have been understood to operate in a democratic context, whether in the contemporary United States or in ancient Athens, where citizens rewarded officials with reappointment to office or punished them with removal from office, fine, imprisonment, or even death.[10] This has led to a general assumption that accountability is democratic, direct, and electoral.[11]

Scholars have identified a wide range of institutions of accountability that operate beyond the realm of direct democratic electoral accountability. Some of these are direct and electoral but are not democratic, such as the semicompetitive elections in authoritarian settings as diverse as Russia under Putin, Egypt under Mubarak, and contemporary rural China.[12] Other institutions of accountability may be nondemocratic, indirect, and nonelectoral, such as when unelected politicians hold unelected bureaucrats accountable for their behavior,[13] or when dictators are accountable to a selectorate, an ombudsman, an anticorruption agency, or a constitutional court.[14] This paper complements previous research findings by incorporating letters to the editor (as a form of citizen complaints) within the range of institutions of accountability in communist regimes.

Proxy accountability is one example of a nondemocratic, indirect, and nonelectoral institution of vertical accountability: it exists in communist autocracies where the involvement of unelected higher-level officials is necessary to incentivize local-level officials to be responsive to citizen demands. Although proxy accountability operates in a nondemocratic context, it shares two important similarities with democratic accountability. The first is that responsiveness and sanctioning exist under both types of accountability. The second is that both types of accountability involve bottom-up (vertical) accountability, where officials are accountable to ordinary citizens.

It would be unreasonable for citizens in an autocracy to expect that the government would be willing to hear all types of complaints. This raises the question of how citizens know the scope of permissible claims. In a communist state, the range of acceptable demands is determined by what scholars have called "the social compact" or "the social contract."[15] Although citizens do not enter into this contract voluntarily, there are nevertheless expectations of how the two parties to the contract should behave: namely, citizens will remain quiescent as long as the regime supplies material benefits and safeguards their basic property rights. Existing scholarship has not provided an explanation as to how the social contract is enforced. But this essay argues that proxy accountability creates an enforcement mechanism. This enforcement mechanism existed under the socialist social contract (in Eastern Europe and China prior to 1989 or in Cuba today) as well as under the market social contract in post-1989 China.

One may wonder what is left of the social contract in contemporary Cuba. At the Sixth Party Congress in 2011, Raúl Castro laid out an ambitious plan for economic reform, featuring price liberalization, the end of rationing, economic decentralization (although large enterprises would continue to be owned by the state), a massive expansion of market activities with the concomitant limiting of the role of the planned economy, and the layoffs of 1.3 million people (20 percent of the Cuban labor force).[16] These reform plans called for nothing short of the dismantling of the socialist social contract.[17] Nevertheless, five years after the Sixth Party Congress, the social contract has survived almost intact.[18] The layoff targets have not been achieved, price liberalization has not occurred, and rationing persists in the form of the ubiquitous *libreta de abastecimientos* (supplies booklet), which entitles every Cuban citizen to purchase from one of the specialized groceries (*bodegas*) their rations of sugar, rice, beans, bread, eggs, poultry, minced meat, pasta, salt, matches, soap, toothpaste, and coffee. These items are sold significantly below cost, with monthly rations available for no more than $3.00, which is about an eighth of the average monthly salary. In addition, phone, electricity, and gas for cooking are available for another $2.50 a month per household. Public transportation, basic medicines, newspapers, books, and theater tickets are also very heavily subsidized. Finally, few Cubans pay rent, since most of them own their housing. Overall, the party-state has proven reluctant to quickly implement bold reforms that would lead to a dismantling of the remnants of the socialist social contract. By signaling to citizens that the regime takes the social contract seriously, published letters to the editor help increase regime legitimacy.

Before we proceed with a discussion of how published letters to the editor in Cuba relate to the social contract, we should briefly reflect on the methodological challenge of studying citizen complaints. We should start by noting that the constitutions in all communist regimes explicitly protected the right to complain.[19] The question, of course, is whether these constitutional guarantees were meaningfully enforced. As this is fundamentally an empirical puzzle, it cannot be answered in the absence of access to archival materials or to a developed secondary literature on the volume and handling of complaints. Research on complaints has been hampered by archival shortcomings, which in turn have produced a modest secondary literature

MARTIN K. DIMITROV

on complaints in mature communist regimes. Students of citizen complaints in Eastern Europe have overwhelmingly focused on one case, namely the Soviet Union during the Stalinist period; Sheila Fitzpatrick's work on complaints and denunciations has produced especially valuable insights.[20] But limited access to archival materials dealing with the post-Stalinist period has made it difficult for scholars to systematically study leadership response to complaints when the Soviet Union exited Stalinism and became a mature communist system. This is a serious limitation, as the importance of obtaining information about citizen preferences by analyzing complaints becomes apparent only when regimes move past the stage when they rule through the habitual use of terror. Future research on complaints can proceed when additional archival materials for later periods of communist rule in Eastern Europe and elsewhere become available.[21]

In the case of Cuba, scholarly access to central-level archival sources on complaints remains impossible. As a second-best option, we can conduct research on the functions of published letters to the editor. These are usually letters of complaint about various aspects of the social contract and, as this essay argues, their publication serves as a signal that the party is open to criticism and that it wants to establish accountability. As more and more critical letters to the editor are printed, citizens collectively let off steam, which results in a net reduction of social tension. This suggests that the publication of readers' letters is valuable to communist regimes as it improves the quality of governance.[22] And yet, the real value of publishing such letters may lie elsewhere: by giving visibility to complaints, the regime can induce citizens to continue to write letters and to thus enable the vertical transmission of information on popular opinion. Although we cannot test this hypothesis for the case of Cuba, we have evidence from other communist regimes that supports such an interpretation of the real (though perhaps not readily apparent) function of the publication of readers' letters in single-party communist regimes.[23]

CARTAS A LA DIRECCIÓN IN CONTEXT

Letters to the editor are not a new phenomenon in Cuba. *Granma* published them decades before it established *Cartas a la Dirección*. And in reform-era Cuba, *Granma* is not the only periodical that features such letters. This section of the essay puts the letters published in *Granma* today in historical context and contrasts them with those published in other contemporary news outlets. These comparisons allow us to highlight what is unique about the letters that appear in *Cartas a la Dirección*.

Granma started to publish responses to citizen queries in 1970 in a tiny column titled *Buzón económico* (Economic Mailbox). Citizens would send in questions (inquiring about such items as the female participation rate in economic activity; the nutritional characteristics and the quality of various types of rice; different ways of organizing the supervision of sugarcane harvesting; and the number of artificially inseminated cattle prior to the triumph of the revolution) and *Granma* would answer (the answer to the last query was: none). These were essentially requests for hard-to-find statistical information, rather than expressions of criticisms, complaints, and suggestions. Another section that was published at irregular intervals throughout the 1970s was titled *Luz roja* (Red Light). It was based on citizen letters but focused exclusively on traffic accidents, traffic safety, and poor transportation infrastructure.

It was not until February 1975, when preparations for the First Congress of the Cuban Communist Party were in full swing, that *Granma* introduced a section titled *A Vuelta de Correo* (By Return Post). The section featured readers' letters (usually redacted), accompanied by a photograph, and rarely by a response. They typically focused on questions like waste of state resources or identified instances of abandoned machinery (bulldozers, tractors, trucks). Occasionally, letters were printed on issues like shortages (of toothpaste, bath soap, and batteries and spare parts for VEF, Sokol, and Orbita radios), the irregular distribution of carbonated drinks, and the poor customer service in upscale hotels. Some letters highlighted abysmal delays in providing services: one reader complained that the Havana watchmaker Slava took two years to clean his Swiss-made Prisma Lux.[24] In another case, readers sounded an alarm about beer that contained "insect eggs, soil particles, and other impurities," including "a crayfish 1.5 inches in length."[25] Typically, no response from those responsible for the infractions was printed. Sometimes there was a reply, but it deflected responsibility or cited "objective difficulties." Other times it said that "necessary steps were taken" to redress the situation. It was highly unusual for letters to be specific as to who was responsible and what measures were taken to hold him or her accountable. One exception that proves the rule is the case of a postman who negligently discarded 12 telegrams in the yard of the Freyre Andrade hospital in Havana; he was terminated and legal proceedings were initiated against him.[26]

A Vuelta de Correo was published irregularly throughout the second half of the 1970s. In 1978, for example, it was not published at all in July and appeared very rarely in May, June, August, and September. However, during the other months of that year, the section might appear as often as five times a week, except during weeks with national holidays or state visits by dignitaries like Mengistu Haile Mariam or Saddam Hussein. For reasons that remain unclear, the section started to appear very infrequently in the 1980s (except for 1984, when it would be published up to three times a week). Other sections based on readers' letters were introduced in the 1980s (*Cartas de Viaje*; *Cartas sin Sobre*), but these lacked the critical element of *A Vuelta de Correo*. In 1988, *Granma* ceased printing letters to the editor altogether. Given the grievances that accumulated in Cuban society since the Special Period (and the short life of *Granma*'s *Abrecartas*, which began to print heavily editorialized letters in 1994 but was closed down in the 2000s), the inauguration of *Cartas a la Dirección* in 2008 was met with keen interest by the citizenry.

Other Print Media that Publish Letters to the Editor

There are at least three other print media in Cuba today that publish readers' letters in one form or another: the daily *Juventud Rebelde*; the weekly newspaper *Tribuna de La Habana*; and the biweekly magazine *Bohemia*. *Juventud Rebelde* publishes a section titled *Acuse de recibo* (Acknowledgment of Receipt) five days a week; the section is managed by José Alejandro Rodríguez, who uses citizen letters for his pieces on various irregularities in the provision of municipal services, excessive bureaucratic regulations, or shortages of certain goods. *Tribuna de La Habana* features a weekly section titled *Tribuna del lector*, which typically includes a redacted letter, a response from the entity that is criticized in the letter, and some editorial commentary. Finally, *Bohemia* runs *Puntillazos*, which are paragraph-long critical commentaries on negative phenomena (noise, accumulation of uncollected trash in the streets, or the poor quality of services) that are written on the basis of readers' letters. These other print media highlight what is unique about the letters published in *Granma*: they are not redacted (apart from grammar and spelling);[27] they are numerous and focus on diverse themes, thus making them more interesting than sections that are limited to one letter on a single issue; and they feature minimal editorial commentary, thus looking more authentic (in part, this authenticity reflects *Granma*'s decision to "improve credibility" by publishing only letters containing a complete name and address from March 14, 2014 onward).[28]

THE EVOLVING CONTENT AND FUNCTIONS OF LETTERS TO THE EDITOR

This section uses a detailed coding of readers' letters, responses, and editorial postscripts published in *Granma* to assess whether the content of these letters has evolved since the inception of *Cartas a la Dirección*. Figure 5.1 pres-

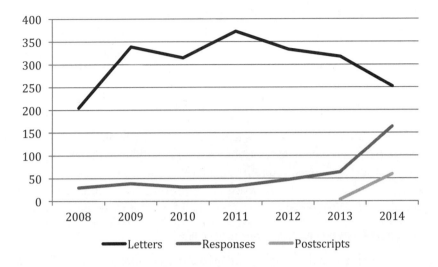

Figure 5.1. Letters, Responses, and *Coletillas*, 2008–2014. Source: Author's dataset.

ents aggregate statistics of the number of letters, responses, and postscripts published between March 2008 and December 2014. Although we do not know how these letters were selected for publication, the data presented in figure 5.1 allow us to make one key observation: namely, over time, the number of responses grew substantially. Along with the introduction of editorial postscripts in November 2013, the increased number of printed responses sends a powerful signal to potential letter writers that *Granma* takes their grievances seriously.

Please note that figure 5.1 reports statistics for only March–December 2008. Elsewhere in this essay, references to 2008 concern the entire one-year period following the inauguration of *Cartas a la Dirección* (March 14, 2008–March 6, 2009).

To have maximum leverage over change over time, I analyze all letters printed in the first year after *Cartas a la Dirección* was introduced (March 14, 2008–March 6, 2009) and in the last complete year when these letters were published (2014). This section of the essay first discusses the categories I developed for coding these letters, paying particular attention to the distinction between critical and noncritical letters. It then provides an overview of how the distribution of letters into these two broad categories has changed over time and discusses the relative share of several subcategories of critical and noncritical letters. After that, the section engages with the question of how the function of readers' letters has changed over time with regard to signaling openness to criticism; demonstrating accountability; and transmitting information about widespread grievances. The section concludes by examining another function of readers' letters, which is suggested by evidence from other single-party communist regimes, but which cannot be definitively ascertained on the basis of the currently available Cuban materials.

Types of Letters Published in *Granma*

We cannot make sense of the letters published in *Granma* without systematic coding rules. After reading each letter, I assigned it to one of two categories: noncritical or critical. Noncritical letters were further subdivided into specific subcategories like: letters praising the party and the revolution; opinions on the pace and direction of reform; opinions on the importance of establishing standardized accounting practices; suggestions about improving work discipline; and letters expressing satisfaction with the quality of goods and services. Critical letters included complaints about the poor quality of goods and services; shortages of goods; excessive bureaucratic regulations; speculative trade; and violations of social order. The largest subcategory—complaints about the quality of services—was subdivided into specific issues, such as: transportation services; medical services; customer service in hard-currency stores; mail delivery services; telephone services; and trash collection. Grouping the letters into these categories allows us to track the critical orientation of *Cartas a la Dirección* over time.

Aggregate Trends in Letters Published in 2008 and 2014

Tables 5.1, 5.2, and 5.3 reveal three important differences between the letters that appeared in *Cartas a la Dirección* in 2008 and those published in 2014. First, table 5.1 indicates that although the absolute number of letters published has stayed relatively constant, the share of noncritical letters has declined from 35.9 percent in 2008 to 17.9 percent in 2014. Especially noteworthy is the decline in letters praising the party and the revolution from 12.2 percent in 2008 to 2.4 percent in 2014 (table 5.3). Second, the ratio of published letters to published responses has decreased fivefold, from 7.5:1 in 2008 to 1.54:1 in 2014 (table 5.2). We should also note that *Granma*'s December 2013 decision to feature "postscripts" (*coletillas*), has led to a marked improvement in the quality of the responses. And third, the share of letters focusing on shortages and the poor quality of goods and services has doubled from 28.5 percent in 2008 to 57.5 percent in 2014 (table 5.3). These three trends indicate that the party wants to send increasingly stronger signals about its openness to criticism, its commitment to establishing accountability, and its willingness to allow the dissemination of information about certain widespread popular grievances.

TABLE 5.1. Critical and Noncritical Letters, 2008 and 2014

	Total letters	Noncritical letters	Critical letters
2008	270	97 (35.9%)	173 (64.1%)
2014	252	45 (17.9%)	207 (82.1%)

Source: Author's dataset.

TABLE 5.2. Letter Volume, Responses, and Postscripts, 2008 and 2014

	Letters	Responses to letters	Letters to responses ratio	Postscripts
2008	270	36	7.5:1	0
2014	252	164	1.54:1	59

Source: Author's dataset.

TABLE 5.3. Letters Praising the Party and Letters about the Quality of Services, 2008 and 2014

	Percent of letters praising the party/revolution	Percent of letters about shortages and the poor quality of goods and services
2008	12.2	28.5
2014	2.4	57.5

Source: Author's dataset.

Openness to Criticism

One of Raúl Castro's strategies for increasing the legitimacy of the Cuban Communist Party was to declare its openness to criticism in early 2008.[29] The very establishment of *Cartas a la Dirección* within weeks of Raúl's speech stands as evidence of such openness. Another indicator is offered by the editorial decisions about the letters that are printed in the section, in particular the gradual decline of noncritical letters between 2008 and 2014. Table 5.4 offers a breakdown of the noncritical letters printed in *Granma* in 2008 and 2014. We need to highlight two trends. One is the already noted sharp reduction in letters praising Fidel, Raúl, the party, the achievements of the revolution, and international solidarity. Although 33 such letters were printed in 2008, by 2014 their number had been reduced to six. Without a doubt, some Cubans must believe in the party and the achievements of the revolution. Yet even if they are genuine, these letters can easily appear doctored, as when the daughter of a convict expresses gratitude to the penitentiary system and tes-

TABLE 5.4. Subcategories of Noncritical Letters, 2008 and 2014

	Absolute number, 2008	As percent of all letters in 2008	Absolute number, 2014	As percent of all letters in 2014
Praise of party/revolution	33	12.2	6	2.4
Opinions on the pace and speed of reform	33	12.2	7	2.8
Opinions on the need to improve enterprise budgeting and introduce uniform accounting standards	17	6.3	3	1.2
Praise of quality of goods/services	5	1.8	14	5.5
Other noncritical	9	3.3	15	5.9
Total	97	35.9	45	17.9

Source: Author's dataset.

tifies to the value of the revolution for her family; or when an inmate thanks the party for converting prisons into schools, thus allowing him to study the revolutionary ideas of Fidel and Raúl and to bring joy to his mother's heart; or when a cancer survivor proclaims that this much love and care for the sick can exist only in the Cuba forged by Fidel.[30] Such overt displays of loyalty to the revolution are suspect; printing them less often can enhance the overall credibility of the letters published in *Cartas a la Dirección*. The second trend is the increase in the number of letters that indicate satisfaction with the quality of goods and services. Whereas in 2008 the letters of this genre printed in *Granma* seemed exaggerated (as, for example, when a complaint about the quality of coffee and chocolate mix resulted in an angry riposte from another reader that she believed it was "unjust to evaluate the chocolate mix negatively"),[31] by 2014 these letters were toned down. And yet, by expressing thanks for exemplary service, they highlighted how rare it is to see a clean bus;[32] to have one's wallet or other lost valuables returned;[33] or to encounter a medical professional who uses gloves (a dental student thanked a veterinarian for draining an abscess on her dog with enthusiasm but without gloves, "his hands covered in blood and pus").[34] Thus, the overall effect of the decline of noncritical letters is to free more space for critical letters and to thus demonstrate the openness of the party to criticism.

Accountability

One problem that communist regimes encounter when soliciting citizen letters is how to ensure a continuous flow of such communications. Even though the introduction of a section that regularly publishes letters to the editor could induce citizens to write to newspapers, over time this willingness might taper off, unless letter writers believe that their complaints can have some meaningful impact on redressing the grievances that they have highlighted. For this reason, the party needs to ensure that responses to some letters are printed. Furthermore, these responses have to specify what measures were taken to investigate the complaints and how those who were responsible were punished for their infractions. To the extent that they do so, they serve as an instrument of accountability.

In 2008, *Granma* published only 36 responses to citizen letters. These were often pro forma, pointing out objective difficulties or the U.S. blockade as the source of the problem. Sometimes the response would indicate that the letter writer was a troublemaker or would entirely negate the complaint, as when Cubacafé said that coffee quality was good or when the post office indicated that an employee suspected of negligence in delivering *Granma* to a subscriber was in fact exemplary.[35] Even when the response acknowledged that there were problems, the solutions offered were nonspecific: following a letter about poor customer service at the ice cream parlor Coppelia, the management blamed the problems on the long-term legacies of the Special Period, stated that the collective was fervently dedicated to its work, and concluded by saying that nevertheless, workers were instructed to commit to offering sterling service.[36] These measures were ineffective, as demonstrated by the ongoing complaints about Coppelia that were published in *Granma* throughout 2008. Overall, the responses printed in 2008 did not convey the impression that the letters that appeared in *Cartas a la Dirección* could function as a mechanism for accountability in Cuba. What made matters worse is that the number of responses stayed very low in 2008–2013, before increasing sharply in 2014 (see figure 5.1).

Granma took several measures to improve the level of responsiveness to citizen complaints. In December 2013, it introduced postscripts to selected readers' letters with an emphasis on inadequate responses. For example, when commenting on the response of a water supply company to a complaint about flooding in Habana del Este due to sloppy maintenance work, *Granma* stated that "objective problems are one thing and poor customer service quite another."[37] Such editorial comments were meant to publicly shame government agencies that were shirking responsibility. Another measure aimed at increasing responsiveness was an overview once every four months of the responses received and a list of the entities that did not respond to printed letters in a timely manner. The result of these efforts was impressive: in the last four months of 2014, *Granma* printed exactly 69 letters and 69 responses. The quality of the responses also improved rapidly: responses are now more likely to specify who was determined to have been responsible for a certain infraction and how he or she was punished. Overall, then, we can conclude that the responses printed in *Granma* in 2014 project a much more convincing image of accountability than did those that appeared in *Cartas a la Dirección* in 2008.

The Horizontal Transmission of Information about Widespread Popular Grievances

The essay has argued that letters to the editor can reduce social tension by transmitting information about widespread popular grievances. This is a counterintuitive claim, as the dissemination of such information can, of course, lead to instability by creating a focal point that allows for collective antiregime mobilization.[38] Therefore, the party needs to carefully manage the information that is circulating by selecting grievances like service quality, shortages of nonessential items, and excessive regulations, which do not allow for collective mobilization, and by appearing to take these grievances seriously by stressing responsiveness. Under those conditions, printing such letters can reduce social tension by allowing citizens to collectively let off steam.

As table 5.5 demonstrates, *Granma* has begun to print more critical letters over time. Two trends need to be highlighted. In 2014, there was a single case when a letter indicating lack of attention to popular input was printed (no such letters were published in 2008). This serves as a strong indicator of how seriously the party takes the importance of appearing receptive to criticism and popular input. Second, issues identified by scholars as likely to spur collective mobilization in other communist regimes that experienced a transition from plan to market (enterprise closure, nonpayment of wages, and unemployment) received no coverage in *Granma* in 2008 and account for barely 4.4 percent of the letters printed in 2014.[39] This suggests that the party is carefully avoiding the transmission of information that can increase the likelihood of collective action. *Granma* focuses instead on "safe" issues like excessive regulations, shortages, and the poor quality of goods and services, which constituted 69 percent of all letters in *Cartas a la Dirección* in 2014, nearly exactly double the volume of such letters in 2008 (36.7 percent). These issues are a source of daily consternation for Cubans. For this reason, printing letters on such themes is very popular.[40]

TABLE 5.5. Subcategories of Critical Letters, 2008 and 2014

	Absolute number, 2008	As percent of all letters in 2008	Absolute number, 2014	As percent of all letters in2014
Excessive bureaucratic regulations	22	8.1	29	11.5
Poor cadre quality/ poor management	16	5.9	1	0.4
Poor work discipline	8	3	0	0
Waste of resources	5	1.8	3	1.2
Use of state assets for private gain	2	0.7	0	0
Enterprise closure, non-payment of wages, and unemployment	0	0	11	4.4
Resellers/speculative trade	18	6.7	9	3.6
Lack of attention to popular input	0	0	1	0.4
Violations of public order	13	4.8	8	3.2
Shortages	6	2.2	24	9.5
Poor quality of goods (including food)	3	1.1	9	3.6
Poor quality of services	68	25.2	112	44.4
Other	12	4.4		
Total	173	64.1	207	82.1

Source: Author's dataset.

Table 5.6 offers a detailed breakdown of the complaints about the poor quality of services, which constituted the single largest group of grievances in both 2008 (25.2 percent of all letters) and 2014 (44.4 percent of all letters). Some items appeared on the list in both years, accounting for a roughly similar share of the total number of service complaints: transportation (irregular bus service; rude drivers pocketing bus fare; buses overridden by vermin); telecommunications; mail delivery; and rude customer service in hard currency stores. Others, like service quality at Coppelia appeared in 2008, but not in 2014. Complaints about medical and dental service and shortages of drugs saw a marked increase in 2014. Finally, one category of service com-

TABLE 5.6. Types of Complaints about Service Quality, 2008 and 2014

	Absolute number, 2008	As percent of all letters about services in 2008	Absolute number, 2014	As percent of all services in 2014
Transportation	13	19.1	26	23.2
Coppelia	4	5.9	0	0
Mail delivery	2	2.9	3	2.7
Telecommunications	4	5.9	5	4.5
Medical/dental/ pharmaceutical	5	7.3	20	17.9
Hard-currency stores	6	8.8	7	6.2
Business hours	5	7.3	0	0
Cinemas	2	2.9	0	0
Trash collection/ur- ban hygiene	2	2.9	11	9.8
Inconsistent prices	0	0	4	3.6
Other	25	36.8	36	32.1
Total	68	100	112	100

Source: Author's dataset.

plaints (inconsistent prices) appeared in 2014 but not in 2008. It would be unreasonable to treat these data as representative of the relative prevalence of different types of concerns about services. The data do, however, illustrate the striking range of poor customer service in contemporary Cuba, thus revealing why service quality may indeed be among the biggest daily concerns of ordinary citizens.

Readers writing about excessive regulations focused on the difficulty of obtaining permits to repair or build new homes; the challenges involved in transferring property; and the difficulty of establishing a successful business as a *cuentapropista* (self-employed individual). These complaints maintained a roughly similar share of all letters printed in *Cartas a la Dirección*: 8.1 percent in 2008 and 11.5 percent in 2014.

With regard to shortages, the number of letters printed increased fourfold from 2.2 percent of the total in 2008 to 9.5 percent in 2014. It is unlikely that this represents a dramatic worsening of the existing shortages in Cuba. Instead, it probably reflects an editorial decision to give a higher profile to shortages, knowing full well how much time ordinary citizens devote to looking for scarce items. In both years, no letters about the irregular supply of essential food items were printed. In 2008, letter writers focused on the shortages of tampons, contact lenses, eyeglasses, and orthopedic shoes.

In 2014, in addition to tampons and orthopedic shoes, citizens complained about the scarcity of condoms, toilet paper, school uniforms, chocolate mix, salt, deodorant, potatoes, pots and pans, light bulbs, batteries for electric bikes, motorcycle tires, animal feed, toothbrushes, and white tooth fillings and resins. For most of those items, explanations from the responsible suppliers were printed, offering specific plans for meeting the existing demand.

As publishing these letters represents the choices of the editorial staff of *Cartas a la Dirección*, we cannot conclude with any certainty whether some daily life problems have become worse between 2008 and 2014. We can infer that *Granma* has made a decision to publicize these grievances and that, instead of fearing that shining a light on these popular grumbles would destabilize the system, it knows that it can reduce social tensions by allowing citizens to collectively let off steam.

Readers' Letters and the Gathering of Information about Popular Discontent

Letters to the editor in communist single-party states like China, the Soviet Union, Bulgaria, and the German Democratic Republic have another function: when systematized and analyzed, they can provide the regime with information about popular opinion, especially with regard to the fulfillment of the social contract.[41] Meaningful analysis requires reading all letters received, and it is no coincidence that the letter departments of the flagship newspapers in communist regimes have the largest staff. One hypothesis that cannot be tested with the currently available materials from Cuba, but that seems warranted given what we know about the handling of citizen complaints in other communist single-party regimes, is that the real purpose of *Cartas a la Dirección* may be to stimulate citizens to send letters to *Granma* so that these letters can be analyzed and information about public opinion can be prepared for transmission to the top leadership. Testing this hypothesis would require access to a very different source of data: the almost 100,000 letters that *Granma* receives on an annual basis, rather than the 250 or so that it decides to publish. For the time being, we can focus on gaining a more complete understanding of the function of published letters to the editor in Cuba.

CONCLUSIONS

This essay has analyzed the functions of readers' letters published in *Granma* since 2008. It has argued that these letters improve the quality of governance in Cuba by signaling the openness of the party to criticism (an important part of Raúl's reforms), by creating a mechanism for accountability, and by allowing citizens to collectively let off steam. The continued willingness of citizens to submit letters to *Granma* will depend on increased responsiveness to the concerns about the fulfillment of the social contract articulated in these letters. As the experience of the East European single-party communist regimes that tried to rapidly dismantle the social contract indicates, the regime may be able to maximize popular support by further delaying bold reforms that would eliminate the entitlements associated with the socialist social contract.

The essay has highlighted important changes over time in the letters that are selected for publication by the editorial staff of *Granma*. The tone, form, and content of these letters have all rapidly evolved. In 2008, *Cartas a la Dirección* contained a hefty dose of gentle admonitions, respectful opinions, and laudatory missives glorifying the party and the revolution. By 2014, the tone was overwhelmingly critical; vague opinion letters had been replaced by concrete requests for rectifying specific problems; and laudatory letters had almost disappeared. To the extent that citizens are influenced by published content and frame their complaints accordingly, the change in tone will incentivize letter writers to send even more critical communications to *Granma*, which can then decide whether it wants to print them.

In many ways, a section of letters to the editor is an anachronism hearkening back to *Granma* of the 1970s or to Soviet models like *Literaturnaia gazeta*.[42] In single-party communist states with high levels of Internet penetration like contemporary China, the functions of *Cartas a la Dirección* are carried out by social media, which allow for the rapid horizontal transmission of information about popular grievances and establish requirements for accountability, thus obviating the need for the publication of readers' letters in newspapers. Should Cuba experience a rapid expansion of internet penetration, this would both make *Granma*'s letters obsolete and would create a new challenge for the communist leadership: namely, how to control a technology that allows for the instantaneous transmission of information on popular opinion and that requires a degree of responsiveness that is higher than the one the party has been providing so far.

NOTES

1. "A nuestros lectores," *Granma*, January 4, 2013, 10.

2. Carl J. Friedrich and Zbigniew K. Brzezinski, *Totalitarian Dictatorship and Autocracy* (2nd rev. ed.) (Cambridge: Harvard University Press, 1965); Timur Kuran, "Now Out of Never: The Element of Surprise in the East European Revolution of 1989," *World Politics* 44, no. 1 (1991): 7–48.

3. Studies have highlighted the role of elections (Beatriz Magaloni, *Voting for Au-*

tocracy: Hegemonic Party Survival and Its Demise in Mexico [New York: Cambridge University Press, 2006]), protests (Peter Lorentzen, "Regularizing Rioting: Permitting Public Protest in an Authoritarian Regime," *Quarterly Journal of Political Science* 8 [2013], 127–58), and commercialized media (Daniela Stockmann, *Media Commercialization and Authoritarian Rule in China* [New York: Cambridge University Press, 2013]).

4. For example, *Granma* received 93,394 letters in 2011 (83,000 letters; 7,069 emails; and 3,325 postcards) and printed 373 of them, which is 0.4 percent ("Un año más de Cartas a la Dirección," *Granma*, March 16, 2012: 10).

5. For an extended treatment of this point, see Martin K. Dimitrov, "Vertical Accountability in Communist Regimes: The Role of Citizen Complaints in Bulgaria and China," in *Why Communism Did Not Collapse: Understanding Authoritarian Regime Resilience in Asia and Europe*, ed. Martin K. Dimitrov (New York: Cambridge University Press, 2013), 276–302.

6. On China, see 2002 and 2008 Asian Barometer survey results at http://www.asianbarometer.org/ (accessed September 16, 2012). On the Soviet Union, see VTsIOM, *Obshchestvennoe mnenie v tsifrakh* no. 8 (15) (April 1990): 15. On Russia, see the results of a Levada Center poll reported in "Russians Trust President and Church Most," March 25, 2004, http://english.pravda.ru/news/russia/25-03-2004/56195-0/ (accessed September 16, 2012).

7. Stoian Mikhailov, "Sotsialni otdushnitsi," *Suvremennik* no. 2 (1985): 347–59, 355.

8. On performance reviews in China, see Susan Whiting, "The Cadre Evaluation System at the Grassroots: The Paradox of Party Rule," in Barry Naughton and Dali Yang, eds., *Holding China Together: Diversity and National Integration in the Post-Deng Era* (New York: Cambridge University Press, 2004), 101–19.

9. This is a minimal definition that would be acceptable even to critics of the concept of accountability. See Edward Rubin, "The Myth of Accountability," *Michigan Law Review* 103, no. 8 (August 2005): 2073–136 and Mark Philp, "Delimiting Democratic Accountability," *Political Studies* 57, no. 1 (2009): 28–53.

10. Jennifer Tolbert Roberts, *Accountability in Athenian Government* (Madison: University of Wisconsin Press, 1982), esp. 14–29.

11. For a critique of this assumption, see Philp, "Delimiting Democratic Accountability."

12. On China, see Melanie Manion, *Information for Autocrats: Representation in Chinese Local Congresses* (New York: Cambridge University Press, 2015).

13. On this process in China, see Pierre F. Landry, *Decentralized Authoritarianism in China: The Communist Party's Control of Local Elites in the Post-Mao Era* (New York: Cambridge University Press, 2008). Of course, indirect accountability also exists in democracies, where elected politicians hold unelected bureaucrats accountable through periodic oversight. See Mathew D. McCubbins and Thomas Schwartz,

"Congressional Oversight Overlooked: Police Patrols Versus Fire Alarms," *American Journal of Political Science* 28, no. 1 (1984): 165–79.

14. Scott Mainwaring and Christopher Welna, eds., *Democratic Accountability in Latin America* (New York: Oxford University Press, 2003).

15. The social contract in a communist society is not a Rousseauian contract into which citizens enter voluntarily. See Linda J. Cook, *The Soviet Social Contract and Why It Failed: Welfare Policy and Workers' Politics from Brezhnev to Yeltsin* (Cambridge: Harvard University Press, 1993) and Linda J. Cook and Martin K. Dimitrov, "The Social Contract Revisited: Evidence from Communist and State Capitalist Economies," *Europe-Asia Studies* 69, no. 1: 8–26.

16. See "Informe Central presentado por el compañero Raúl" (Central Report Presented by Comrade Raúl), April 17, 2011. http://www.granma.cubaweb.cu /secciones/6to-congreso-pcc/artic-04.html.

17. Carmelo Mesa-Lago, *Cuba en la era de Raúl Castro: Reformas económico-sociales y sus efectos* (Madrid: Colibrí, 2012).

18. Statement based on research conducted in Havana, May–June 2015.

19. Such provisions exist in Article 63 of the 1992 Cuban Constitution. They are also included in the constitutions of the USSR (Article 49 of the 1977 Constitution), Bulgaria (Article 55 of the 1971 Constitution), Czechoslovakia (Article 29), the GDR (Articles 104–05), Hungary (Article 68.2), Poland (Article 73), and Romania (Article 34). See also Article 41 of the 1999 Chinese Constitution, Articles 53 and 74 of the 2001 Vietnamese Constitution, Article 27 of the 1991 Lao People's Democratic Republic Constitution, and Article 69 of the 1998 North Korean Constitution (for more details on petitions in North Korea, see Yonhap News Agency [Seoul], *North Korea Handbook* [Armonk: M. E. Sharpe, 2003], 153).

20. Sheila Fitzpatrick, *Tear Off the Masks! Identity and Imposture in Twentieth-Century Russia* (Princeton: Princeton University Press, 2005). See also Merle Fainsod, *Smolensk under Soviet Rule* (Cambridge: Harvard University Press, 1958), 378–408.

21. For examples of new research on complaints in English that does not focus on the Soviet Union under Stalin, see Martin K. Dimitrov, "Internal Assessments of the Quality of Governance in China," *Studies in Comparative International Development* 50, no. 1 (2015): 50–72 and Luminita Gatejel, "Appealing for a Car: Consumption Policies and Entitlement in the USSR, the GDR, and Romania, 1950s–1980s," *Slavic Review* 75, no. 1 (2016): 122–45.

22. On the utility of complaints information for improving the quality of governance, see Dimitrov, "Internal Assessments of the Quality of Governance in China."

23. Martin K. Dimitrov, *Dictatorship and Information: Autocratic Regime Resilience in Communist Europe and China* (book manuscript in progress).

24. *Granma* (October 10, 1978), 5.

25. *Granma* (March 22, 1984), 3.

26. *Granma* (January 19, 1978), 3.

27. *Granma* (March 14, 2014), 10.

28. *Granma* (March 14, 2014), 10.

29. Raul Castro speech to the Seventh National Assembly, February 24, 2008. http://www.cubaminrex.cu/es/discurso-pronunciado-por-raul-castro-ruz-presidente -de-los-consejos-de-estado-y-de-ministros-en-las (accessed April 10, 2015); see also Mesa Lago, *Cuba en la era de Raúl Castro*, 242–43.

30. *Granma* (October 3, 2014), 11; *Granma* (May 2, 2014), 11; *Granma* (October 17, 2014), 11.

31. *Granma* (August 15, 2008), 11.

32. *Granma* (June 27, 2014), 11.

33. *Granma* (June 20, 2014), 11.

34. *Granma* (April 11, 2014), 11.

35. *Granma* (October 24, 2008), 11; *Granma* (August 29, 2008), 10; *Granma* (August 22, 2008), 10.

36. *Granma* (July 25, 2008), 10.

37. *Granma* (July 18, 2014), 10.

38. Kuran, "Now Out of Never"; Gary King, Jennifer Pan, and Margaret E. Roberts, "How Censorship in China Allows Government Criticism but Silences Collective Expression," *American Political Science Review* 107, no. 2 (May 2013), 326–43.

39. On China, see for example Yongshun Cai, *Collective Resistance in China: Why Popular Protests Succeed or Fail* (Stanford: Stanford University Press, 2010).

40. Interview with a Cuban journalist, June 16, 2015 (Havana).

41. Martin K. Dimitrov, "What the Party Wanted to Know: Citizen Complaints as a 'Barometer of Public Opinion' in Communist Bulgaria," *East European Politics and Societies and Cultures* 28, no. 2 (May 2014), 271–95; Martin K. Dimitrov, "Stimmungsberichterstattung in Bulgarien und China," in *Dem Volk auf der Spur . . . Staatliche Berichterstattung über Bevölkerungsstimmungen im 20. Jahrhundert. Deutschland, Osteuropa, China*, ed. Daniela Münkel and Henrik Bispinck (Göttingen: Vandenhoeck und Ruprecht, 2017), 157-177; Dimitrov, "Internal Government Assessments of the Quality of Governance in China"; and Dimitrov, *Dictatorship and Information*.

42. On *Literaturnaia gazeta*, see Martin K. Dimitrov, "Tracking Public Opinion under Authoritarianism: The Case of the Soviet Union under Brezhnev," *Russian History* 41, no. 3 (2014), 329–53.

LARRY CATÁ BACKER

THE CUBAN COMMUNIST PARTY AT THE CUSP OF CHANGE

The Cuban Communist Party (Partido Comunista de Cuba or PCC) stands at the cusp of great changes. The protective insulation that was provided to the Republic of Cuba by its Soviet protectors and the U.S. embargo has disappeared. Its new protectors—principally Brazil, Venezuela, and China—have been less eager to shield Cuba from the realities of emerging global political and economic realities. The great revolutionary leaders around which both state and party were organized, and through which both were able to defy expectations of integration in the 1990s,[1] are about to leave the scene. The 2015 reestablishment of diplomatic relations with the United States capped off this slow transition out of protective isolation.[2] All these changes have exposed the current governance order of the Republic of Cuba to its greatest strain since the disappearance of the Soviet Union nearly a generation ago. The challenge for the Cuban state is to preserve its current overall framework as it is required to embed itself more robustly in global economic, social, and political currents, and to be able to retain its autonomy and legitimacy in the face of interactions with transnational economic, political, and social actors.

These challenges fall squarely on the vanguard party in Cuba. No longer able to operate within its own space-time continuum, oblivious to changing global and national conditions, the PCC must evolve. The alternatives to evolution are not easy: either the PCC will perish as did the European and Soviet sister systems or the system itself will produce a substantial instability, as is increasingly evident in Venezuela, as Cuba seeks a new equilibrium point within the logic of political possibilities on the Island. There are any number of actors that would work toward that end. The United States and its European allies have made it clear that evolution away from any sort of party-state system is preferable to any modification in the present system that serves to strengthen the current political order.

But even evolution presents its challenges and dangers. Evolution Soviet style—one that focuses on political reform—could well plunge the state into a period of instability, with no guarantee of a Western-style democratic government at its end.[3] In any case, Soviet-style Marxism-Leninism remains substantially discredited as ideology and as a viable institutional form of government.[4] Evolution Chinese-style—one that focuses on economic development first overseen through an the institutionalized diffusion of power within an autonomous corporate vanguard party apparatus[5]—could turn the PCC on itself as old guard *nomenklatura* might seek to subvert reform, and in the process also produce the sort of instability that might lead to military dictatorship. But Marxism-Leninism is itself evolving to meet new challenges.[6] And it is clear that the PCC would have a substantial amount of catching up to do, not just institutionally but also in terms of embedding changing ideological approaches to its institutional structures.[7] And the party-state system itself carries its own set of dangers—bureaucratism, cults of personality, and ideological rigidity among them.[8]

For all the risk, evolution is inevitable in the face of the demands and expectations of both the Cuban people and the international community. Indeed, the process of evolution has already been given form and a rough measure of direction since the beginning of the second decade of the twenty-first century. With the Sixth PCC Congress, long overdue, the PCC itself recognized not merely the need to evolve if it was to survive, but its choice of the way forward. The Seventh PCC Congress promised greater reform. In mid-2015 it was reported that such reform would take Cuba in a direction neither Soviet nor Chinese in its approach to the development of the PCC and state apparatus: holding a popular vote to elect the next president; reforming and empowering the National Assembly; devolving power to the provinces and municipalities; and the electoral and constitutional reform necessary to institutionalize these changes within the government apparatus.[9] However, the Seventh Congress delivered what can only be understood as a firm defense of

LARRY CATÁ BACKER

the status quo against the inevitability of a reluctant recognition of the need to avoid economic collapse. By the middle of 2016 it became clear that economic reform would not venture far from the central planning care that had been at the center of macroeconomic policy since the 1960s.[10] By the end of 2016, any hope of political reform appears stalled as well by an ironic combination of fears of the consequences of U.S.–Cuban normalization, the death of Fidel Castro near the end of 2016, and substantial economic stagnation.[11]

This chapter briefly considers the issues facing the PCC as it seeks to emerge as an autonomous institutional force, free of the control of its creators and the personal power of those revolutionary leaders whose conflation of party and personality deeply affected the character and development of the PCC through its first half century. The section that follows examines the history of the PCC in the context of its current challenges. The next section considers the application of ideology to political construction of the party-state apparatus. The last section discusses the current state of PCC approaches to the challenges that face the party-state apparatus if it is to retain its legitimacy and viability in the current stage of development into which Cuba will be thrust in the next decade. It focuses on some of the potential changes that may figure in the years to come. The chapter concludes that Cuba has finally embraced the possibility of advancing both the ideological base on which its system is founded and to apply it to make potentially substantial changes in the state and party apparatus.

THE PCC IN IDEOLOGICAL-HISTORICAL CONTEXT

The PCC, the vanguard party of Cuba, was founded in its present form in 1965. Its establishment culminated in an initial unifying process of older parties and other groups starting after Fidel Castro and other revolutionary forces ousted the Batista government in January 1959.[12] The first step toward the creation of the party was the formation of the Organizaciones Revolucionarias Integradas (ORI).[13] The ORI was founded in 1961 and was composed of the Movimiento Revolucionario 26 de Julio, which was led by Fidel Castro, the Partido Socialista Popular (PSP), and the Directorio Revolucionario 13 de Marzo.[14] The second step toward the creation of the party was the formation of the Partido Unido de la Revolución Socialista de Cuba (PURSC), which was established in 1962.[15] With the creation of this predecessor to the PCC, the framework for the party was established. Finally, on October 3, 1965, the first central committee meeting of the PCC took place.[16]

In the 1960s, the PCC was weak because of its weak apparatus and its incapacity to assert a leading role in the politics of Cuba.[17] The party suffered from a limited ability to mobilize masses and a limited infrastructure.

LeoGrande posits that these weaknesses were due to several factors: 1) the small size of the party; 2) "the limited coverage of the population afforded by the Party's meager apparatus"; 3) "a persistent shortage of competent cadres due to the low educational level of the Party membership"; and 4) "a serious lack of internal organization and co-ordination both within and between Party organs."[18] But of course, there was another reason that drove the others. In the 1960s Cuba, like the Soviet Union, China, and Vietnam, still layered an ideology of personality cult, focused on the leader of the vanguard party, as the principal basis for ideological and institutional development.[19] The cults of Stalin, Mao, and Castro in some ways resembled each other in the sense that in each case the party and its apparatus was conflated within the body of the leader. Each came perilously close to the situation in Africa during the 1960s where party-state systems evolved as little more than the personal political machine of the leader.[20] And the institutionalization of PCC apparatus had to compete, in part, with the power and institutional structures of the military apparatus, whose central role in defending the republic against invasion, as a principal force for the projection of Cuban power abroad in the 1970s–1980s, and as the most highly developed autonomous economic force in Cuba, made the construction of a paramount role for the vanguard party more difficult.[21]

After nearly a decade of playing a minimal role in Cuba in the 1960s, the 1970s saw a move toward greater institutionalization of the PCC. With that change came an expansion of PCC membership. By the time of the First Party Congress in 1975, the PCC had grown from 55,000 members in 1969 to a reported 202,807.[22] Membership has continued to be small, rising to almost 520,000 in 1986.[23] Built more to serve as a revolutionary vanguard than as a party in power, the leanness of the PCC permits it to remain highly hierarchical in structure and operation. There is little devolution of authority, except for the application of discretionary authority specified from authorities in Havana. The PCC's Central Committee began regularly meeting and its role "in the overall political process" became more defined.[24] But those meetings were dominated by the históricos and the revolutionary leaders who embodied both ideology and vanguard power grounded in the revolutionary experience of the 1950s and 1960s.

Since the late 1960s the PCC has continued to adhere to a European- and Soviet-style approach to Marxist-Leninism-Stalinism,[25] but one in which the military also plays a substantial role.[26] That adherence survived the collapse of the Soviet Union. The preservation of that system has produced much of the gyrations of policy and experimentation that marked Cuban internal policy since the late 1980s. But it has also resulted in a failure because of its

LARRY CATÁ BACKER

inability to reconcile the contradictions with Cuba's realities and its ideological verities. This approach to Marxism-Leninism makes the objective of preserving the revolution, this become "the paramount ideological stance."[27] The PCC doesn't engage in theorizing so much as it guards the revolutionary legacy even against efforts to modernize coming from its.[28] It remains very much a revolutionary party in the sense of embedding its identity in the revolutionary struggle. "The revolutionary moment remains a palpable concept—it has been detached from history and governs all aspects of the operation of governance—political or administrative—within Cuba."[29] In other words, the PCC attempts to preserve the status quo at the moment the revolution succeeded in overthrowing the Batista government.[30]

WHAT IDEOLOGY HAS WROUGHT—THE PRESENT STATE OF CUBAN GOVERNANCE

The Cuban party-state apparatus continues to reflect a highly centralized intermeshed bureaucratic structure controlled at the very center by the leader of the PCC itself, its first secretary. In that respect the transfer of power from Fidel to Raúl Castro did little to change the fundamental structure of the political apparatus of either the state or the party that dominates the state apparatus. Nor will the resignation of Raúl Castro from the Cuban presidency alter power as long as he remains first secretary. And these transfers of power affected even less the structures of the military's organization and authority within Cuba. The leader continues to control selection for membership in the Politburo, and through that maintains control of the PCC and the state apparatus.[31]

The Cuban Constitution creates mutually reinforcing structures of authority among the state apparatus and the PCC, constrained only by a constitutional obligation to further "socialism" guided by the "ideology of José Martí, and the sociopolitical ideas of Marx, Engels, and Lenin."[32] This provides an ideological base distinct from that of either China or European Marxism. There are three key structural provisions in the constitution.[33] The first is Article 1, which declares a political basis in nationalist class struggle. The second is Article 3, which creates the form of the state apparatus—all popular (worker) power is exercised through a national assembly and those organs of state created through it, whose principal responsibilities center around the defense of the nation (and its political system) and the institution of socialism. The third is Article 5, in which the PCC is recognized—as a constitutional matter—as the leading force of society and the state. This last provision is particularly interesting for its constraining language with respect to the character of the PCC and its role. The PCC is bounded by the ideology of José Martí and Marxism-Leninism (a kind of nationalist socialism). It retains its authority only as long as it serves as the vanguard of the Cuban nation (workers in a class struggle context). And last, its object is focused on the construction of socialism with the goal of advancing toward a (nationalist) communist society. To this end, the PCC also controls the means of production (through the state apparatus) and all means of mass social movements.

The PCC is structured, like other Marxist-Leninist vanguard parties, on principles of democratic centralism,[34] collective action and individual responsibility,[35] and avoidance of factionalism.[36] All these techniques converge in the supreme organ of PCC governance, the PCC Congress, which elects the Central Committee of the PCC.[37] The PCC Congress is the supreme organ of the PCC and has authority to set the course of PCC activities, ideologies and policy.[38] It is to be held at regular intervals at least every five years,[39] though this has not been followed in practice. Indeed, since its establishment, the PCC has held seven congresses, the last held in 2016. Most have been held at roughly five-year intervals with the exception of the establishment of the PCC and the First PCC Congress (1975) and the fourteen years between the Fifth and Sixth PCC Congress. Each congress has served as a vehicle for the announcement of significant shifts in PCC policy and given direction to the work of governmental organs that were to be charged with the implementation of these changes.[40] These shifts either appear to move policy toward reform (e.g., the Sixth Congress and its Lineamientos) or it acts decisively to preserve the traditional structures of economy and politics (e.g., the Seventh PCC Congress).[41]

The Central Committee, in turn, has substantial governance authority within the PCC itself, including authority to manage the PCC Congress.[42] It exercises supreme authority when the PCC Congress is not convened,[43] meeting more regularly.[44] But real power resides in the Politburo, which exercises supreme power when neither central committee nor PCC committees are convened.[45] Power within the Politburo, in turn, is exercised by an executive committee presided over by the first secretary of the Central Committee.[46] And it is in this way that democratic centralism in ideological work is translated into a working style of institutional operation. Through these devices the first secretary has been able, over the past half century, to continue to exercise effective personal authority. Until recently, such a structure has permitted the first secretary to assert a personal ruling style, acting through both Politburo and Central Committee as convenient, and through the PCC Congress only as necessary to effectuate more broadly important changes in policy or ideology. And indeed, stronger institutionalization of the PCC beyond its organization at the highest levels appears to have begun more vigorously only well after the reins of authority passed from Fidel to Raúl

Castro. The 2012 National Congress of the PCC provides a window on that development and its difficulties, discussed further below.[47]

Intermediate PCC organizations mirror those of the center and are entirely dependent on central control for the exercise of any authority.[48] The PCC asserts control of the military and maintains cells at all levels of military organization,[49] all of which are directed by the first secretary of the Central Committee.[50] Social control is maintained through authority over all mass organizations in Cuba. That control permits the PCC to determine and constrain civil society organizations and to ensure that civil society may not become completely autonomous of the PCC's oversight. With respect to formally constituted mass organizations, these managerial constraints are well developed. Article 47 of the PCC's Reglamento[51] states that the organizations at the base of the party that are constituted in the central bodies of the state or their delegations do not control the activity of their direction.[52] Article 48 states that the superior bodies of the direction of the party, in completing their responsibilities with the central bodies of the state, help themselves with the base organizations that are constituted in them. In other words, those party members that hold leadership positions in state organizations can rely on the PCC's base organizations.[53] Finally, Article 37 of the PCC's Estatutos similarly states that the base organizations of the PCC constituted in the bodies of the central administration of the state and their delegations do not control their activity of direction.[54]

The PCC's Estatuto also makes clear the relationship between party and state organs, augmenting the provisions in the constitution. The PCC is declared to be the only legitimate expression of popular sovereignty and the sole source for the articulation of communist ideology—at least ideology that can be merged within the nationalism of José Martí.[55] Its authority depends both on its representation of a majority of people and its constitution as the embodiment of the Cuban nation. That unity is the foundation for its leadership role in the state—as the entity to which all state organs are accountable, and whose policies and ideologies the state apparatus, as representative of the people (through the party) must implement.[56]

These provisions provide the basis on which the PCC and the state have constructed a symbolic and intermeshed relationship.[57] Those in the top party positions also hold top positions in crucial state institutions. For example, in 2016 the first secretary of the PCC, Raúl Castro, is also the president of the "Consejos de Estado y de Ministros." The second secretary, José Ramón Machado Ventura, is the vice president of the "Consejo de Estado y de Ministros."[58] The rest of the members who make up the Political Bureau of the Central Committee of the PCC also hold leadership positions in important state institutions.[59] The same is true of members of the Secretariat of the PCC's Central Committee[60] and the members of the Central Committee[61] itself. Another example is committee member Esteban Lazo Hernández, who is also president of the Asamblea Nacional del Poder Popular. As a result of this interlocking structure, the decision-making power may be understood as subsumed within the PCC's structures.[62] And because Cuba is a small state, it is more possible for informal structures to obliterate the fine distinctions between PCC and state positions.

Cuba has been challenged with the elaboration of post-Leninist approaches to the refinement of their respective party-state systems. More specifically, Cuba has been facing the problem of the management and allocation of power between the party and the state. Cuba has adhered formally at least to the old Leninist line that the state and party functions ought to be kept separate except at the highest levels of authority where the two merge. The reality has been somewhat messier at the levels below the leadership levels. The connection between state and party is diffuse and it has been unclear what the division of authority may be. The resulting difficulties are ameliorated to the extent that the equivalent offices of state and party are filled by the same set of individuals. Yet that mediating effect also substantially erodes the institutional autonomy of both organizations in ways that make it hard for the PCC to focus on its role as the vanguard party, leaving to the state the more technical task of administration. The Leninist repercussions of these approaches are also clear—a tendency to favor administrative discretion in rule making, the use of taxation to extract "surplus" from nonstate sector activities, licensing of virtually all activities as a means of controlling their actualization, and the overarching assumption that any deviation from the classic state planned economic model is temporary and might be undone by the state at any time.

Jorge Domínguez has argued that Raúl Castro's initiative to reduce the direct administrative role of the PCC, that the PCC should not be "in charge of administration or the direct implementation of government policy," will be a difficult change to implement.[63] However, Domínguez also claims that this initiative proves to be confusing because as a result of the Sixth Party Congress, Raúl Castro consults a team and holds weekly meetings. Raúl meets with the executive committee of the PCC's Political Bureau and the executive committee of the Council of Ministers.[64] He also holds monthly meetings with the Council of Ministers, and sometimes the Political Bureau, the Secretariat, and the Council of State participate in these joint meetings. Domínguez argues that these joint meetings give "confusing signals" because "there is no difference between party, government, or state institutions."[65] Yet ultimately reform becomes difficult not merely because of the tightness of

LARRY CATÁ BACKER

control from the top, but because of the ossification of leadership and the indifference of younger people to the benefits of joining the PCC. The problem is not merely Cuban—the Vietnamese Communist Party is also said to suffer from the same malady, and paralysis.[66]

But there is another consequence to stodginess. Even this system, which is organized to reinforce centralization of party and state, and the further centralization of the party within the structures controlled by the first secretary may be challenged from a different source—from the lower levels of the PCC itself. Pedro Campos has noted the potentially serious split within the PCC between the old line Stalinists who continue to control the upper levels of state and party, and the grassroots cadres—the regional and local members who may be actively seeking a different direction for the PCC.[67] In contrast to the ossifying bureaucratic nomenklatura of the upper levels of the PCC, Campos asserts that, "at base-level, we have the other, the true Communist Party, made up of party members at production and services centers, some in the Party's bureaucratic apparatus and so-called "Zone Departments," which includes pensioners, where many criticize the bureaucratic system that has been imposed on the people in the name of socialism and the obstacles stemming from the state-command system, constantly advancing proposals (which are seldom heard and rarely addressed) about how to confront community, production, or service-related problems through innovative means."[68] This split, with roots in the debates about reform in the wake of the Fourth Party Congress,[69] reappeared with some force during the Sixth Party Congress and the debates about the course of future economic policy and political reform (within and beyond the PCC itself) and had made it harder for old-line PCC leaders to control opinion in organizations like the Young Communists League.[70] However, it is strong enough to move Campos to assert: "Today, it has become clear that the bureaucratic leadership of the Cuban Communist Party is heading in one direction while much of the rank-and-file is heading in a different one. That is why I speak of two Communist Parties"[71]—it is not yet strong enough to command the direction of policy and reform in Cuba. And the Seventh Party Congress saw the reassertion of power of the antireform faction, with a reassertion of the traditional antimarket notions and the reaffirmation of the centrality of old-style central planning.

As such, for the moment, this movement toward PCC reform remains at the periphery. Ideology and institutions at the highest levels continue to be bent in the service of a unified structure whose touchstone is the legitimating victory of the revolution that overthrew the Batista dictatorship—years before the institution of either the party or its ideological foundations. That inversion has given rise to a political structure that is dependent on the institutionalization of single-person control, through the first secretary of the Politburo, and whose foundation is built on the conflation of people and party. That conflation of people and party provides the basis for the intermeshing of popular action (through the party) and the obligations of the representative organs of state—representative of the people through the organs of the party. These cross-hatched representations construct a set of incarnations—the people in the party, the nation in the state apparatus.[72] In both cases, both popular will and governmental action must be guided by the ideology that legitimates these conflations and incarnations—a particular reading of the nationalism of José Martí and the political ideology of Marxism-Leninism. It is to that reading, and to the challenges of the half century of rigid fidelity to that reading, that we turn to next.

WHAT THE FUTURE BRINGS: FROM THE SEVENTH PCC CONFERENCE TO AN UNCERTAIN FUTURE

The key to the long-term success of any state organized along party-state lines is the organization and operation of the vanguard (Communist) Party. That is the essential insight of the Leninist part of Marxist-Leninist theory— if Marxism provides the baseline political ideology and objectives of the state, Leninism provides the foundations of its organizational principles.[73] But baseline principles do not necessarily suggest an end to ideological development, much less an engagement with the implementation of foundational principles within the specific context of a particular state. Indeed, the fear of theoretical ossification has dogged Leninism (and its Marxist foundations) almost from the beginning of post-Marxist theoretical work.[74] And in Cuba's case, the melding of Marxism-Leninism with the nationalist ideology of José Martí adds a wrinkle to institution building that poses both opportunities and challenges—both of which have been realized only in part.

Cuba's *organization* remains deeply Leninist, even as the scope of its activities are affected by Martian nationalism. Fidel Castro for decades continued to refer to himself as a professional revolutionary—which was interpreted by some to refer to his antipathy for injustice,[75] though it was more accurately a direct reference to the Leninist notion of professional revolutionary as a necessary ingredient in communist revolution.[76] The irony, of course, is that this reference to the essential character of the communist as a professional revolutionary was never successfully transposed into postrevolutionary Leninism. The exception perhaps was to reimagine notions of the communist international, formally dead after 1943, the spirit of which the PCC and Castro continue to embrace, though now without the European mechanisms for its institutionalization and in the form of an internationalized class struggle ideology grounded in the imperatives of proletarian revolution.[77] Its current incarnation is reflected in the ideology of ALBA.[78]

But Cuba has become an outlier among Marxist-Leninist states, reflecting a rigid and antiquarian form of this method of state organization—the way that the eighteenth-century British system might appear to modern-day U.K. citizens. China has become among the most influential leading forces in advancing the development of Marxist-Leninist party-state government. The Chinese have adapted Leninism in quite distinct ways. Though both the PCC and the Chinese Communist Party (CCP) are Leninist parties, their institutionalization of Leninist principles has produced quite distinct vanguard parties. The CCP has sought to progress beyond the revolutionary party organizational focus of Leninism to what is increasingly referenced as socialist democracy. In the case of China, those normative elements of Marxism have been refined within the notions of socialist modernization:[79] the motive power of the reform of the Chinese Communist Party is further developing the productive force and improving the construction of the party by consolidating the foundation of economy.

The focus of the reform of the Chinese political system is the division of party and administrative power. This represents a fundamental shift in the application of Marxist-Leninist theory to the problem of governing the state and its relation to the vanguard party. In China, there has been a move toward a separation of powers grounded in a split between political power—which rests with the vanguard party and exists beyond the constitution—and the administrative power, which is exercised through the state organs and subject to the constraints of the national constitution. The object is to ensure that the political work of the party as an institution is distinct from the work of the state as the apparatus through which such political work is implemented. That provides a basis for some separation of political issues, open only to party members and the intraparty mechanisms of democratic centralism, from administrative issues, for which popular participation may be encouraged as an instrument for ensuring administrative efficiency. The national constitution is understood as the supreme law over the administrative apparatus, but it is also the application of the party line and is understood as the substantive principles of the party's politics, as principle but not law is applicable to the CCP.[80] More important is the move toward what the Chinese call socialist democracy—an effort to routinize and institutionalize intraparty democracy in collective decision making and the development of a theory that makes this effort compatible with basic principles of Marxism-Leninism.[81]

Indeed, the concept of socialist modernization, key to the scientific development of CCP political lines, is noticeably absent from a PCC discussion. And it is absent precisely because the ideological center of Cuban Marxism remains rooted in state planning. That is the cornerstone of both its internal and external economic model. Its opening up, then, remains mediated by its own approach to economic organization, one that makes it more difficult to achieve compatibility with the global system rules with which it interacts. But that is also an important element of resistance that has been a cornerstone of Fidel Castro's ideological glosses on the relationship between Cuban communism and globalization.

But the core difference is in the way in which the Chinese and the Cubans approach the issue of the role of the vanguard party. In China the notion is that this role is dynamic and changes, along with the vanguard party's basic line, in accord with changing historical stages. That was made clear after the Nineteenth CCP Congress in October 2017, at which the CCP introduced sweeping changes in the wake of its recognition of a "New Era" and a new stage in the development of the Chinese state (and party).[82] In contrast, the PCC remains very much a *revolutionary party*, rather than a party in power. It is a Leninist party still geared for (perpetual) revolution long after the moment of its historical occurrence. The revolutionary moment remains a palpable concept—it has been detached form history and governs over all aspects of the operation of governance—political or administrative within Cuba.[83] Perhaps this single-minded focus on organization grounded in the spirit of the moment of revolutionary triumph is made necessary by the constant opposition of the United States, perhaps not. But that focus remains the bedrock of the organization of state and party in ways that substantially limit the ability of the PCC to organize itself as other than a vanguard party frozen at the moment of its accession to power. As a result it has been difficult for the PCC to change with the times, Chinese style, and assume the role of the vanguard party tasked with the governance of a state that is the instrument of the objective to eventually reach a level of development that makes the communist ideal attainable.

And indeed, connected with the avoidance of historical perspective or context at the heart of the "eternalization" of the revolutionary moment for PCC organization is the idea that at that moment of triumph the communist ideal was also within reach. This is a substantially different premise than that embraced by the CCP and accounts for a significant difference in both the PCC's organization, and aims. The CCP *looks forward* to attainment of a communist society. That is the core of the CCP's socialist modernization basic line. In contrast, the PCC assumes that its role is to *preserve* the communist society it achieved at the moment of revolutionary triumph. That distinction will have significant effects on the way in which the PCC approaches its relationships with outsiders and its internal governance.

Preservation requires a single-minded focus on the consolidation of PCC power, though effectuated through the personalities of its leaders rather than through strong institutional structures.[84] Preservationism might be understood as a window onto the stubborn Stalinist streak in Cuban institutionalizing ideology. The PCC is also Stalinist in the sense of the driving force of personality over institution.[85] Institutions are essential instruments for the implementation of collective will, but that will is manifested through the politics of personality rather than situated within a matrix of rules that reflect collective application of ideological frameworks on individual issues. This succinctly describes the structural repercussions of the Latinized European Soviet style of Leninism and its reflections on the institution of the Communist Party after the moment of revolutionary triumph. That tension may be reflected, as well in the irregularity of holding Communist Party congresses in Cuba.[86]

But there are certain unique conditions to the PCC that also affect its character and structure, and the nature of the hold of revolutionary ideology in its operation. The PCC is the rare example of a communist party established after a successful communist revolution.[87] The task of building a communist party, then, became bound up in the work of building a socialist state after the attainment of power. The real institutional glue during this process was the military—a condition that continues to mark the relations among the military and bureaucratic establishment in Cuba. The military PCC relations born of an unacknowledged history also set it apart from that of the CCP, for example. Institutionalization came late and was relatively weak. The First PCC Party Congress was not held until 1975, after the apparatus of the revolution was already well in place.[88] At the time, in his address to the participants Fidel Castro emphasized the value of the party's institutionalization, evidenced by the congress for the purpose of stability, though noting that the ideological work for the congress ought to be focused on implementation.[89] Yet behind the institutionalization, the force of personality remained vigorous. While China began moving toward a depersonalized CCP apparatus, Cuba would reinforce the personal element in party organization—the essential role of the Leninist professional revolutionaries in postrevolutionary Cuba as the glue to keep the structures of state and party stable. Most of the party congresses after the collapse of the Soviet Union, in contrast, have been called to deal with the issue of preservation and adjustment. The idea in Cuba is that prior to 1989, Cuba had its internal ideological house in order—and that the function of the state and of the party apparatus was to resist change, for any change would signal a retreat from the revolutionary ideal. That factor has also shaped the organization of the PCC and its internal ruling style.

The cult of personality issue is still a very delicate subject in Cuba, in part because unlike China, where such discussion was more open after the passing of the revolutionary generation, that is still difficult in Cuba. While the official position of the state and party disfavors personality cults, at least in its most blatant Soviet Stalinist forms, the reverence with which the founding generation are held, at least in official circles, suggests a tension between official reality and facts on the ground.[90] Only recently Raúl Castro spoke in general terms of unspecified terms for the succession of leadership within the PCC.[91] But that speech itself suggested a lack of effort to institutionalize leadership changes, and a continuation of the focus on personality and its bourgeois democratic implications. Still, the role of Fidel Castro Ruz, who led the state and party apparatus for a half century, not only looms large over both administrative cultures and party ideology; "[e]ven with the institutionalization of the late 1970s and early 1980s, there was little doubt that PCC cadres served at the pleasure of the maximum leader. He was not constrained by its routines or bureaucracy, and he answered to no one else in the Party leadership."[92]

Since the passing of Mao Zedong and the leadership of Deng Xiaoping, China has become particularly sensitive to issue of cult of personality, and its implications for the development of a socialist rule of law state.[93] The CCP has thought to theorize the leadership of Mao Zedong for the lessons it provided a dynamic Leninist element in party organization.[94] Much current theorizing about the bureaucratization and institutionalization of political power within the CCP and the democratization of its exercise internally is guided by the need to ensure that Mao-style cults do not reappear.[95] It also underlies, to some extent, the Chinese embrace of law—and rule of law concepts—as part of their administrative operations, especially within the state apparatus. This insight does not shape only the succession within the vanguard party, but also provides a measure of stability between periodic and stable changes within the party's leadership. It also permits a greater focus toward anticorruption efforts, and perhaps the institutionalization of a large and increasingly effective intraparty mechanism for anticorruption efforts, though one that itself is subject to criticism.[96]

It is not clear that the death of Fidel Castro in 2016 will have the same effect as that of Mao Zedong. Unlike Mao, Fidel has not been humanized by the experiences of the Cultural Revolution and its rejection after 1978. On the other hand, Fidel's death creates more room for his brother to continue a slow but steady effort to tilt a little toward the Chinese path. Raúl Castro, for example, has been moving toward embracing a Chinese path to institutional succession. In February 2013, he announced plans to begin to modify succession and its institutionalization in Cuba.[97] Most important, perhaps, was the announcement, in the style of Deng Xiaoping, of his retirement, projected to occur in 2018. "And yet, on an island where a Castro has been in charge since 1959, he also seemed intent on changing how his successors will rule. In an announcement more surprising than his retirement plan, Mr. Castro said he hoped to establish term limits and age caps for political offices, including the presidency. Some broad constitutional changes, he said, will even require a referendum."[98] But even here he was careful to ensure the selection of successors who could mediate the interests of the state and party apparatus against those of the military.[99] Changes to the Constitution of China in 2018 suggest that the issue of longevity and term limits in China may be changing as well.[100]

Yet the differences between Cuban and Chinese Marxism-Leninism could not be clearer. The basic principles of the PCC reflect the focus on the revolution and revolutionary values that are meant to take on a transformative and transrevolutionary character—a static dynamism that is meant to capture and hold steady the moment of revolutionary triumph. The PCC centers its revolutionary ideology around the following points: First, absolute loyalty to the interests of the working class and other working people; Second, unwavering opposition to the capitalist system and any other systems with exploitation; Third, creatively applying Marxist-Leninist theory to the specific conditions in Cuba and experiencing it according to their own experiences and other fraternal parties' experiences. Fourth, loyalty to proletarian internationalism and opposition to manifestations of nationalism and chauvinism, fighting alongside all other communists and opposition forces of reactionaries and imperialism, and supporting the struggle against the capitalist exploitation of the working people of other countries. Fifth, close ties with people.

It is in this context that one can consider the thrust of the choices that the PCC most recently made as it sought to move forward in ways that preserve the current system but permit that system to evolve, and perhaps evolve in substantial respects without losing its essential character. The direction of those choices had been hinted at in the proposed agenda of the Seventh PCC Congress and appeared to seek to reaffirm traditional values over Chinese-style Marxist markets approaches.[101] The Seventh PCC Congress was to be important from a transitional point of view for two distinct reasons. First, it appears that it would "assess the implementation of the agreements of the Fourth Congress and the First National Conference of the Party, [and] specify the way to continue improving the Cuban economic and social model."[102] The second reason touches on the extent of structural changes that the PCC might propose to change the institutions of governance in Cuba. Both were hinted at in reports of the Thirteenth Plenum of the PCC Central Committee. The Plenum considered a report on economic and social development through 2030,[103] one that appeared to echo similar approaches in China.[104] It also reflected on the slow realization of the recommendations in the Lineamientos, of which only 21 percent of the recommendations has been implemented in the five years since their adoption in the Sixth PCC Congress.[105]

The suggestion of reference to the Fourth PCC Congress is telling and important. This was the first PCC Congress held as the Soviet Union was disintegrating and many of the communist regimes in Eastern Europe had been overthrown.[106] And it was a critical step in the process of ossification of Cuban nationalist Marxist-Leninism—it was here that the preservationist cult manifested itself in its most complete form. It was from this point to the present that both party and state were turned to the task, not of furthering the development of socialism, but of preserving the development from the corrupting dangers of development itself. The fear that gave rise to this ossification was all around the PCC, especially as an evisceration of what had appeared to be stable and progressive Marxist-Leninist regimes in Eastern Europe. And the PCC, at the behest of its then first secretary and commander in chief, rejected outright as a betrayal of Marxism itself, the new path that Deng Xiaoping was forging in post–Mao Zedong China.[107] Fidel Castro himself set the tone for the congress by rejecting both political and economic reform, the former dismissed as contrary to the ideology of both Lenin and Martí (who had tolerated only a single party for independence in Castro's view) and the latter dismissed as capitalism by other means:

> No habrá economía de mercado, o como quiera llamársele a ese mejunje que no tiene nada que ver con el socialismo. Nuestra economía será una economía programada, planificada, no caeremos en las locuras de creer que mediante mecanismos espontáneos se va a desarrollar el país; y mientras más limitados sean los recursos más decisivo es saber usarlos de manera racional y óptima. De modo que nuestra Revolución no hará concesiones de principios, y es bueno que se sepa, porque a cada rato surgen salvadores, consejeros, no sé qué, quienes hablan de hacerle concesiones al imperialismo, como si se hubiera salvado en la historia alguna vez un proceso revolucionario haciendo concesiones.[108]

Indeed, the Fourth PCC Congress has been understood as the augmentation of a rectification campaign well in progress by the late 1980s that then swelled to include a campaign to restore orthodoxy to the PCC in the face of changes sweeping the communist world.[109] "El neoliberalismo, el capitalismo y el imperialismo no hacen concesiones. ¡El socialismo no puede hacer concesiones, nuestro socialismo no hará jamás concesiones de principios!"[110] To the extent that the Seventh PCC Congress would revisit the Fourth PCC Congress, it appears that it might seek to revisit orthodoxy and its expression. If that were the case, it is possible to produce either a reaffirmation or an opening up of orthodoxy. In either case, the official line might well have to be read in conjunction with the effective consequences of that statement—a reaffirmation of orthodoxy as the system of central planning is weakened will speak volumes. But orthodoxy might be as well preserved by *rejecting the idea* of central planning as the unmovable cornerstone of a Marxist ideology and *embracing the idea* of markets as compatible with socialism and a movement toward Chinese-style theorizing about Marxist orthodoxy. The Fourth Congress's preservationism remains the block on the ability of the PCC to move beyond the nineteenth century in terms of Marxist economics and beyond the twentieth century in terms of postrevolutionary conceptions of the role of a vanguard as a party in power. But given the timidity of the Sixth PCC Congress in matters of economics,[111] it is no surprise that the Seventh PCC Congress was not used to move away from the core ideology of the Fourth PCC Congress. Though the PCC's left wing was nervous indeed that was the course the PCC would take as younger cadres begin to assert influence,[112] as the platform for the rejection of preservationist Marxism-Leninism in Cuba.

Ironically, that this did not happen could be ascribed, in part, to an unintended consequence of normalization of U.S –Cuba relations. On the eve of the Seventh Congress, Fidel Castro himself chided President Obama for his interference in Cuban internal politics in his earlier visit: "My modest suggestion is that he gives it thought and does not attempt now to elaborate theories on Cuban policy."[113] This was followed by a harshly critical news commentary by the influential writer Darío Machado.[114] Raúl Castro noted Cuban frustration with and suspicion of the pace and direction of normalization at the start of the Seventh PCC Congress.[115] And the foreign minister characterized the visit as " a deep attack on our ideas, our history, our culture and our symbols."[116] What these attacks reveal is not so much aggression as it reveals fear, the fear that the United States might overwhelm the ability of the Cuban state to continue to be the master of its own political and macroeconomic project. To ensure control, the PCC might have succumbed to the temptation to preserve those key points that made it different—a rejection of markets and of the sort of popular democracy so dear to the United States.

To that end, the Fourth Congress is important for another reason; its ideology would serve as a useful resistance template. Its reforms eventually led to changes in the Cuban state constitution.[117] The confirmation of orthodoxy that emerged from the Seventh Congress will likely also require constitutional realignment as well, but not before Raúl Castro institutionally solidifies the succession. That would produce a substantial break with the past, but a necessary one if Cuba is to preserve any remnant of its current party-state system. What those constitutional provisions might include could be gleaned from some of the possibilities for structural reform that have been suggested. All of them show a tendency toward deeper institutionalization of the party-state system in ways that engage the polity more directly. But few of them actually touch on the issue of greatest moment to that polity—substantial economic reform. It would seem, then, that the PCC may be choosing the European rather than the Chinese path toward reform. A risky proposition indeed, but one that the Cuban leadership believes it can control—especially in the context of its negotiations on normalization of relations with the great adversary—the United States.[118] Yet by the middle of 2017 all of these calculations had proven wrong. The Affair of the Sonic Weapons Attack and the election of Donald Trump to the U.S. presidency in November 2016 effectively froze the process of normalization and in some respects rolled it back a little.

The speculation about the scope of the substantive changes centered on political reform.[119] One of the most important involved speculation to permit popular election of the highest state officials—notably the president and vice president. Most likely this will be a ceremonial change—permitting the electorate to ratify the choices made by the Politburo and its first secretary.[120] Voting serves purposes well beyond those of actually exercising robust political power.[121] But in Marxist-Leninist states such elections might be contrary to the fundamental political ordering of the state, in which political authority (and the placement of effective discursive power) is centered within the vanguard party as the incarnation of the popular will.[122] Thus in that context elections of this sort have revolutionary potential, should popular discourse be permitted in the context of the election. But elections of this kind do little to change the underlying structures of control—the first secretary still wields enormous power. It provides, then, the illusion of participation. This might well be the worst of all worlds. It weakens the application of the ideology of vanguard party leadership without changing its effects. It creates a gap between the idea of the representational capacity of the vanguard and the exercise of elections. But it effects no internal change in the PCC. Yet it might be more important to develop intra-PCC democracy—and thus strengthen and deepen the institutional viability of the PCC rather than expend energy on Potemkin village exercises that do little to develop the PCC's vanguard obligation to listen to popular sentiment and to incorporate it in their leadership role. It is all speculation, built on the promise of possible reform that will be produced only in the run-up to the 2018 elections. "In fact, the Cuban government recently announced that it would roll out a new electoral law following the congress. This, together with previous changes that limited top political posts to two terms of five years each, has sparked speculation among intellectuals, dissidents and Cuban citizens in general about how far the electoral reforms will go."[123]

The Chinese approach might better serve both the PCC and the people. That approach targets both popular engagement through a reworking of the "mass line,"[124] and institutional stability through effective measures to increase dialog within the party along with vigorous anticorruption campaigns. Political reform, if it is to be effective in strengthening the party-state system, must begin by strengthening the character, institutional operations, and responsiveness of the vanguard party. In effect, political reform requires the opening up to the necessity of developing Leninism to meet the current conditions of Cuba. That is the effect that the PCC has avoided through its long-term preservationism. The gesture of popular elections exacerbates rather than ameliorates this problem. It seeks to use the veil of a form of popular participation to mask the ossification of the institutional holder of political power in Cuba. And this will only serve to accelerate the process of degeneration that will lead to a Soviet-style end of the system. The Chinese have understood better (though still imperfectly) that within Leninist party-state systems, the engine of democratization must be centered on the vanguard party. That democratization must focus on collectivity in decision making rather than the forms of election.[125] Internal democratization within a Leninist party-state system ought to focus the Seventh PCC Congress on the power structures that limit the authority of the first secretary and embed it within the collective deliberations of the Politburo and Central Committee. It ought to provide a more effective political role for the Central Committee, and eventually to the PCC Congress itself. And it ought to seek to vigorously expand membership in the PCC itself. Ultimately democratization in a Leninist system implies that the vanguard will expand to include all the population of the state. If that fails to happen the vanguard has failed in its fundamental duty.

And political reform must focus on the internal integrity of the vanguard party itself. That requires a vigorous anticorruption effort, like that currently undertaken in China. But it also requires a change in the approach to the exercise of power by PCC cadres in their party and ministerial roles. This is particularly the case with respect to law making that effectively does little more than provide officials with a largely unconstrained discretion. Such discretionary legislation—usually evidenced by statutes that require application by individuals and review—produce little certainly in rule structures (they advance the notion that the application of law is personal even if the law is formally neutral). Such discretionary systems of law invite corruption—because to apply the law requires the exercise of discretion that is unlikely to be reviewable by any sort of standard reference. Thus, intraparty democratization without a significant development of the PCC's working style will produce an empty political reform that will contribute to the further ossification of the PCC as an effective Leninist organ. But these efforts have yet to materialize in a sustained way in Cuba. There is no Chinese-style effort to root out corruption or to establish any sort of supervision agency of the type that has proven effective and popular in China.

Another object of reform was thought to have been the National Assembly. Though in the end there was no reform, the speculation revealed the splits in political thinking among PCC factions. It had been speculated that the Seventh PCC Congress will consider changing the character of the National Assembly from a rubber stamp organ meeting a few days a year to a more muscular organ for the consideration of and debate about legislature measures. The object is to embrace a variant of the Vietnamese model and might reflect a growing relationship that has been encouraged between the Vietnamese and Cuban National Assemblies.[126] This serves a useful purpose. But its potential cannot be realized without a vigorous reform of the PCC's own governance approaches and its development of a more refined notion of the role of a vanguard party as the collective that exercises political authority, but that leaves the administrative and ministerial functions to the organs of state. That requires a willingness to implement a stricter separation of powers in Cuba between the PCC apparatus and the administrative apparatus of the state. It requires the PCC, and especially its cadres, to avoid meddling with administrative functions, especially those exercised by others, within the cage of rules that the administrative apparatus develops to implement the political will of the PCC. The Lineamientos was a good first step in the direction of this sort of governmental reform—the PCC developed political policy, and the administrative implementation was left to the state organs. But further work is necessary if this change to the authority and functioning of the National Assembly is to have any positive functional effect. Yet here the vectors of these reforms converge with those of democratization of the PCC and its rule systems. A National Assembly that is incapable of developing rules beyond those that preserve substantial administrative discretion fail in their ultimate purpose. Rule systems that are not responsive to current conditions also fail.

But ultimately the major constraint remains the unwillingness of the PCC to move beyond the ideological framework of the Fourth Party Congress with respect to the fundamental orientation of economic reform, that is, to develop the seeds that were planted but have yet to sprout from the Sixth PCC Conference. Until that bridge is crossed, political reform will always appear to be more gesture than substance. That bridge, however, was not crossed by action at the Seventh PCC Congress, and will likely await the changes in leadership slated for 2018. The PCC remains committed to a centrally planned economy in which the bulk of capital is managed through the state bureaucracy and related enterprises, in which foreign investment is kept within a cordon sanitaire and in which the private sector remains small and tightly controlled.

Related to the reform of the National Assembly is speculation, though one that appears well founded in recent movements by central authorities, to devolve more authority to provinces and municipalities. This reflects what appears to be a positive response to the experiment in devolving power that was effectuated in Artemisa and Mayabeque provinces in 2011.[127] It was hoped that some form of devolution would be incorporated in the proceedings of the Seventh PCC Congress. However, devolution remains experimental and limited in scope. In any case, that devolution, efficient in theory, leaves untouched the underlying structural problems that gave rise to devolution as a remedy—"bureaucratic sloth and silence"[128] Devolution merely diffuses the problem of governance in Cuba—the intermingling of administrative and PCC organs, a state of law grounded in rules that sometimes accomplish little more than the management of unconstrained administrative discretion, and the proliferation of administrative choke points in decision making that effectively crimps governance, raises the transaction costs of action and provides fertile ground for corruption. This is not a Marxist-Leninist problem, though Cuba provides a model of governance structures that nurture the corruption-discretion axis.[129] More important, perhaps, and more profoundly important, may be a move to shift taxation powers to the provinces as well. This provides a necessary measure of flexibility to meet quite distinct needs across Cuba. But it also provides more fertile ground for corruption in the absence of a strong reform of the bureaucracy—and especially of the interlinking between state organs and the PCC. In the end, the reform may serve as a means of reducing the size of the national bureaucracy by effectively transferring personnel down to the provincial level. But this change will again be more of a gesture than effective reform if the structures of governance remains intact. And it might do little to reduce the size of the bureaucracy in the aggregate—just provide a basis for reporting that the national bureaucratic structures have indeed been reformed.

Taken together, one sees an uneven and fairly risky picture emerging. The PCC has become more conservative since the 1990s, and more reactive. It has become less willing to treat its ideology—and the implementation of that ideology—to suit the historical stage for which these are deployed—as an evolving normative structure. Instead, the PCC appears to have begun to treat its foundational ideologies like divine script—unchangeable and immovable—a text for all ages beyond which it is impossible to move. Yet ideological growth is a necessary foundation of any Leninist project, and indeed evolution toward an ultimate objective is a central tenet of Marxism itself. There is nothing sacred about central planning, there is nothing inevitable about cults of personality within Leninist collective structures of governance, there is nothing inherently Marxist about rejection of firm regulatory structures and rule of law principles bent toward socialist objectives; markets do not have political or ideological affiliations, and capital does not assert political power.

Even the idea of class struggle, so deeply rooted in PCC ideology, is ripe for change—the PCC continues to adhere, without any thought, to ancient notions of personal service as a nondetachable part of labor. Yet little work has been done to confront the issue of the personality of labor and to detach the value of a task from the individual obligations of those who provide it. Until that occurs, Marxism, like capitalism, continues to face the issue of the inherently exploitative nature of labor service. Yet we see no effort to even begin theorizing these core problems of vanguard party obligation. Indeed, while the PCC continues to adhere to the idea that class struggle and proletarian revolution comprise the central contradiction that must be overcome, the CCP has moved first from the idea of class struggle to that of socialist modernization (the development of productive forces in the service of the masses) during Deng Xiaoping's leadership to post-Nineteenth CCP Congress New Era thinking. After 2017, the central contradiction on which the CCP focuses is neither class struggle nor socialist modernization but rather that "the principal contradiction facing Chinese society in the new era is that between unbalanced and inadequate development and the people's ever-growing needs for a better life."[130]

That continued focus on ancient revolutionary objectives has frozen the PCC in a place far removed from the reality of its own governance. It has produced a Marxism in which the state itself has become the incarnation of the ultimately exploitative capitalist class. And it has produced a PCC that is still engaged in a class struggle where by dint of its own revolutionary victory it has become the class against which it must fight. The rejection of that idea of evolution, where both polity and theory grow toward the establishment of a communist society built on the accumulated wealth of the nation, will increase the likelihood that Cuban nationalist Marxism will continue on the road toward irrelevance as it becomes increasingly remote from the realities of the challenges that face the state and nation—and party. In an effort to preserve its history and its ideology, the PCC is in danger of losing both, even as other Marxist-Leninist states evidence the possibilities of alternative paths.

CONCLUSION

Today the PCC stands at a great crossroads—one that will determine its future and the future character of the operational ideology of the Cuban state. The internal self-contradictions of European Marxism were brought to full flower within the unsustainable ideology of Stalinism, which itself was sustained only by an excess of bureaucratism and cult of personality. These self-contradictions, embraced by the PCC, combined with the ossification of Cuban Marxism—an almost obsessive reflex to use the entire resources of the nation to stop time on January 1, 1959 (an obsession mirrored perversely by their adversaries within certain elements of the Cuban exile community)—threaten the viability of the PCC more than any threat by the Americans and the Cuban exile community, both of which have remained substantially impotent, ideologically and in terms of power politics, to affect facts on the ground in Cuba to come close to their own objectives. The failures and ideological gaps in the moves toward economic reform of the past five years suggests the problem.

Unable to escape the logic and tensions of the ideological stasis grounded in an unchanging approach to an understanding of Marxist-Leninist theory, and even of the Castroism that sought to apply its logic to the context of Cuba, any effort to structure deep economic reform will necessary flounder, its ability to conform to the realities of the Cuban situation irreconcilable with an ideological base that appears to be unchanging and indifferent to the scientific development inherent in the founding ideology itself. The problem of reform in Cuba, then, focuses on the unwillingness of the PCC to confront its own ideological structures and to be willing to develop these to meet the realities of the current context. The result is the application and reapplication of an ossified Leninism that fails to reflect both the possibilities of engagement by a vanguard party and the fundamental nature of Leninism—collectivity, responsibility, leadership, and responsiveness in the service of the greater object of moving Cuba forward toward a better life for its people. That requires not so much sacrifice in the service of ideology but ideology in the service of the core objective of the vanguard party—not class struggle (a revolutionary phase in ideology) but the appropriate development of the productive forces of the people.

These problems of the PCC are of their own making. The PCC has the power to move beyond them. That requires, beyond the institutionalization of the PCC itself (a vast and complex task in its own right), the depersonification of the structures of party rule, and the institution of rule of law cultures within the party, in the PCC's relationship with the state apparatus, and in the behaviors of the state apparatus itself. While the PCC as a vanguard party is expected to set policy and the objectives that the state ought to attain, Cuban Marxism fails by continuing the unsustainable policies of a half century ago that suggested that law and politics converge, that the party must govern as well as direct, and that there should not be a separation between administration and governance. The Chinese and the Vietnamese have shown, however much these systems still must develop and evolve, that it is possible to develop a Marxist system compatible with markets without overweening state control of economic activity (though of policy), one that separates the party from the administrative organs of state, and that eventually provides a space for popular engagement with state administration, while opening political participation more generally to all levels of party members.

Yet even the PCC itself might be ready to confront these contradictions as it seeks to preserve its governance and economic systems—that is, as it seeks to find a way to preserve the basic premises of its politics and economics while conceding the necessity of changing its institutions and operations.

> The "Cuban revolution," which some understand as the events of the 1960s, linked to a group of historical figures who sought to impose a neo-Stalinist form of socialism on the country, has been left behind by history and lives on only in the memories of the older generations and the media controlled by the Party bureaucracy. The other, the true revolution, the revolution that entails the democratization of politics and the socialization of the economy, enjoys broad support and is alive at the Party base and society in general.[131]

Cuba appears ready to engage in some political reform, reform that might decenter the PCC as a Leninist vanguard party in favor of more direct political relationships between the people and the state apparatus. Though that relationship will still be tightly controlled, the PCC has chosen political reform rather than economic reform. It appears to be moving in that direction at a time of economic crisis, and in the context of Cuban reengagement in global economic structures. Perhaps the PCC's inability to stray farther from orthodoxy than the slight movement represented by the Sixth Party Congress Lineamientos was as far as the PCC could tolerate Marxism's development away from its mid-twentieth-century European roots. The Seventh PCC Congress suggested the limits of the toleration of reform, the caution that is slowing its pace, the ironically perverse effects of opening up to the United States on the scope of reform. It appears likely that the PCC will choose to continue down the path of political reform in order to preserve the orthodoxy of socialist central planning and a small and tightly controlled private sector. Perhaps it suggests a high-risk gambit, which, when tried in Europe a generation ago, led to the sweeping away of the party-state systems in Eastern Europe.

NOTES

My thanks to my research assistant Angelo Mancini (Penn State JD, 2017 expected) for his usual exceptional work.

1. See, e.g., Carmelo Mesa-Lago, ed., *Cuba After the Cold War* (Pittsburgh: University of Pittsburgh Press, 1993).

2. See, e.g., Larry Catá Backer, "On Cuban Normalization," *Opinio Juris* (January 5, 2015). http://opiniojuris.org/2015/01/05/guest-post-cuban-normalization/.

3. This though the Cuban party-state architecture was able to survive the initial collapse in the 1990s. See, e.g., Jorge I. Domínguez, "The Political Impact on Cuba of the Reform and Collapse of Communist Regimes," in Carmelo Mesa-Lago, ed., *Cuba After the Cold War,* 99–131 (Pittsburgh: University of Pittsburgh Press, 1993).

4. See, e.g., Lezek Kolakowski, *Main Currents of Marxism* (New York: W. W. Norton, 2005).

5. See, e.g., Constitution of the Communist Party of China, General Program.

6. See, e.g., Larry Catá Backer, "Crafting a Theory of Socialist Democracy for China in the 21st Century: Considering Hu Angang's Theory of Collective Presidency in the Context of the Emerging Chinese Constitutional State," *Asian-Pacific Law and Policy Journal* 16, no 1 (2014): 29–82.

7. See, e.g., Backer, "Crafting a Theory of Socialist Democracy for China in the 21st Century."

8. See, e.g., Hu Angang, *The Modernization of China's State Governance* (Beijing: Institute for Contemporary Studies, Tsinghua University, 2014); Hu Angang, *China's Collective Presidency* (Dordrecht: Springer, 2014).

9. Diego Moya-Ocampos, "Potential Changes to Cuba's Political System in 2016 to Lower Government Stability Risks But Democratic Reform Unlikely," *IHS Jane's Intelligence Weekly* (June 10, 2015). http://www.janes.com/article/52181/potential-changes

-to-cuba-s-political-system-in-2016-to-lower-government-stability-risks-but-democratic
-reform-unlikely.

10. See *Conceptualización del modelo económico y social cubano de desarrollo socialista*, VI Congreso del Partido Comunista de Cuba [hereafter *Conceptualización*]. http://www.thecpe.org/wp-content/uploads/2016/05/Conceptualizacion-del-modelo-economico-PCC-Cuba-2016.pdf. As one commentator noted: "In addition to approving greater restrictions on the self employed, the Congress decided not only to ban the concentration of private property, but also wealth (riquezas), a word that was not included in the Guidelines of the 2011 Congress. As did his brother Fidel in 1968, now, well into the 21st century, General Castro accused entrepreneurs of having 'unscrupulous attitudes,' and thinking only about 'making more and more.'" Roberto Álvarez Quiñones, "The 7th Congress: A Reality Check," *Diario de Cuba* (April 21, 2016). http://www.diariodecuba.com/cuba/1461241072_21833.html.

11. "But with the economy in crisis and failing to produce employment for vast numbers of Cubans, many regional analysts expect a scenario under which economic reform accelerates even as the one-party political system remains untouched." Howard LaFranchi, "Cuba after Fidel: Economic reform? Sí. Political reform? No." *Christian Science Monitor,* November 28, 2016.

12. See, e.g., http://www.pcc.cu/i_historia.php.

13. See e.g., http://www.pcc.cu/i_historia.php.

14. See e.g., http://www.pcc.cu/i_historia.php.

15. See e.g., http://www.pcc.cu/i_historia.php.

16. See e.g., http://www.pcc.cu/i_historia.php.

17. See e.g., William M. LeoGrande, "The Communist Party of Cuba since the First Congress," *Journal of Latin American Studies* 12 (1980): 397, 399.

18. See e.g., LeoGrande, "The Communist Party of Cuba since the First Congress," 397, 399.

19. See, e.g., José Ramón Ponce Solozabal, "Castro's Tactics of Control in Cuba," *Military Review* 86, no. 4 (July–August 2006): 90–100.

20. See Andrés Suárez, "Leadership, Ideology and Political Party," in Carmelo Mesa-Lago, ed., *Revolutionary Change in Cuba* (Pittsburgh: University of Pittsburgh Press, 1971), 3–21, 9.

21. See, e.g., Jaime Suchlicki, "Challenges to a Post-Castro Cuba," *Harvard International Law Review* 2007. http://ctp.iccas.miami.edu/website_documents/Challenges.pdf.

22. See, e.g., LeoGrande, The Communist Party of Cuba since the First Congress."

23. See Mauricio A. Font, "Perspective on a Changing Cuba," in *Handbook of Contemporary Cuba: Economy, Politics, Civil Society and Globalization,* 9–21, 14 (Boulder: Paradigm Publishers, 2013); Communist Party of Cuba, Global Security. org. http://www.globalsecurity.org/military/world/cuba/communist-party.htm.

24. See, e.g., LeoGrande, The Communist Party of Cuba since the First Congress," 407.

25. See, e.g., Suárez, "Leadership, Ideology and Political Party," 5.

26. See, e.g., Frank O. Mora, "A Comparative Study of Civil-Military Relations in Cuba and China: The Effects of Bingshang," *Armed Forces and Society* 28, no. 2 (2002):185–209; John Hoyt Williams, "Cuba: Havana's Military Machine," *The Atlantic,* August 1988. http://www.theatlantic.com/magazine/archive/1988/08/cuba-havanas -military-machine/305932/.

27. See, e.g., Larry Catá Backer, "The Cuban Communist Party at the Center of Political and Economic Reform: Current Status and Future Reform," *Northwestern Interdisciplinary Law Review* 8 (2015): 71, 86.

28. Discussed below in "What the Future Brings."

29. See, e.g., Backer, *The Cuban Communist Party.*

30. See, e.g., Backer, *The Cuban Communist Party.*

31. See "Cuba's Government," Global Security.org. http://www.globalsecurity.org /military/world/cuba/government.htm.

32. See Constitution of Cuba, Preamble. http://www.constitutionnet.org/files /Cuba%20Constitution.pdf.

33. See http://www.cuba.cu/gobierno/cuba.htm.

34. Estatuto del Partido Comunista de Cuba, art. 15. http://www.pcc.cu/pdf/docu mentos/estatutos/estatutos6c.pdf.

35. Estatuto del Partido Comunista de Cuba, art 17.

36. Estatuto del Partido Comunista de Cuba, art. 18.

37. Estatuto del Partido Comunista de Cuba, art. 19.

38. Estatuto del Partido Comunista de Cuba, art. 45.

39. Estatuto del Partido Comunista de Cuba, art. 46.

40. See, e.g., IV Congreso PCC, Resolución sobre los estatutos del Partido Comunista de Cuba, in *Granma* (October 13, 1991). http://congresopcc.cip.cu/wp-content /uploads/2011/02/IV-congreso_Resoluci%C3%B3n-Reglamento.pdf.

41. Conceptualización del modelo económico y social Cubano de desarrollo socialista: Plan nacional de desarrollo económico y social hasta 2030: Propuesta de visión de la nación, ejes y sectores estratégicos. http://www.thecpe.org/wp-content /uploads/2016/05/Conceptualizacion-del-modelo-economico-PCC-Cuba-2016.pdf. Discussed in Larry Catá Backer, "Embracing a 21st Century Planning Marxism Model: The Cuban Communist Party Confronts Crisis, Challenge and Change in Its 7th Congress," *Cuba in Transition* 26 (2016): 188–208

42. Estatuto del Partido Comunista de Cuba, art. 18–29, 46.

43. Estatuto del Partido Comunista de Cuba, art. 49.

44. Estatuto del Partido Comunista de Cuba, art. 49–50.

45. Estatuto del Partido Comunista de Cuba, art. 52.

46. Estatuto del Partido Comunista de Cuba, art. 53.

47. Objetivos del trabajo del PCC aprobados en la Conferencia Nacional, *Cuba Debate* (February 1, 2012). http://www.cubadebate.cu/especiales/2012/02/01/objetivos-de
-trabajo-del-pcc-aprobados-en-la-conferencia-nacional-pdf/#.Vowe0PHo1PM.

48. Estatuto del Partido Comunista de Cuba, art. 30–42.

49. Estatuto del Partido Comunista de Cuba, art. 54–58.

50. Estatuto del Partido Comunista de Cuba, art. 59.

51. Reglamento de las organizaciones de base del Partido Comunista de Cuba (April 2013). http://www.pcc.cu/pdf/documentos/reglamento/base.pdf.

52. See http://www.pcc.cu/pdf/documentos/reglamento/base.pdf.

53. See http://www.pcc.cu/pdf/documentos/reglamento/base.pdf.

54. See http://www.pcc.cu/pdf/documentos/estatutos/estatutos6c.pdf.

55. Estatuto del Partido Comunista de Cuba, Cap. I.

56. Estatuto del Partido Comunista de Cuba, Cap. I.

57. See, e.g., Ilja A. Luciak, "Party and State in Cuba: Gender Equality in Political Decision Making," *Politics and Gender* 1 (2005): 241, 244.

58. See, e.g., http://www.pcc.cu/eo_buro_politico.php.

59. See, e.g., http://www.pcc.cu/eo_buro_politico.php.

60. See http://www.pcc.cu/eo_secretariado.php.

61. See http://www.pcc.cu/eo_miembros.php.

62. See, e.g., Luciak, "Party and State in Cuba," n. 19.

63. See, e.g., Jorge I. Domínguez, "Introduction: On the Brink of Change: Cuba's Economy and Society at the Start of the 2010s," in *Cuban Economic and Social Development: Policy Reforms and Challenges in the 21st Century*, eds. Jorge I. Domínguez et al. (Cambridge: David Rockefeller Center for Latin American Studies and Harvard University Press, 2012), 1–18

64. Domínguez, "Introduction."

65. Domínguez, "Introduction," 13.

66. In complaining about the unwillingness of young people, blue-collar workers, and intellectuals to join the party, Pham Van Dong, Vietnam's prime minister for 33 years, was quoted as saying "These three types of people don't want to join the party, because they see many members as undeserving." Mark McDonald, "Vietnam's Communist party struggles to attract youths," *San Jose Mercury News*, February 6, 2000, in *Communist Party Statistics, Adherents.com*. http://www.adherents.com/largecom
/communist_parties.html. It also noted "his trend that Dong despairs about—a sort of self-perpetuating stodginess in the party—also worries the current leadership. A party boss in Thai Nguyen recently complained that the average age of party members in his province is now over 55."

67. Pedro Campos, "Cuba's Two Communist Parties," *Havana Times*, January 29, 2015. http://www.havanatimes.org/?p=108972.

68. Campos, "Cuba's Two Communist Parties."

69. Discussed in Section III.

70. Campos, "Cuba's Two Communist Parties."

71. Campos, "Cuba's Two Communist Parties."

72. Thus, in 2012 the PCC National Congress noted: "El Partido Comunista de Cuba, marxista, leninista y martiano, en su condición de Partido único de la nación cubana, tiene como fortaleza y misión principal la de unir a todos los patriotas y sumarlos a los intereses supremos de construir el Socialismo, preservar las conquistas de la Revolución y continuar luchando por nuestros sueños de justicia para Cuba y la humanidad toda" (Objetivos del trabajo del PCC aprobados en la Conferencia Nacional, *Cuba Debate*, February 1, 2012).

73. Discussed more fully in Larry Catá Backer, "Crafting a Theory of Socialist Democracy for China in the 21st Century: Considering Hu Angang's Theory of Collective Presidency in the Context of the Emerging Chinese Constitutional State," *Asian-Pacific Law and Policy Journal* 16 (2014), no. 1.

74. Indeed, Lenin began one of his most influential works by confronting the issue of theoretical ossification in Marxism—in 1901.

See Vladimir I. Lenin, *What Is to Be Done?: Burning Questions of Our Movement* (New York: International Publishers, 1929, 1943) (in the context of freedom of criticism, 12–25).

75. Sheldon B. Liss, *Castro!: Castro's Political and Social Thought* (Boulder: Westview Press, 1994), 4.

76. Lenin, *What Is to Be Done?* 116.

77. See, e.g., H. Michael Erisman, *Cuba's International Relations: The Anatomy of a Nationalistic Foreign Policy* (Boulder: Westview Press, 1985), 8.

78. Larry Catá Backer and Augusto Molina, "Cuba and the Construction of Alternative Global Trade Systems: ALBA and Free Trade in the Americas," *University of Pennsylvania Journal of International Law* 31, no. 3: 679–752 (2010).

79. Jiang Zemin, "Build a Well-off Society in an All-Round Way and Create a New Situation in Building Socialism with Chinese Characteristics," Report to the 16th Party Congress of the CCP (2002). http://english.peopledaily.com.cn/200211/18/eng20021118_106983.shtml.

80. Discussed in Larry Catá Backer and Keren Wang, "The Emerging Structures of Socialist Constitutionalism with Chinese Characteristics: Extra-Judicial Detention (Laojiao and Shuanggui) and the Chinese Constitutional Order," *Pacific Rim Law & Policy Journal* 23, no. 2 (2014): 251–341.

81. See Hu Angang, *Collective Presidency in China* (Beijing: Tsinghua Institute for Contemporary China Studies, 2013).

82. Xi Jinping, "Secure a Decisive Victory in Building a Moderately Prosperous Society in All Respects and Strive for the Great Success of Socialism with Chinese

Characteristics for a New Era: Delivered at the 19th National Congress of the Communist Party of China October 18, 2017." http://www.xinhuanet.com/english/down load/Xi_Jinping's_report_at_19th_CPC_National_Congress.pdf.

83. This historical rootedness in approach is well reflected in a 2015 speech by a leading figure of the PCC, José Ramón Machado Ventura, "The Communist Party of Cuba Will Always Be the Backbone of the Ciuban Nation's Resistance," *Granma*, October 6, 2105. http://en.granma.cu/cuba/2015–10–06/the-communist-party-of-cuba -will-always-be-the-backbone-of-the-cuban-nations-resistance.

84. See, e.g., Eusebio Mujal-León and Joshua W. Busby, *Much Ado About Something?: Regime Change in Cuba, in Cuban Communism, 1959–2003* (Irving Louis Horowitz and Jaime Suchlicki, eds., Transaction Publishers, 2003), 491–512.

85. But not without some questioning very recently, and tentatively. See, e.g., W. T. Whitney, Jr., "Cuba, Culture and the Battle of Ideas," *People's World,* April 25, 2014. http://peoplesworld.org/cuba-culture-and-the-battle-of-ideas/.

86. The PCC has held six party congresses at irregular intervals since 1959. See Partido Comunista de Cuba, Congresos del Partido Comunista de Cuba. http://www .pcc.cu/cong_asamb.php. In contrast, the CCP has held party congresses at regular four-year intervals almost since the founding of the People's Republic in 1949. News of the Communist Party of China, Party Congress Review. http://english.cpc.people .com.cn/206972/207190/index.html.

87. See, e.g., William M. LeoGrande, *The Cuban Communist Party and Electoral Politics: Adaptation, Succession, and Transition* (Miami: Institute for Cuban and Cuban-American Studies, 2002), 3.

88. See I Congreso del Partido Comunista de Cuba. http://www.pcc.cu/cong1 .php.

89. Fidel Castro Ruz, Discurso pronunciado por el Comandante en Jefe Fidel Castro Ruz, primer secretario del Comité Central del Partido Comunista de Cuba y primer ministro del gobierno revolucionario, en el acto en que le fueran entregados los compromisos del pueblo en saludo al Primer Congreso del Partido por parte de los dirigentes de las organizaciones de masas, en el Palacio de la Revolución, el 29 de mayo de 1975. http://congresopcc.cip.cu/wp-content/uploads/2011/02 /DISCURSO-DE-FIDEL-EN-EL-ACTO-EN-QUE-LE-FUERAN-ENTREGADOS -LOS-COMPROMISOS-DEL-PUEBLO-EN-SALUDO-AL-PRIMER-CONGRESO -DEL-PARTIDO.pdf.

90. See, e.g., "The Castro Cult: Fidel's Fanclub," *The Economist*, April 26, 2011. http://www.economist.com/blogs/americasview/2011/04/castro_cult.

91. See Marc Frank, "Cuba's Raúl Castro Promises Succession Has Started," *Reuters,* July 26, 2013. http://www.reuters.com/article/2013/07/26/us-cuba-castro -anniversary-idUSBRE96P0UD20130726.

92. Mujal-León and Busby, *Much Ado About Something?*, 494–95. "Castro's conti-

nuing presence and his constant exhortations to revolutionary struggle and ideology place strict, if formally undefined, limits on how far government and Party functionaries can deviate from the official canon of nationalism, anticapitalism, and anti-Americanism," Mujal-León and Busby, 500.

93. Indeed, this has been a subject of importance in China and an important part of the CCP's ideological line as it moves away from personality as the driver of politics and focuses on the dynamics of collective action through rules. See, e.g., Mo Zhang, "The Socialist Legal System with Chinese Characteristics: China's Discourse for the Rule of Law and a Bitter Experience," *Temple International & Comparative Law Journal* 24, no. 1 (2010). As the discussion at the Eighteenth CCP Party Congress suggests, the efforts to develop socialist rule of law remains very much a work in progress.

94. "Mao Zedong made 'mistakes,' says Chinese President Xi Jinping," Press Trust of India, December 26, 2013. http://www.ndtv.com/article/world/mao-zedong-made-mistakes-says-chinese-president-xi-jinping-463497. See "1980: Deng Xiaoping comments on Mao Zedong Thought," Seventeenth National Congress of the Communist Party of China, October 25, 2007. http://www.china.org.cn/english/congress/229773.htm. It must be remembered that Xi Jinping was himself identified as at the core of the CPC Central Committee in 2016, though the implications are unclear. "CPC Central Committee with Xi as 'Core' Leads China to Centenary Goals," Xinhuanet, Oct. 27, 2016. http://www.xinhuanet.com/english/2016-10/28/c_135785846.htm.

95. Hu Angang, *Collective Presidency in China* (Beijing: Tsinghua Institute for Contemporary China Studies, 2013), criticizing Mao Zedong's personal leadership style after the Great Leap Forward: "As a result, the Standing Committee of the Political Bureau of the Central Committee of the CPC was downgraded to an institution that simply implemented the personal instructions of Mao Zedong. The membership of the Standing Committee underwent frequent changes in a non-institutionalized manner; the collective leadership of the CPC was seriously impaired, and existed in name only." Hu Angang, *Collective Presidency in China*, 26.

96. Discussed in Catá Backer and Wang, "The Emerging Structures of Socialist Constitutionalism."

97. See Damien Cave, "Raúl Castro Says His New 5-Year Term as Cuba's President Will Be His Last," *The New York Times*, February 24, 2013. http://www.nytimes.com/2013/02/25/world/americas/raul-castro-to-step-down-as-cubas-president-in-2018.html?_r=0.

98. http://www.nytimes.com/2013/02/25/world/americas/raul-castro-to-step-down-as-cubas-president-in-2018.html?_r=0.

99. http://www.nytimes.com/2013/02/25/world/americas/raul-castro-to-step-down-as-cubas-president-in-2018.html?_r=0 ("He was a senior Communist Party official for Villa Clara and Holguin provinces, where there were important openings with

foreign investment in tourism," said Mr. López Levy. He added that Mr. Díaz-Canel often worked as an intermediary between the central government and the military, which has taken an expanded role in tourism under Raúl Castro. "In that sense," Mr. López Levy said, "he will face the challenge and opportunity to prepare a smooth landing for a new type of civil-military relationship in the future.").

100. Chris Buckley and Keith Brandisher, "China Moves to Let Xi Stay in Power by Abolishing Term Limit," *The New York Times,* February 25, 2018. https://www.nytimes.com/2018/02/25/world/asia/china-xi-jinping.html.

101. "Evaluó Pleno del Comité Central documentos que serán debatidos en el VII Congreso del Partido," *Granma,* January 15, 2016. http://www.granma.cu/cuba/2016-01-15/evaluo-pleno-del-comite-central-documentos-que-seran-debatidos-en-el-vii-congreso-del-partido-15-01-2016-00-01-11.

102. "7th Cuba Communist Party Congress Summoned for 2016," *Prensa Latina News Service* (July 16, 2015). http://en.escambray.cu/2015/7th-cuba-communist-party-congress-summoned-for-2016/.

103. "Programa de Desarrollo Económico y Social hasta el 2030. Propuesta de Visión de la Nación, Ejes Estratégicos, Objetivos y Sectores Estratégicos," described in http://en.escambray.cu/2015/7th-cuba-communist-party-congress-summoned-for-2016/.

104. Compare Hu Angang, Yilong Yan and Xing Wei, *China 2030* (Springer 2012).

105. "Evaluó Pleno del Comité Central documentos que serán debatidos en el VII Congreso del Partido."

106. See Juan M. Del Aguila, "The Party, the Fourth Congress, and the Process of Counter-Reform," *Cuban Studies* 23 (Jorge Pérez-López, ed. Pittsburgh: University of Pittsburgh Press, 1993), 71–90.

107. See Larry Catá Backer, "Fidel Castro on Deng Xiaoping and Erich Honecker—Understanding the Foundations of Cuban Political and Economic Policy," *Law at the End of the Day* August 19, 2012. http://lcbackerblog.blogspot.com/2012/08/fidel-castro-on-deng-xiaoping-and-erich.html.

108. Discurso pronunciado por el Comandante en Jefe Fidel Castro Ruz, Primer Secretario del Comité Central del Partido Comunista de Cuba y Presidente de los Consejos de Estado y de Ministros, en el acto central conmemorativo del XXX aniversario de la victoria de Playa Girón, efectuado en el teatro "Carlos Marx," el 19 de abril de 1991. http://www.cuba.cu/gobierno/discursos/1991/esp/f190491e.html.

109. Del Aguila, "The Party, the Fourth Congress, and the Process of Counter-Reform," 74–76 ("In short, there were enough signs of internal decay, corruption, and organizational weakness for the leadership to act upon them, and to do so in a manner that would restore discipline, and efficiency, as well as impose political orthodoxy." Del Aguila, 75).

110. Discurso pronunciado por el Comandante en Jefe Fidel Castro Ruz (note 105).

111. See, e.g., Larry Catá Backer, "The Cooperative as Proletarian Corporation: Property Rights Between Corporation, Cooperatives and Globalization in Cuba," *Northwestern Journal of International Law and Business* 33 (2013): 527–618.

112. See discussion in Samuel Farber, "The Future of the Cuban Revolution," *Jacobin* (January 2014). https://www.jacobinmag.com/2014/01/the-cuban-revolution/ ("Cuban social scientist Camila Piñeiro Harnecker, in particular, has discussed the influence of 'statist' elements whom she describes as a group of 'middle-level administrators and state functionaries who fear losing their jobs and the ability to benefit from the state through corruption.' They advocate for the improvement, as opposed to the elimination, of state socialism along these self-interested lines.")

113. Fidel Castro Ruz, "Brother Obama," *Granma,* March 28, 2016. http://en.granma.cu/cuba/2016-03-28/brother-obama.

114. Darío Machado, "The 'Good' Obama," *Granma,* March 30, 2016. http://en.granma.cu/cuba/2016-03-30/the-good-obama ("Meanwhile, it was clear that he does not want to cooperate with Cuba, but rather with that part of our society which offers the best conditions for the strategic interests he represents. . . . He hoped to contribute to the fragmentation of Cuban society in order to recover U.S. hegemony here and in our region.").

115. See William M. LeoGrande, "Cuba's Communists Face Contradiction of Economic Reform vs. Ideology," *World Politics Review,* April 22, 2016. http://www.worldpoliticsreview.com/articles/18571/cuba-s-communists-face-contradiction-of-economic-reform-vs-ideology.

116. "Cuban Officials Call Obama Visit 'a Deep Attack,'" *NewsMax,* April 19, 2016. http://www.newsmax.com/Newsfront/cuban-officials-obama-visit/2016/04/19/id/724742/.

117. See Rafael Rojas, "Cultura e ideología en el poscomunismo Cubano," in *Cuba: sociedad, cultura y política en tiempos de globalización* (Mauricio de Miranda Parrondo, ed. Bogotá: Centro Editorial Javeriano, 2003), 79–94; 81.

118. See "Cuba will not renounce the principles and ideals for which generations of Cubans have fought," *Periódico26.cu,* December 31, 2015. ("Regarding the issue of relations with the United States, President Raúl Castro stressed . . . 'as I explained in my statement in the Council of Ministers on the 18th, during which I also reaffirmed that Cuba should not be asked to abandon its independence cause, or renounce the principles and ideals for which generations of Cubans have fought, for a century and a half.'"). http://www.periodico26.cu/index.php/en/giants/20485-cuba-will-not-renounce-the-principles-and-ideals-for-which-generations-of-cubans-have-fought.

119. Moya-Ocampos, "Potential Changes to Cuba's Political System" (see note 10).

120. See, e.g., Larry Catá Backer, "Democracy Part 31: In a World Premised on

Exogenous Democracy Is a Theory of Endogenous Democracy Possible?" *Law at the End of the Day*, January 17, 2015. http://lcbackerblog.blogspot.com/2015/01/democracy -part-31-in-world-premised-on.html.

121. See, e.g., Larry Catá Backer, "Democracy Part XXVII—The Utility of Voting in the Shadow of the Administrative State," *Law at the End of the Day*, July 27, 2012. http://lcbackerblog.blogspot.com/2012/07/demcracy-part-xxvii-utility-of-voting .html.

122. See Backer and Wang, "The Emerging Structures of Socialist Constitutiona- lism."

123. Ted A. Henken and Armando Chaguaceda, "Between Reforms and Repres- sion, Can Cuba's New Forces of Change Succeed?" *World Politics Review*, May 10, 2016.

124. See Brenden Ford, "China's 'Mass Line' Campaign," *The Diplomat* September 9, 2013 ("The campaign is predicated in the political notion of the 'mass line,' descri- bed as a 'guideline under which Party officials and members are required to prioritize the interests of the people and persist in representing them and working on their behalf.'"). http://thediplomat.com/2013/09/chinas-mass-line-campaign-2/.

125. See, e.g., Hu Angang, *China's Collective Presidency* (Dordrecht: Springer, 2014).

126. Esteban Lazo, president of the Cuban National Assembly, was quoted as follows: "The Cuban National Assembly is determined to work together with its Vietnamese counterpart to enhance the bilateral relations, especially in economy, trade and investment, and at inter-parliamentary organisations, striving to make the legislative ties a crucial factor in the special Viet Nam-Cuba relationship, he stressed." "Vietnam Resolved to Deepen Ties with Cuba: State President," *Viet Nam News*, September 30, 2015. http://vietnamnews.vn/politics-laws/276452/viet-nam -resolved-to-deepen-ties-with-cuba-state-president.html. See also, "Esteban Lazo Receives President of Vietnam," *Granma*, September 29, 2015. http://en.granma.cu /cuba/2015–09–29/esteban-lazo-receives-president-of-vietnam; "Vice Chairwoman of National Assembly Nguyen Thi Kim Ngan has talks with Head of Cuban Par- ty Central Committee's Department of International Relations and Vice President of Cuban Parliament," Vietnamese Embassy in Bangladesh-Vietnamese Diploma- tic Missions, June 12, 2011. http://www.vietnamembassy-bangladesh.org/vnemb.vn /tin_hddn/ns111207154725.

127. Arlin Alberty Loforte and Alberto G. Walon, "Exponen avances y retos de la experiencia de Artemisa y Maybeque," *Granma*, May 28, 2015. http://www.granma .cu/cuba/2015–05–28/exponen-avances-y-retos-de-la-experiencia-de-artemisa-y -mayabeque.

128. José Alejandro Rodríguez, "Cuba: Democratic Reforms Go Deep," *Green Left*, August 28, 2011. https://www.greenleft.org.au/node/48669.

129. Beina Xu, "Governance in India: Corruption," *Council of Foreign Relations Backgrounder*, September 4, 2014. ("But many analysts believe India's sprawling bureaucracy and weak institutions—the police and judiciary were ranked as the second and third most corrupt institutions in India, respectively, after political parties—have thwarted convictions, and arguably increased incentives for bribery.") http://www.cfr.org/corruption-and-bribery/governance-india-corruption/p31823.

130. Xi Jinping, "Secure a Decisive Victory."

131. Campos, *Cuba's Two Communist Parties*.

ANÍBAL PÉREZ-LIÑÁN AND SCOTT MAINWARING

THE PROSPECTS FOR CUBAN DEMOCRACY IN THE POST-TRANSITION ERA

Scholarly debates about the future of Cuba often focus on the possibility (and the timing) of a democratic transition. In this chapter we focus on a different question. Assuming that a transition to competitive politics will—sooner or later—take place, what kind of democracy can we expect to emerge?

We address this question by analyzing the experience of other Latin American countries. By the early twenty-first century, every country in Latin America except Cuba had been a democracy since at least 1978 (Costa Rica, Colombia, and Venezuela) or had experienced a transition to a competitive regime during the third wave of democratization that started in that year (16 countries). But the outcomes of these transitions varied widely. At one pole, countries such as Nicaragua, Paraguay, and Guatemala established competitive regimes that today remain fraught by limited accountability, weak judiciaries, frequent state abuses of power, and weak protection of political rights. At the other end of this spectrum, Chile (after 1990) and Uruguay (after 1985) joined Costa Rica as stable, robust democracies with solid mechanisms of intrastate accountability, effective rule of law, and solid respect for civil and political rights.

An even more dramatic dispersion of regime outcomes has occurred in parts of the world that used to be dominated by single-party systems. In post-Soviet countries, many transitions ultimately failed, resulting in a burgeoning number of competitive authoritarian regimes that sponsor controlled elections. Other transitions, such as those in Poland, the Czech Republic, or—until recently—Hungary, resulted in robust democracies.[1] The wide variation in democratic outcomes after transitions poses a question of great relevance for the future of Cuba: Why have some countries blossomed into stable and robust democracies, while other regimes remain (at best) semidemocratic? These other transitions suggest some lessons for Cuba's post-transition politics.

Our main argument in this chapter is that prior experiences with democracy matter greatly for the post-transition context. Given its limited democratic history, Cuba will confront important challenges to build a vibrant democratic regime after the end of authoritarian rule. Authoritarian regimes prevailed in Cuba during the twentieth century, increasing their power and survival capacity over time. The dictatorship of Gerardo Machado (1925–1933) lasted for eight years. The rule of Fulgencio Batista, counting his days as strongman (1933–1944) and as dictator (1952–1959), accumulated 18 years. As of this writing (March 2018), the revolutionary regime inaugurated in 1959 had survived in power 59 years and counting. Only the brief period of Auténtico rule—a bit short of 7 ½ years between 1944 and 1952—can be considered an early democratic experiment by modern standards.[2]

The comparative context suggests that this limited experience with democracy will be troubling for Cuba. In the first three sections of the chapter we show that Latin American countries with stronger histories of democracy between 1900 and 1977 are more democratic today. The only countries that have attained a very high level of democracy in contemporary Latin America—Chile, Costa Rica, and Uruguay—had the region's strongest democratic legacies from 1900 until 1977. Most countries that had highly authoritarian pasts have transitioned to competitive political regimes, but the level of democracy in these regimes is much lower.

In the last two sections of the chapter we offer an explanation for this phenomenon, and show that regime legacies were partly reproduced over time through political parties and legal institutions. This argument does not imply that institutional conditions are constant or irreversible. Latin American political regimes in many countries underwent a profound transformation in the post-1977 period. Because the notion of "path dependence" implies too much linearity, we instead developed the concept of regime legacies. Our findings indicate that a potential transition to democracy could be success-

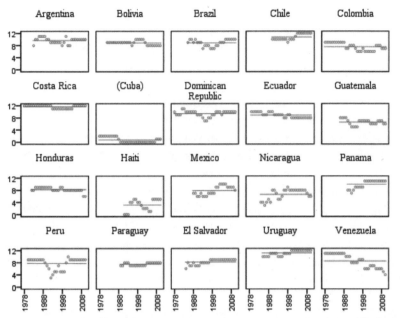

Note: Vertical axis reflects Freedom House scores, starting with the democratic transition. Cuba and Haiti included in the graphic for comparative purposes, but not in the analysis.

Figure 7.1. Freedom House Scores in the Post-Transition Era, 1978–2010.

Note: Vertical axis reflects Freedom House scores, starting with the democratic transition.

Cuda and Haiti included in the graphic for comparative purposes but no in the analysis.

ful in Cuba, yet the country will probably struggle to establish high-quality democracy. If Cuba is able to make a transition, the country's limited democratic experience will present, at least in the early years, a liability for the new regime.

LEVELS OF DEMOCRACY IN CONTEMPORARY LÁTIN AMERICA

The post-1977 wave of democratization profoundly transformed Latin America. For the first time ever, almost all countries in the region have had competitive political regimes for a long time. But the level or quality of democracy (we use the two terms interchangeably) has varied widely. We focus on the most conventional aspects of democratic quality—civil liberties and political rights—to compare levels of democracy achieved in the post-transition era using Freedom House scores. Although not free from problems, Freedom House scores are a conventionally accepted measure of democracy.[3] We also employ alternative measures of democracy to assess past experiences with democratization.

ANÍBAL PÉREZ-LIÑÁN AND SCOTT MAINWARING

Figure 7.1 depicts the evolution of Freedom House scores for Latin American countries between the year of the transition from authoritarian rule (or 1978 for Costa Rica, Colombia, and Venezuela) and 2010.[4] The dots represent the observed Freedom House scores, and horizontal lines indicate mean values for the period. With the exception of Cuba, countries enter the sample in the year when a competitive political regime existed for the first time in the post-1977 period. Because our dependent variable is post-transition levels of democracy, we include Cuba for reference in the figure, but do not include the country in the empirical analysis conducted below. (Haiti is also excluded due to missing data for some important variables.)

In the third wave, Chile, Costa Rica, and Uruguay stand out as the Latin American countries with the highest levels of democracy. They are the only countries in Latin America that have ever registered the highest possible Freedom House score. Nicaragua and Guatemala anchor the other end of the spectrum with much lower mean Freedom House scores.

Figure 7.2 plots the average Freedom House score (represented by the horizontal lines in figure 7.1) against the average Polity scores prior to the third wave of democratization, in 1900–1977 (figure 7.2a) and 1900–1944 (figure 7.2b). The Polity index ranges from –10, indicating an extreme autocracy, to 10, indicating a high-level democracy.[5] The plots suggest an intriguing relationship, depicted by the upward trend, between early democratic experiences and the average level of democracy after the most recent democratic transitions initiated in 1978. Average Freedom House scores for 1978–2010 correlate at .69 (p < .01) with Polity scores for 1900–1977 and at .64 (p < .01) with earlier Polity scores for 1900–1944.

The vertical line in each panel roughly indicates the expected location of Cuba in the Freedom House scale after a hypothetical post-1978 transition, given its experience during the first and second waves of democratization. The expected value in figure 7.2a, based on the first wave of democratization (1900–44), is optimistic because Polity gives Cuba a lenient score (+3) until 1927. The lower predicted value in figure 7.2b illustrates how the accumulated experience of authoritarian rule after 1952 further undermines the chances for high-quality democracy in the contemporary era.

Figure 7.2 does not provide conclusive evidence of long-term regime legacies for two reasons. First, average Freedom House scores mask within-country variation in levels of democracy during the post-1977 period. A few countries (Peru, Venezuela, and Nicaragua) have exhibited pronounced shifts over time. Second and most important, apparent regime legacies may result from long-term forces driving latent continuities at the national level. It is possible that some stable conditions—enduring social cleavages or cul-

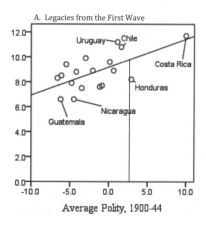
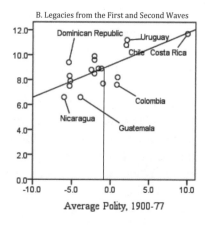

A. Legacies from the First Wave

B. Legacies from the First and Second Waves

Average Polity, 1900-44

Average Polity, 1900-77

Figure 7.2. Regime Legacies on the Third Wave of Democracy (Freedom House Scores).

tural traits—have affected the level of democratization in a consistent manner over the past century. Likewise, it is possible that a consistently higher level of development, rather than legacies of the political regime, explains why some countries have on average been more democratic than others both since 1977 and from 1900 to 1977. Our focus on Latin America rules out some likely candidates for this type of explanation (colonial legacies, religious worldviews) that show little variance in this region. We address this problem more systematically in the next section.

EXPLAINING POST-TRANSITION LEVELS OF DEMOCRACY

To verify the legacy of past political regimes on the current level of democracy in Latin America, we employ a time-series cross-section model. Each country in a given year is one observation. Because we focus on the third wave of democratization, Costa Rica, Colombia, and Venezuela enter the dataset in 1978 even though they inaugurated competitive political regimes well before that (1949, 1958, and 1959, respectively).

Figure 7.1 indicates that although some countries have shown considerable fluctuations in democratic quality, differences among countries are more important to understand the level of democracy in the region than change over time within countries. Because democracy scores are quite stable for many countries, entrenched country characteristics may shape the overall level of democracy in the long run.

Figure 7.1 raises two related questions: Why do some countries enjoy high levels of democracy on average, while others are less democratic? And why

ANÍBAL PÉREZ-LIÑÁN AND SCOTT MAINWARING

do countries rise above or fall below those historical averages during particular periods? While the latter question can be answered by looking at time-varying explanatory factors (for instance, a period of economic decline may trigger an erosion in the level of democracy), the former calls for the analysis of stable country characteristics—including historical legacies—that help explain variation across countries.

Invoking country characteristics as causal factors does not mean that some countries are culturally predetermined to be more or less democratic. Rather, we seek to identify stable conditions that affect the level of democracy in the long run. This approach precludes the use of a cross-sectional analysis or a standard fixed-effects model. We therefore estimate the impact of our independent variables using a "hybrid" fixed-effects estimator developed by Paul D. Allison.[6] To estimate this model, we perform two tasks. First, we compute the deviation of all time-varying predictors from their country averages (i.e., we group-center or de-mean the variables). Second, we estimate a random-effects model in which the centered variables are included in the equation along with their country-level averages and other time-invariant predictors.[7]

Our analysis includes a measure of regime legacies (computed according to three alternative sources) and several additional predictors, including rarely-changing and time-varying covariates. Our quantitative analysis extends to 2004.

Regime Legacies

To capture regime legacies, we created a variable for the average level of democracy for each country between 1900 and 1977, as depicted in figure 7.2. Although widely used in political science, Polity scores in figure 7.2 are of questionable validity for many Latin American countries for the first decades of the twentieth century. For example, against the comparative historiography, Polity scores suggest that Honduras and Cuba were more democratic than Chile and Uruguay in the first half of the century, and Costa Rica has an untainted score of 10 throughout the twentieth century despite a military dictatorship from 1917 to 1919 and civil war in 1948.[8] Given these shortcomings, we also rely on two additional indicators of democratic legacies.[9]

Mainwaring, Brinks, and Pérez-Liñán coded all Latin American countries as democratic, semidemocratic, or authoritarian.[10] We recoded their scale as Democracy=1, Semidemocracy=0.5, and Authoritarian=0, so that the average value for each historical period could be roughly interpreted as the proportion of years that a country was democratic. Smith classified Latin

American regimes into four categories: democratic, semidemocratic, oligarchic, and authoritarian.[11] We again gave democracies a score of 1, dictatorships a score of 0, and semidemocracies or oligarchic regimes as score of 0.5.

Other Predictors

We include several independent variables to capture the impact of economic conditions: the natural logarithm of per capita GDP,[12] the share of the
economically active population in manufacturing,[13] the proportion of gross
national income represented by exports of fuel and minerals,[14] per-capita income growth (as a proportion of GDP), and inflation.[15] The last two variables
are measured as ten-year running averages beginning with the transition to
the new regime.

To assess political conditions, we use a dummy variable for multiparty
systems (an effective number of parties of 3 or greater) to test if multipar-
tism influences the level of democracy, the average Freedom House score of
a country's immediate neighbors during the previous year,[16] and ethnolinguistic fractionalization—a time-invariant index that approaches a value of
zero when the country is highly homogenous and a value of one when the
country is highly fractionalized.[17] In addition, because conditions varied over
time, we include year fixed-effects in our models.

STATISTICAL EVIDENCE OF REGIME LEGACIES

Table 7.1 presents the analysis of statistical models predicting post-transition
levels of democracy. The upper panel presents the estimates of fixed effects
based on the centered, time-varying predictors, while the lower panel presents the estimates for stable country-level variables. Country averages for
time-varying covariates were included for proper specification, but coefficients are not reported to save space.

Model 1.1 presents conventional fixed-effects estimates for reference. Two
independent variables (democracy from 1900 to 1977, and ethnic fractionalization) are time-invariant and thus drop from the conventional fixed-effects
estimation. Models 1.2 to 1.4 present the coefficients for the hybrid estimator
using three different measures of regime legacies. Even after controlling for a
large number of alternative explanations, an early history of democracy has
a powerful impact on levels of democracy among contemporary competitive
regimes.

In model 1.2, an increase of 1 point in the 21-point Polity scale for 1900–77
is associated with an increase of 0.21 points in the 13-point Freedom House
scale for the post-1977 period. In model 1.3, a unit increase in the Mainwar-

ANÍBAL PÉREZ-LIÑÁN AND SCOTT MAINWARING

TABLE 7.1. Test of Regime Legacies (Dependent Variable is FH Scores)

	1.1. Fixed-effects		1.2. polity		1.3. Mainwaring		1.4. Smith	
	coef.	s.e.	Coef.	s.e.	Coef.	s.e.	Coef.	s.e.
Fixed effects estimates:								
Per capita GDP, ln	2.05**	0.68	2.02**	0.68	2.01**	0.68	2.02**	0.68
Labor force in industry	0.08**	0.02	0.08**	0.02	0.08**	0.02	0.08**	0.02
Fuel and mineral exports	−4.18*	2.04	−4.16*	2.04	−4.15*	2.04	−4.17*	2.04
Growth, 10 years	17.51**	5.03	17.49**	5.03	17.44**	5.03	17.43**	5.03
Inflation, 10 years	−0.02	0.17	−0.02	0.17	−0.02	0.17	−0.02	0.17
Multipartism	−0.10	0.18	−0.11	0.17	−0.11	0.17	−0.11	0.17
Democracy neighbors	−0.15**	0.06	−0.15**	0.06	−0.15**	0.06	−0.15**	0.06
Country-level variables:								
Ethnic fractionalization			−2.70	1.45	−2.26	1.36	−3.02	1.70
Democracy (1900–1977)			0.21**	0.05	4.40**	1.01	4.57**	1.54
Intercept	−7.22	5.12	6.09*	2.89	6.06*	2.68	6.86*	3.42
Std. deviation of intercept			0.70*	0.19	0.65*	0.18	0.84*	0.22
N	390		390		390		390	
R² (within)	0.353							

Notes: Entries are coefficients for fixed-effects model in 1.1 and coefficients for Allison's hybrid estimator in models 1.2–1.4. Entries in the top panel represent fixed-effects (within) coefficients and entries in the bottom panel represent cross-sectional (between) coefficients. Country-level averages for the time-varying covariates and year dummies were omitted to save space.
* Significant at $p < .05$ ** $p < .01$

Source: "Regime Legacies and Levels of Democracy: Evidence from Latin America." *Comparative Politics* 45 (July 2013), 386.

ing et al. classification for 1900–77 (that is, a change in conditions from a country that was always authoritarian between 1900 and 1977 to one that was always democratic) predicts a substantial increase of 4.4 points on the inverted Freedom House scale for contemporary competitive regimes. In model 1.4, using Smith's classification of political regimes, a country that was consistently democratic from 1900 to 1977 would have a predicted Freedom House score a very sizeably 4.6 points higher for the post-1977 period than a country that was consistently authoritarian. The impact of past democracy on the current level of democracy is consistent with the result obtained by Bratton and van de Walle for 47 African countries; a past history of more elections and more electoral participation favored a higher level of democracy in Africa in 1994.[18]

Other variables have effects in the expected direction: a higher level of development has not increased the likelihood of transitions,[19] but an increase in the level of development has favored a higher level of democracy among competitive regimes in the post-1977 period. Increases in the rate of economic growth and in the share of the labor force in manufacturing boost democracy, while an increase in reliance on fuel and mineral exports weakens it.[20] The only variable that presents an unexpected effect is the influence of increases in the level of democracy among neighbors, which counterintuitively are associated with a decrease in the level of democracy in the given country. Although democratic neighbors help promote transitions to democracy, countries follow independent and often contradictory trajectories after their transitions take place.

The estimates in table 7.1 suggest that regime legacies are one of the main factors that explain the post-1978 level of democracy. An authoritarian past did not prevent Latin American countries from developing competitive political regimes in the post-1977 period, but it did tend to limit the quality of democracy. Countries with a past democratic heritage had a significant advantage in building a high-quality democracy in contemporary Latin America. This is true even when, such as in Chile (1973–1990) and Uruguay (1973–1985), military dictatorships attempted to radically stamp out the democratic past.

WHY PAST REGIMES MATTER FOR THE FUTURE

In short, a democratic past predicts a high post-transition level of democracy in the post-1977 period; this finding augurs poorly for Cuba. The statistical results, however, do not explain the causal mechanism that lies behind the impact of regime heritage on the contemporary level of democracy. Our finding about the enduring impact of early democratization has some similarities to arguments about path dependence in social science.[21] Levi defines path dependence as meaning that "once a country or region has started down a track, the costs of reversal are very high." Events in one historical moment greatly alter the distribution of possible and probable outcomes into the long-term future.[22]

Our statistical results show a similar story: the early history of political regimes affects the current level of democracy. Two countries similar on all other independent variables would have different predicted levels of democracy today if one had a more democratic past than the other. However, a claim about path dependence does not indicate how regime legacies are reproduced over time.

In Latin America, regime change in every country except Colombia, Cos-

ANÍBAL PÉREZ-LIÑÁN AND SCOTT MAINWARING

ta Rica, and Cuba since the 1970s undermines strong claims about path dependence. Authoritarian disruptions in countries with long democratic traditions, such as the ones that occurred in Chile (1973–1990) and Uruguay (1973–1984), involved sudden profound ruptures rather than a linear history. Likewise, in the post-1977 period, several countries (Bolivia, the Dominican Republic, El Salvador, Guatemala, Mexico, Nicaragua, and Paraguay) shifted from almost uninterrupted histories of authoritarian rule to somewhat durable competitive regimes (Nicaragua, until the authoritarian turn in the 2010s). The latter pattern of change is of crucial importance for the Cuban case. Path dependence cannot explain so many radical departures from the past.

Moreover, the concept of path dependence is too vague to explain the historical continuities documented by our statistical analysis. Any explanation of regime legacies can be logically sound and historically credible only if we identify an intertemporal bridging mechanism that accounts for how legacies of a distant era can carry influence into the present, even overcoming a long interlude of authoritarian rule.

In some cases, the intertemporal bridging mechanism is given by the survival of individual leaders. Patricio Aylwin and Julio María Sanguinetti were up-and-coming party leaders in Chile and Uruguay before military coups imposed repressive dictatorships in 1973, and they returned as inaugural presidents after the transition took place in each country.[23] But the survival of individuals cannot fully explain the long-lasting legacies of the first wave of democratization depicted in figure 7.2. Lengthy dictatorships should have depleted the pool of democratic leaders, not only because authoritarian rulers repressed them but also because aging individuals retired from politics or died over time.[24]

We hypothesize that *an early history of democracy favored the building of formal institutions, such as political parties and the legal system, that are favorable to a higher level of democracy in the contemporary period.* In established democratic regimes, parties and heads of government are usually recruited through parties. They usually have a strong interest in restoring or expanding democracy. Parties socialize their members in particular values, policy preferences, and tactics that are preserved across generations with a certain probability. Yet parties are not static—ideas may evolve over time and organizations may change.[25]

The justice system also operates as an institutional carrier of regime legacies. Throughout the twentieth century, presidents were unlikely to reshuffle supreme courts in countries with strong democratic traditions, such as Chile, Costa Rica, and Uruguay.[26] Today, according to the World Bank Governance

Indicators, these three countries have by far the best perceptions for rule of law and control of corruption in the region. Conversely, justice systems that historically were bulwarks of authoritarian regimes have been obstacles to creating high-level democracies in the third wave. Given a past of either unstable and shackled judiciaries or judiciaries appointed under authoritarian rule, it has been difficult to build a justice system that helps generate strong democratic rule of law.

EVIDENCE OF INSTITUTIONAL MECHANISMS

In this section we test the impact of institutional mechanisms by adding new indicators of democratic party and court institutionalization to the empirical models of regime legacies presented in table 7.1. If our hypothesis is correct and regime legacies are preserved by institutional carriers, the new predictors should be statistically significant, and their inclusion should reduce the coefficients for measures of past democracy.

Our empirical test of this proposition focuses on two institutions: political parties and the legal system. If our understanding of regime legacies is correct, well-established parties will favor a higher level of democracy only if these parties functioned under democratic regimes. A party that was institutionalized under democracy should be an asset for a higher level of democracy. In contrast, an institutionalized governing party that sustained an authoritarian regime—such as the PRI (Partido Revolucionario Institucional) in Mexico or the Colorados in Paraguay–will not. Cuban leaders socialized into politics by the Communist Party of Cuba (PCC) are more likely to be an obstacle than an asset for democracy after a potential transition takes place.

To capture the *institutionalization of democratic parties* during the twentieth century, we created an indicator that reflects the democratic experience of the parties in congress for each country after 1977, weighted by their seat share. We count the number of years each party existed under a democratic or semidemocratic regime (according to the Mainwaring et al. classification) since 1900. Because age is a nonlinear indicator of party institutionalization, we take the square root of age before weighting this value by the share of seats controlled by the party in congress. The index is therefore a weighted average of the (square root of the democratic) age of parties in congress.[27]

We constructed a similar index to assess *democratic institutionalization in the judiciary* by focusing on each country's supreme court. This index captures the length of the tenure for all sitting justices in the court appointed by democratic governments. As with the party index, we take the square root of the number of years before calculating the average tenure for the whole

ANÍBAL PÉREZ-LIÑÁN AND SCOTT MAINWARING

court. Judges appointed by authoritarian governments are not included in the calculation.[28]

In order to disentangle the effects of institutional legacies from the potential consequences of national political culture, we also incorporate country-level measures of elite and mass support for democracy in the analysis. We use information from similar questionnaire items employed by the Survey of Latin American Parliamentary Elites (PELA, its Spanish acronym) and by national public opinion surveys conducted by Latinobarómetro.[29] Both projects asked respondents whether they agreed with the statement, "Democracy is preferable to any other form of government" (as opposed to a statement indicating conditional support for authoritarian rule). Our indicator of *elite support for democracy* is the average percentage of legislators who agreed with the statement in each country between 1995 and 2005. The indicator of *mass attitudes* is the average percentage of respondents who agreed with the statement in each country between 1995 and 2006. We treated national averages for both variables as country-level measures of stable cultural traits.

Table 7.2 includes these new covariates designed to capture specific causal mechanisms in addition to the general measure of regime legacies for 1900–1977. Model 2.1 reports the results of a conventional fixed effects model for reference, and thus omits the country-level variables. Models 2.2 through 2.4 present the result of Allison's hybrid estimator using the three different measures of democracy for 1900–1977.

The indicators of democratic party and court institutionalization present positive and significant effects on current levels of democracy in all models. By contrast, the proxies for mass and elite political culture fail to achieve conventional levels of significance. As expected, coefficients for the measure of regime legacies decline by 12 percent in model 2.2 (compared to model 1.2), by 29 percent in model 2.3 (compared to model 1.3), and by 22 percent in model 2.4 (compared to 1.4). Moreover, the coefficient for the previous history of democracy is not significant in the last two models. The reduction in the size of the effects suggests that the indicators of democratic institutionalization capture part of the process that creates regime legacies. The coefficient remains positive and significant in model 2.2, so other unspecified mechanisms may operate as well. After we control for the new variables, the coefficients for fuel and mineral exports and the size of the industrial labor force lose statistical significance, qualifying some of the results in table 7.1.

IMPLICATIONS FOR THE CUBAN CASE

The analysis of Latin American countries that underwent democratic transitions after 1977 offers lessons for the future of Cuba. Countries with a strong past of competitive politics built higher-quality democracies after the transition, while countries with little prior experience during the twentieth century generally established weaker democracies with lower levels of civil liberties and political rights.

This finding suggests that Cuban democrats will confront important challenges after the end of the current regime. They will face the complex task of building a democratic regime on weak historical foundations: the distant memory of the early republican years—tainted by U.S. intervention—and the short democratic experience of 1944–1952—tainted by memories of corruption and violence. No country in Latin America that has a history as authoritarian as Cuba's has succeeded in building a high-quality democracy. The closest cases in this respect are El Salvador and Mexico, both of which had highly authoritarian pasts and have built democracies since 1994 and 2000, respectively. However, chronic infringements of civil liberties and political rights in many parts of both countries have limited the quality of democracy, as figure 7.1 shows. A similar result obtains in the postcommunist countries; only countries that had some history of democracy before communism (such as the Baltic republics, and Czechoslovakia) managed to construct high-quality democracies after 1989.

Holding free and fair elections is not an easy task, but it can be accomplished in a short time. In contrast, building a high-quality democracy requires institutions that protect citizen rights and opposition rights. This process takes time, and it involves constant pushback from entrenched actors.

Our analysis does not suggest that the task of democratization in Cuba will be impossible or doomed to failure. It shows, however, that early stages of democratization could be disappointing for a society that will probably have high expectations after generations of authoritarian rule. The absence of institutional structures, such as political parties and courts, with a stronger democratic tradition will create a more difficult setting for the new regime.

Democratic parties develop interests, norms, and preferences that typically favor some continuity in regime legacies. They have a reservoir of inherited interests, normative principles, policy preferences, and operational rules—an institutional "common sense"—that provides a historical underpinning to their strategic considerations. Likewise, the probability that courts will sustain higher levels of democracy is greater if justices were appointed during democratic periods and trained in the protection of individual rights.[30] Dictatorships in Chile (1973–1990) and Uruguay (1973–1984) crushed the capacity of the court system to stand up for democracy. Even so, new democratic regimes after 1990 and 1985, respectively, drew on the tradition of a solid court system. In part because many judges from the earlier democratic

ANÍBAL PÉREZ-LIÑÁN AND SCOTT MAINWARING

TABLE 7.2. Test of Institutional Mechanisms (Dependent Variable Is FH Scores)

	2.1. Fixed-effects		2.2. Polity		2.3. Mainwaring		2.4. Smith	
	coef.	s.e.	coef.	s.e.	coef.	s.e.	coef.	s.e.
Fixed-effects estimates:								
Party institutionalization	**0.39****	**0.09**	**0.39****	**0.09**	**0.39****	**0.09**	**0.39****	**0.09**
Court institutionalization	**0.44****	**0.10**	**0.44****	**0.10**	**0.44****	**0.10**	**0.44****	**0.10**
Per capita GDP, ln	1.31*	0.64	1.30*	0.64	1.31*	0.64	1.31*	0.64
Labor force in industry	0.03	0.02	0.03	0.02	0.03	0.02	0.03	0.02
Fuel and mineral exports	−2.25	1.93	−2.25	1.93	−2.26	1.93	−2.26	1.93
Growth, 10 years	23.72**	4.73	23.67**	4.73	23.66**	4.73	23.64**	4.73
Inflation, 10 years	−0.00	0.16	V0.00	0.16	−0.00	0.16	−0.00	0.16
Multipartism	0.14	0.16	0.13	0.16	0.13	0.16	0.13	0.16
Democracy neighbors	−0.17**	0.05	−0.17**	0.05	−0.17**	0.05	−0.17**	0.05
Country-level variables:								
Ethnic fractionalization			−2.16	1.37	−1.99	1.67	−2.37	1.85
Mass support for democracy			0.05	0.03	0.04	0.04	0.06	0.03
Elite support for democracy			−0.10	0.16	0.02	0.16	0.03	0.17
Democracy (1900–1977)			0.18*	0.09	3.14	2.57	3.55	3.54
Intercept	−2.41	4.80	12.61	10.02	5.31	10.43	5.60	11.70
Std. deviation of intercept			0.63*	0.24	0.78*	0.29	0.82*	0.31
N	390	390	390	390				
R² (within)	0.452							

Notes: Entries are coefficients for fixed-effects model in 2.1 and coefficients for Allison's hybrid estimator in models 2.2–2.4 (standard errors on the right). Dependent variable is Freedom House Scores. Country-level averages for the time-varying covariates and year dummies were omitted to save space.

* Significant at p < .05 ** p < .01

Source: "Regime Legacies and Levels of Democracy: Evidence from Latin America." *Comparative Politics* 45 (July 2013), 39.

regimes remained in the court system, the current democratic regimes in both countries relatively quickly rebuilt a judicial system that could sustain a democratic rule of law. For both reasons, the cumulative experience of past generations affects the level of democracy in contemporary political regimes. The level of Latin American democracies after 1977 has offered a prime example of this causal mechanism.

Our argument does not mean that historical legacies are irreversible or inescapable. A transition in Cuba would have the negative weight of a deeply authoritarian past. However, the wealth and the (mostly) democratic credentials of the large emigrant population residing in the United States, much of which retains important ties to the island, could partially offset this burden from the past.

Notwithstanding some important resemblances between path dependence and regime legacy arguments, we distinguish between the two. Although the existing literature does not agree on how broadly or narrowly it defines path dependence, path dependence generally means that switching courses is costly and relatively unlikely. The concept implies greater stability than is the case with Latin American political regimes. The stunning and unpredicted transformations of many political regimes in Latin America are inconsistent with the idea of path dependence as advocated by Pierson, Levi, and North [see the full references in notes 22 and 23].[31]

The history of political regimes in Latin America is inconsistent with path dependent or deterministic arguments. A regime legacies argument places less emphasis on the improbability of profound shifts, and greater emphasis on the probability of *recovering* an early democratic trajectory. In post-1977 Latin America, regime legacies have significantly affected the level of democracy, but many countries have established and preserved competitive political regimes despite an authoritarian past. Countries with less pre-1978 democratic experience than Cuba, such as El Salvador and Paraguay, have established durable competitive regimes in recent decades. Building democratic institutions remains the task ahead.

NOTES

This chapter is based on our article, Aníbal Pérez-Liñán and Scott Mainwaring, "Regime Legacies and Levels of Democracy: Evidence from Latin America." *Comparative Politics* 45 (July 2013): 379–97. Parts of it were originally published in this article and *Comparative Politics* and are reprinted with the permission of *Comparative Politics*.

1. Keith Darden and Anna Grzymala-Busse, "The Great Divide: Literacy, Nationa-

lism, and the Communist Collapse," *World Politics*, 59 (October 2006): 83–115; Larry J. Diamond, "Thinking about Hybrid Regimes," *The Journal of Democracy* 13 (April 2002): 21–35; David L. Epstein, Robert Bates, Jack Goldstone, Ida Kristensen, and Sharyn O'Halloran, "Democratic Transitions," *American Journal of Political Science* 50 (July 2006): 551–69; Jeffrey Kopstein and David Reilly, "Geographic Diffusion and the Transformation of the Postcommunist World," *World Politics* 53 (October 2000): 1–37; Steven Levitsky and Lucan A. Way, *Competitive Authoritarianism: Hybrid Regimes After the Cold War* (Cambridge: Cambridge University Press, 2010); Kelly McMann, *Economic Autonomy and Democracy: Hybrid Regimes in Russia and Kyrgyzstan* (Cambridge: Cambridge University Press, 2006); Marina Ottaway, *Democracy Challenged: The Rise of Semi-Authoritarianism* (Washington, DC: The Carnegie Endowment for International Peace, 2003).

2. Charles D. Ameringer, *The Cuban Democratic Experience: The Auténtico Years, 1944–1952* (Gainesville: University Press of Florida, 2000).

3. Every year since 1972, Freedom House has ranked countries on two scales measuring civil liberties and political rights (www.freedomhouse.org). Both scales range from 1 to 7, with 1 being the most democratic outcome.

4. We created an aggregate score of democracy by adding the measures of civil liberties and political rights, and inverted the scale so that 0 indicates a fully authoritarian situation and 12 indicates the highest level of democracy.

5. Monty G. Marshall and Keith Jaggers, *Polity IV Project: Political Regime Characteristics and Transitions, 1800–2010* (cited December 2011). http://www.systemic peace.org/polity/polity4.htm.

6. Paul D. Allison, *Fixed Effects Regression Methods for Longitudinal Data Using SAS* (Cary: SAS Publishing, 2005); Paul D. Allison, *Fixed Effects Regression Models* (Quantitative Application in the Social Sciences, no. 160. Los Angeles: SAGE, 2009), pp. 23–26.

7. An alternative to estimate the effect of country-level covariates is the fixed-effects vector decomposition estimator. Estimates for our models using this technique generated equivalent results.

8. Kirk Bowman, Fabrice Lehoucq, and James Mahoney, "Measuring Political Democracy: Case Expertise, Data Adequacy, and Central America," *Comparative Political Studies* 38 (October 2005): 939–70.

9. Marshall and Jaggers, *Polity IV Project*; Scott Mainwaring, Daniel Brinks, and Aníbal Pérez-Liñán, "Classifying Political Regimes in Latin America, 1945–2004," in Gerardo Munck, ed., *Regimes and Democracy in Latin America: Theories and Methods* (Oxford: Oxford University Press, 2007), pp. 121–60; Peter H. Smith, *Democracy in Latin America: Political Change in Comparative Perspective* (Oxford: Oxford University Press, 2005).

10. Mainwaring et al. classify Latin American countries in 1945–2007 based on whether (1) the president and congress are elected in free and fair elections; (2) the franchise is inclusive; (3) civil liberties are respected; and (4) elected officials actually control the government. If all four conditions are present, the country is coded as democratic. If one condition is fully absent, the country is coded as authoritarian. If any condition presents a "partial violation," the country is treated as semi-democratic. We extended the scale back to 1900.

11. Smith coded as democracies cases in which elections were free and fair, semi-democracies cases in which elections were free but not fair, oligarchic regimes cases in which elections were fair but not free (due to exclusions for candidates or voters), and authoritarian regimes cases in which elections (if existed) were neither free nor fair.

12. Ottaway, *Democracy Challenged*, 161–89; Adam Przeworski, Michael E. Alvarez, José Antonio Cheibub, and Fernando Limongi, *Democracy and Development: Political Institutions and Well-Being in the World, 1950–1990* (Cambridge: Cambridge University Press, 2000).

13. Rueschemeyer, Dietrich, Evelyn Huber Stephens, and John D. Stephens, *Capitalist Development and Democracy* (Chicago: University of Chicago Press, 1992).

14. Michael L. Ross, "Does Oil Hinder Democracy?" *World Politics* 53 (April 2001): 325–61; but see Stephen Haber and Victor Menaldo, "Do Natural Resources Fuel Authoritarianism? A Reappraisal of the Resource Curse," *American Political Science Review* 105 (February 2011): 1–26.

15. To avoid undue influence of extreme values, we took the natural logarithm of annual changes in the consumer price index (CPI), computing $i = \ln(1+CPI/100)$ for years of inflation and $i = -1*\ln(1+|CPI/100|)$ for years of deflation.

16. Daniel Brinks and Michael Coppedge, "Diffusion Is No Illusion: Neighbor Emulation in the Third Wave of Democracy," *Comparative Political Studies* 39 (May 2006): 463–89; Kristian Skrede Gleditsch, *All International Politics is Local: The Diffusion of Conflict, Integration, and Democratization* (Ann Arbor: University of Michigan Press, 2002); Levitsky and Way, *Competitive Authoritarianism*; Kopstein and Reilly, "Geographic Diffusion and the Transformation of the Postcommunist World."

17. The index is constructed as $1 - \Sigma p^2$, where p is the proportion of the population comprised by each group. Anthony Annett, "Social Fractionalization, Political Instability and the Size of Government," *IMF Staff Papers* 48, no. 3 (2001): 561–92; James D. Fearon and David D. Laitin, "Ethnicity, Insurgency and Civil War," *American Political Science Review* 97 (February 2003): 75–90.

18. Michael Bratton and Nicolas van de Walle, *Democratic Experiments in Africa: Regime Transitions in Comparative Perspective* (Cambridge: Cambridge University Press, 1997), 223–25.

19. Scott Mainwaring and Aníbal Pérez-Liñán, *Democracies and Dictatorships in Latin America: Emergence, Survival, and Fall* (New York: Cambridge University Press, 2013).

20. We also ran model 1.2, including a series on income inequality (N declined to 371). The coefficient for regime legacies remained large and significant but the fixed-effects coefficient for income inequality was not significant.

21. Ruth Berins Collier and David Collier, *Shaping the Political Arena: Critical Junctures, the Labor Movement, and Regime Dynamics in Latin America* (Princeton: Princeton University Press, 1991); James Mahoney, "Path Dependence in Historical Sociology," *Theory and Society* 29 (August 2000): 507–48; Douglass C. North, *Institutions, Institutional Change and Economic Performance* (Cambridge: Cambridge University Press, 1990), 92–100; Paul Pierson, *Politics in Time: History, Institutions, and Social Analysis* (Princeton: Princeton University Press, 2004), 17–78; Kathleen Thelen, "Historical Institutionalism in Comparative Politics," *Annual Review of Political Science* 2 (1999): 369–404.

22. Margaret Levi, "A Model, a Map, and a Method: Rational Choice in Comparative Politics," in Mark I. Lichbach and Alan S. Zuckerman, eds., *Comparative Politics: Rationality, Culture, and Structure* (Cambridge: Cambridge University Press, 1997), 28. See also Pierson, *Politics in Time*, 20–22.

23. J. Samuel Valenzuela, "Transición por Redemocratización: El Frente Nacional Colombiano en una Reflexión Teórica y Comparativa," *Kellogg Institute Working Paper* #380 (November 2011). http://kellogg.nd.edu/publications/workingpapers/index.shtml

24. Stylized representations of path dependence based on the Polya urn ignore generational replacement, because balls are never removed from the urn. Brian Arthur, *Increasing Returns and Path Dependence in the Economy* (Ann Arbor: University of Michigan Press, 1994); Scott E. Page, "Path Dependence," *Quarterly Journal of Political Science* 1 (January 2006): 87–115.

25. James Mahoney and Kathleen Thelen, "A Theory of Gradual Institutional Change," in James Mahoney and Kathleen Thelen, *Explaining Institutional Change: Ambiguity, Agency, and Power* (Cambridge: Cambridge University Press, 2010), 1–37; Wolfgang Streeck and Kathleen Ann Thelen, eds., *Beyond Continuity: Institutional Change in Advanced Political Economies* (Oxford: Oxford University Press, 2005), 22–23.

26. Aníbal Pérez-Liñán and Andrea Castagnola, "Presidential Control of High Courts in Latin America: A Long-Term View (1904–2006)," *Journal of Politics in Latin America* 1, no. 2 (2009): 87–114.

27. $DPI_{it} = \Sigma(a_{jt}^{\frac{1}{2}})s_{jt}$ where *DPI* is the democratic party institutionalization score; *s* is the share of seats of party *j* in the lower house, and *a* is the number of years the party existed under a competitive regime between the time of its founding (or 1900) and year t.

28. $DCI_{it} = \Sigma(d_{jt}^{\frac{1}{2}})/n_t$ where DCI is the score for country i; n_t is the number of judges sitting in the Supreme Court in year t, and d_{jt} is the number of years that a justice appointed by a competitive regime has been in office. If a justice j was appointed by an authoritarian regime, the duration term is treated as zero.

29. On PELA, see Fátima García Díez and Araceli Mateos Díaz, "El Proyecto Elites Parlamentarias Latinoamericanas: Continuidades y Cambios (1994–2005)," in Manuel Alcántara, ed., *Políticos y política en América Latina* (Madrid: Siglo XXI, 2006), 3–29. http://americo.usal.es/oir/Elites/index.htm. On Latinobarómetro, see *Informe Latinobarómetro 2006* (Santiago: Latinobarómetro Corporation, 2006), 72. http://www.latinobarometro.org/latino/LATContenidos.jsp.

30. See J. Samuel Valenzuela, "Los Derechos humanos y la redemocratización en Chile," in Manuel Alcántara Sáez and Leticia M. Rodríguez, eds., *Chile: Política y modernización democrática* (Barcelona: Edicions Bellaterra, 2006), 269–312.

31. Levi, "A Model, a Map, and a Method: Rational Choice in Comparative Politics"; North, *Institutions, Institutional Change and Economic Performance*; Pierson, *Politics in Time*.

CARMELO MESA-LAGO

CUBAN SOCIAL SECURITY REFORMS COMPARED WITH LATIN AMERICA, CHINA, AND VIETNAM

Cuba's social security system embraces three key programs: 1) social-insurance contributory pensions (old-age, disability, survivors), state managed and mainly financed by state enterprises and the government, with small contributions from a minority of workers; 2) a public health care system that provides universal free services entirely financed by the state (there is no national health insurance); and 3) social assistance for vulnerable groups (mainly noncontributory pensions for the elderly in need) that lack social insurance coverage, also fully state financed. There is neither unemployment insurance (a small benefit is paid to redundant state employees laid off) nor family allowances; employment injuries and children's protection are not discussed herein due to space limitations. This chapter reviews Cuba's social security evolution, analyzes in detail its three main programs under the structural reforms of Raúl Castro, compares Cuban reforms with those in Latin America, China, and Vietnam, evaluates social security costs and long-run financial sustainability, and provides suggestions for the system's improvement.[1]

Cuba's social security system progressed impressively in 1959–1989. On the eve of the collapse of the USSR and the socialist camp (which provided trade, oil, aid, and price subsidies), Cuban social indicators led most of Latin America and socialist countries, the result of the government commitment to social security and the sizable and munificent Soviet aid.[2] The severe crisis (Special Period in Time of Peace) of the early 1990s badly affected social security. The slow, partial economic recovery that began in 1996 brought some relief, but the huge social gap of the first half of the 1990s was expanded by the Great Recession, resulting in the further deterioration of the system. Social security costs kept rising with a weak foundation (an inefficient economic system grounded on central planning and virtual state ownership of all means of production) and despite the two crises that dwindled resources. In the first 47 years of the revolution, serious economic and social problems accumulated. Due to his grave illness, in 2006 Fidel transferred power to his brother Raúl and he began to implement "structural reforms" in 2007, later endorsed by the Sixth Communist Party Congress of 2011. Such reforms include a reduction in social security expenditures to make the system financially sustainable.[3]

CONTRIBUTORY PENSIONS
Evolution

In 1961–1963, the revolutionary government unified 54 standing social insurance pension schemes, standardized their entitlement conditions, appropriated their funds, and centralized their management.[4] Coverage rose from 63 percent of the labor force in 1958—one of the highest in the region—to 91 percent, the highest. Small private farmers, the self-employed, and unpaid family workers lacked mandatory coverage but could join the pension scheme voluntarily. In 1989, Cuba's pension system was among the widest in coverage, the most generous and costliest in Latin America: a) retirement ages were very low: 60 for men and 55 for women; b) this meant that average retirement spans were respectively 20 and 26 years, the longest in the region; c) state enterprises contributed 12 percent of the payroll but workers did not make contributions; d) pensions were meager but supplemented by a social protection network.[5] Armed forces and state-security personnel enjoyed a separate, more generous pension scheme than the general pension system, which was basically state financed;[6] its cost in 1995 equaled the total deficit of the general pension system covering most of the labor force.

The severe economic crisis of the 1990s undermined many of the positive features of the pension system. The number of private sector workers jumped from 4 percent to 15 percent of the labor force in 1989–2001, increas-

CARMELO MESA-LAGO

ing the number of those not mandatorily covered. Voluntarily affiliated self-employed workers and small private farmers were required to pay 10 percent of their earnings, twice the rate of state workers and a disincentive for affiliation. The 1994 tax law required all workers to pay pension contributions, but its application was first suspended for sociopolitical reasons and then implemented gradually; only wage earners under the "Enterprise Improvement System" (*Sistema de Perfeccionamiento Empresarial*), operating in one-fifth of state enterprises, had 5 percent of their wages withheld as social security contributions.

In 2008, the monthly average nominal pension was 235 pesos (CUP), equivalent to $9.40.[7] The real value of such pension (adjusted for inflation) declined by 60 percent in 1989–2007 (see figure 8.1) and the purchasing power loss was aggravated by other factors: state-subsidized rationed food covered only the first seven to ten days of the month and cost 30 to 40 CUP; the monthly electricity tariff was 10 to 20 CUP; telephone and water from 8 to 10 CUP per month; and bus fares from 12 to 20 CUP per month; although 85 percent of the population owned a home, a minority paid an average rent of 33 CUP monthly. All these expenses added up from 60 to 123 CUP per month; the remaining 112 to 175 CUP of the pension had to buy food needs for the 20–23 days not supplied by rationing, bought in free agricultural markets and hard-currency state shops (TRD), at very high prices (Mesa-Lago and Pérez-López 2013).[8]

The social protection network that existed for nearly four decades has deteriorated due to the decrease in goods supplied by rationing, reduction in access to and quality of health care services (see section 2), and increase in public utility tariffs. It is impossible for those who receive the minimum or average pension to survive if they do not get foreign remittances or family help. Many pensioners work as street vendors or carry out other activities to survive. In 2000, one poll in Havana city showed that the elderly were among the poorest groups: 88 percent lived in mediocre or bad housing, 78 percent considered their income insufficient to meet basic living expenses; and they complained about expensive transportation, difficult access to health care, and lack of homes for the elderly (Espina 2008; ONEI 2008b, 2009b). Due to generous entitlement conditions, maturity of the pension system, rapid aging of the population and insufficient financing, pension expenditures rose from 5.8 percent to 7.1 percent of GDP in 1989–2008, driving the scheme's fiscal deficit from 38.2 percent to 40.5 percent of total pension expenditures. The ratio of active workers per pensioner shrank from 3.6 to 3.1 in that period (table 8.2).

TABLE 8.1. Population Aging in Cuba, 1953–2025 (per 100 inhabitants)

Years	Births[a]	Net emigration	Pop. growth	Age > 60[b]	Mortality
1953	2.50		2.11	6.9	
1970	2.20	-0.06	2.16	9.1	5.1
1981	1.40	-0.15	1.14	10.9	5.9
2002	1.26	-0.13	0.66	14.7	7.2
2012	1.13	-1.10	-0.02	18.7	8.0
2013	1.12	0.00	0.33	18.7	8.2
2014	1.09	0.02	0.25	19.0	8.6
2025[c]			-0.20	25.9	

Notes: Blank spaces: data not available.
[a] In 2014 the range went from 0.9 percent in Havana to 1.4 percent in Guantánamo, the second poorest province.
[b] Percent of total population.
[c] Projection based on 2012 census.

Sources: Author's calculations based on ONEI, 2008a, 2015a, 2015b.

Reforms

The pension reform of 2008 confronted some, but not all, of the problems afflicting the pension system: 1) it increased the retirement age by five years for both sexes (from 55 to 60 for women and from 60 to 65 for men) gradually, over a period of seven years[9] (those who retire during this period with ages under 60/65 will receive lower pensions); 2) calculated the pension based on the monthly average of wages for the previous five years and applied to this average a replacement rate of 60 percent (higher than the previous 50 percent), and raised the number of required work years to qualify for a pension from 25 to 30; 3) raised the pension amount for each year that retirement is postponed; d) increased nominal pensions: the minimum pension by 22 percent and others from 10 percent to 20 percent (the higher the pension amount, the lower the increase), and; 4) imposed a wage contribution by workers of 5 percent, to be paid gradually as their salaries rise.

The reform measures were well thought out but insufficient to turn around the insolvency of the pension system. Cuba is now tied with Uruguay in having the oldest population in Latin America:[10] the birth rate fell from 2.5 percent to 1 percent in 1953–2014 (the fertility rate has been below the replacement rate since 1978 and the lowest in the hemisphere), the net emigration rate rose from –0.06 percent to –0.1 percent in 1970–2012, the population growth rate shrank from 2.2 percent to –0.02 percent (in absolute terms, the population declined in 2007–2010).[11] The cohort age 60 and above

CARMELO MESA-LAGO

TABLE 8.2. Pension Scheme Financial Imbalance in Cuba, 1989 and 2006–2014

Indicators	1989	2008	2009	2010	2011	2012	2013	2014
Pension cost (percent GDP)	5.8	7.1	7.6	7.6	7.4	7.3	7.2	6.9
Pension deficit								
Financed by state (percent expenses)	38.2	40.5	41.5	39.1	41.0	43.1	43.8	35.2
Percent of GDP	2.2	2.9	3.2	3.0	3.0	3.1	3.2	2.4
Employer contribution								
Current percent of payroll	10.0	12.0	12.0	12.0	12.0	12.0	12.0	12.0
Percent needed to eliminate deficit	16.2	20.2	20.5	19.7	20.3	21.0	21.3	18.5
No. of active workers per pensioner	3.6	3.1	3.1	3.0	3.0	2.9	2.9	3.0

Sources: 1989 from Mesa-Lago and Pérez-López 2013; the rest, author's estimates based on ONEI, 2009a to 2014.

jumped from 9 percent to 19 percent of the total population in 1970–2014 and is projected to reach 26 percent by 2025 (one elderly person for every four inhabitants). These changes have led to a rising mortality rate, from 5.1 percent to 8.6 percent (table 8.1). As population ages and the pension scheme matures, the ratio of active workers for one pensioner falls and eventually will force higher contributions/retirement ages, cuts in the meager pensions, or a combination of both policies.

Despite the 2008 pension reform, the pension deficit financed by the state climbed in 2008–2013, from 40.5 percent to 43.8 percent of total expenses and from 2.9 percent to 3.2 percent of GDP (table 8.2). The gradual increase in the retirement age to 60/65 (women/men) was completed in 2015 but its full effects will take longer. Due to the aging process, the productive age segment (15–60 years) will contract from 64.3 percent in 2014 to 57.7 percent in 2025, making it more difficult to finance pensions: the ratio of active workers to one pensioner fell from 3.1 to 2.9 in 2008–2014. The worker contribution of 5 percent should be gradually imposed in tandem with wage increases, but the real wage shrunk by 72 percent in 1989–2013. Even if the entire labor force had paid the 5 percent contribution in 2013, the total contribution (jointly with 12 percent from enterprises) would be 17 percent, vis-à-vis an estimated 21 percent required to financially balance the system in that year (table 8.2).

The nonstate sector (self-employed, coop members and those working for private sector employers) rose from 17 percent to 26 percent of the labor force in 2008–2013, which could jeopardize coverage by the pension system. And yet legislation in 2013–2014 made coverage mandatory to part of the self-employed and members of new nonagricultural cooperatives, thus approaching full coverage of the labor force. Despite nominal increases, the average pension in 2013 was $10, grossly insufficient to satisfy basic needs. Cuba is one of four countries in Latin America that does not mandate a yearly cost-of-living adjustment of pensions adjusted to inflation; the pension in 2013 was half of the 1989 level and has been stagnant in the past five years (figure 8.1).

Comparisons

Latin American countries usually have social insurance schemes on pensions, health care, and employment injury; most of them also have a public health system for the uninsured population; some have unemployment insurance. The Cuban pension scheme is unique in the region because it is fully managed and mostly financed by the state, lacking even a contingency reserve. Cuba's 2008 pension reform was parametric (and modest) rather than structural. In contrast, 11 countries in Latin America fully or partially privatized social insurance pensions in 1981–2011, following three models: (1) fully replacing the pay-as-you-go (PAYG), defined benefit, publicly managed system with a fully funded, defined contribution, privately managed system (Chile, Bolivia, Dominican Republic, El Salvador, and Mexico); (2) a mixed system with two pillars, namely PAYG and individual accounts (Argentina, Costa Rica, Panama, and Uruguay); and (3) a parallel model that kept PAYG and added individual accounts, both competing (Colombia and Peru). The structural reforms improved efficiency, the relationship between contribution and pension levels, and capital accumulation. However, these reforms failed to expand labor-force coverage, social solidarity was absent in the private system, gender inequality worsened, competition did not work in most cases, administrative charges were very high, and transition costs have been much greater and longer than initially projected. Re-reforms in Argentina and Chile in 2008 and in Bolivia in 2010 enlarged the state role in such pensions and improved social elements. Argentina and Bolivia closed the private system and moved all the insured and their funds to the public system, with important social progress but questionable financial sustainability. Meanwhile, Chile kept the private system but improved it with better pensions, enhanced social solidarity, gender equity, and competition, while ensuring financial sustainability.[12] With respect to the half of the region with public pension systems, most face growing financial/actuarial deficit, inefficiencies, and low benefits (Mesa-Lago 2012, 2014b, 2016b; Mesa-Lago and Bertranou 2016).

Statistics on Cuban pension coverage of the labor force have never been released, but available data suggest that it is probably at a similar level to

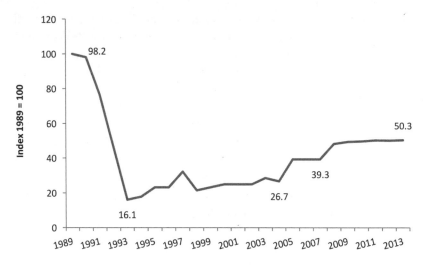

Figure 8.1: Evolution of the Real Pension in Cuba, 1989–2013

Uruguay (80 percent), and higher than Chile (65 percent), Costa Rica (64 percent) and Argentina (50 percent) (Lazo 2014; CCSS 2015; Bertranou et al. 2018; Mesa-Lago and Bertranou 2016). Cuba also ranks high on social solidarity. Conversely, Cuba's average pension benefit is among the lowest in the region (save for least developed countries like Haiti, Bolivia, Honduras, and Nicaragua), there is no benefit indexation as in most countries, and its financial deficit is among the worst (Mesa-Lago 2012, 2013). Cuba's replacement rate of 60 percent on the most recent five-year average earnings is relatively high but based on very low wages that lead to meager pensions.

China's social security has the three key programs (pensions, health care, and employment injury) and unemployment insurance (absent in Cuba).[13] Under Mao Zedong, pension and health systems were tied to large urban state enterprises now largely decentralized, as well as rural communes now disbanded. China' pension reforms were influenced by the structural reforms in Latin America, specifically the mixed model. The system is highly fragmented, exacerbates inequalities among groups, and generates regressive effects: it rewards the privileged rather than the disadvantaged (Leung and Xu 2015). There are four old-age pension schemes: 1) a mandatory pension for urban workers, the main scheme, has two pillars: PAYG entirely financed by employers' 20 percent contribution, and funded individual accounts wholly financed by employees' 8 percent contribution; it covers 62 percent of total insured; 2) a voluntary rural pension also has two pillars: a basic pension financed by local and central governments and individual accounts; affiliates select among five contribution scales and local governments are urged to match; it covers 27 percent of total insured;[14] 3) a mandatory pension for civil servants (including armed forces) and public service units, a PAYG system, provides the most generous entitlement conditions and benefits,[15] entirely financed by public funds; it covers 11 percent of total insured; since 2008 the central government has tried to align this costly and unequal scheme with the rest, but resistance of powerful groups has impeded it; 4) a voluntary urban resident pension, with a similar structure of the rural scheme, geared to those who are either unemployed and do not qualify for the urban employee scheme or informal workers; no data are available for its coverage. In addition, there is a third voluntary supplementary pillar, funded and defined contribution, for private employees, but this has not been very successful (Fang 2014; Leung and Xu 2015). Estimates of coverage of the total labor force by the pension schemes in 2010–2011 are diverse: Fang, excluding voluntary urban residents, estimates it at 39 percent; adding the excluded scheme, this author assesses 55 percent; the ILO (2014) calculates 74 percent; and Leung and Xu (2015) estimates urban coverage at 70 percent and rural at 4 percent; all are lower than Cuba's. Those excluded are half the rural labor force, rural migrant workers working in urban settings,[16] the self-employed and other informal workers; the target of 95 percent coverage in 2020 will be quite difficult to meet. Expanding coverage is difficult because one-third of the labor force in six urban areas is informal and much higher nationally (ILO/ WIEGO 2013). Retirement ages are 60 for men and 55 for women (as in Cuba before 2008) and 15 years of contributions are required for eligibility. The basic monthly public pension averaged $266 in the mandatory scheme and $11.43 in the voluntary schemes (a huge gap), to which is added the pension from individual accounts (Leung and Xu 2015), whereas Cuba's average pension was $10 (as in Cuba, pensions are not indexed to inflation). The cost of social insurance (not only pensions) was 3 percent in 2011 vis-à-vis Cuba's 7 percent. In contrast to Cuba, China has notably reduced poverty (Gao 2013).

Vietnam has essentially the same social security schemes as China. The current social insurance law,[17] enacted in 2006, has two schemes: compulsory for public sector (including the armed forces and the party) and salaried-private and coop workers (excluding workers with less than a three-month contract); and voluntary for nonsalaried workers, e.g., workers with contracts under three months, the self-employed, and workers without wages (National Assembly 2006). Contributions to the compulsory scheme in 2014 were 14 percent by employers and 8 percent by workers; voluntary affiliates pay 22 percent, a heavy burden. A new supplementary pension fund for large enterprises is apparently financed by employers and employees. Compulsory coverage is 20 percent of the labor force, much less than China's and Cuba's;

voluntary coverage is low: 0.25 percent of the target group. The informal sector in Vietnam is 44 percent of the nonagricultural labor force, higher than China and even more than Cuba (ILO/WIEGO 2013). As in China, Vietnam has attained a sizable reduction in poverty, contrary to Cuba's increasing trend. Ages of retirement are the same as in China. The average replacement rate in 2013 was 45 percent based on 15 years of contributions; additional years get 2 percent for men and 3 percent for women with a maximum of 75 percent. The monthly pension in the compulsory scheme was $123 in 2012, 12-fold the Cuban pension (Huöng et al. 2013). The cost of pensions was 3.1 percent of GDP in 2010 vis-à-vis Cuba's 7 percent (ILO 2014).

HEALTH CARE
Evolution

Prior to the revolution, Cuba lacked a national social insurance health care scheme, a common characteristic of Latin American countries. Urban areas relied on a public health system fairly developed and virtually free, combined with a network of health care cooperatives and mutual aid societies that charged low premiums; this partly explains why Cuban health indicators were among the best in Latin America. Rural public health facilities and indicators were notably inferior, however. In 1961, the state expropriated all health care cooperatives, mutual aid societies, and private facilities, and prohibited the private practice of medicine. A national unified public health system with universal and free access was created that significantly reduced the urban–rural gap in facilities, personnel, and quality of services.[18] The government built a large number of hospitals, especially in the countryside;[19] launched a nationwide immunization campaign against contagious diseases; and trained a vast number of physicians and other health care professionals tuition-free at public universities and with scholarships (including room and board) for students without resources. The public system, however, was capital intensive as it emphasized hospitals, equipment, and physicians. The innovative family doctor program established in 1984 provided patients with greater local access to primary care but was also quite expensive.[20] The health policy was a success for three decades: in 1959–1989, the ratio of physicians jumped from 9.2 to 33 per 10,000 inhabitants, hospital beds from 4.2 to 5.1 per 1,000 inhabitants, and real expenses per inhabitant by 162 percent. Infant mortality fell from 33.4 to 11.1 per 1,000 children born alive, maternal mortality plunged from 125.3 to 29.2 per 100,000 births, and mortality of the cohort aged 65 years and above receded from 52.9 to 46.3 per 1,000. Most contagious diseases (e.g., diphtheria, measles, paratyphoid, poliomyelitis, whooping cough) were eradicated, but the incidence of chickenpox, venereal diseases (including AIDS), and hepatitis, as well as diarrheic and acute repatory diseases, increased.

The economic crisis of the first half of the 1990s virtually halted imports of medical supplies, medicine, equipment, and other medical inputs from the USSR and the socialist camp, inducing severe shortages, and real health expenditures per capita shrunk by 75 percent. Therefore, maternal mortality rose from 29.2 to 65.2 per 100,000 births and elderly mortality from 46.3 to 55.7 per 1,000. Conversely, the ratio of physicians climbed from 33 to 52 per 10,000 inhabitants (the highest in Latin America) and hospital beds from 5.1 to 6 per 1,000 inhabitants, whereas infant mortality shrank from 11.1 to 9.4 per 1,000 children born alive (lowest in the region). The latter accomplishments, however, were paired with an irrational allocation of scarce resources. The costly training of physicians continued even though many doctors abandoned the profession. Hospital beds kept raising, but their occupation average fell from 83.9 percent to 71.3 percent (even lower in pediatric and neonatal hospitals), while the already high average days of hospital stay rose from 9.9 to 10.4. The struggle to reduce the low infant mortality persisted, with the government investing scarce resources[21] desperately required to meet more urgent needs, such as overhauling the severely deteriorated potable water-sewerage infrastructure and immunization of the population (which had dangerously decreased).[22] Eradicated diseases did not reappear, except for tuberculosis, but those previously showing a growing trend increased notably. The lack of prophylactics and rise in prostitution boosted venereal diseases, the cut in immunization swelled chickenpox and tuberculosis, contaminated water brought about hepatitis and acute diarrhea; acute respiratory diseases also increased. Food shortages resulted in malnutrition expanding from 5 percent to 13 percent of the population; the lack of vitamins caused a blindness epidemic, and family doctors lacked vital medicines.

During the recovery, infant mortality continued its decline to 5.3 per 1,000 children born alive in 2006 (the lowest in the hemisphere after Canada) but maternal mortality peaked at 51.4 per 100,000 births and the ratio of hospital beds per 1,000 inhabitants fell to 4.1. The ratio of physicians rose from 54.6 to 63.6 per 10,000 inhabitants in 1996–2006, leading the region and among the highest in the world (UNDP 2007); but one-third of the physicians worked abroad. These factors resulted in a shortage of doctors, a decrease in the people's access to services, and long waiting lists for surgery. Immunization declined, especially the triple vaccine (diphtheria, pertussis [whooping cough], and tetanus) and against tuberculosis. And yet, apart from the eradicated diseases, in 1996–2005 Cuba's reported rates showed more infectious diseases falling than rising. On the other hand, there were 23,000 foreign students

CARMELO MESA-LAGO

TABLE 8.3. Health Care Indicators in Cuba, 1989 and 2006–2014

Indicators	1989	2006	2007	2008	2009	2010	2011	2012	2013	2014	Change (percent)[a]	
											2014/1989	2014/2006
Infant mortality[b]	11.1	5.3	5.3	4.7	4.8	4.5	4.9	4.6	4.2	4.2	–7	–1
Maternal mortality[c]	29.2	51.4[e]	31.1[f]	46.5	46.9	43.1	40.6	33.4	38.9	35.1	6	–16
No. of hospitals	265	243	222	217	219	215	161	152	152	152	–113	–91
Of which rural	66	38	21	17	17	16	0	0	0	0	–66	–38
No. of rural posts	229	138	138	120	127	134	0	0	0	0	–229	–138
Hospital beds[d]	5.1	4.1	3.9	3.9	3.8	3.8	3.7	3.6	3.5	3.6	–1.5	–0.5

Notes: peak year in dark font.
[a] Difference between two years.
[b] Per 1,000 born alive.
[c] Per 100,000 births.
[d] Average real beds per 1,000 inhabitants.
[e] 2005.
[f] Underestimated ratio due to exclusion of category "others."

Source: 1989 from CCE, 191; rest from ONEI, 2012, 2014, 2015a.

on scholarship pursuing health careers in Cuba, which cost around $300 million annually.

Reforms

Raúl's reforms aimed to reduce health care cost and enhance efficiency. Health expenses were cut by 2 percentage points of GDP in 2006–2013; the number of hospitals was reduced by 37 percent, and all rural hospitals and health posts were closed (table 8.3). Since 2011, rural hospitals/posts have been classified as polyclinics but the latter number actually fell in that year and then stagnated (ONEI 2015a). The hospital infrastructure worsened, and relatives of patients had to provide them with sheets, pillows, pillowcases, medicine, and food. Due to poor asepsis (e.g., insufficient sterile gloves, soap), 55,000 hospital infections were reported in 2014, one-third life threatening (*Cubanet* Havana, March 12, 2014). The ratio of hospital beds decreased from 4.1 to 3.6 per 1,000 inhabitants, far below 5.1 in 1989 (table 8.3). There is a severe scarcity of medicine, with most medicine only available at high prices at the TRD.

The number of health professionals steadily shrank in 2008–2014: 21 percent overall personnel, 50 percent technicians, and 16 percent nurses (figure 8.2). The number of physicians rose 16 percent but an increasing number have been sent abroad to earn hard currency for the government: exports of professional services brought Cuba $8.2 billion in 2014, about 40 percent of all exports (Frank 2014; *Granma* Havana, March 21, 2014). Out of a total 83,698

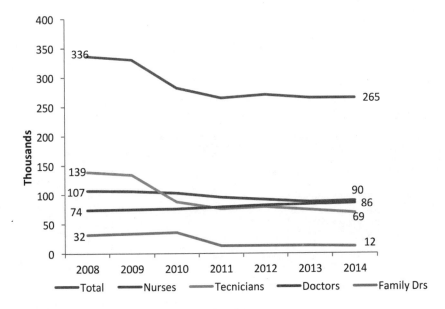

Figure 8.2. Health Care Personnel in Cuba, 2008–2014

physicians in 2013, about 40,000 worked mainly in Venezuela (25,000) and Brazil (14,456), Ecuador, Angola, and 60 other countries (*Juventud Rebelde* Havana, June 9, 2013).[23] Subtracting those abroad, the ratio of physicians per 10,000 inhabitants is halved from 74.7 to 35.7, without counting doctors that shifted to occupations in the expanding private sector, which pays higher salaries than the state. Family doctors dropped 62 percent, significantly reducing access to primary care.[24]

Cuba's water system is between 50 and 100 years old; due to leaks, half of the pumped water is lost; 58 percent in Havana (*Juventud Rebelde* Havana, January 24, 2013). Sewerage pipes leak into potable water pipes; the latter burst and trickle into the streets, creating pools where mosquitoes carrying illnesses incubate.[25] Garbage accumulates in the streets due to insufficient collection trucks and dumpsters to deposit it, as well as bulldozers to bury it; 20,000 metric tons of garbage is daily accumulated in Havana but only 40 percent is collected; rats and insects, thrive generating health risks (*Bohemia* Havana, August 23, 2012; *Cubanet* Havana, August 29, 2014).

Diseases eradicated earlier did not reappear in the period, but out of the 14 remaining infectious diseases, the rates for seven declined (e.g., hepatitis, gonorrhea, chickenpox, acute diarrhea) whereas for seven others they rose (e.g., acute respiratory diseases, scarlet fever, syphilis, bacterial meningoencephalitis) or were stagnant (ONEI 2012, 2014, 2015a). Scarcity of vitamins

CARMELO MESA-LAGO

causes optical neuritis. There have been recurrent epidemics of dengue fever and cholera, the latter not occurring since the late nineteenth century. In 2013, the Ministry of Public Health identified 51 cases of cholera in various Havana municipalities and referred to previous outbreaks in other regions (MINSAP 2013). Similar outbreaks were reported in the province of Guantánamo due to contaminated waters, as well as in Manzanillo, Camagüey, Ciego de Avila, and Santiago de Cuba (*El Médico* July 29–31, 2013; *Venceremos* Guantánamo, October 31, 2013). The Panamerican Health Organization confirmed that Cuba had exported cases of cholera to three foreign countries and reported 163 domestic cases (PAHO 2013a, 2013b). An outbreak of cholera reappeared in 2014 in Villaclara, with 55 percent of the province having cases, as well as in Camagüey and Artemisa (*Diario de Cuba* Santa Clara, July 9, 2014). After 15 years without cases of dengue (transmitted by the mosquito *Aedes aegyti*), an epidemic struck in 1997, transmitted endogenously and including the hemorrhagic type; outbreaks followed almost annually; the one in 2006 took place in 11 out of the 14 provinces and the latest was in 2013–2014. A Cuban expert, in an article published in the Island's principal public health journal, judged the disease "a grave epidemiological problem in Cuba," and referred to a dengue "epidemiological silence," due to lack of official reports or reports not as frequently as needed, which "neither contributes to the control of suspicious cases and infected people nor to a real perception of the potential danger of the disease and the need to eliminate the transmission agent" (Suárez 2013). In 2014, the Municipal Director of Hygiene and Epidemiology of Cienfuegos reported 3,500 cases of dengue in the city (*Nuevo Herald* Miami, May 11, 2014).

Despite the above analysis, infant mortality officially continued its decline from 5.3 per 1,000 children born alive in 2006 to 4.2 in 2014, now reportedly the lowest in the western hemisphere (*Granma* Havana, January 2, 2014; see below), whereas maternal mortality dwindled from 51.5 to 35.1 per 100,000 births, but still above 29.2 in 1989. Recent data/research offer new light on these figures. A ground-breaking study shows that the infant mortality rate (IMR) reported by Cuba is misleading; after exploring the sharp discrepancy between late fetal and early neonatal deaths, a method for adjusting the IMR reveals that the rate is twice the one reported officially, calling into question the common view that Cuba's IMR is comparable to that of developed countries, albeit lower than in the region (Gonzalez 2015). The latest national survey of fertility found that 21 percent of women of ages 15–54 have had at least one abortion, and the average was 1.6 abortions per woman (ONEI 2010b). Dr. Jorge Peláez, gynecologist at the Ministry of Public Health, acknowledged that the procedure is common due to insufficient prophylactics; he also noted that some of his patients had had as many as six abortions (García 2014). Most maternal deaths occur during childbirth or in the subsequent 48 hours due to uterine hemorrhages or postpartum infections. Complications arising from abortion and its aftereffects increase the mortality rate (Mesa-Lago and Pérez-López 2013).

Efficiency-seeking reforms include regionalization of health care, concentrating patients in regional hospitals (reducing expenses but increasing travel time for patients), and use of acupuncture and traditional and herbal medicine. At a Council of Ministers meeting held in 2013, Marino Murillo revealed flaws in the Plan for Natural and Traditional Medicine: it was not given priority; it has deficiencies in organization, training, equipment, and resources for production and distribution of the raw materials (herbs); prices are high; and the quality of the product is inadequate (*Granma* Havana, September 24, 2013). Not publicly discussed is the great need to allocate scarce resources more rationally, e.g., the costly effort to reduce infant mortality continues, although Cuba supposedly has the lowest ratio in the continent, but the infrastructure of potable water and sewage is badly in need of repair/ reconstruction. Gynecology and pediatric hospitals have a low occupational rate but their number has hardly decreased, whereas there is a significant need for geriatric hospitals due to the rapid aging of the population (see "Contributory Pensions").

Comparisons

In Latin American countries, the health system is normally fragmented with diverse schemes for various groups in the population: social insurance for the formal labor force, public health care for the uninsured, and special regimes for the armed forces and other powerful sectors. Brazil has a public system, but it is quite patchy and contracts with private providers. Costa Rica is unique, with a nationally unified health social insurance covering all the population, including the poor (CCSS 2015); there is no public system. Structural health care reforms that began in the 1980s and expanded thereafter introduced in many countries competing private for-profit corporations (HMOs) that were expected to improve care and reduce costs, but in practice charged high premiums and copayments, excluded preexisting conditions, and imposed higher fees for fertility-age women and the elderly. In pioneer Chile, services in the public health sector deteriorated and later required a sizable investment; as they improved, the population enrolled in HMOs declined from 25 percent to 16 percent, whereas the public sector expanded; a re-reform in 2004 revamped the system, establishing minimum guaranteed services for all (Mesa-Lago 2012).

China's highly fragmented health system comprises four insurance schemes: 1) mandatory for urban employees (accounting for two-thirds of total health expenses) with two tiers: social pooling financed by 1.8 percent contribution by employers and 2 percent by employees, and individual accounts with 4.8 percent contributions from employers plus contributions from the insured; reimbursements paid by the pooling have a ceiling on wages, expenses above the ceiling come from the accounts, copayments, out of pocket or private medical insurance; 2) mandatory for public employees, financed by the central and local governments; it is being gradually merged with the first scheme; 3) voluntary for urban residents who are outside the formal labor force (informal workers, some students), funded by participating households and government subsidies;[26] 4) voluntary for rural coops, covering mostly inpatient costs; central and local governments reimburse 30 percent while the patient has a copayment of 70 percent. This program covers 95 percent of the rural population (Leung and Xu 2015; Dillon 2016; for health assistance to the poor see "Social Assistance"). Although statistics are unavailable, Leung and Xu (2015: 84) assert that China "has attained almost full [health care] coverage of the national population," but there are huge differences among all schemes in terms of access, covered treatments, quality of services, and financing. China's total health care cost was 1.27 percent of GDP in 2011 vis-à-vis 8 percent Cuba's (Gao 2013).

The Vietnamese health system is somewhere between Cuba's and China's. The system is public and relatively unified, with emphasis on primary care; 70 percent of the population is covered (less than Cuba); of the 30 percent uncovered, 87 percent are near poor, and 66 percent are workers in cooperatives. Inequalities in access exist across groups by income, ethnicity, location (mountain areas have more limited access), and gender. Almost all districts (communes) have primary health care posts but only 46 percent of them meet national standards; many posts are deteriorating and face a shortage of or poorly qualified medical personnel. Higher-level hospitals are overcrowded due to underutilization of local-level services. Despite significant improvements (e.g., vaccinations), children's malnutrition is still high, as is the rate of some infectious diseases such as tuberculosis with rates among the 20 highest in the world (infectious diseases rates are much higher than Cuba's).[27] Free insurance cards are granted to civil servants, armed forces, and war veterans, as well as to the poor or near poor and children under 6 years of age. About 78 percent of all participants receive government subsidies for their insurance cards, 83 percent among ethnic minorities (Fifth Plenum . . . 2012; Huöng et al. 2013). Each insured and their dependents are assigned to a public local clinic that provides primary care; if they go to said 'clinic a 5 percent copayment is charged; when special treatment is needed, the doctor refers patients to a hospital and a basic 5 percent fee is also paid, but the proportion increases with more costly treatment. If the insured goes to another clinic he/she pays 70 percent of all costs. For children age 6–18, the state pays 30 percent and parents 70 percent (De Miranda and Yamaoka 2014). Health care costs were 2.54 percent of GDP in 2010, twice China's but one-third Cuba's.

SOCIAL ASSISTANCE
Evolution

The revolution provided social assistance to various "vulnerable groups": elderly, disabled, single mothers, children, and parents dependent on deceased workers, low-benefit pensioners, and workers without a pension. The poor who do not own a dwelling and rent from the state are exempted from paying more than 10 percent of their salaries in rent. In almost 56 years since the revolution, the government has not published poverty statistics and has claimed that it eradicated poverty.

As a result of the economic crisis of the 1990s, the urban population "at risk of having a basic need uncovered" (a euphemism for poverty) rose from 6.3 percent to 14.7 percent in 1988–1996. Havana's "at risk" population augmented more than threefold: from 6 percent to 20 percent in 1988–2002; a poll on poverty self-perception showed that 23 percent of the people considered themselves "poor," and another 23 percent "nearly poor" (Añé 2007). The poor were mainly composed of women, the elderly, Afro-Cubans, migrants from eastern provinces, those with only primary-school education or living in homes with six or more people, and the unemployed (Espina 2008). The city of Havana is the most economically and socially developed province and hence it is appropriate to conclude that the poverty rate in the other 14 provinces and Cuba as a whole was higher.

Despite the poverty increase and due to lack of resources, the average social assistance real pension (granted at age 60/65 to those without resources and family to take care of them) decreased 82 percent in 1989–1994—the peak period of the crisis. The nominal monthly average social assistance pension in 2000 was only 105 pesos ($4.20), not enough to purchase one or two days of food in nonrationed markets. However, as the economy improved and more resources were available, in 2000–2006 the number of social assistance beneficiaries jumped threefold while as a percentage of the total population it grew from 1.8 percent to 5.3 percent. Social assistance expenditures stagnated at 0.5 percent of GDP in 1989–2000, but gradually increased to 2.2 percent in 2006 (see figure 8.3).

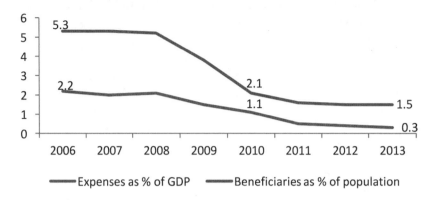

Figure 8.3. Decline of Social Assistance in Cuba, 2006–2013

Reforms

Raúl's economic reforms are needed and rational but have expanded poverty for various reasons: removal of subsidized goods from the rationing list and their sale at market prices three-to-four times higher than rationed prices; social-services cuts, such as shown in health care; abolition of subsidized meals for workers in workplace cafeterias (workers currently receive a voucher insufficient to buy lunch); increases in public utility tariffs and goods sold at TRDs with a markup of 230 percent; and rising open unemployment from 1.6 percent to 3.3 percent (ONEI, 2014).

Since 1995, Cuban economists correctly recommended the replacement of universal subsidies to goods (rationing), received even by high-income groups with regressive effects, by social assistance targeted to the needy, both to conserve fiscal resources and because they would have progressive effects on distribution. In 2008, Raúl accepted such advice and promised that no one in need would be unprotected. And yet, in 2011 the Party Congress approved a resolution terminating social assistance to beneficiaries with families able to help them. Detecting and eliminating "free riders" (those who do not need assistance) is a commonly-accepted international policy but said resolution is unreasonable in Cuba's milieu of expanding poverty and generalized level of need. A sweeping reversal in social assistance took place in 2006–2013: the number of beneficiaries shrunk from 5.3 percent to 1.5 percent of the population whereas the number of the poor expanded, hence most of the needy lack social assistance (figure 8.3). Furthermore, based on the 20 percent poverty rate in 2002, which must have risen during the structural reforms, the author roughly estimates that the poor covered by social assistance shrank from 19

TABLE 8.4. Estimates of Poor Population Covered by Social Assistance in Cuba and Havana, 2009 and 2013

Estimations	2009		2013	
	Cuba	Havana	Cuba	Havana
Total population (thousands)	11 243	2 142	11,210	2,117
20 percent living in poverty[a]	2 248	428	2,242	423
Social assistance beneficiaries	426	66	171	41
Poor people covered (percent)	19.0	15.4	7.6	9.7

Note: [a] On the basis of 2002 data, the 2013 rate should be higher.

Source: Author's calculations based on ONEI, 2011, 2014; 2002 poverty rate from text.

percent to 7.6 percent in 2009–2013, whereas in Havana they fell from 15.4 percent to 9.7 percent (table 8.4). Coverage of the elderly by social assistance (mostly pensions) in 2013 is estimated at 8 percent (based on ONEI 2014).[28]

In 2006–2013, the budget amount allocated to social assistance (the smallest budget allocation among all social services) dropped from 2.2 percent to 0.3 percent of GDP (figure 8.3). The monthly average social assistance benefit was 128 pesos in 2013 or $5, an increase of $1 over 13 years; it accounts for half the average social-insurance pension, hence it does not cover basic food needs. In addition, the following cuts were implemented: 21 percent in social assistance hospital beds for the elderly and the disabled; 21 percent in homes for the old;[29] and 63 percent in assistance for the elderly in need (ONEI 2008b to 2014).

Comparisons

In Latin America, 15 countries provide social assistance pensions of various types,[30] all of them targeting the poor except for Bolivia, which grants a universal pension to all the elderly regardless of their income. Bolivia, one of the least developed counties in the region, pays a universal pension of $40 monthly, sixfold Cuba's pension, whereas Costa Rica's targeted pension of $140 is 28-fold. Cuba's coverage of the elderly population by social assistance pensions (2.5 percent) is much lower than in Bolivia (97 percent); conservatively assuming that 20 percent of the elderly are poor in Cuba, 12 percent would be covered vis-à-vis 97 percent in Uruguay and Argentina, 84–86 percent in Brazil and Chile, 57 percent in Costa Rica, and 45 percent in Panama (IADB 2014; Lazo 2014; CCSS 2015; ONEI 2015a; Bertranou et al. 2018; Mesa-Lago and Bertranou 2016). The most successful antipoverty programs, however, are the conditional cash transfers that most countries in the region have, although not Cuba.

China's social assistance system has multiple schemes; the main one is cash transfers to low-income households to meet basic survival needs (urban and rural *dibao)*, which accounts for 69 percent of total assistance expenditures; recipients' income must be under a social assistance threshold (the aid fills the gap) and undertake an annual means test.[31] Other schemes are: aid to survivors and veterans; cash transfers to rural elderly, disabled, and children, all without working capacity, income, and a guardian. Financing is about 72 percent from the central government and the rest from local governments. A medical assistance scheme targets the extreme poor, incapable of paying high medical bills; at the start only inpatient care was provided but it has expanded to some outpatient care; the government reimburses most expenses but the beneficiary has to pay a part. Targeting is a major problem in all these schemes and fraud is common (Leung and Wu 2015). According to ILO (2014), coverage of the elderly by noncontributory pensions was 42 percent in 2010, 17 times that of Cuba (2.5 percent). The rural *dibao,* however, covers only about 10 percent of the poor, whereas more than half the recipients are not poor. The average monthly assistance paid in 2013 was $32 (sixfold Cuba's average of $5), but $41 in urban areas and $18 in rural areas (Leung and Wu 2015). Social assistance cost was 0.5 percent of GDP in 2010 (Gao 2013), lower than Cuba's in that year (1.1 percent), but it includes some services not available in the latter.[32]

In Vietnam, all persons age 80 and above who are not in the public sector and lack a pension and family support receive a noncontributory pension of $9 monthly; in 2014 the National Assembly approved a raise to $13.50 (both higher than Cuba's). The elderly under the poverty line[33] and lacking family support receive such a pension at age 60. In addition, assistance is granted to other groups in need, most living in poor households and lacking capacity to work: the disabled, the mentally ill, those infected by HIV/AIDS, single mothers, children of low-income families or with no supporting adults, and those who adopt orphans or abandoned children. Coverage by all these programs extends to 24 percent of the total population, three times that of Cuba (De Miranda and Yamaoka 2014); however, based on the elderly, coverage was 8.7 percent (ILO 2014) vis-à-vis 2.5 percent in Cuba. The cost of social assistance for the elderly was 0.1 percent in 2010, one-tenth that of Cuba in that year and also lower than that of China (ILO 2014).

SOCIAL SECURITY COSTS AND FINANCIAL SUSTAINABILITY
Evolution

In 2009, Cuba's cost of social security peaked at 20.4 percent of GDP, the highest in Latin America.[34] Such an outcome was due to the financial commitment of the revolution to expand social protection of the population, which in turn became a source of people's support. But such costs proved to be financially unsustainable, aggravated by both internal and external adverse factors; among the former are rapid population aging and rising life expectancy (both increasing the costs of pensions and health care);[35] external factors are: the collapse of the socialist camp and the world financial crisis, despite substantial Venezuelan aid since 2003.

Reforms

The challenging economic situation therefore forced Raúl in 2009–2013 to cut social security costs by 4.7 percentage points (pp) of GDP from 20.4 percent to 15.7 percent (figure 8.4). Most affected were health care (–3.3 pp), followed by social assistance (–1.8 pp) whereas pensions were only reduced 0.4 pp and still are slightly higher than in 2008. As already shown, those cuts have hurt the population.

The Cuban economy lacks the capacity to sustain the high cost of social security. The GDP growth rate slowed down from 12.1 percent to 1.3 percent in 2006–2014[36] (the growth rate averaged 2 percent per annum in the last six years), systematically below official targets and among the lowest in the region. Gross fixed capital formation fell from 10.4 percent to 8.3 percent of GDP in 2006–2013 (compared with 25.6 percent in 1989 and a regional average of 20 percent in 2014); Cuban economists estimate that 25 percent is needed to sustain economic growth. The agricultural production index in 2013 was below the 2005 level, except for three crops, and the industrial production index declined 45.4 percent in 1989–2013. In 2006–2013, the goods trade balance ended in deficit, peaking at $10.6 billion in 2008; after a brief decline it resumed its growth and reached $9.4 billion in 2013, the second largest in history (ONEI 2014; ECLAC 2014). Food imports cover 70 percent of domestic consumption and grew from $1.5 to $2 billion in the last three years. Conversely, Cuba enjoys a surplus in its balance of services, mostly generated by the export of medical services mainly to Venezuela; such surplus often offsets the deficit in the goods balance but leads to a strong economic dependence on Venezuela. The author estimated the combined value of the entire economic relationship with Venezuela at $13 billion in 2010, tantamount to 21 percent of Cuban GDP (Mesa-Lago 2013). The risk of

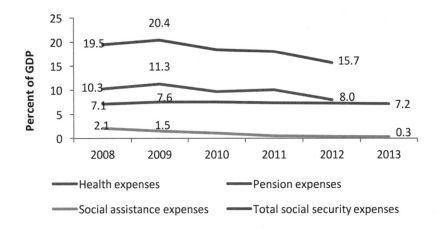

Figure 8.4. The Cost of Social Security in Cuba, 2006–2013a

this dependence increases with Venezuela's severe economic crisis. On December 17, 2014, Presidents Obama and Castro agreed to normalize relations between the two countries. Obama relaxed somewhat the restrictions on trade and travel to Cuba, took the island off the list of countries that sponsor terrorism, and embassies were opened in Havana and Washington. It is too soon to assert if detente would substantially help the Cuban economy, diminish its dependency on Venezuela, and improve social security.

Comparisons

Despite Cuban cuts in social security costs, they continue to be among the highest in the region. The latest comparative data (for 2010, before the sharpest costs occurred in Cuba) placed that country at the top, closely followed by Argentina, Brazil, and Uruguay (ILO 2014). Most public systems in Latin America usually suffer from severe actuarial disequilibrium; private systems are based on individual accounts and are less affected by that problem although they are not immune to population aging. The re-reforms in Argentina and Bolivia face financial problems in the long run (Mesa-Lago 2014b, 2016b; Bertranou et al. 2018).

China, the second largest economy in the world, lags well behind developed countries on social security, whose cost—subtracting education and housing—was 4.7 percent of GDP in 2010, less than one-third of Cuba's 15.7 percent (ILO 2014).[37] But as the official policy goal shifts from economic growth to social expenditures, more public resources are being allocated to the latter. Funds of individual accounts of the urban pension scheme were transferred to the PAYG tier, hence depleting those accounts; since 2000 both pillars are separated; still, in 2011 accounts were 89 percent behind the target and 14 provinces had deficits (Leung and Xu 2015). Population aging is accelerated by the one-child policy; ratios of active insured to one pensioner were 3.1 in the urban pension scheme, 2.8 in the rural scheme (both similar to Cuba's 2.9), and probably less than 2 in the civil servants scheme. Still the percentage of the population age 60 and above was 14.9 percent in 2013 vis-à-vis 19 percent in Cuba. Due to the lack of a mature financial market, funds in the individual accounts are invested in public debt and bank deposits with either small or negative returns, which could reduce future pension benefits. The total contribution to the urban pension scheme is 28 percent, relatively high compared with that of OECD countries and much higher than Cuba's (Fang 2014; Leung and Xu 2015). The health system is financed by employers and insured contributions that add up to 43 percent of wages (32 percent by employers); not-reimbursable costs demand copayments, out-of-pocket expenses, and private insurance; subsidies from the central and local governments have been increasing, placing into question sustainability. Social assistance financing from the central government has risen to 72 percent; the rest comes from local governments.

Vietnam's reforms have been similar to China's. Vietnam's social security costs, excluding other schemes, were 5.7 percent in 2010 (ILO 2014) higher than in China but much lower than in Cuba. The pension scheme is financed by a contribution of 22 percent vis-à-vis 12 percent by employers in Cuba and only a minority of workers contributing 5 percent; the system is PAYG but with is a sizable collective fund (absent in Cuba) which currently generates a surplus. In order to keep the fund in equilibrium, a 1 percent increase in contribution is planned every two years; but investment real returns in 2001–2010 averaged –4 percent, hence a future deficit is expected and reserves are expected to last until 2024, thereafter forcing state subsidies or higher contributions[38] (Huöng et al. 2013; De Miranda and Yamaoka 2014). The health care scheme is public and partly financed by the state and minor copayments at the primary level but increasing to a majority at higher levels if the insured chooses a provider other than the one assigned. Social assistance is fully state financed as in Cuba and China. The 2012–2020 social-protection plan stipulates a cut in state-budget expenses on the elderly to ensure sustainability, as in Cuba (Huöng et al. 2013).[39]

CONCLUSIONS AND SUGGESTIONS FOR IMPROVEMENT

This section evaluates Cuba's social security performance on the basis of ILO principles (see Mesa-Lago 2012) and does the same with respect to the other reference countries. It also analyzes the impact of the reforms on the social security system and provides policy suggestions to improve Cuba's situation.

Conclusions

Building upon a previous relatively advanced system in the context of the Latin American region (save for social assistance), Cuba's revolutionary government in its first three decades built a universal and virtually free social security system (at a level comparable to some developed countries) with generous entitlement conditions and benefits, based on the government commitment and huge Soviet aid, and without taking into account financial sustainability in the long run. The collapse of the USSR and the socialist camp radically changed the situation; the economic crises of 1990–1995 and 2008–2009 eroded social security and aggravated the system's unsustainability. Raúl Castro's structural reforms subordinated social security to economic growth and available fiscal resources, cutting expenses, diminishing access, and reducing benefits. Conversely, China and Vietnam started almost from scratch and initially gave priority to economic development, subordinating social security to growth and fiscal capacity, establishing a bare minimum social security system that took four and two decades, respectively, to take off and still is gradually and slowly expanding.[40] Such disparate paths could result in a convergence of the three systems (Dillon 2018.

a) *Unity and uniform treatment.* Cuba's social security system is ahead of the other countries because its pension and health care systems are unified and entitlement conditions are uniform with the exception of 1) the schemes for armed forces and security personnel, which have better conditions and more generous and costly benefits than the general system; and 2) separate health care treatment of hard-currency-paying foreigners. Latin America has experienced a gradual process of social security unification-normalization but still fragmentation persists in many countries and the large majority retains separate schemes for the armed forces, even in Chile, where the military regime imposed full privatization of pensions and partial privatization of health care, while keeping its separate privileged schemes. China and Vietnam have very fragmented social security systems in the three key programs.

b) *Coverage and access.* Cuba's contributive pension coverage is quasi universal (aided by having the smallest informal labor sector among all compared countries) and only a minority of workers pays pension contributions, placing Cuba ahead of most of Latin America, China and Vietnam. Coverage of Cuba's public health care system is universal and free for the population, higher than in all countries referenced. And yet, effective access to health care has dwindled due to the export of medical personnel to earn hard currency (primary-care family doctors have halved), overall deterioration of services, and severe scarcity of medicine and other inputs. Although comparisons on social assistance coverage are difficult due to the diverse programs involved, Cuba's is lower than in most Latin American countries, as well as in Vietnam and China; furthermore, it is being sharply cut despite an expanding vulnerable population, whereas it is expanding in the two Asian countries whose poverty incidence is declining.

c) *Benefit sufficiency.* Cuba's average monthly pension in 2013 was equivalent to $10, grossly insufficient to cover basic food needs; the average real pension fell by one half in 1989–2013. The social assistance average monthly benefit was the equivalent of $5, half of the average pension, and hence even more insufficient to cover food needs. Pensioners and social assistance beneficiaries are among the poorest groups in the population and survive due to foreign remittances, getting help from relatives, and doing some work for pay. Cuba's average contributory and noncontributory pension benefits are below those in most of Latin America. China's and Vietnam's average pensions in the mandatory scheme are respectively 26- and 12-fold Cuba's, whereas average social assistance benefits are six- and three-fold Cuba's.[41] Ages of retirement in China and Vietnam are five years lower in each sex than Cuba, and require fewer years of contribution (15 fewer years). The replacement rate in Cuba is 60 percent of the average earnings for five years, higher than in China and Vietnam (45 percent of 15-year average wages). The large majority of Latin American countries adjust pensions annually for cost of living, whereas Cuba, China and Vietnam do not.

d) *Social solidarity and gender equity.* No social security scheme has been privatized or "marketized" in Cuba; social security is public and mostly state financed, hence social solidarity is maximized, with transfers among generations, genders and income groups (save for the armed forces). In Latin America, social solidarity and gender equity are enhanced in public and social insurance systems but excluded in pension individual accounts and HMOs; social solidarity is exogenous through state provision of minimum pensions and social assistance; re-reforms in three countries have improved social solidarity and gender equity. Because of China's highly fragmented pension and health care systems, social solidarity is low; central and local government subsidies, particularly in social assistance, infuse some solidarity. Vietnam allows for solidarity among generations in the pension scheme, and also grants women 1 percent more than men in the pension for each additional year of contribution after the statutory age.

e) *Administration.* Cuba's social security system is excessively centralized in a state monopoly that bans private, cooperative and individual practice,

CARMELO MESA-LAGO

without effective workers' participation in its management, monitoring and evaluation, hence the system is in need of decentralization and social participation. The ILO-recommended tripartite approach to administer social security is absent as workers do not have any participation in the management of the public pension and health systems. Administrative costs are impossible to estimate as they are not transparent and the government does not provide data. Latin America has a wide variety of systems; half the countries have privately managed pension funds, half have publicly administered ones; most countries have HMOs although health care social insurance leads. Tripartite participation (workers, employers, and government) functions in public social insurance schemes, but not in private systems. Most countries are moving toward decentralization. Vietnam, and particularly China, have decentralized systems; the central government delineates broad guiding principles for the reform (indicative rather than mandatory) and local governments are encouraged to experiment with diverse solutions according to their particular circumstances, taking responsibility in management and decision making. In China, social organizations' participation has increased since 2012; village committees play a significant role in selecting *dibao* beneficiaries. In Vietnam there is less participation than in China but more than in Cuba, with representatives of the labor confederation and cooperatives on the board; management costs are high and compliance low (Huöng et al. 2013). In both countries there has been a "marketization" of social security with mixed pension and health care schemes, combining partial central and local government funding with insured contributions and copayments.

f) *Financial sustainability.* Cuba's total contributions to social security amounts to 12 percent by enterprises to the pension scheme (17 percent if we include the 5 percent paid by a tiny minority of workers). The state subsidized the resulting deficit with the equivalent of 9.3 percent of wages in 2013 (much more to achieve equilibrium in the medium term) for a total of 21.3 percent; health care is free. China's contributions are 28 percent for the urban pension and 43 percent for the health care system; in addition, central and state governments make increasing transfers to balance the system. Vietnam's contribution to the pension scheme is 22 percent (projected to rise 1 percent annually); and about 5 percent copayments to the health care system. Therefore, Cuba's contribution is the lowest among the three countries and also lower than that of Latin American countries at a similar level of social development, like Uruguay, Argentina, Brazil, and Costa Rica. The total cost of social security in Cuba is 15.7 percent of GDP (despite a cut of 3 percentage points by Raúl's reforms) vis-à-vis 4.7 percent in China and 5.7 percent in Vietnam, about one-third of Cuba's level. [42] Therefore Cuba has the highest costs and the lowest contributions; hence the actuarial deficit should be enormous. At the same time access and quality of benefits have deteriorated. Pension and health care costs will keep climbing due to population aging, currently the oldest population in the region tied with Uruguay. China is aging faster than Vietnam but still well behind Cuba. Vietnam's active to passive ratio is twice Cuba's. Latin American private pension systems are less affected by aging but not exempted in the long term: to cover a longer period of retirement, the "defined" contribution has to be increased, the age raised, or the benefit reduced. Some public systems are undertaking parametric reforms to make them more sustainable but still confront actuarial disequilibrium.

In summary, Cuba is ahead of other countries in unity-uniformity and coverage (except for social assistance and eroding in health care), social solidarity and gender equity, but behind the rest on benefit sufficiency, administration, and financial sustainability.

Some Suggestions to Improve Social Security

Generally, Cuba should ask the ILO to conduct an assessment of the state of social protection floor on minimum contributory pensions, basic health care, and social assistance for the elderly, including an exercise based on a national dialogue to generate consensus, as already done in many countries. The ILO should also conduct a costing exercise to determine the available and necessary fiscal space for needed social security improvements over a ten-year period, with a choice between low- and high-cost packages, hence providing the government with a range of options, costs related to GDP and alternative funding sources (Schmitt and Chadwick 2014). Specific suggestions are listed below.

a) *Pension system:* Conduct a household survey to estimate total coverage of the labor force by contributory pensions and also of the elderly by non-contributory pensions, in order to identify the uninsured and ways to incorporate them (self-employed, usufruct and private farmers, and employees in microbusinesses); integrate into the general pension system the costly armed forces and internal security pension schemes; consider a pension reform either creating a new PAYG scheme or a mixed system as in China and Costa Rica. Should new resources become available, raise pension levels and adjust them to the cost of living.

b) *Health care:* Maintain the public health care system but with needed changes: give priority to potable-water and sewage infrastructure; reallocate scarce resources more rationally, e.g., instead of continuing the effort to reduce infant mortality (a problem basically already solved) shift those funds to improve the water sewage infrastructure, medicine imports, and other areas of greater need; discontinue free fellowships for foreign medical students and health care aid to other countries (a humane task, but not affordable when there are domestic gaps that need to be filled); convert maternity and pediatric hospitals with low occupancy rates into geriatric hospitals and; charge the full cost (or at least a copayment) of curative health services to the highest income strata and slowly charge copayments to the top middle income strata, as done in China, Vietnam, and some Latin American countries; attract more foreigners to receive medical attention in Cuba in facilities that generate hard currency; reduce the number of family doctors abroad as they are essential to provide primary care; authorize self-employment of health professionals as well as health-care cooperatives that compete with state services.

c) *Social assistance:* Through the household survey suggested above, estimate the people in real need of help, design a targeting tool similar to those used in several Latin American countries; start providing social assistance to the population in extreme poverty and, as resources become available, gradually incorporate all the poor;[43] once the social safety net is in place, continue phasing out the rationing system; permit churches and NGOs to receive direct foreign aid in order to establish and expand free old age homes for the needy, as well as to help other groups in the vulnerable population.

d) *Financial sustainability:* Carry out an actuarial valuation to determine the present and long run pension disequilibrium and identify alternative policies to improve the situation; one option might be to close the current general pension system to new entrants, make the state responsible for ongoing pensions, and create a new public system for young workers already insured in the old system as well as all new workers, with a reserve that is invested to generate returns and help in the long-term financing and improvement of pensions; enforce and gradually increase the personal income tax set in the tax reform and assign part of the new revenue to social security; generate savings from the integration of the armed forces schemes into the general system; invest the potential dividend from normalizing relations with the United States (in the form of reductions in defense) in improving the financial health of the social security system, setting priorities on assistance to address the most urgent needs.

Cuba's social security is unique in Latin America, and compared with China and Vietnam, for its universal and free features. Despite paying meager benefits, Cuba's system is financially unsustainable; current reforms are painfully cutting away expenses but the long-term sustainability is dire. Comparisons with China and Vietnam herein and in other chapters of this book show that the two Asian countries have achieved remarkable economic success by implementing more profound and faster economic reforms than Cuba, which have resulted in a mixed socialist market system. While they are behind Cuba in social security coverage and unity-uniformity, their systems are more financially sustainable and are expanding gradually according to available resources. To sum up, first, the only way for Cuba to escape from the current economic abyss is to deepen and accelerate the structural reforms that Raúl has been implementing for eight years (slowly and with many obstacles and disincentives) in order to substantially transform the current inefficient economic system, characterized by predominance of central planning and state ownership of the means of production over the market and nonstate ownership, into a mixed system able to generate high and sustainable growth. Second, Raúl's social security reforms are painful but necessary; they are currently subordinated to economic capacity but, as suggested in this section, multiple measures could be implemented to improve efficiency, benefits, and sustainability and thus enhance social security.

NOTES

1. This chapter significantly expands and updates to mid-2015 several of the author's works on the topic (Mesa-Lago 2013, 2014a, 2015) and adds systematic international comparisons; information without a source herein is from those works. Statistics mainly come from Cuba's National Office of Statistics and Information (ONEI) and focus on the 2006–2015 period under Raúl Castro. The author alone is responsible for the contents of this chapter, but gratefully acknowledges Jorge Pérez-López and Scott Morgenstern for many useful comments; Mauricio De Miranda and Tanako Yamaoka for the interview they conducted with a high official in Hanoi; and Thomas Rawski for guiding me on the Chinese bibliography;

2. The USSR granted $65 billion to Cuba in 1960–1990, 60.5 percent in donations and price subsidies and 39.5 percent in loans, of which Cuba paid back only 0.7 percent.

3. For detailed analysis of Raúl's reforms see: Mesa-Lago 2014a; Mesa-Lago and Pérez-López 2013.

4. In January 1959, the author was appointed by the revolutionary government to reform the old pension system and unify the diverse schemes; aided by the ILO, the Cuban Institute of Social Insurance was established and the unification process began.

5. Subsidized prices for rationed goods, free health care, owned or low-priced rental housing, and inexpensive public utilities.

6. For example, a man who enters the army at age 17 can retire after 25 years of

service, at age 42, and receive a pension of 100 percent of his last year's salary for an average retirement period of 37 years.

7. Cuba has two currencies: the national peso (CUP) and the convertible peso (CUC). The CUC is equal to 25 CUP; the CUC's value is fairly close to the US dollar. Conversions of CUP to US dollar herein are based on the exchange rate 1$=25 CUP.

8. One pound of ham takes the entire minimum pension of 200 CUP ($8); an energy-saving light bulb is half of such a pension.

9. In some of his writings, the author recommended a period from 10 to 20 years for the gradual increase in the retirement age in order to lessen its impact. However, Raúl Castro (2008) decided that the financial crisis of the pension scheme required it to be done in just seven years.

10. It was projected that this would occur in 2015 but in 2014 Cuba tied Uruguay, with 13.8 percent of its population of age 65 and above (Lazo 2014; ONEI 2015).

11. Contrary to the steady decline in the birth rate, official data shows 0.33 percent population growth in 2013 and 0.25 percent in 2014 resulting from zero net emigration in 2013 and a net positive of 0.02 percent in 2014. And yet, those leaving the island by boats and rafts have steadily increased. It seems that ONEI reports only emigrants who depart legally.

12. In 2014, President Michele Bachelet appointed a Presidential Commission on Pensions to assess the results of her first re-reform and recommend measures to correct the remaining flaws; the author was a member of that commission, which delivered its report in September 2015.

13. The most important social welfare component is education, which takes almost half of total expenditures.

14. In Latin America, management is private in the funded system/pillar; in China it is public, managed by local governments.

15. Pensions under this scheme average two to three times those of employees in the private sector (Fang 2014).

16. A special national scheme was created for this group with a combination of PAYG and individual accounts, enterprises contribute 12 percent (but 86 percent evade such contributions) and workers from 4 percent to 8 percent (Leung and Xu 2015).

17. Social insurance provides old-age/survivors pensions (the main component), sickness-maternity and employment risks.

18. Exempted from the unified system are armed forces, state security, and top government and Communist Party officials, who have a different health care network. In the 1990s, another separate program was set to serve foreigners paying in hard currency. Both programs provide higher-quality services than the general health care system available to the population.

19. In 1959–1989, the number of rural hospitals rose from 1 to 70 and the total number of hospitals from 230 to 264.

20. For every several urban blocks, a dwelling was built with facilities in the ground floor, staffed by a physician and a nurse.

21. As infant mortality shrinks, it becomes more difficult and costly to reduce it, requiring sonograms to detect congenital problems, special care of pregnant women, and performance of an abortion when the fetus faces serious risks. Cuba has the highest abortion rate in the region.

22. In 1989–1995, the immunized population fell 56 percent for tuberculosis, 50 percent for tetanus, 45 percent for typhoid, and 27 percent for polio.

23. Data from Venezuela from President Nicolás Maduro (www.noticierodigital .com, Caracas, February 28, 2014) and from Brazil by *Associated Press*, November 4, 2014.

24. After a cut in the number of graduates in schools of medicine, a sharp increase has occurred since 2008–2009 (ONEI 2014).

25. An important advance was the renovation in 2014 of Santiago de Cuba's aqueduct.

26. Migrant workers are allowed to choose between the first and third schemes.

27. The 2012 morbidity rate per 100,000 inhabitants for tuberculosis was 215 in Vietnam and 6.7 in Cuba (ONEI 2014); Huöng et al. (2013).

28. Coverage of the elderly: 170,674 (social assistance beneficiaries) divided by 2,135,280 (population age 60 and above) x 100 = 8 percent.

29. Only 15,825 slots were available in asylums and nurseries, but 480,000 persons age 60 and above need care.

30. The countries are: Argentina, Bolivia, Brazil, Chile, Colombia, Costa Rica, Cuba, Ecuador, El Salvador, Guatemala, Mexico, Panama, Peru, Uruguay, and Venezuela. Only the least developed countries do not provide such pension (IADB 2014).

31. The *wubao* assistance scheme for the rural elderly in need is being replaced by the *dibao*.

32. ILO (2014) estimated 0.22 percent of GDP for 2010.

33. The poverty line in urban areas is $25 monthly and in rural areas $20, both higher than the average pension in Cuba.

34. As a percentage of current expenditures in the state budget, however, expenditures peaked at 29.5 percent in 2011 and were 29.3 percent in 2013, because current expenditures over GDP fell 10 percentage points in that period (ONEI 2014),

35. Reportedly, in 2014 life expectancy in Cuba was 78.45 years, the highest in Latin America after Costa Rica, and also higher than in China, 74.8 years (Leung and Xu 2015). Cuba's active/passive ratio is 2.9, and 6 in Costa Rica (CCSS 2015).

36. ECLAC (2014) estimates 1.1 percent, the fifth-lowest rate among 35 countries of Latin America and the Caribbean.

37. According to Gao (2013) it was 4.5 percent in 2011.

38. Because the compulsory fund is very young, the ratio of active insured to one pensioner was 5.3 to 1 in 2011 (almost twice Cuba's ratio) but declining fast. In the voluntary program, the ratio was 0.6 to 1 (Huöng et al. 2013; ratios estimated by author).

39. Vietnam's social protection eight-year plan aims to achieve a universal system by 2020, targeting those in especially difficult circumstances: children in need, low-income elderly, severely disabled persons, and the poor (Fifth Plenum 2012). The ILO estimates that closing the social gap will cost between 1.98 percent and 6.06 percent of GDP by 2020 (Schmitt and Chadwick 2014).

40. China's first social security law was enacted in 1951, Cuba's in 1963.

41. Chile's average social assistance pension in 2013 was 26-fold Cuba's.

42. Despite the tightening of the pension scheme, the state-financed deficit has grown.

43. If Cuba were to expand social assistance to protect all those in need, costs would jump tenfold, from 0.3 percent to 3 percent of GDP. But a targeted assistance to those with highest need, e.g., living in extreme poverty, would cost less and significantly reduce poverty.

BIBLIOGRAPHY

Añé, Lía. "Contribución a los Estudios de Pobreza en Cuba." Ponencia Congreso de LASA. Montreal: September 6–8, 2007.

Bertranou, Fabio, et al. "Country Case-Studies on Recent Reversals of Pension Privatisation: Argentina." In *Reversing Pension Privatization in the World*. Edited by Isabel Ortiz. Geneva: ILO, 2018.

Caja Costarricense de Seguro Social—CCSS. *Información estadística*. San José, September 2, 2015.

Castro, Raúl. "Discurso en las Conclusiones de la Primera Sesión Ordinaria de la Asamblea Nacional del Poder Popular," Havana, July 11, 2008.

Comité Estatal de Estadísticas—CEE. *Anuario Estadístico de Cuba 1989*. Havana, 1991.

De Miranda, Mauricio, and Kanako Yamaoka. Author's interview with a top official (who requested anonymity) of the Social Security Policy Studies, Institute of Labor Science and Social Affairs, Vietnam's Ministry of Labor, Hanoi, October 30, 2014.

Dillon, Nara. "Two Worlds of Welfare Communism: China and Cuba Compared." In Martin Dimitrov, ed., *China–Cuba: Trajectories of Post-Revolutionary Governance*, 2018.

Economic Commission for Latin American and the Caribbean—ECLAC. *Preliminary Overview of the Economies of Latin American and the Caribbean 2014*. Santiago de Chile, 2014.

Espina, Mayra. *Políticas de Atención a la Pobreza y la Desigualdad: Examinando el Rol del Estado en la Experiencia Cubana*. Buenos Aires: CLACSO, 2008.

Fang, Lianquan. "Towards Universal Coverage: A Macro Analysis of China's Public Pension Program." In *Reforming Pensions in Developing and Transition Countries*. Edited by Katja Hujo, 187–219. Basingstoke: UNRISD, Palgrave Macmillan, 2014.

Fifth Plenum 11th Central Committee. *Resolution No. 15-NQ/TW Vietnam Social Policies for 2012–2020*. Hanoi, 2012.

Frank, Marc. "Health Service Exports to Top $8 billion." Havana, *Reuters,* March 21, 2014.

Gao, Qin. "Size and Structure of the Chinese Welfare System: Evidence from Macro Data." Paper presented at the American Association of Chinese Studies, 55th Annual Conference, Rutgers University, October 11–13, 2013.

García, Ivan. Article in *D'Lamé*, January 22, 2014.

Gonzalez, Roberto M. "Infant Mortality in Cuba." *Cuban Studies* 43, 19–39. Pittsburgh: University of Pittsburgh Press, 2015.

Huông, Nguyen Thi Lan, et al. *Development of the Social Protection System in Vietnam Until 2020*. Hanoi: Institute of Labor Science and Social Affairs, July 2013.

Inter-American Development Bank—IADB. *Panorama de las Pensiones en América Latina y el Caribe*. Washington, DC, 2014.

International Labor Organization—ILO. *Social Protection for Older Persons: Key Trends and Statistics*. Geneva: ILO, 2014.

International Labor Organization and WIEGO—ILO-WIEGO. *Women and Men in Informal Employment: A Statistical Picture*, 2nd ed. Geneva: ILO, 2013.

Lazo, Alicia M. "Análisis de Cobertura del Régimen Previsional Uruguayo." Montevideo, December 2014.

Leung, Joe C. B., and Yuebin Xu. *China's Social Welfare: The Third Turning Point*. Cambridge: Polity Press, 2015.

Mesa-Lago, Carmelo. *Reassembling Social Security: A Survey of Pension and Health Care Reforms*, 2nd ed. Oxford: Oxford University Press, 2012.

Mesa-Lago, Carmelo. *Social Protection Systems in Latin America and the Caribbean: Cuba*. Santiago: ECLAC, 2013.

Mesa-Lago, Carmelo. "Institutional Changes in Cuba's Economic and Social Reforms." In *Cuba Economic Change in Comparative Perspective*. Edited by Richard Feinberg and Ted Piccone, 49–69. Washington, DC: Brookings Institution and Universidad de La Habana, 2014a.

Mesa-Lago, Carmelo. *Reversing Pension Privatization: The Experience of Argentina, Bolivia, Chile and Hungary*. Geneva: ILO, 2014b.

Mesa-Lago, Carmelo. "The Cuban Social Welfare System: Universalism-Gratuity and Economic Sustainability." In *Social Welfare Systems in the World*. Edited by Christian Aspalter. Ashgate, 2015.

Mesa-Lago, Carmelo. "A Comparative Analyses of Structural Reforms in Cuba and China." In *China–Cuba: Trajectories of Post-Revolutionary Governance*. Edited by Martin Dimitrov. 2018.

Mesa-Lago, Carmelo. "Reversing Pension Privatization in Bolivia," in Isabel Ortiz (ed.) *Reversing Pension Privatization in the World*. Geneva: ILO, 2018.

Mesa-Lago, Carmelo, and Jorge Pérez-López. *Cuba Under Raúl Castro: Assessing the Reforms*. Boulder–London: Lynne Rienner Publishers, 2013.

Mesa-Lago, Carmelo, and Fabio Bertranou. "Pension Reforms in Chile and Social Security Principles, 1981–2015." *International Social Security Review* 69, no.1, January–March 2016, pp. 25–45.

Ministry of Public Health—MINSAP. *Nota Informativa a la Población*. Havana, January 15, 2013.

MINSAP. *Anuario Estadístico de Salud 2013*. Havana, 2014.

National Assembly Vietnam. Social Insurance Law No. 71. Hanoi, 2006.

Oficina Nacional de Estadísticas e Información—ONEI. *Anuario Estadístico de Cuba 2006, 2007, 2008, 2009, 2010, 2011, 2012, 2013, 2014*. Havana, 2007, 2008, 2009, 2010, 2011, 2012, 2013, 2014, 2015.

ONEI. *El Estado Actual y Perspectivo de la Población Cubana: Un Reto para el Desarrollo Territorial Sostenible*. Havana, 2008b.

ONEI. *El Envejecimiento de la Población Cubana 2008*. Havana, 2009b.

ONEI. *Encuesta Nacional de Fecundidad Informe de Resultados 2009*. Havana, 2010b.

ONEI. *Panorama Económico y Social Cuba 2014*. Havana, 2015b.

ONEI. *Anuario Demográfico de Cuba 2014*. Havana, 2015c.

Pan American Health Organization—PAHO. "Alerta Epidemiológica en Cuba." www .paho.org, August 14, 2013a.

PAHO. *Boletín de la OPS*, August 23, 2013b.

Roffman, Rafael, and Maria L. Oliveri. *Pension Coverage in Latin America: Trends and Determinants*. Washington, DC: World Bank, 2012.

Sánchez Rosas, Luis. "El Silencio Epidemiológico y la Etica de la Salud Pública Cubana." *Revista Cubana de Salud Pública*, 39, no. 3 (August 2013).

Schmitt, Valéry, and Rachael Chadwick. "Social Protection-Assessment Based National Dialogues Exercises: Cambodia, Indonesia, Thailand, Vietnam." *International Social Security Review* 67, no. 1 (2014): 95–119.

United Nations Development Program—UNDP. *Human Development Report 2007/2008*. New York, 2007.

Xianglin, Mao. Latin American Institute, Chinese Academy of Social Sciences, Answers to author's questions on China reforms. Beijing, November 8, 2013.

JAVIER VÁZQUEZ-D'ELÍA

THE FUTURE OF CUBAN SOCIAL PROTECTION

ANALYSIS FROM THE LATIN AMERICAN WINDOW

Fidel Castro's succession by his brother, a number of subsequent reforms affecting the institutional frames of economic activity, and the recent evolution of diplomatic relations with the United States have fed expectations that significant changes may be on Cuba's horizon. This chapter seeks to identify possible trends of change of the Cuban system of social protection by taking a comparative glance at the main regional trends over the past three decades. Its central assumption is that some of the macrostructural forces, conflicts, and institutional dynamics that have shaped the reforms of social protection systems in the region are likely to play relevant roles in Cuba's future evolution as well. I will not attempt to predict future directions of change; more modestly, the purpose here is to use the results of recent research on the comparative political economy of welfare reform in Latin America to identify potential directions for change in Cuba, accounting for differences in institutional and contextual configurations.

Systems of social protection provide a reliable map of the distribution of power in any society, and in turn define institutional frameworks, decisively constraining and shaping the political mobilization of important collective actors. In addition, the context of "permanent austerity" that followed the exhaustion of the cycle of postwar economic expansion has made welfare reform an almost permanent object of acute political contention all around the world.

In the Cuban case, some specific circumstances add to those omnipresent determinants of the directions for change in the social welfare system. The impressive achievements of social policies have historically been one of the most solid sources of international and domestic legitimacy for the postrevolutionary order. Since 1989, the persistent stagnation of the Cuban economy has progressively undermined the sustainability of those policies and their results. The consequences of that deterioration do not only entail potential effects on Cubans' evaluations of the performance of their government and on the legitimacy of the regime, but also have critical implications for the viability of any sustainable program of economic recovery and long-term development.

The theme of Cuba's exceptionalism has a long history and remains well alive, and I will refer to it throughout this chapter. The country's special circumstances imply that neither the conceptual approach nor, as a consequence, the choice of relevant cases for purposes of comparison, is obvious. There are several alternatives. Should we revisit the literature on the tensions and synergies resulting from the simultaneity of regime transition and market-oriented reform? How much light can we cast on the Cuban case from the experiences of "third-wave democracies" in Latin America, on the one hand, and the former communist bloc, on the other hand? Or should we consider the regimes of "market-Leninism"[1] emerging from the protracted processes of China and Vietnam?

I will contend that the multiple uncertainties surrounding the current stage of the Cuban process, as well as the limitations of the information we can reliably build upon, would provide too shaky a foundation for any effort of systematic comparison aiming at theory testing. Given the scarcity of data plus the variety of alternative paths to consider, such an attempt would equal an exercise in science fiction. That said, a glance from different windows can help to identify the analytical problems and need for information necessary to develop a research agenda. With this purpose in mind, I find that looking at the transformations experienced by welfare regimes in Latin America throughout the past three decades is a source of useful insight.

As evidenced in the literature on the comparative political economy of the welfare state, all countries face some similar challenges with regards to social protection, and there are also some general world trends. However, that literature also shows that the specific forms in which those trends combine in each case, the varying degrees to which the same type of general transformation affects different countries, and the specific institutional crystallization that eventually consolidates changes, are highly context and path dependent. While the singularity of the Cuban welfare regime in the Latin American context complicates the comparisons, also evident are similarities in terms of the levels of economic (under) development, demographic configurations, limitations in infrastructure, and initial development of systems of social security.

My premise is that these similarities entail comparable challenges for the sustainability of systems of social protection, which in turn should result in lines of fracture or cleavages within the political system. True, there is conclusive evidence showing that such translations are by no means automatic, but decisively shaped by configurations of institutions and actors marked by a strong path dependence. Looking at the institutions and actors that have proved most influential in other cases in the region can allow reasonable speculation on likely paths for the Cuban system to follow.

This chapter intends to build upon the fine dissection provided by Mesa-Lago in chapter 8 of this volume, using comparative analysis as an exploratory tool. The chapter proceeds through the following steps:

a) A brief enumeration of the main structural forces behind the most important transformations in the welfare systems of the region;

b) Identification of the most extended trends of transformation and outcomes of reform;

c) Identification of the most relevant cleavages and actors that have shaped the political processes leading to those outcomes; and

d) A summary assessment of the potential relevance that analogous cleavages and actors may have for Cuba's future.

A FEW THEORETICAL CONSIDERATIONS

A central proposition of this study is that systems of social protection[2] have *political* significance. Beyond their immediate impact in terms of management of social risks and, in some cases, redistribution of income, they define an essential dimension of citizenship, and as a result, these systems articulate between society and state. In other words, welfare states are *welfare* states, but also welfare *states*. Considered under this light, processes of reform of social protection systems constitute exercises in statecraft. They create or redefine the limits of different constituencies (they may facilitate their integration, fragmentation, or mobilization), thus shaping the very terms of distributive

JAVIER VÁZQUEZ-D'ELÍA

conflict in particular and providing an essential instrument for the regulation of political conflict in general, as well as for the production of political legitimacy. As James Malloy once said, the fiscal foundations and distribution of benefits of any system of social protection provide a very reliable map of the distribution of political power in the respective society.[3]

For the analytical purposes of this chapter, I will propose a scheme to discuss reform paths that has been built through a comparison of social policy reform in 11 Latin American countries between 1980 and 2010.[4] From a theoretical point of view, the main points of the argument are the following:

1. Systems of social protection constitute highly resilient institutional conglomerates. Their remarkable inertia mainly rests on the strength of coalitions of insiders, specialized bureaucracies in charge of their administration, and politicians profiting from the electoral support of those constituencies.

2. The main forces with the potential to shake and remove that inertia are the following:

   - changes in the socioeconomic structure eventually resulting in the emergence of new social risks not covered by existing policies, compromising the financial viability of the latter, or redistributing power among different types of stakeholders;

   - endogenous processes of maturation of existing systems that may complicate their financial sustainability.

3. Even when socioeconomic change or, more precisely, the resulting disjunctures between institutions and the structure of social risks constitute the primary force of friction and pressures for reform, the concrete terms in which reforms enter the public agenda and become a matter of political contention are shaped by institutional factors and political strategies. In other words, socioeconomic transformations may favor the displacement of cleavages, the emergence of new lines of fracture, or the formation of new constituencies; however, the political activation and mobilization of cleavages and constituencies is always institutionally mediated.

4. Institutional effects are not mechanical. They operate by shaping the configuration of political actors and their respective structures of political opportunity.

5. The political dynamics of social protection reforms are decisively shaped by the configuration of the institutional conglomerates that regulate the interactions between: a) political parties; b) interest groups representing risk

categories covered by existing social protection (insiders); c) expert bureaucracies; and d) social or political collective actors mobilizing support from risk groups not covered by existing schemes of social protection (outsiders).

MAIN TRENDS OF REFORM IN LATIN AMERICAN SOCIAL PROTECTION SYSTEMS (1980–2010)

The current situation: postreform welfare regimes[5]

Compared with the picture of the 1980s, the current kaleidoscope of systems of social protection shows important degrees of continuity. Welfare regimes, however, have experienced important changes. In many cases, important alterations in the balance between state and market ending in recommodification have occurred. But even the most stubbornly resilient systems have in the end been forced to give some response to pressing changes in the social structure. The drastic expansion of social assistance and the resulting dualization constitute the most notorious common denominator, shared by all countries to variable degrees. I propose a classification based on five types: exclusionary/assistential, conservative/assistential, liberal assistential, segmented universalism, and incomplete universalism (see table 9.1, pg. 265).

The purpose behind the inclusion of this typology is not to fit Cuba into a pigeonhole. Quite the contrary, my contention will be that, in spite of the diversity of the menu, Cuba cannot be reasonably squeezed into any of the following ideal types. Instead, I begin by showing the diversity both of results and of the multiple paths that led to them, for which I will provide a quick overview. But the argument also has a positivist side: by analyzing the main structural and institutional variables underlying those multiple paths, I will argue that although each welfare system has its specific mix, a few critical ingredients have been present pretty much everywhere. Since many of those ingredients are also present in Cuba, understanding the ways in which they have interacted throughout the region may provide valuable insight for hypothesizing likely paths for the Cuban situation.

EXCLUSIONARY/ASSISTENTIAL

This category includes the cases of Bolivia, Ecuador, and Peru. The welfare mix includes a high level of informality, states with an important assistential role but limited capacities, poorly institutionalized markets, and a small and highly segmented contributions-based component. This is the most markedly truncated type, and also the one with the lowest level of decommodification and highest familialism. Truncation provides the most visible line of a brutally simplified stratification.

CONSERVATIVE/ASSISTENTIAL

Venezuela fits this category. It includes a highly deteriorated but highly resilient, highly segmented contributory core, where neither marketization nor universalization have made advances. Truncation is less brutal than in the previous category, but dualization is—in part due to political dynamics—even more marked. It is also the case in which assistance is most extended, segmented, and poorly institutionalized. The state is the central component of the mix, but somewhat paradoxically the informal sector is also important. Decommodification is significant, but limited in its reproduction and potential long-term effects by fragmentation and informality.

LIBERAL/ASSISTENTIAL

This type includes Chile, Colombia, and Mexico. Its mix is the one with most pronounced marketization, but the informal sector remains an important component. The result has been high recommodification. Stratification follows two main lines. First, the stratifying effect of the market operates more or less directly, only very tenuously mediated by marginal risk pooling. Second, those same stratifying effects make social assistance important. Its impact, however, varies considerably within the category, due to very diverse levels of informalization.

SEGMENTED UNIVERSALISM

This includes Argentina and Uruguay. The state remains the most influential component of the mix, but both the market and the family play important roles. The informal sector is considerably less extended than in other types but is nevertheless significant compared to the past configuration of these countries. Correspondingly, assistance is reduced in comparison to the old corporatist core of the system of social protection, but is by no means negligible. As a result, the pattern of stratification is probably the most complex, since it combines in a relatively balanced cocktail the considerable segmentation of the social insurance system, the effects of the recently expanded private component, and the consequences of moderate truncation.

INCOMPLETE UNIVERSALISM

This last category includes Brazil and Costa Rica. It is the type with the most robust participation of the state, and as a result the one with the most significant level of decommodification. Universal rights play an important role as determinants of access to benefits, but universalism remains incomplete in two senses. First, its logic is unevenly influential across policy domains—in both cases, less for pensions than for healthcare. Second, informality also constitutes an important limitation, although it is significantly moderated by multiple noncontributory benefits. Stratification effects are thus uneven across policy areas.

Structural changes underlying recent reforms of Latin American welfare regimes

In the model proposed in this paper, welfare reforms primarily enter the political agenda as a result of changes in the socioeconomic structure that in turn result in disjunctures between the architecture of social risk and the institutions put in place to cope with them. The important cross-national variation among the solutions implemented to cope with those disjunctures reflects the diversity of paths followed by welfare regime reforms. These, in turn, are shaped by highly variable and specific combinations of institutional legacies and conjunctural equations of political actors. However, at the root of these diverging paths we find a common denominator of challenges originated by a relatively small number of structural transformations that are common to all cases. What follows is an enumeration of the most influential of such transformations, with no pretension of exhaustive elaboration on their multiple interactions.[6]

First, especially in the most mature regimes, there has been a *demographic transition* that has damaged the ratios of dependents to paying workers (Riesco and Draibe 2007). Second, a *crisis of the patriarchal family model* that, combined with an accelerated *feminization of the labor force*, has created multiple points of friction with the familialist bias of existing welfare mixes (Filgueira 1996). That change has decisively accentuated the incidence of gender-based stratification effects. Third, an *expansion of informal economic activity* has highlighted the extent to which welfare regimes reach only limited parts of the citizenry throughout the region. With increasing numbers of people working outside formal economic sectors, there has been increasing pressure on social protection systems, showing needs to: a) drastically expand noncontributory forms of social assistance; b) contract the fiscal basis of social security programs funded through payroll taxes; and c) narrow the population matching conditions of eligibility for social security benefits. Fourth, processes of *massive rural–urban migration* have contributed to the overflowing of urban infrastructure and diverse public services have accentuated the incidence of a number of social risks, especially those associated with insufficient sanitation. Fifth, the growth of *structural, long-term unemployment*—itself one of the forces feeding informalization—and of *precarious employment*, has simultaneously constituted a source of new social risks and negatively impacted fiscal revenue.

JAVIER VÁZQUEZ-D'ELÍA

While these trends affect most countries, there is also an important caveat: the configurations of factors pressuring the welfare regimes are unstable. In other words, there are multiple patterns of (in)stability. As a result, while some countries have gone through cycles of radical reform followed by equally radical backlashes, others have exhibited far more gradual and cumulative patterns.

Mesa-Lago has provided abundant evidence of the extent to which Cuba shares most of these structural trends. Here I will only remind the reader that perhaps concomitant to its position at the vanguard of processes of demographic aging in the region, poor economic opportunities, and decreasing welfare protections, Cubans have crafted creative survival mechanisms, especially in the area of the informal and underground economy. This has not only supported growth in production and employment, it has also narrowed the fiscal basis of the country's social protection scheme.

Main directions of reform common to the region

While there are common sociopolitical trends, data on changes in legislation and institutions dealing with social protection point in contradictory directions. There are some common trends, but there is still wide variation among final policies implemented across the region in the past thirty years of transformations. An elementary grouping of countries based on a quantitative comparison of levels of welfare effort around 2006, without being drastically different from the one we found around 1980, shows important displacements,[7] suggesting that prereform welfare regimes, while strongly influencing reform trajectories and outcomes, did not completely determine them. The inconsistent paths suggest the importance of analyzing interactions between regimes and other institutional configurations to explain the changes. Here I will point to a particular formula for explaining reform trends, but limit myself to identifying variables that affect change and pointing to regionwide trends.

Although there is variance in terms of chronology and intensity, at least nine clear master lineages of policy change have pervaded the whole region throughout the past three decades. First, there has been an extended and on average *steady increase* of aggregated social spending. Second, many countries have *constitutionalized* entitlements to different forms of social protection in terms of universal citizenship rights. Third, and in many cases in flagrant contradiction with the previous trend, states have *retrenched* participation in the welfare mix, and there has been a correlative expansion of the role of markets in the provision of social protection.[8] Fourth, there has been a qualitative displacement of predominant *forms of states' intervention,* from provision to regulation, coordination, and last-resort insurance; and a correlative increase in the importance of private providers. Fifth, the region has seen a significant *homogenization*—at least formally—of the *menu* of programs forming part of social security systems.[9] Sixth, almost all countries have *expanded the assistential component* of social protection by means of diverse types of means-tested programs. Seventh, and strongly associated with the previous aspect, there have been *important gains in terms of access* (especially to primary health care) that nevertheless frequently coexist with very *uneven distributions in terms of the quality* of services. Eighth, most countries have *relaxed the degree of regulation* of labor markets in general, and of the *protection of jobs* in particular. Ninth, and directly associated with that, there has been an important *decline of the importance of employment* as the anchor of social protection.[10]

Overview of intraregional variations on common themes

At first sight, the current panorama of welfare policies in Latin America looks messy and extremely diverse, but it is not much different than the range within the OECD world. What is clear is that neither the wave of market-oriented reforms, nor the backlash that followed it, entailed uniform patterns of transformation.

Change has occurred pretty much everywhere, and it has been significant. Some of the oldest and most extended original cores, characterized by their extreme fragmentation and problems of financial sustainability, have proved very resilient (Argentina, Uruguay, and to a lesser extent Brazil), but others were dismantled or drastically transformed (Chile, Mexico). Or perhaps it would be more accurate to say that established coalitions of insiders have very often proved more resilient than the general configurations of the systems to which they owed their benefits. The price of structural change has been more often than not the need for reformers to negotiate with those coalitions and accept some of their demands, thus compromising to an important extent the scope originally intended for reforms and the internal coherence of their results. A direct consequence of the need to preserve the privileges of the beneficiaries of the previous systems has been the predominance of trajectories of change leading to institutional layering.[11] The institutional fragmentation produced by the accumulation of "layers" based on different principles and logics has made coordination problems probably the most extended common denominator across systems of social protection in the region. It is worth noticing that this capacity of insiders to form coalitions who can frustrate reformist projects is not alien to the Cuban experience, considering the capacity of privileged pension systems with a contributory basis to navigate a

JAVIER VÁZQUEZ-D'ELÍA

revolution in the name of a very different set of principles than the initiatives sponsored by the Washington Consensus.

It is not, of course, that the neoliberal wave that passed over the region starting in the 1980s had no durable consequences. The posthumous balance of the Washington Consensus probably disappoints its formerly most enthusiastic advocates, who would have liked it to go deeper. Still, the balance between states and markets changed drastically in favor of the latter in several cases. This has been the case both for pensions (Argentina, Bolivia, Chile, Colombia, Mexico, Peru, Uruguay), and for health care systems (Chile, Colombia, Mexico, Peru).[12]

However, we can find changes in the opposite direction too. The state has sometimes recovered ground after drastic and sometimes very ephemeral withdrawals—as in the cases of pension systems in Argentina, Ecuador, and Venezuela—restoring something very close to a status quo ante. At other times, the pendulum swung back as violently as it had previously done toward the market, but the resulting configuration is a new one—the case of pensions in Bolivia. Yet in other—admittedly few—cases, the strengthening of the public component of the mix was not part of a backlash, but of gradual processes of reconfiguration of its mode of operation: cases of health care in Brazil, Costa Rica, and Uruguay. What is clear is that, if the old state-centric matrix is gone for good, a "market society" model—in the Polanyian sense—has not replaced it.

Still, the progress of decommodification has been moderate at best. While, as previously noted, there has been progress in terms of adding social rights in constitutions, only rarely have there been ruptures with the contributory principle in the direction of an effectively rights-based approach.[13] Across the region there have been multiple reforms in health care systems and in some cases the reforms have had important impacts on some aggregate indicators (McGuire 2010). However, most health care systems are still organized according to the region's historical basic blueprint. If anything, there has been an important de facto recommodification of health care systems, and that trend has been even clearer in the case of pensions, where eight of the 11 countries here considered have introduced structural changes entailing privatization and the narrowing or complete suppression of solidarity by risk pooling. With a few exceptions, most progress in terms of the coverage of social protection has occurred through means-tested social assistance.

In spite of varying systems, there is some consensus about basic benefits, which somewhat resembles the Cuban scenario. Most visibly, all systems have noncontributive pensions, standard packages of minimum health care benefits, and guaranteed coverage from "catastrophic illnesses."[14] Although the importance of these developments should by no means be underestimated, their impact is frequently undermined by their insertion in systems that maintain their fundamental principles. There has also been considerable convergence around the tightening of some basic parameters of retirement schemes—mainly minimal retirement ages and ratios between contributions and benefits. The distribution of the contributory burden, however, remains diverse.[15]

The effects of persistence of the contributory principle are magnified because Latin American countries tend to experience persistent difficulties in expanding their tax bases or requiring greater individual contributions for their social protection systems. The lack of resources to support the welfare systems is one of the central differences between Latin America and more developed regions.

The *dualization* of social protection is the most obvious and important consequence, where there is one system for the wealthy and another for everyone else. It has had its most transparent institutional expression in the omnipresence of those ministries of social development that it would probably have been politically incorrect but not inaccurate to name "ministries of the poor." From a certain angle—particularly relevant for those qualifying for social assistance—the dualization of social protection represents progress with respect to their truncation. But it adds to the stratifying effects of the respective welfare regimes—or, more accurately, it displaces it, turning the "outsiders" of the social protection system into "second-class insiders." This is an outcome that, even if through different processes and with important differences from a quantitative point of view, has not been absent in Cuba. Actually, the gap shows serious potential for growth, as long as the decline of benefits and quality of services at the bottom continues to happen in parallel with a proliferation of privileged packages for those formally employed in the sectors of the economy open to foreign entrepreneurial activity, at the top. The magnitude of that gap is less in Cuba, but the central political puzzle would be the same for hypothetical Cuban reformers aiming at more equality: Will those dual systems facilitate the formation of coalitions that demand the reduction of inequalities in the distribution of benefits? A priori at least, the institutional crystallization of the line separating insured groups from those covered by social assistance does not seem to contribute to that type of coalitional dynamics.[16]

The commonalities summarized in this section predominantly result from similar structural problems, on the one hand, and the homogeneity of the analytical frameworks that shaped diagnoses and policy recommendations, on the other. Regarding the former, suffice it to say that the aftermath

JAVIER VÁZQUEZ-D'ELÍA

of the debt crisis led to reforms consistent with the Washington Consensus. However, this is only half of a story that also includes the diversification obtained once those highly homogeneous models experienced refraction through the prism of domestic institutions and distributions of political power. The final results were, as a consequence, extremely differentiated, and the next section is an attempt to briefly summarize that heterogeneity. It is important to remark how different the intellectual and international stage for an eventual process of welfare reforms in Cuba is likely to be. At the peak of the intellectual hegemony of the Washington Consensus, during the 1990s, debates on reforms were shaped to a considerable degree by efforts by international financial institutions to promote "one size fits all" solutions as evidenced by efforts to export the Chilean pension model to every corner of the region. However, after two decades of disappointing neoliberal experiments followed to variable degrees by a backlash of "left turns," no blueprint has enjoyed a remotely comparable predominance.

Continuity and change in national systems of social protection

The previous section focused on similar pressures on welfare regimes resulting from common trends of socioeconomic change. This section provides details about diverging paths and outcomes of reform resulting from different political dynamics. It aims at showing, through a descriptive glance at the diversity of concrete directions and contents of reform chosen by different countries, how outcomes have been extremely heterogeneous and far from linear. Not only it is possible to find countries with similar levels of development and social spending that nevertheless have chosen to spend in different ways and according to diverse priorities; in some cases we can even find substantial variation across policy areas within a single country. These realities have, in turn, direct implications regarding the premises from which speculation on potential orientations of reform in Cuba should—or at least should not—be attempted. We should assume neither the existence of "obvious" blueprints, nor the internal consistency of solutions or the coherence of models across policy areas. Instead, the evidence in this section suggests that perhaps we should expect, for Cuba or elsewhere, that reform processes will be contentious and messy; outcomes will be decided through the politics of "muddling through" varying configurations of actors and institutions. These, in turn, are contingent upon a more general political context that remains fluid and uncertain.

First, *Bolivia, Ecuador, and Peru,* the countries at the bottom in terms of social spending (online appendix, table 1), have been unable to break certain vicious circles in spite of some concerted efforts at reform. To a great extent, the three countries maintain the exclusionary nature of the respective earlier systems of social insurance. Bolivia has recently reversed the privatization of its pension system that occurred under Sánchez de Lozada (1997), but has maintained the structure of individual savings accounts, and the most important innovation has been the creation of a solidarity fund for purposes of assistance. The creation of a unified health care system is part of the agenda of the Morales administration, but things still look uncertain. Similar considerations apply to the projected health care reform of Rafael Correa's government in Ecuador. Ecuador's experiment of structural pension reform was born virtually dead—the reform was annulled by the constitutional court. So far, the effective reach of social insurance remains extremely limited in both cases. The same basic considerations apply to Peru, where in 1993 the Fujimori administration created a parallel system of privately managed individual retirement accounts. Not only has the global coverage of social insurance remained extremely narrow, but most of the important parametric adjustments of the last decade have been patchwork, aiming to remedying the short-term financial health of the new system.

The main innovation is the expansion of means-tested cash transfers and services both in Bolivia and Ecuador—particularly the latter's *Bono de Desarrollo Humano*. The immediate impact of those programs in terms of poverty alleviation has been important—we could say that, due to the extremely modest coverage of social insurance, they have become the core of the respective systems of social protection. Precisely for that reason, the possibility may exist to turn those extensive social assistance programs into a door to transition to more permanent universal solutions with an emphasis on social investment. Such a possibility, however, would be contingent to a great extent on the removal of two types of bottlenecks: First, the development of the extensive infrastructure of services required for the effective attainment of goals that the programs have on paper regarding the development of human capital, and second, the limited inclination shown by the respective governments to consolidate the institutional frames and long-term financial sustainability of their social policies. In any case, both situations are too recent and remain too uncertain to anticipate directions of change.

At the medium level of social spending are Colombia and Mexico. *Colombia* is, among members of the original category of exclusionary regimes, the one that may have been experiencing changes leading to a category switch. Apart from the expansion of social security spending, it has introduced important changes in the central principles guiding access to social protection. The constitutional reform of the early 1990s provided the opportunity for an intense debate, with ranging participation of diverse interest groups and

JAVIER VÁZQUEZ-D'ELÍA

social movements. The result was a comprehensive reform of the social protection system that tipped the welfare mix decidedly in favor of the market—although not with the dogmatic enthusiasm of other experiences.

Mexico has to an important degree converged toward a similar orientation. However, different points of departure resulted in different trajectories. In the Colombian case, due to the initial underdevelopment of social protection, the trajectory entailed an expansion based on commodification. In the case of Mexico, the path toward market-based social protection entailed a process of recommodification, given the relative important development of the Bismarckian component of its dual prereform regime. The change, in the last case, did not go too far beyond the original limits of social insurance—although, as was also the case in Colombia, it made more progress in the area of basic health care than in the pension system. As a result, the Mexican welfare regime is still a dual one, but the massive expansion of social assistance has changed the nature of its duality. Through PRONASOL, PROGRESA, and *Oportunidades*—products of the partial recycling and expansion of social assistance by successive administrations—targeted programs have become a stable and increasingly important component of social protection in Mexico. Recently, important progress has been made in the direction of suppressing some of the lines of segmentation introduced in the pension system in order to protect some special regimes from the effects of privatization. However, both the Mexican and Colombian pension systems remain highly fragmented.

That is perhaps one of the main differences with *Chile*, but not the only one. To some extent, the Chilean case is in a class by itself. It certainly has gone the farthest in terms of the predominance of the market component of its welfare mix, which was possible given the willingness of the dictatorship to remove privileges for special groups. The Chilean system of social protection thus has an uncommon degree of internal cohesiveness and homogeneity of principles across policy areas. It also benefits from the economy with the lowest levels of informality, which increases taxes and facilitates enrollment of the population. However, the same factors underlying the consistency of the regime explain the levels of inequality and poverty that were also part of the "Chilean miracle." That has allowed for an important role of social assistance in the welfare equation of the country. The other singularity of its situation was the long continuity—briefly interrupted and recently reinitiated—of center-left administrations that developed an incremental effort to reinforce public participation in the production of welfare. However, the limits of that effort have been consistent as well, and both the pension and the health care system maintain a clear predominance of the market.

If anything, social assistance had an even more explosive—although also considerably more erratic and uncoordinated—expansion in *Venezuela*. What is also characteristic of the Venezuelan path is the continuity of the highly fragmented core of social insurance. Considered as a whole, the evolution of the Venezuelan system of social protection resembles in some aspects the Mexican configuration—a dual structure with the novelty of a massive expansion of social assistance programs. However, the former did not experience anything remotely similar to the latter's process of privatization of the formal core—the promarket reform attempted by the Caldera administration (1999) constituted a sort of swan's song of the Punto Fijo system, which was reversed before being implemented.

Brazil is probably the most important case of migration from the group of conservative/informal welfare systems, but in the opposite direction to the one followed by Mexico. While Mexico tends to converge with Colombia by developing a new type of dual system with a liberal core and an assistential periphery, Brazil tends to move upward in the direction of Costa Rica's incomplete universalism. The Brazilian pattern has three components: the preservation through reform of its highly fragmented pension system; the reform of health care in the direction of a unified universal system; and the development of what is, together with the Mexican program, the most successful massive program of targeted assistance through conditional cash transfers.

Brazil is, with Costa Rica, the case of most consistent incremental rupture with the contributory principle in the domain of health care—although the situation is different in the Brazilian pension system. In Brazil, however, it was the military dictatorship that introduced the first turning point of the process by introducing a program of noncontributory benefits for rural workers. The other turning point was the 1988 constitutional reform, which played a "foundational" role in terms of health care, analogous to the one observed in the Colombian case. However, the constitution also confirmed the strong segmentation of the pension system. This has combined with the scale and federal nature of the Brazilian state, and with the extreme inequalities of the Brazilian social structure, to exacerbate the fragmentation among programs and subregimes operating at the state and municipal level.

It is also important to recall that the building of the unified national health system had to find ways of compromising with a preexisting powerful private sector—something that *Costa Rica* has never had. Indeed, if both health care systems have dual structures with public predominance, the complementary role of the private sector is considerably more marginal in this case. On

JAVIER VÁZQUEZ-D'ELÍA

the other hand, the Costa Rican pension system was not capable of surviving without the introduction of a private pillar. Still, its public component is considerably more homogeneous and has a less stratified distribution of benefits. On the other hand, the more integrated and egalitarian Costa Rican social structure has required a far more modest development of targeted programs—although noncontributory pensions are an important part of the system of social insurance.

Finally, the extended conservative regimes of *Argentina* and *Uruguay* are perhaps the cases of most stubborn continuity of extended but highly fragmented legacies. Still, both introduced significant structural alterations in the 1990s through the creation of mixed pension systems. In both cases, however, the strength of the respective coalitions of insiders imposed considerable fragmentation on the final outcome. The process was recently reversed in Argentina, resulting in an imperfect return to the prereform configuration, which looks institutionally uncertain and financially unsustainable. Both countries maintain tripartite health care systems,[17] with important private components of a sui generis nature—the respective central actors, the Argentinean *obras sociales* and the Uruguayan *instituciones de asistencia mutua*—constitute nonprofit entities. It is also true that the financial difficulties of many of those institutions has brought important displacements into the mix, favoring the expansion of profit-oriented schemes of private insurance. The aggregated result has been the accentuation of the complex fragmentation of both systems.

Both countries recently witnessed efforts to reinforce the regulatory role of the state. So far, the Uruguayan experience has been the most successful one. Building upon a fiscal reform that expanded the contributory base of the system, it included the creation of a solidarity fund through which risk pooling and coverage had an important expansion, although access remains in the end tied to formal employment. While the system remains complex and segmented, the mix has been altered in favor of the state.

The expansion of informality has been behind the increased importance of social assistance in both cases. The process was more marked in Argentina, where the depth of the crisis in the early 2000s and its consequences in terms of social agitation led to considerably larger and long-lasting anti-poverty programs. However, there has also been an important effort to turn temporary solutions into permanent universalist programs—this has been the process behind the universalization of family allowances, which was replicated in Uruguay.

Brief observations on the political dynamics of reform

The extreme diversity in the directions of reform reflects the intricacies of the respective country-specific political configurations of institutions and actors. However, while we find significant differences across countries and policy areas in terms of timing, sequence, actors involved, and institutional change, a detailed analysis of reform processes reveals some repeated patterns in the political dynamics. The rest of this section characterizes the similarities by focusing on "political-process building blocks"; the final section of this chapter will assess the likelihood of the emergence of analogous actors and strategies in some hypothetical Cuban futures.

1. Coalitions of beneficiaries have been effective at preserving privileged schemes of insurance. Social welfare regimes create core constituencies, but because they have privileged some groups more than others they have also created a strong opposition. Still, when in power the core constituencies have been successful at blocking structural reforms from the opposition. Frequently, the core constituencies have pushed reforms that have favored their own groups, thus augmenting the segmentation.

2. Processes of structural retrenchment have predominantly included exclusionary patterns of technocratic policy making. Some of the extreme versions of this strategy—the unusual Chilean case aside—have proved notoriously fragile and unstable, giving way to strong backlashes (Argentina, Bolivia, Ecuador, Venezuela).

3. Established specialized bureaucracies have frequently played an important role in many reforms. However, they have not shown univocal preferences regarding directions of reform: while providing intellectual leadership throughout the crafting of projects with a universalizing orientation, they have also put their expertise at the service of the protection of established systems of privilege.

4. Partisan actors capable of the articulation of majorities based on coalitions of insiders and outsiders have been essential for the viability of processes of structural expansion.

5. Intragovernmental conflicts between expert teams controlling macroeconomic policy, on the one hand, and reformist teams leading social policy reforms, on the other, have been omnipresent. The existence of linkages between ruling parties and interest groups that could provide the latter with ways of influencing policy-making processes have played an important role in the definition of those conflicts.

JAVIER VÁZQUEZ-D'ELÍA

6. Social assistance has been used as an instrument for political mobilization in several cases. However, there has been an important degree of variation in the ways in which the programs have been used to mobilized their supporting publics. Although our current knowledge of the respective political processes is still fragmentary and the availability of comparable data has important limitations, it seems clear that the main factors determining the variation in who is mobilized, how they mobilized, and the shape of mobilized coalitions are—apart from the design of programs themselves—the systemic structuration of party competition, the organizational structure of ruling parties, and the bureaucratic capacities of the respective states.

7. Decentralized innovation, at the local or provincial level, has played a central role in several processes resulting in the expansion of health care coverage. The scaling-up of those reforms to the national level, however, has not always been successful.

THE CUBAN SITUATION IN COMPARATIVE PERSPECTIVE
Structural challenges to the sustainability of the system of social protection

Perhaps the most basic finding from research on the political economy of welfare state reform in Latin America is that regardless of ideological inclinations, political elites are almost universally averse to the political risks entailed by any reform involving rolling back social protection by reducing benefits or tightening conditions for access. With such an aversion, retrenchment is unlikely to reach the top of public agendas before severe financial constraints threaten the mid- or short-term sustainability of the system, and structural reform is only likely to be considered once the whole range of options for parametric adjustment has been exhausted. As chapter 8 in this volume shows, Cuba has clearly reached that point.

Indeed, the most striking impression from a first glance at the current situation of social protection in Cuba against the backdrop of its regional context, is the contrast between 1) exceptional progress in the direction of the universalization of coverage and equal treatment; 2) the degree to which effective access, the quality of services, and the sustainability of the system is challenged by a series of factors very similar to all its regional peers. All the mentioned socioeconomic trends that continue to pressure countries toward some types of reform observed are evident, perhaps abundant, in Cuba. These include:

1. Extremely low and erratically oscillating levels of economic growth that for several decades have been shrinking the resources necessary to merely

maintain the levels of access and quality of services that Cuba reached three decades ago.

2. Cuba's demographic structure is heavily biased by the predominance of older age groups, thus setting an extremely low ceiling for the possibilities of productive expansion. That balance also negatively affects the ratio of active and passive citizens, thus necessitating new financial models.

3. The fast expansion of Cuba's informal sector is conspiring against the expansion of the fiscal bases for social protection, because workers in that sector avoid paying taxes.

4. Rising costs of medical technology accentuate the problems of a health care system already long suffering from insufficient investment toward the preservation and improvement of basic infrastructure.

5. A taxation system with some important regressive aspects will magnify some of the consequences of the mentioned challenges.

Potential political cleavages and relevant actors

The problems afflicting pensions and healthcare systems are not identical. As in other Latin American countries, the Cuban pension system, first, faces a financial squeeze due to the combined effects of a legacy of extremely generous retirement conditions and benefits, the age structure of Cuban demography, and the expansion of informal employment. Cuba's initial response to the crisis also fits that of other countries in that they made some parametric adjustments that provided, at best, some oxygen in the very short term. Since the health care system has operated on universal principles for decades, its most salient and urgent problems are less about the principles guiding the general architecture than about the limited availability of resources, obsolescent infrastructure, and the need for more efficient strategies of micromanagement.

Of course, the long-term financial health of the pension system depends on sustained growth employment in the formal sector. As we noted in the previous section, most new jobs have been created in the informal sector; thus, it seems very unlikely that Cuba will enact structural reforms to the pension regime, at least in the short term. A privatization (total or partial) that would create individual capital accounts would entail prohibitive transition costs, on top of a frontal clash with the regime's general ideological orientation. A transformation in the opposite direction, where the current contribution-based scheme would be replaced by one financed through gen-

JAVIER VÁZQUEZ-D'ELÍA

eral revenue and perhaps also by suppressing privileged retirement schemes for specific professional categories, does not look politically feasible either. As elsewhere in the region, we should expect that the current beneficiaries of special programs would block initiatives aiming at any significant reduction of internal segmentation.

Based on a superficial analysis, the argument could be made that the very absence of electoral risk, together with the concentration of executive power inherent in an authoritarian situation, might create the conditions to overrule the veto powers of privileged corporations; the experiences of the Brazilian and Chilean military dictatorships come to mind in this respect. However, the two key privileged categories constitute critical pillars of the stability of the Cuban dictatorship, namely the armed forces and the civil service. The political leverage of the Cuban armed forces—"the most solid institution," according to Mesa-Lago—is probably unparalleled in the region.[18] On the other hand, the lack of political independence among Cuban unions does not entail a complete lack of political "voice," and there is evidence that they possess a limited but nevertheless real capacity to limit the scope of some reformist initiatives directly threatening their interests.[19] Actually, what appears as more likely is an eventual accentuation of the fragmentation of the system due to the development of parallel, company-specific schemes of insurance for privileged segments of the workforce operating within the bubbles of outward-oriented economic activity allowed by the government for the arrival of foreign direct investment.

I have already alluded to the predominance of "quantitative" matters among the problems that affect the health care system. In spite of the very visible deterioration of outcomes and standards of attention, the Cuban health care system still resists comparisons with regional standards, and it is precisely its key defining feature—universalism—that has recently been reaffirmed by multiple experts as a goal for the countries of the region to pursue that is critical, yet politically difficult to achieve.

It makes sense to ask about the likelihood of an eventual choice for the development of a sector of competing providers of medical services. Medical professionals currently constitute a substantial budgetary asset for the Cuban government, which has found an important source of complementary revenue in the exportation of medical expertise throughout the region. It is worth noticing that medical missions constitute a vehicle for the transmission of expertise and know-how that may operate in both directions, since it allows Cuban doctors the opportunity of direct contact with alternative forms of institutional organization of the healthcare sector. Through this channel, the multiple experiences in the region with medical cooperatives might capture the interest of Cuban policy makers. However, it is also reasonable to expect a regime that makes the preservation of gate-keeping capacity its priority, to be reluctant to allow the medical profession—one of the most pervasive obstacles to universalist reforms throughout the world—some institutional bases for the eventual development of corporate autonomy.

The expansion of the unemployed and underemployed population resulting from the reduction of the state's payroll and the lack of dynamism in the private sector to create jobs has the potential for becoming politically explosive. Given the budgetary constraints, focused social assistance appears as the most likely response—actually, the only viable one. Even such a limited response, however, will require both fresh resources and efficient targeting. There are open questions about the source of such funding and whether the administration has the information and the bureaucratic capacity that targeted social policies require.[20]

How significant might the initiation of a transitional process that enables more extended political participation and contestation be for the development of new social welfare policies? A more open and competitive political environment would probably stimulate the expression of demands; other countries have shown, however, how difficult it has been to aggregate interests of outsiders and insiders in pursuit of profound reform. This is particularly unclear, since a transition will affect both the bureaucracy and society in unknown ways. An important question, then—for which I lack the data to fully answer—is the likelihood of the reconfiguration of those actors in an eventual transition to perform those tasks. Cuba, further, has an additional actor, the armed forces, that would likely set an insuperable limit for the elimination of privileged schemes. Still, the transitions to democracy in Latin America have sometimes provided new ways of access to the policy-making process for the voices of outsiders.

If Cuba were to suffer a more "catastrophic transition"—that is, one closer to the Soviet and Eastern European pattern than to the Chinese one—new actors could come to the stage. Among them, the current opposition of exiled Cubans, and diverse sources of financial cooperation and expertise (the United States, naturally, among them) could play an important role in eventual processes of reform of social protection. In that scenario, the intellectual hegemony enjoyed by radical market-oriented reform paradigms throughout the 1990s seems to be in the past. However, the specifics of the Cuban situation might favor a more prevalent role for a direct influence of the U.S. business community and the multiple networks of think tanks associated with it.

In sum, applying the Latin American experiences with the welfare system

TABLE 9.1. Types of welfare regime in Latin America, around 2010

Type of welfare regime	Welfare mix	Outcomes	Stratification	Cases
Exclusionary/assistential	Truncated development of state and market. Important informal sector.	Low decommodification. Low defamilialization.	Between outsiders and insiders, due to subsisting truncation of social protection. Among insiders, between those insured and the ones relying on assistance.	Bolivia, Ecuador, Peru
Conservative/assistential	State and market are more developed, but still high levels of informality.	Medium decommodification. Low defamilialization. Focalized CCTs simultaneously introduce moderate decommodification and reinforce familialism.	Between recipients of social assistance and the insured. Among the insured, high fragmentation among occupational categories.	Venezuela
Liberal/assistential	Predominance of market, although with a still important residual of state participation. Subsistence of important levels of informality	Medium/low decommodification, depending on policy domain. Low defamilialization.	Between recipients of social assistance and the insured. Among the insured, due to special regimes and marketization. Among generations, due to the segmentation of pension privatization. In healthcare, significant variation in quality and coverage of services across regions.	Chile, Mexico, Colombia
Segmented universalism	Predominance of the state. Important marketization. Informality still significant.	Medium decommodification, depending on policy. Scanty elements of defamilialization.	Between recipients of social assistance and the insured. Among the insured, high segmentation in special regimes. Stratification from marketization in some policy domains. Among generations, from segmented pension privatization.	Argentina, Uruguay
Incomplete universalism	State is predominant. Significant informality; partially moderated by universal programs.	High/medium decommodification, depending on policy domain.	Between recipients of social assistance and the insured in some policy domains. Segmentation persists in some domains (pensions).	Brazil, Costa Rica

to the Cuban situation suggest that a more open political process will bring new pressures on the regime. Further, we should expect particularly strong pressures in the Cuban case, given the interplay of social, economic, and perhaps international pressures. Some of those pressures, however, will work at opposing purposes, with powerful groups pushing for expansion of benefits and others trying to preserve their special positions. Expanding benefits for all, unfortunately, will not likely be a realistic option, given the economic limitations. Rising pressures without the means to meet them could be an explosive cocktail.

NOTES

Space limitations make it impossible to include all the tables to present the evidence supporting the arguments developed here. They are available as an online Appendix to this chapter through my page at Research Gate; I will also be glad to provide them upon request to javiervazquezdelia@gmail.com.

1. Regarding the concept of "market Leninism" see, for example, London (2008; 2014).

2. Throughout this chapter, social protection will be understood as "public actions taken in response to levels of vulnerability, risk and deprivation, which are deemed unacceptable within a given polity and society" (Barrientos and Santibáñez 2009). Systems of social protection are typically formed by three components that run across diverse policy domains: social insurance, social assistance, and labor market regulations. Social insurance designates a series of programs that provide protection against life course and employment hazards, and are financed with variable combinations of contributions from employers, workers, and governments. In most developed systems it covers occupational risks; health care and cash benefits for maternity and nonwork accidents and diseases; old age, disability, and survivors' pensions; family allowances; and unemployment. There are also a number of additional benefits that are frequently included under the umbrella of social insurance systems—e.g., funeral aid, personal and mortgage loans, and day care centers (Mesa-Lago 1989). Social assistance, instead, is financed by the government out of general revenue, and includes those programs oriented to support populations in situation of poverty (e.g., means-tested noncontributory health care and pension programs). Finally, there is a third component, which will not be considered here: labor market regulations aim to protect the right to voice and representation of workers, in the first place by providing guarantees against unfair dismissal.

A second group of central concepts that I repeatedly use aims at the identification of transformations affecting social security systems and some of the cleavages that may arise from them. Decommodification refers to those reforms that, by turning the protection from a social risk into a right, puts the responsibility for its provision in the hands of the state, thus preventing its contingency on market oscillations. The notion of truncation points to the inclusiveness of systems of social insurance, defining the lower boundaries of their respective coverage—in other words, their eventual failure to achieve universal coverage. The existence of a dual system of social protection is a direct result of truncation, and may eventually define a politically relevant line of cleavage by opposing insiders and outsiders to the former. Skimming refers to the process by which the private components of systems of social protection drain the respective public ones from the top by capturing the membership of upper income strata—which are, in contribution-based systems, crucial for long-term financial sustainability. Segmentation, in turn, focuses on inequalities affecting different fractions of the total insured population—it refers to differences regarding qualifying conditions for benefits, levels of benefits, quality of services, etc.

3. See Malloy (1979).

4. For further elaboration and bibliographical suggestions, see Vázquez-D'Elía (2014).

5. The typology of welfare regimes in this section should be complemented by one summarizing the situation before the past 30 years of reforms, which is summarized as Table 1 in the online appendix. Space limitations make it impossible to include both typologies. See Vázquez-D'Elía (2014) for that typology, plus a comparative discussion of changes and continuities, as well as detailed descriptions of the specific characteristics of each country.

6. On the different processes listed below and their multiple interconnections, see (CEPAL 2002; Chackiel 2001; Fernández-Kelly and Shefner 2006; Repetto 1996; Roberts 1979, 1995, 1998).

7. See table 1 in online appendix.

8. This is most clear in the case of pension systems; see tables 2 and 3 in the online appendix for a summary of outcomes of pension reform. On the general structure of health care systems, see table 4; on the proportion between public and private spending on health care see table 5.

9. See table 6 in the online appendix.

10. In the online appendix see table 7 for the evolution of the population contributing to social security; and Table 8 on the expansion of noncontributory benefits.

11. "Layering" designates a pattern of gradual institutional change singularized by the fact that innovations do not replace but add "layers" to existing institutions. See Van der Heijden (2011) for an introductory review and discussion of the concept.

12. See tables 2 to 4 in the online appendix.

13. For a detailed discussion in these terms, see Cecchini and Martínez 2012.

14. See table 4 in the online appendix. Also, but with considerably lower frequen-

cy, the prohibition of exclusion from insurance based on preexisting conditions, as a way to prevent practices of adverse selection (Mesa-Lago 2008).

15. See table 7 in the online appendix.

16. I explore this question in Vazquez-D'Elía (2014), chapters 6 and 7.

17. Implying that the system is funded with contributions from the state, employers, and employees.

18. See Corrales (2005a).

19. See, for example, Morris (2014).

20. Some aspects of reforms introduced in the taxation system are revealing in this respect. See Morris (2014: 24).

BIBLIOGRAPHY

Barrientos, Armando, and Claudio Santibáñez. "New Forms of Social Assistance and the Evolution of Social Protection in Latin America." *Journal of Latin American Studies* 41 (2009): 1–26.

Cecchini, Simone, and Rodrigo Martínez. *Inclusive Social Protection in Latin America: A Comprehensive, Rights-based Approach*. Santiago: United Nations, 2012.

Centeno, Miguel Angel. "Society for Latin American Studies 2004 Plenary Lecture The Return of Cuba to Latin America: The End of Cuban Exceptionalism?" *Bulletin of Latin American Research* 23, no. 4 (2004): 403–13.

CEPAL. *Vulnerabilidad demográfica: viejos y nuevos riesgos para comunidades, hogares y personas*. Santiago: CEPAL, 2002.

Chackiel, Juan. "El envejecimiento de la población latinoamericana." In *Sociología del Desarrollo, Políticas Sociales y Democracia*. Edited by Rolando Franco. Mexico: Siglo XXI—CEPAL, 2001.

Cook, Linda J. "Negotiating Welfare in Postcommunist States." *Comparative Politics* 2007: 41–62.

Corrales, Javier. "Strong Societies, Weak Parties: Regime Change in Cuba and Venezuela in the 1950s and Today." *Latin American Politics and Society* 2001: 81–113.

Corrales, Javier. "The Gatekeeper State: Limited Economic Reforms and Regime Survival in Cuba, 1989–2002." *Latin American Research Review* 39, no. 2 (2004): 35–65.

Corrales, Javier. "Civil Society in Cuba: Internal Exile." In J. Tulchin et al., *Changes in Cuban Society since the Nineties*, 207–29. Washington, DC: Woodrow Wilson Center for International Scholars, 2005a.

Corrales, Javier. "Cuba after Fidel." *Current History* 104, no. 679 (2005b): 69–76.

Díaz-Briquets, Sergio, and Jorge Pérez-López. *Corruption in Cuba: Castro and Beyond*. University of Texas Press, 2006.

Draibe, Sonia M., and Manuel Riesco. "Latin America: a new developmental welfare state in the making?" *Latin America*. Palgrave Macmillan, London, 2007. 21-113.

Eckstein, Susan. "The Transformation of the Diaspora and the Transformation of Cuba." In *Changes in Cuban Society since the Nineties*. Edited by Joseph S. Tulchin et al., 207–29. Washington, DC: Woodrow Wilson Center for International Scholars, 2005.

Eckstein, Susan. *The Immigrant Divide*. New York: Routledge, 2009.

Fernández-Kelly, María Patricia, and Jon Shefner. *Out of the Shadows: Political Action and the Informal Economy in Latin America*. University Park: Pennsylvania State University Press, 2006.

Filgueira, Carlos. *Sobre revoluciones ocultas: la familia en el Uruguay*. Montevideo: CEPAL, 1996.

Hoffmann, Bert. "Emigration and Regime Stability: the Persistence of Cuban Socialism." *Journal of Communist Studies and Transition Politics* 21, no. 4 (2005): 436–61.

Hoffmann, Bert. "Charismatic Authority and Leadership Change: Lessons from Cuba's Post-Fidel Succession." *International Political Science Review* 30, no. 3 (2009): 229–48.

Hoffmann, Bert, and Laurence Whitehead. *Debating Cuban Exceptionalism*. New York: Palgrave Macmillan, 2007.

London, Jonathan D. "Reasserting the State in Viet Nam Health Care and the Logics of Market-Leninism." *Policy and Society* 27, no. 2 (2008): 115–28.

London, Jonathan D. "Welfare Regimes in China and Vietnam." *Journal of Contemporary Asia* 44, no. 1 (2014): 84–107.

Ludlam, Steve. "Cuban Labor at 50: What about the Workers?" *Bulletin of Latin American Research* 28, no. 4 (2009): 542–57.

Malloy, James M. *The Politics of Social Security in Brazil*. Pittsburgh: University of Pittsburgh Press, 1979.

Mazzei, Julie. "Negotiating Domestic Socialism with Global Capitalism: So-Called Tourist Apartheid in Cuba." *Communist and Post-Communist Studies* 45, no.1 (2012): 91–103.

McGuire, James. *Wealth, Health and Democracy in East Asia and Latin America*. Cambridge: Cambridge University Press, 2010.

Mesa-Lago, Carmelo. "Cuba's Economic CounteRreform (Rectificactión): Causes, Policies and Effects." *Journal of Communist Studies* 5, no. 4 (1989): 98–139.

Mesa-Lago, Carmelo. *Breve historia económica de la Cuba socialista: políticas, resultados y perspectivas*. Madrid: Alianza Editorial, 1994.

Mesa-Lago, Carmelo. *Reassembling social security: a survey of pensions and health care reforms in Latin America*. Oxford: Oxford University Press, 2008.

Mesa-Lago, Carmelo. "Cincuenta años de servicios sociales en Cuba." *Temas* 64 (2010): 45–56.

Mesa-Lago, Carmelo, and Jorge Pérez-López. *Cuba's Aborted Reform: Socioeconomic Effects, International Comparisons, and Transition Policies*. Gainesville: University Press of Florida, 2005.

Mora, Frank O. "From Fidelismo to Raulismo—Civilian Control of the Military in Cuba." *Problems of Post-Communism* 46, no. 2 (1999): 25–38.

Mora, Frank O. "Military Business: Explaining Support for Policy Change in China, Cuba, and Vietnam." *Problems of Post-Communism* 51, no. 6 (2004a): 44–63.

Mora, Frank O. "The FAR and Its Economic Role: From Civic to Technocrat-Soldier." ICCAS Occasional Paper Series. University of Miami (June 2004) (2004b).

Morris, Emily. "Unexpected Cuba." *New Left Review* 88 (2014): 5–45.

Reed, Gail. *Island in the Storm: The Cuban Communist Party's Fourth Congress*. Ocean Press, 1992.

Repetto, Fabián. "Estado y pobreza en América Latina: perspectivas de un vínculo en transformación." *Perfiles Latinoamericanos* 8 (January–July 1996):173–200.

Riesco, Manuel, and Sonia M. Draibe, eds. *Latin America: A New Developmental Welfare State Model in the Making?* New York: Palgrave Macmillan, 2007.

Roberts, Bryan R. *Cities of Peasants: The Political Economy of Urbanization in the Third World. Explorations in Urban Analysis*. Beverly Hills: SAGE Publications 1979.

Roberts, Bryan R. *The Making of Citizens: Cities of Peasants Revisited*. 2nd ed. London: Halsted Press, 1995.

Roberts, Bryan R. *Ciudadanía y política social*. 1st ed. *Centroamérica en reestructuración*. San José: FLACSO, 1998.

Van der Heijden, Jeroen. "Institutional Layering: A Review of the Use of the Concept." *Politics* 31, no. 1 (2011): 9–18.

Vazquez-D'Elía, Javier. "(Re-)shaping the Political Arena? A Comparative Study of Welfare Regime Reforms in Latin America, 1980–2010." Ph.D. diss., University of Pittsburgh, 2014.

RONALD H. LINDEN

10

AFTER THE FALL

POSTCOMMUNIST DYNAMICS IN
CENTRAL AND EASTERN EUROPE
AND THEIR IMPLICATIONS FOR CUBA

What happens now, or, more properly, what will happen next in Cuba? Its path, of course, will be unique, determined by a distinctive—and changing—mixture of internal and external factors. Prediction with multiple variables is fraught with uncertainties—even when focusing on just one case—and must be accompanied by requisite social science caveats. Still, we might derive some expectations about Cuba and its future by looking at how other countries have moved from state-dominated, one-party, quasi-ideological systems toward more politically and economically pluralistic regimes.

The countries of Central and Eastern Europe (CEE) form an excellent comparative set for this purpose, because of their relatively small size and similar experience with multiple generations of communist rule. Comparison with these cases is more plausible, for example, than comparing Cuba to China or Russia. Even more fortuitous, these countries form an almost perfect political science laboratory in which to test possible explanatory factors for the outcomes that have emerged. All of the CEE states were governed since the end of the Second World War by communist regimes. Their leaderships were committed to state control of the economy and all were governed by one dominant party that countenanced no genuine opposition parties or expression of preference for alternatives to their rule. All used repressive measures to ensure not just political quiescence but social conformity.

At the same time, there was enough divergence in the actual practice of communist rule in the region to allow for fruitful comparison. The populations of some of the CEE were Roman Catholic, for example (Poland, Slovakia) while others were Eastern Orthodox (Romania, Bulgaria) and some were mixed (Yugoslavia). Most were Slavic, but some (e.g., Hungary) were not. Some took advantage of a substantial and attentive diasporas (e.g., Poland) while no such external constituencies existed for others (e.g., Romania, Albania). Some were federal systems (e.g., Yugoslavia) and some were unitary (e.g., Poland). The economies of a few allowed for limited independent actors at some points (Yugoslavia, Hungary) while others tolerated virtually no activity—political, social, or economic—not controlled by the state (Romania, Albania).

Probably the most significant difference between the CEE and Cuba lies in their respective external environments. For most Central and Eastern European regimes, the USSR acted as a hegemonic enforcer of the status quo. Intrusive and occasionally invasive, until 1989 Moscow made it clear that uncontrolled change or challenges to communist rule would not be tolerated. Hence all the regimes had to balance internal dynamics that might have compelled change—for example, economic slowdown—against the obsessive attention and threat of (as well as actual) intervention against change coming from Moscow.[1] Cuba, on the other hand, is located in an environment in which the dominant hegemon, the United States, was until recently committed to revising the status quo and supporting efforts—both public and secret—to remove the communist regime.[2]

After the fall of communism in CEE, the external environment changed in two key ways: 1) the disappearance of the hegemon's willingness and capacity to intervene in the region, followed by the disappearance of the hegemon itself; and 2) the emergence of powerful regional actor, the European Union, willing and able to exert influence on the direction of developments inside the countries and to offer membership in a prosperous, democratic community.

This chapter will not focus primarily on Cuba but instead will consider the direction of developments in Central and Eastern Europe in the first two decades after the fall of communism. It will demonstrate the diversity of these directions and offer some suggestive possibilities that might explain these different outcomes. It will also take a brief look at the most recent pe-

RONALD H. LINDEN

riod as a way of highlighting possible factors that might change the path of postcommunist countries over an extended period of time. We will conclude by considering the implications of postcommunist developments in Central and Eastern Europe for Cuba.

CENTRAL AND EASTERN EUROPE SINCE 1989

Due to a variety of factors, both persistent and proximate, the communist regimes of CEE, which had been in power since just after the Second World War, crumbled. In roughly three months, one-party regimes from Warsaw to Bucharest were driven from office by popular uprisings or palace coups. Soon after, upheaval reached Albania—the most isolated country in Europe—and tore apart Yugoslavia.[3] Then, on Christmas Day, 1991, the USSR—which had been created nearly 70 years before and had endured radical transformation, devastation in the Second World War, recovery, and a long and costly Cold War—ceased to exist. In CEE the call was for a "return to Europe," for democracy, freedom and a society free of intrusive government control.[4]

Over the next 20 years, the former communist countries were transformed by a "triple transition": 1) establishing a democratic form of governance, allowing for political competition, multiple legitimate parties, rule of law, independent judiciary, and accountable governments; 2) creation of economic dynamics in which private actors as well as market forces played a role while the share of the state in the economy shrunk; and 3) encouragement of attitudes and behavior in society that support the structure and practice of democracy building, including: tolerance, participation in the deliberations and acceptance of outcomes of the democratic determination of policy, and recognition of the governing system's legitimacy—as opposed to sheer power—of rule.[5]

As table 10.1 shows, progress in the first 20 years on the dimension of democracy varied considerably. Under the Freedom House evaluations of political rights and civil liberties, with 1 being the most democratic and 7 the least, the CEE group alone showed scores ranging from 1 to 4 and, if Russia is included, to 5 and 6. Fourteen of these states were deemed "Free" and seven "Partly Free." In the economic realm, using the measurements of the European Bank for Reconstruction and Development (EBRD) on economic reform, specifically large and small-scale privatization and economic restructuring, the postcommunist states show less variation, from 3 to 4+ (low to high). Thus, one comparative conclusion emerges right away: economic restructuring moved more quickly and was accomplished more thoroughly and region-wide than political reformation.

Other rough comparisons can be enabled by resetting the table from high-

TABLE 10.1. Political and Economic Variation in Eastern and Southeastern Europe (as of 2009)

Country	Freedom House ranking*			EBRD ranking**			
	Pol. rights	Civil lib.	Rating	Lg.	Priv.	Sm.	Restruct.
Albania	3	3	Partly free	3+	4		2+
Bos.-Herz.	4	3	Partly free	3	3		2
Bulgaria	2	2	Free	4	4		3-
Croatia	1	2	Free	3+	4+		3
Czech Rep.	1	1	Free	4	4+		3+
Estonia	1	1	Free	4	4+		4-
Georgia	4	4	Partly free	4	4		2+
Greece	1	2	Free	NA	NA		NA
Hungary	1	1	Free	4	4+		4-
Latvia	2	1	Free	4-	4+		3
Lithuania	1	1	Free	4	4+		3
Macedonia	3	3	Partly free	3+	4		3-
Moldova	4	4	Partly free	3	4		2
Montenegro	3	3	Partly free	3+	4-		2
Poland	1	1	Free	3+	4+		4-
Romania	2	2	Free	4-	4-		3-
Russia	6	5	Not free	3	4		2+
Serbia	2	2	Free	3-	4-		2+
Slovakia	1	1	Free	4	4+		4-
Slovenia	1	1	Free	3	4+		3
Turkey	3	3	Partly free	NA	NA		NA
Ukraine	3	2	Free	3	4		2

Notes: *1=most free, 7=least free. Rankings on Political Rights and Civil Liberties.
**Rankings for Large and Small Privatization, Government and Enterprise Restructuring; 1=no change from centrally planned economy, 4+=standards of an industrialized market economy.

Sources: Arch Puddington, "The Freedom House Survey for 2009," *Journal of Democracy* 21, no. 2 (April 2010), 142–43; European Bank for Reconstruction and Development, *Transition Report 2008* (London: EBRD, 2008), 4.

est, i.e., best performing on the democracy scale, to lowest (table 10.2). Here a geographic pattern emerges: states in Central Europe, such as Poland, the Czech Republic, and Hungary, did the best in the first 20 years, while those in the Balkans, such as Bosnia, Montenegro, and Macedonia, fared worse. Table 10.3 offers both a broader and a more detailed comparison, adding in more states from the former Soviet Union and more dimensions of democracy. Most former Soviet republics rated poorly after 20 years. But status as

RONALD H. LINDEN

TABLE 10.2. Economic and Political Variation in East and Southeastern Europe, Sorted by Ranking (as of 2009)

Country	Freedom House Ranking*			EBRD Ranking**			
	Pol. Rights	Civil Lib.	Rating	Lg.	Priv.	Sm.	Restruct.
Czech Rep.	1	1	Free	4	4+		3+
Estonia	1	1	Free	4	4+		4-
Hungary	1	1	Free	4	4+		4-
Lithuania	1	1	Free	4	4+		3
Poland	1	1	Free	3+	4+		4-
Slovakia	1	1	Free	4	4+		4-
Slovenia	1	1	Free	3	4+		3
Latvia	1	1	Free	4-	4+		3
Greece	1	2	Free	NA	NA		NA
Croatia	2	2	Free	4	4		3-
Bulgaria	1	2	Free	3+	4+		3
Romania	2	2	Free	4-	4-		3
Serbia	3	2	Free	3-	4-		2+
Ukraine	3	2	Free	3	4		2
Albania	3	3	Partly Free	3+	4		2+
Macedonia	3	3	Partly Free	3+	4		3-
Turkey	3	3	Partly Free	NA	NA		NA
Montenegro	3	3	Partly Free	3+	4-		2
Bos.-Herz.	3	3	Partly Free	3	3		2
Georgia	3	3	Partly Free	4	4		2+
Moldova	3	4	Partly Free	3	4		2
Russia	6	5	Not Free	3	4		2+

Notes: *1=Most Free, 7=Least Free. Rankings on Political Rights and Civil Liberties.
**Rankings for Large and Small Privatization, Government and Enterprise Restructuring; 1=no change from centrally planned economy, 4+=standards of an industrialized market economy.

Sources: Arch Puddington, "The Freedom House Survey for 2009," *Journal of Democracy*, Vol. 21, No. 2 (April) 2010, pp. 142-43; European Bank for Reconstruction and Development, *Transition Report 2008* (London: EBRD, 2008), p. 4.

a former Soviet republic is clearly not determinate, as Lithuania, Latvia, and Estonia, which had shared the same fate, scored well.

It is also clear from this comparison that during the first decades after the fall of communism, those states that began and completed the process of joining the EU did significantly better in constructing democracy than did either southeast European countries with no EU "prospect" (the Balkans) or non-Baltic members of the FSU.

TABLE 10.3. Progress in Democracy in Central and Eastern Europe, Southeastern Europe, and the Former Soviet Union

	1999–2000	2001	2002	2003	2004	2005	2006	2007	2008	2009
New EU members										
Bulgaria	3.58	3.42	3.33	3.38	3.25	3.18	2.93	2.89	2.86	3.04
Czech Republic	2.08	2.25	2.46	2.33	2.33	2.29	2.25	2.25	2.14	2.18
Estonia	2.25	2.13	2.00	2.00	1.92	1.96	1.96	1.96	1.93	1.93
Hungary	1.88	2.13	2.13	1.96	1.96	1.96	2.00	2.14	2.14	2.29
Latvia	2.29	2.21	2.25	2.25	2.17	2.14	2.07	2.07	2.07	2.18
Lithuania	2.29	2.21	2.21	2.13	2.13	2.21	2.21	2.29	2.25	2.29
Poland	1.58	1.58	1.63	1.75	1.75	2.00	2.14	2.36	2.39	2.25
Romania	3.54	3.67	3.71	3.63	3.58	3.39	3.39	3.29	3.36	3.36
Slovakia	2.71	2.50	2.17	2.08	2.08	2.00	1.96	2.14	2.29	2.46
Slovenia	1.88	1.88	1.83	1.79	1.75	1.68	1.75	1.82	1.86	1.93
Average	2.41	2.40	2.37	2.33	2.29	2.28	2.27	2.32	2.33	2.39
Median	2.27	2.21	2.19	2.10	2.10	2.11	2.20	2.20	2.20	2.27
Balkans										
Albania	4.75	4.42	4.25	4.17	4.13	4.04	3.79	3.82	3.82	3.82
Bosnia	5.42	5.17	4.83	4.54	4.29	4.18	4.07	4.04	4.11	4.18
Croatia	4.46	3.54	3.54	3.79	3.83	3.75	3.71	3.75	3.64	3.71
Macedonia	3.83	4.04	4.46	4.29	4.00	3.89	3.82	3.82	3.86	3.86
Yugoslavia	5.67	5.04	4.00	3.88	N/A	N/A	N/A	N/A	N/A	N/A
Serbia	N/A	N/A	N/A	N/A	3.83	3.75	3.71	3.68	3.79	3.79
Montenegro	N/A	N/A	N/A	N/A	3.83	3.79	3.89	3.93	3.79	3.79
Kosovo	N/A	N/A	N/A	N/A	5.50	5.32	5.36	5.36	5.21	5.11
Average	4.83	4.44	4.22	4.13	4.20	4.10	4.05	4.06	4.03	4.04
Median	4.75	4.42	4.25	4.17	4.00	3.89	3.82	3.82	3.82	3.82
Non-Baltic former Soviet states										
Armenia	4.79	4.83	4.83	4.92	5.00	5.18	5.14	5.21	5.21	5.39
Azerbaijan	5.58	5.63	5.54	5.46	5.63	5.86	5.93	6.00	6.00	6.25
Belarus	6.25	6.38	6.38	6.46	6.54	6.64	6.71	6.68	6.71	6.57
Georgia	4.17	4.33	4.58	4.83	4.83	4.96	4.86	4.68	4.79	4.93
Kazakhstan	5.50	5.71	5.96	6.17	6.25	6.29	6.39	6.39	6.39	6.32
Kyrgyzstan	5.08	5.29	5.46	5.67	5.67	5.64	5.68	5.68	5.93	6.04
Moldova	4.25	4.29	4.50	4.71	4.88	5.07	4.96	4.96	5.00	5.07
Russia	4.58	4.88	5.00	4.96	5.25	5.61	5.75	5.86	5.96	6.11
Tajikistan	5.75	5.58	5.63	5.63	5.71	5.79	5.93	5.96	6.07	6.14
Turkmenistan	6.75	6.83	6.83	6.83	6.88	6.93	6.96	6.96	6.93	6.93
Ukraine	4.63	4.71	4.92	4.71	4.88	4.50	4.21	4.25	4.25	4.39
Uzbekistan	6.38	6.42	6.46	6.46	6.46	6.43	6.82	6.82	6.86	6.89
Average	5.31	5.41	5.51	5.57	5.66	5.74	5.78	5.79	5.84	5.92
Median	5.29	5.44	5.50	5.54	5.65	5.72	5.84	5.91	5.98	6.13

Sources: https://freedomhouse.org/report/nations-transit-2009/ratings-tables. Democracy Scores are from Table 9 and range from 1 (free) to 7 (not free). Scores are explained in detail at: https://freedomhouse.org/sites/default/files/Freedom%20in%20the%20World%20FAQs%202016_0.pdf.

POSSIBLE EXPLANATIONS

Why should this be so? Why should countries and societies with roughly the same communist, one-party state past—at least in Eastern and Southern Europe—diverge in their creation of a democratic postcommunist polity? For some observers, the answer is "civilizational." Some aspect of a society's historical and cultural orientation, in this view, made them more or less ready for the democratic project and more or less successful in constructing its mechanisms. Samuel Huntington's famous essay "Clash of Civilizations" included a map dividing Western, Roman Catholic and Protestant, Europe from Eastern, Orthodox and Muslim parts.[6] The latter group, Huntington argued, "historically belonged to the Ottoman or Tsarist empires and were only lightly touched by the shaping events in the rest of Europe; they are generally less advanced economically; they seem much less likely to develop stable democratic political systems."[7]

While appealing at first glance, Huntington's argument suffers from several flaws. For example, depending on the time period chosen, the pattern of democratic or nondemocratic polities changes. In the post-1989 period, Orthodox Romania clearly trailed its postcommunist partners, but so did Catholic Slovakia, at least according to EU assessments.[8] Until 1975, decidedly nondemocratic but Catholic Spain and Portugal were kept out of Europe-only organizations. Further, a "civilizational" axis lumps together other factors that are likely to have an effect on postcommunist development. For example, the history of Ukraine, Belarus, and Moldova is one of enduring economic isolation and backwardness, compared to Central Europe; moreover, these three new states had no experience as independent states (unlike Poland and Hungary). Such factors are likely to be as determinative as religious practice—especially in cases where such practice was suppressed.

When studied empirically in the postcommunist world, Huntington's putative link between culture and democracy is only partially borne out and hard to distinguish from other factors. As Huntington largely used religion as a proxy for culture, Mungiu-Pippidi and Mindruta studied attitudes toward democracy among different populations in predominantly Orthodox Romania, Orthodox and Muslim Bulgaria, and Catholic Slovakia. They found that "religion and ethnicity were not significantly associated with democratic orientations. . . . Neither religion nor ethnicity were predictors of democratic orientation even when tested separately."[9] They conclude that "There is no evidence . . . that an East European is more likely to be a democrat if he or she belongs to any of these religious groups, or to an ethnic group."[10] Instead, Mungiu-Pippidi and Mindruta found that age, years of socialization under communism, and ideological self-placement determined attitudes toward democracy. Similar conclusions about historical periods, economic development, and individual experience and attitudes appear in other studies, though the effect of religious doctrine in individual orientation and the role of the church in the state do not wash out entirely.[11]

Whatever the cause, the rough geographic pattern displayed in table 10.3 seems evident. When Kopstein and Reilly group the CEE states in terms of "distance from the West," geography is strongly associated with democratic progress. Those states closer to Western Europe score higher in both political and economic reform.[12] The correlation is not perfect; Mongolia, very far from the West, nevertheless scored very well and Bosnia-Herzegovina, in the geographically closest group, did poorly. Kopstein and Reilly do not posit that distance alone accounts for this trend line. Instead they argue that geographically closer neighbors can have an influence in the building of democracy if: 1) they themselves are committed to that process and 2) the postcommunist country in question is open to the effect of this outside influence. Belarus, for example, is virtually as close to the West as Estonia or Latvia, and was, like those Baltic states, a former Soviet republic. Yet its regime has been—and continues to be—hostile to outside involvement or influence, especially when that influence suggests a democratic direction.

Huntington's civilizational argument and the Kopstein–Reilly geography study represent one key distinction among the explanatory variables used to understand the variation seen in democratic development in postcommunist Eastern Europe: that between essentially internal factors and forces external to the state. A further important internal distinction is the presence or absence of violent conflict in the recent pasts. Virtually all the CEE states were able to move along the transition path without such conflict, while others, notably in what had been Yugoslavia, suffered upheaval, violent conflict, and civil war.

Shale Horowitz, in his study of developments in the 1990s, suggests that the presence of internal conflict had a significant and negative effect on the process of democracy building.[13] If we chart level of democratic progress against the presence or absence of conflict, the results are striking. Virtually none of the top performers saw internal conflict while almost all those who lag behind endured such developments. Along these lines but focusing on competition short of violent conflict, Vachudova demonstrates that the successful establishment and persistence of democratic practices is, to some extent, the product of the experience, level, and quality of domestic political competition, contrasting Poland, for example, with Romania.[14]

RONALD H. LINDEN

Turning to the external environment, virtually all studies of the progress of postcommunist Central and Eastern Europe recognize the importance of key "normative hegemons."[15] The most prominent of these likely to have had an effect on the democratic development in the region was the European Union and, to a lesser extent, NATO. The populations of all the East European countries were eager to "rejoin Europe," which meant becoming a member of its most prominent institutions. The CEE states quickly joined the Council of Europe to demonstrate their democratic bona fides and then lined up to apply to join both the EU and NATO. In the 1990s both organizations held their suitors at arms' length and, especially in the case of the EU, applied rigorous and detailed criteria to ensure the creation and implementation of democratic practices inside the states. Only when these were satisfied could negotiations begin and when successful, the applicant was offered membership. For eight of the postcommunist states, this occurred in 2004 and for Romania and Bulgaria, 2007.[16]

EU influence was exercised in several key ways: 1) normative validation, i.e., by accepting the new democracies as part of "Europe;" 2) use of specific evaluative instruments, e.g., the *acquis communautaire*, annual reports; 3) provision of substantial financial support—some $30 billion over more than 15 years; and 4) the leverage of a membership "prospect." The cost for joining was high and the economic dislocation for the formerly protected and nonmarket based economies was significant. But by the end of the first decade economic growth had returned, ties with Western Europe were solidified, and after 15 years the new democracies became full members. When membership dates are added to the ranking of the countries on democratic development (see table 10.4), the divide between those with a membership prospect and those without one is clear.

The literature on the impact of EU accession on postcommunist East European democracy is vast and has added an important nuance to our understanding of the power and sustainability of the process.[17] Overall, the conclusion of most work is that the promise of membership and the process of achieving it (accession) exercised substantial influence on these countries' transition from one-party dictatorship to multiparty systems and to help put in place authentic democratic institutions.[18] Most studies stipulate that the membership offer itself was key, which suggests that such leverage is a wasting asset whose power might decline once membership is achieved. This will be considered later in the chapter with a brief look at the post-2009 period in the region.

Country	EU membership status (as of 2009)	Freedom House ranking*			EBRD ranking**		
		Pol. rights	Civil lib.	Rating	Lg. Priv.	Sm.	Restruct.
Czech Rep.	2004	1	1	Free	4	4+	3+
Estonia	2004	1	1	Free	4	4+	4-
Hungary	2004	1	1	Free	4	4+	4-
Lithuania	2004	1	1	Free	4	4+	3
Poland	2004	1	1	Free	3+	4+	4-
Slovakia	2004	1	1	Free	4	4+	4-
Slovenia	2004	1	1	Free	3	4+	3
Latvia	2004	1	1	Free	4-	4+	3
Greece	1981	1	2	Free	NA	NA	NA
Croatia	Candidate[1]	2	2	Free	4	4	3-
Bulgaria	2007	1	2	Free	3+	4+	3
Romania	2007	2	2	Free	4-	4-	3
Serbia	Pot. cand.[2]	3	2	Free	3-	4-	2+
Ukraine	ENP[3]	3	2	Free	3	4	2
Albania	SAA[4]	3	3	Partly free	3+	4	2+
Macedonia	Candidate	3	3	Partly free	3+	4	3-
Turkey	Candidate	3	3	Partly free	NA	NA	NA
Montenegro	SAA[5]	3	3	Partly free	3+	4-	2
Bos.-Herz.	Pot. cand.[6]	3	3	Partly free	3	3	2
Georgia	ENP	3	3	Partly free	4	4	2+
Moldova	ENP	3	4	Partly Free	3	4	2
Russia	PCA[7]	6	5	Not Free	3	4	2+

Notes: *1=most free, 7=least free. Rankings on Political Rights and Civil Liberties.
**Rankings for Large and Small Privatization, Government and Enterprise Restructuring; 1=no change from centrally planned economy, 4+=standards of an industrialized market economy.
1. Became member 2013.
2. "Potential candidate" status; became candidate 2012.
3. European Neighborhood Policy; does not include membership prospect.
4. Stabilization and Association Agreement; became candidate 2014.
5. Stabilization and Association Agreement (entered into force 2010); became candidate 2010.
6. "Potential candidate" status; SAA entered into force 2015.
7. Partnership and Cooperation Agreement, does not include membership prospect.

Sources: Arch Puddington, "The Freedom House Survey for 2009," *Journal of Democracy* 21, no. 2 (April 2010), 142–43; European Bank for Reconstruction and Development, *Transition Report 2008* (London: EBRD, 2008), p. 4; European Commission.

LEGACY OR PATH?

Internal explanations for the East European postcommunist period usually take one of two approaches. Some emphasize that the political dynamics we see are a product, a legacy, of what the regimes were before communism fell. From this perspective, we know what ruling structures or ideologies were under communism and thus we have reasons to predict certain outcomes afterward. These might vary somewhat but can be attributed fundamentally to the communist, one-party state legacy.[19]

Others argue that while legacy might be a powerful determinant, the path taken from dictatorship to democracy can have an important, maybe decisive, impact. It makes a difference, for example, whether the "revolution" that occurred in 1989 was a genuine bottom-up eruption, as happened in East Germany, for example, or a "switch at the top," as happened in Bulgaria. Also, the dynamics of the change itself were negotiated in some cases between partners of roughly equal power, e.g., in Poland, but in others were imposed more rapidly by those who moved over from the old regime, as in Romania. Such transition-based arguments focus much more on the particular path taken toward the transition.[20]

While this chapter cannot consider or test all such arguments, we can consider a few, related to political dynamics. Table 10.5 demonstrates four types of expectations in the political system of postcommunist states. One-party rule, for example, can be expected to lead to weak, fragmented party development and a volatile electoral environment. This is due to a lack of experience with the formation of legitimate, public political parties and a deep social skepticism about fake parties created by communist rulers to give the appearance—while preventing the reality—of multiparty competition. The outcome in Eastern Europe indeed showed weak and volatile party—and electoral—development, at least in the first years after the revolutions.[21] Though there was variation on both accounts, party fragmentation and electoral volatility occurred throughout the region, both in cases in which the transition path included broad social participation and in others in which a narrower coup occurred, suggesting a legacy explanation.[22] Nevertheless, to carry the comparison one step further, the effect on democracy over time seems to be low. Both Poland and Hungary, for example, saw high party volatility and relatively weak parties yet showed substantial democratic progress—at least until recently. This suggests that electoral design as well as the gradual emergence of social or political bases for party division—common in Western Europe—can make a difference to democratic development.[23]

Similarly, all the communist states had governing systems that privileged

TABLE 10.5. Legacy and Path: Impact on Democracy—Political System

Legacy	Expected impact	Outcome	Explanation	Effect on democracy
One-party rule	Weak party development; volatile elections	Weak party development; volatile elections	Legacy	Low
Strong executive	Weak executive; parliamentary dominance	Weak executive; parliamentary dominance	Legacy	Moderate positive
Narrow elite path	Narrow political elites; broader economic elites	Circulation of elites	Path (nature of revolution)	Moderate positive
Pervasive politics	Weak civil society	Moderately active civil society	Path (revolutions, mobilizations)	High posttive

a strong executive. The head of the party ruled, whether or not he was invested with the formal title of head of state (president) or government (prime minister). Parliaments were inauthentic (though occasional rebellions did occur) and the first or general secretary of the party stayed in power as long as he wanted and could please, coopt, or intimidate the political oligarchy around him. We might expect, then, that movements that overthrew communism would be allergic to such a structure. We would expect postcommunist systems to feature leaders who were typically beholden to an elected legislature rather than the other way around. Indeed, that has been the case throughout virtually all of Eastern Europe, irrespective of the transition path and even when the country's postcommunist leader—e.g., Vaclav Havel or Lech Walesa—brought enormous normative power with him because of his own legacy.[24] This is clearly a legacy argument and the impact on democracy is positive. In fact, the erosion of this dynamic, in the form of the emergence of a powerful single leader (think Vladimir Putin) is almost always detrimental to democratic development.[25]

All of the communist one-party states of Eastern Europe shared two other characteristics: 1) the path to leadership was exceptionally narrow. It ran through the party and rewarded loyalty over technical skills, in general. In some cases, such as Hungary, economic elites were somewhat broader but overall these were not fluid, accessible systems.[26] At the same time, the typical CEE regime's concern with maintaining its power—both for its own sake and to stave off Russian attention and possible intervention—meant keeping civil society weak. Independent political—and in most cases even social—organizations were strictly regulated by the regime and subject to top-down mobilization not independent action.[27]

RONALD H. LINDEN

Our expectations with regard to elites and to broader civil society once communism had been overthrown might be for the opposite to occur. That is, we might expect that after the overthrow of the regimes, elite circulation (i.e., movement into and out of the top) would spread out. For one thing, with greater economic freedom and the appearance of private economic actors, we might expect a differentiation of political from economic elites. At the same time, with the functioning of a democratic process—governing parties winning and losing—there would be, at the very least, some circulation of political elites. At the societal level, after years of exclusion and marginalization, we might expect the emergence of an active, engaged civil society in postcommunist countries after 1989.

This expectation is not fulfilled, however. Elite circulation across Eastern Europe has varied tremendously, with economic actors having independent access and influence in some cases and with political control—especially exercised through state-directed privatization schemes—being maintained in others. While private and foreign investors and corporations made their presence felt in Hungary, for example, that was not the case in Romania. Romanians (and Bulgarians) were treated to the persistence of prerevolutionary political elites who controlled the distribution of resources and their own access to power. In Romania, people ruefully grumbled that privatization was *"Din noi, la noi"* ("From us to us").

At the same time, the expected explosion of civil society actors and influence has not been uniform across the region. According to Howard, civil society has remained remarkably weak after the great changes of 1989.[28] Others point out, however, that the results vary based on available domestic and international resources[29] and that civil society measures, in comparison to those in Western Europe, suggest a somewhat stronger case than Howard would draw.[30]

Assuming that these results are empirically valid, the patterns of varied civil society and elite circulation would seem to be a function more of transition path than predemocratic legacy. In both Hungary and Poland, for example, the actual collapse of communist power took place over a more extended period of time than in Romania or Bulgaria. The transition of power was negotiated in both cases with powerful civil society groups, such as Solidarity in Poland or nascent political organizations in Hungary. Neither of these was present in either Romania or Bulgaria or had the opportunity to participate in any negotiations. In both Romania and Bulgaria a brief and intense popular eruption was followed by an oligarchic coup that left most of the ruling political elites in place. In Romania, former Communist Party Central Committee member Ion Iliescu and his National Salvation Front won the first sets of elections in 1990 and 1992; it was not until 1996 that an opposition coalition could take office. Except for a brief period of opposition rule, communist-era elites were not voted out in Bulgaria until 1997. In contrast, in Poland a decade-long struggle before 1989 had created an ongoing political organization (Solidarity) and recognized alternative leaders who were ready to take power and govern, which they did in the summer of 1989. Free elections putting a coalition of opposition parties in power took place in 1991. Czechoslovakia (which became the Czech Republic and Slovakia in 1993) also had both an alternative conscience movement (Charter 77) and an available charismatic leader (Havel) who brought with him new cohorts. Such forces were not available in other cases and the particular path the transition took there did not facilitate their emergence, with apparently lasting effects.

DEMOCRACY FATIGUE?

This chapter has surveyed the first 20 years of postcommunist development in Central and Eastern Europe; a more complete test might want to add another five years to this assessment. But even if we look only at 2009, we note that troubling prospects were present. For one thing, support for the building blocks of democracy had begun to weaken. According to a Pew study (see table 10.6), support for a multiparty system had already declined across the region, in some cases dramatically. At the same time, when people were asked about key aspects of democracy, they generally did *not* think that they were operating in their own country (see table 10.7). In CEE, only in the case of freedom of religion did close to half the respondents (44 percent) think democracy was operating in their country. The Pew study also showed substantial dissatisfaction with the performance of the system throughout the region, including in those states approved earliest for membership in the EU, like Lithuania and Hungary (see figure 10.1). Jacques Rupnik calls such phenomena "early-onset democracy fatigue."[31]

Since then, the operation of democracy itself has softened in most postcommunist countries. As figure 10.2 shows, the Freedom House scores for 2015 show a decline in all postcommunist countries, with the Balkans relatively stable and declines in Eurasia greater than those in CEE. In this region, Hungary's retreat from democracy has been the most dramatic. There the electoral success of Viktor Orban's Fidesz Party has led to attacks on numerous institutions of representative government, including the judiciary, the media, and the constitution itself.[32] Likewise, in Poland the election of the Law and Justice Party in 2016 was quickly followed by the imposition of similar measures, designed to ensure one-party dominance and reduce the ability

TABLE 10.6. Decline in Support for Multiparty Systems, 2009 (percent approval)

	1991	Approve 2009	Change
Ukraine	72	30	–42
Bulgaria	76	52	–24
Lithuania	75	55	–20
Hungary	74	56	–18
Russia	61	53	–8
East Germany	91	85	–6
Czech Rep.	80	80	0
Slovakia	70	71	+1
Poland	66	70	+4

Note: Question 12. Question wording varies slightly among countries.

Source: *The Pulse of Europe 2009: 20 Years after the Fall of the Berlin Wall* (Washington, DC: Pew Global Attitudes Project, 2009), 30.

TABLE 10.7. Democracy in One's Own Country

Do democratic principles describe our country? Percent answering "very well"						
	Fair judiciary	Multiparty elections	Free media	Free religion	Free speech	Civilian control of military	MEDIAN
Czech Rep.	5	48	17	59	27	12	22
Poland	11	29	24	44	18	15	21
Russia	19	16	15	43	22	12	18
Slovakia	5	37	18	46	18	11	18
Hungary	32	17	16	48	13	16	17
Bulgaria	8	16	13	42	29	14	15
Lithuania	5	14	14	44	15	9	14
Ukraine	11	11	13	31	22	7	12
Median	10	17	16	44	20	12	

Note: Questions 42a through 42f.

Source: *The Pulse of Europe 2009: 20 Years after the Fall of the Berlin Wall* (Washington, DC: Pew Global Attitudes Project, 2009), 23.

Satisfaction With Democracy

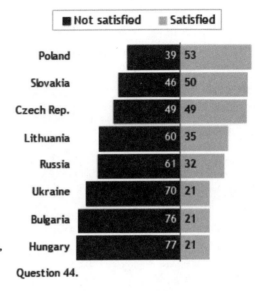

■ Not satisfied ▨ Satisfied

	Not satisfied	Satisfied
Poland	39	53
Slovakia	46	50
Czech Rep.	49	49
Lithuania	60	35
Russia	61	32
Ukraine	70	21
Bulgaria	76	21
Hungary	77	21

Figure 10.1. Satisfaction with Democracy. Source: *The Pulse of Europe 2009: 20 Years After the Fall of the Berlin Wall* (Washington, DC: Pew Global Attitudes Project, 2009), 32. Question 44.

of political, economic, or social actors to function independent of government authority.[33] So serious were these moves that in both cases the EU has attempted to utilize both its normative power and some leverage, including threats to EU privileges, in an attempt restore democratic balance.[34]

At first glance, causation for such a direction might be attributed to the great recession of 2008 and its aftermath, as economic growth in all of Europe, including CEE, was hurt. But this does not hold for Poland, where growth remained robust. Moreover, economic decline was even steeper in the Baltic states and little backtracking on democratic processes seems to be in evidence. The Polish and Hungarian cases, rather, seem to be part of a continentwide rise in populism, unhappiness with the democratic process, and skepticism about the ability of existing domestic and international institutions to effectively manage crises, real or feared. For the postcommunist states, new and old, the question now is whether hard-won gains in democratic governance will endure or be reversed.[35]

CONCLUSION: IMPLICATIONS FOR CUBA'S FUTURE

This chapter has not been about Cuba but instead has focused on the cases of postcommunist political and economic development in Central and Eastern Europe. These cases are, at least in terms of fundamentals, comparable to Cuba and, as a guide to our analysis of the postcommunist period there, they

RONALD H. LINDEN

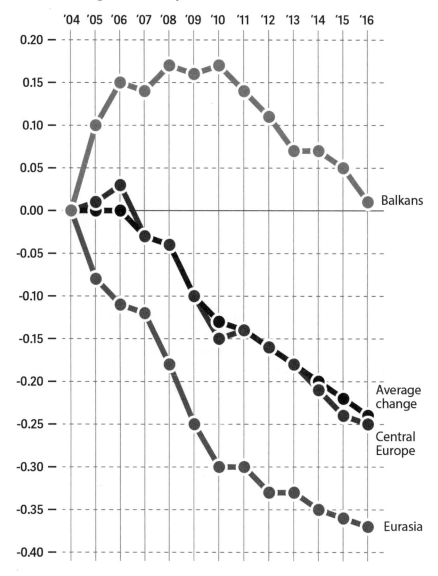

NATIONS IN TRANSIT 2016: CHANGE IN DEMOCRACY SCORE AVERAGES BY REGION

Normalized subregional Democracy Scores

Figure 10.2. Decline in Democracy in Postcommunist States. Source: *Freedom House, Nations in Transit 2016* (Washington, DC: Freedom House, 2016), 3.

suggest some intriguing questions. Seeking the answers will require a longer period to unfold in Cuba and more expertise than the author of this chapter has at hand, but can nevertheless offer a useful set of lenses through which to watch those developments.

Grouping key factors roughly into domestic and international categories and beginning with the former, we might ask: What role, if any, will the presence of internal conflict play in Cuban developments? That is, does the struggle against the Castro regime and the process that is ending it carry within it effects comparable to the civil conflict that occurred in some parts of Eastern Europe? While Cuba is not fragmented ethnically like, say, Bosnia, it did divide along political lines, creating deep enmities. Those on one side of this divide—anticommunists or anti-Castroites—were mostly gone from Cuba during communism and their numbers are now reduced by generational turnover. Still, the return of "exiles" and the attitudes they bring and bequeath to others is likely to have an impact on the chances for internal conflict and thus democratic development.[36] Questions here might focus on what role such people might play and how their power as well as their narratives of the past, present, and future of Cuba might affect the development of Cuban postcommunist democracy?

This leads to some broader questions regarding the evolving domestic scene. If we think about key "legacies" that the CEE setting included, we can ask some reasonable questions about Cuba. For example, as in Eastern Europe, the communist period in Cuba saw the emergence of a dominant leader. Fidel Castro certainly depended on the support of those close to him and the party, but there is no doubt he was the dominant leader during this period. Indeed, it is his partial departure from the scene that has triggered or allowed whatever movement into postcommunism that has developed.[37] So in Cuba our expectation might be that a reaction against one-person rule will support the construction of stronger parliamentary or judicial structures. Will Cuba show itself to be as allergic to strong-man rule as Central and Eastern Europe has been? We may not know until both Fidel and Raúl have left the scene.

Viewed this way, postcommunist development in Cuba might embody a desire to *prevent* something that Cuba, like CEE, has had—that is, one-man rule. At the same time, we can expect to see the *creation* of something lacking under Cuban communism—for example, political parties, maybe in large numbers. If so, where will they come from? Will they reflect such social cleavages as are present in Cuba or will they be primarily ideological? We might not expect to see cultural viewpoints reflected in political parties, as in Western Europe, but we might expect to see parties develop on the basis of

RONALD H. LINDEN

interpretations of the preferred future of Cuban society, for example.[38]

And who will do the interpreting? We have seen that elite presence and circulation is an important, though varying, factor in postcommunist development in Eastern Europe. As in that region, elite circulation in Cuba under communism was controlled, narrow, and based on political criteria. An opening up of society, both political and economic, to autonomous actors (companies, parties) also widens (potentially) the elite path to power. For Cuba, with political power in flux, this will be a crucial dynamic to watch, with significant implications for democracy in the country.[39]

Among the most important of the legacies found in Eastern Europe was the generations-long absence of a vigorous, legitimate civil society. Civil society in that region has struggled to regain health—though perhaps not so much as some would think—and a key seems to have been the route or path of the country's transition to democracy, e.g., compare Poland to Romania. To date, the Cuban route seems to be more one of negotiation (as in Hungary) than upheaval (Romania). That would suggest that a more robust civil society, and therefore democracy, might emerge in Cuba. Some analyses suggest the sources there could be religious, cultural, or the outgrowth of a pluralization of Cuban society as a result of reforms.[40] But in the Polish and Czech cases at least, there were also powerful, if illegal, counterorganizations and people with whom the regime could negotiate. It will be important to know if, in the Cuban case, the cultural and perhaps informational sources can develop the organizational leverage they might need to challenge the regime.[41] Are there charismatic noncommunist leaders with social support, comparable to Lech Walesa or Vaclav Havel, who will do the negotiating? Who are these leaders and will they or their organizations be the vehicle by which a vigorous, democratic civil society emerges in Cuba?[42]

The leadership question raises an interesting comparison—especially for Cuba. Throughout the post-Soviet region, antiregime leaders who had spent the communist years outside their home countries came back once communism fell. They tried to take positions of influence and power in their home country and seemed to assume that they would be welcomed back. But some, such as those in Romania or Poland, found that the new generations—even those who were hostile to the communist regime—did not know them or find their personal biographies or causes appealing. Judging by elections results in many cases, the leadership of returnees was rejected. In other cases, most prominently the Baltic former Soviet republics, reintegration was more successful. At least one exile, Toomas Ilves of Estonia, became president of his newly independent and democratic country.[43]

Who such returning elites might be and what the reaction to them will be in Cuba is worth study in itself, but it also leads us to consider the second basket of factors affecting democracy, those originating outside the country. In the case of Central and Eastern Europe, clearly the role of external actors in support of democracy, most notably the EU, was very powerful. At the same time, the negative role the USSR played was crucial in the course of developments in the region. Given the region's history, movements for democracy in Eastern Europe were also movements *against* the USSR. In this region, Russia was the reason these states and people were cut off from Europe and lacked postwar democracy. Regimes there began with a fundamental lack of governing legitimacy owing to their external, "alien" source.

In the Cuban case, in contrast, the major external actor, the United States, was devoted not to preserving the Castro regime but to removing it. Thus, supporting communism and Castro, especially in the face of U.S.-backed sanctions, blended with Cuban nationalism in a way that was not true in Eastern Europe. To support the regime in Cuba was to support it against the major regional hegemon; in Eastern Europe, to support the regime was to support that hegemon. The question for democratic development in Cuba will be: Can the new regime and the new society see building democracy not as capitulation to an American challenge but compatible with a major theme in the country's 55-year social and political narrative—that of fierce independence?

In designing their democracy, Cuba will not have as attractive, powerful, and intrusive an external benefactor as Eastern Europe had in the EU. But keeping in mind the "geographic" factor noted earlier, it will have a generally supportive, accepting, and mostly democratic "neighborhood." While the nature and approach of a new American administration will matter, it is unlikely that Washington could offer, or have Cuba accept, a detailed *acquis communautaire* to follow as a blueprint for democracy. But with Cuban membership in the Organization of American States now possible (since 2009), might this organization implement the conditionality that was so effective in Central and Eastern Europe? The instruments available to the EU (see section above, "Possible Explanations") were powerful and their absence may hurt democratic development in Cuba. At the same time, it will reinforce the authenticity of the Cuban democracy project as it will not be subject to claims that outside actors (or the regional hegemon) are forcing their will on Cuba.

Finally, one thing we know from postcommunism in Central and Eastern Europe is that a romance with democracy does not last forever—or even for a decade. The decline in support for democracy and its attendant mechanisms is on display in CEE—in some cases egregiously. The openness of democrat-

RONALD H. LINDEN

ic processes, the challenges and uncertainties of economic change, and the presence of probably unrealistic expectations regarding democracy's speed and output can lead to a certain "democracy fatigue." This might be followed, as we have seen in Russia and in parts of Central and Eastern Europe, by energetic support for populists and demagogues, with the unhappy result of an erosion of democratic processes and the undoing of the democratic revolutions that made these changes possible. As we contemplate Cuba's future, it will be useful to keep in mind Chris Hughes's reflection that "although history is universal and forward-moving, it is not linear and not always forward-moving."[44]

NOTES

1. Ronald H. Linden, "The Security Bind in East Europe," *International Studies Quarterly* 26, no. 2 (June 1982): 155–89.

2. There were, nevertheless, behind-the-scenes attempts to improve relations; see William LeoGrande and Peter Kornbluh, *Back Channel to Cuba* (Chapel Hill: University of North Carolina Press, 2014).

3. Gale Stokes, *The Walls Came Tumbling Down: Collapse and Rebirth in Eastern Europe* 2nd ed. (New York: Oxford University Press, 2011).

4. J. F. Brown, *Surge to Freedom* (Durham: Duke University Press, 1991).

5. This notion differs somewhat from notions of transition that add "stateness" as the third transition. See Taras Kuzio, "Transition in Postcommunist States: Triple or Quadruple?" *Politics* 21, no. 3 (2001): 168–77.

6. Samuel Huntington, "Clash of Civilizations?" *Foreign Affairs* 72, no. 3 (Summer 1993): 30.

7. Huntington, "Clash of Civilizations?": 30–31.

8. The European Commission's Progress Reports on the CEE candidate countries can be found at the Archive of European Integration, University of Pittsburgh at: http://aei.pitt.edu/view/euar/.

9. Alina Mungiu-Pippidi and Denisa Mindruta, "Was Huntington Right? Testing the Cultural Legacies and the Civilizational Border," *International Politics* 39, no. 2 (June 2002): 201.

10. Mungiu-Pippidi and Mindruta, "Was Huntington Right?" 202.

11. Hans-Dieter Klingemann, Dieter Fuchs and Jan Zielonka, eds., *Democracy and Political Culture in Eastern Europe* (London: Routledge, 2006); Alfred Stepan, "Religion, Democracy and the 'Twin Tolerations,'" *Journal of Democracy* 11, no. 4 (October 2000): 37–57; Michael Minkenberg, "Democracy and Religion: Theoretical and Empirical Observations on the Relationship between Christianity, Islam and Liberal Democracy," *Journal of Ethnic and Migration Studies*: 33, no. 6 (August 2007): 887–909.

12. Jeffrey Kopstein and David Reilly, "A Political Geography Approach to Explaining Postcommunist Outcomes," in Grzegorz Ekiert and Stephen Hanson, eds., *Capitalism and Democracy in Central and Eastern Europe* (Cambridge: Cambridge University Press, 2003), 120–54. Kopstein and Reilly use Polity scores for these dimensions.

13. Shale Horowitz, "Sources of Post-communist Democratization: Economic Structure, Political Culture, War, and Political Institutions," *Nationalities Papers*, June 2003.

14. Milada Vachudova, *Europe Undivided: Democracy, Leverage, and Integration After Communism* (Oxford: Oxford University Press, 2005).

15. Hiski Haukkala, "The European Union as a Regional Normative Hegemon: The Case of European Neighbourhood Policy," *Europe-Asia Studies* 60, no. 9 (November 2008): 1601–22; Thomas Diez, "Normative Power as Hegemony," *Cooperation and Conflict* 48, no. 2 (June 2013): 194–210.

16. This process is discussed for eight of the states in Vachudova, *Europe Undivided*, pp. 105–38, and in Heather Grabbe, *The EU's Transformative Power* (Houndsmill: Palgrave Macmillan, 2006). For Romania and Bulgaria, see Ronald H. Linden, "The Burden of Belonging: Romanian and Bulgarian Foreign Policy in the New Era," *Journal of Balkan and Near Eastern Studies* 11, no. 3: 269–91.

17. In addition to Vachudova, *Europe Undivided*, and Grabbe, *The EU's Transformative Power*, see Wade Jacoby, *The Enlargement of the European Union and NATO: Ordering from the Menu in Central Europe* (Cambridge: Cambridge University Press, 2004); Ronald H. Linden, ed., *Norms and Nannies: The Impact of International Organizations on the Central and East European States* (Lanham: Rowman and Littlefield, 2002); Frank Schimmelfennig and Ulrich Sedelmeier, *The Europeanizaion of Central and Eastern Europe* (Ithaca: Cornell University Press, 2005).

18. See, for example, Tim Haughton, "When Does the EU Make a Difference? Conditionality and the Accession Process in Central and Eastern Europe," *Political Studies Review* 5 (2007): 233–46; Geoffrey Pridham, "European Union Accession Dynamics and Democratization in Central and Eastern Europe: Past and Future Perspectives," *Government and Opposition* 41, no. 3 (2006: 373–400; Judith Kelley, "International Actors on the Domestic Scene: Membership Conditionality and Socialization by International Institutions," *International Organization* 58 (Summer 2004): 425–57.

19. Anna Seleny, "Communism's Many Legacies in East-Central Europe," *Journal of Democracy* 18, no. 3 (July 2007): 156–70; Grigore Pop-Eleches, "Historical Legacies and Postcommunist Regime Change," *The Journal of Politics* 69, no. 4 (November 2007): 908–26; Valerie Bunce, "The National Idea: Imperial Legacies and Postcommunist Pathways in Eastern Europe," *East European Politics and Societies* 19, no. 3 (Summer 2005): 406–42.

20. Michael McFaul, "The Fourth Wave of Democracy and Dictatorship: Noncoo-perative Transitions in the Postcommunist World," in Michael McFaul and Kathryn Stoner-Weiss, eds., *After the Collapse of Communism: Comparative Lessons of Transition* (Cambridge: Cambridge University Press, 2004), 58–95; Graeme Gill, *Democracy and Post-Communism: Political Change in the Postcommunist World* (London: Routledge, 2002); Michel Dobry, ed., *Democratic and Capitalist Transitions in Eastern Europe* (Dordrecht: Kluwer Academic Publishers, 2000); David Stark and Laszlo Bruszt, *Postsocialist Pathways* (Cambridge: Cambridge University Press, 1998). Some of this literature also contests the very concept of "transition." See, for example, Thomas Carothers, "The End of the Transition Paradigm," *Journal of Democracy* 13, no. 1 (January 2002): 5–21.

21. Richard Rose, *Understanding Postcommunist Transformation* (New York: Routledge, 2009), 135–52; Paul Lewis, ed., *Party Development and Democratic Change in Postcommunist Europe: The First Decade* (London: Frank Cass, 2000). Brad Epperly, "Institutions and Legacies: Electoral Volatility in the Postcommunist World," *Comparative Political Studies* 44, no. 7 (April 2011): 829–53.

22. Zsolt Enyedi and Fernando Bertoa, "Patterns of Party Competition (1990–2009)," in Paul Lewis and Radoslaw Markowski, eds., *Europeanising Party Politics: Comparative Perspectives on Central and Eastern Europe* (Manchester: Manchester University Press, 2011): 116–42; see also Paul Lewis, "Introduction: Europeanising Party Politics? Central and Eastern Europe after EU Enlargement," in Lewis and Markowski, *Europeanising Party Politics*: 1–24.

23. On electoral design, see Robert Moser, "Electoral Systems and the Number of Parties in Postcommunist States," *World Politics* 51, no. 3 (April 1999): 359–84. On the evolution of social cleavages, see Geoffrey Evans, "The Social Bases of Political Divisions in Postcommunist Eastern Europe," in *Annual Review of Sociology* 32 (2006): 245–70; Ian McAllister and Stephen White, "Political Parties and Democratic Consolidation in Postcommunist Societies," *Party Politics* 13, no. 2 (2007): 197–26. On parties and democratic consolidation, see Robert Rohrschneider and Stephen Whitefield, "Understanding Cleavages in Party Systems: Issue Position and Issue Salience in 13 Postcommunist Democracies," *Comparative Political Studies* 42, no. 2 (February 2009): 280–313.

24. Petra Schleiter and Edward Morgan-Jones, "Who's in Charge? Presidents, Assemblies, and the Political Control of Semipresidential Cabinets," *Comparative Political Studies* 43, no. 11 (November 2010): 1415–41; Thomas Baylis, "Embattled Executives: Prime Ministerial Weakness in East Central Europe," *Communist and Postcommunist Studies* 40 (200): 81–106.

25. Ray Taras's review of executive systems in the first postcommunist decade demonstrates this link. See Ray Taras, "Executive Leadership: Presidents and Governments," in Stephen White, Judy Batt, and Paul Lewis, eds., *Developments in Central*

and East European Politics 3 (Durham: Duke University Press, 2003), 115–32, especially the chart on p. 118.

26. Ronald H. Linden and Bert A. Rockman, eds., *Elite Studies and Communist Politics* (Pittsburgh: University Center for International Studies, 1984).

27. Mark Pittaway, *Eastern Europe 1939–2000* (London: Arnold, 2004), ch. 6. The classic description of this system is T. H. Rigby, "Politics in the Mono-Organizational Society," in Andrew Janos, ed., *Authoritarian Politics in Communist Europe: Uniformity and Diversity in One-Party States* (Berkeley: University of California Press, 1976), 31–80.

28. Marc Morje Howard, "The Weakness of Postcommunist Civil Society," *Journal of Democracy* 13, no. 1 (January 2002): 157–69.

29. Velina Petrova, "Civil Society in Postcommunist Eastern Europe and Eurasia: A Cross-National Analysis of Micro-and Macro-Factors," *World Development* 35, no. 7 (2007): 1277–1305.

30. Claire Wallace, Florian Pichler, and Christian Haerpfer, "Changing Patterns of Civil Society in Europe and America 1995–2005: Is Eastern Europe Different?" *East European Politics & Societies* 26, no. 1 (February 2012): 3–19.

31. Jacques Rupnik, "In Search of a New Model," *Journal of Democracy* 21, no. 1 (January 2010): 107.

32. Daniel Hegedüs, "Hungary," *Nations in Transit, 2017* (Washington, DC: Freedom House, 2017); Balázs Áron Kovács et al., "Hungary," *Nations in Transit, 2015* (Washington, DC: Freedom House, 2015).

33. Henry Foy and Duncan Robinson, "Stand-off in the East," *Financial Times*, January 16–17, 2016.

34. Heather Grabbe and Stefan Lehne, "Defending EU Values in Poland and Hungary," *Carnegie Europe*, September 24, 2017; Alexandra Wiktorek Sarlo and Maia Otarashvili, "Can the EU Rescue Democracy in Hungary?" *Eurasia Review*, August 2013; Jennifer Rankin and Alex Duval Smith, "Poland Gets Official Warning from EU over Constitutional Court Changes" *The Guardian*, June 1, 2016.

35. James Dawson and Seán Hanley, "The Fading Mirage of the 'Liberal Consensus,'" *Journal of Democracy*, 27, no. 1 (2016), 20–34.

36. For evidence of a change in attitudes toward U.S. interaction with Cuba among Miami Cubans, see *2016 FIU Cuba Poll: How Cuban Americans in Miami View US Policies Toward Cuba* (Miami: Florida International University, 2016). https://cri.fiu.edu/research/cuba-poll/2016-cuba-poll.pdf.

37. For a review of changes under Raúl Castro, see Bert Hoffmann, "Bureaucratic Socialism in Reform Mode: The Changing Politics of Cuba's Post-Fidel Era," *Third World Quarterly* 37, no. 9 (2016).

38. Camila Piñeiro Harnecker, "Cuba's New Socialism: Different Visions Shaping Current Changes," in Philip Brenner, Marguerite Rose Jiménez, John M. Kirk, and

William M. LeoGrande, eds., *A Contemporary Cuba Reader: The Revolution under Raúl Castro* (New York: Rowman & Littlefield, Kindle edition, 2015).

39. William M. LeoGrande, "Cuba's Perilous Political Transition to the Post-Castro Era," *Journal of Latin American Studies* 47: 377–45.

40. Velia Cecilia Bobes, "Cuban Civil Society during and beyond the Special Period," *International Journal of Cuban Studies* 5.2 (Summer 2013). See also Alexander Gray and Antoni Kapcia, *The Changing Dynamic of Cuban Civil Society* (Gainesville: University Press of Florida, 2008).

41. For discussions of recent developments in Cuban civil society, see Margaret E. Crahan, "Religion and Civil Society in Cuba, 1959–2013," and Ted A. Henken and Sjamme van de Voort, "From Cyberspace to Public Space? The Emergent Blogosphere and Cuban Civil Society," both in Brenner, Jiménez, Kirk, and LeoGrande, eds., *A Contemporary Cuba Reader.*

42. See the chapter by Larry Catá Backer, "The Cuban Communist Party at the Cusp of Change," in this volume.

43. For a discussion of different patterns of receptivity to returnees, see Michael Radu, "Western Diasporas in Post-Communist Transitions," *Problems of Post-Communism* 42, no. 3 (May–June 1995): 57–63.

44. Chris Hughes, *Liberal Democracy as the End of History* (New York: Routledge, 2012). Indeed, he quotes (145) Francis Fukuyama from his famous tract *The End of History and the Last Man* to the effect that "we should not be surprised if all of the formerly communist countries do not make a rapid and smooth transition to stable democracy."

PART 3

CITIZENS AND SOCIETY

ALAN WEST-DURÁN

THE LIVING LIE AND THE LIVING EYE

CUBA'S REFORMS AND THE RACIAL CONTRACT

Neither mockery nor tears but understanding.
—Spinoza

In March 2013 Roberto Zurbano, then director of publications for Casa de las Américas, published an op-ed piece in *The New York Times*. It also appeared in Cuba, published in a widely available cultural magazine, *La Jiribilla*. Both its content and especially its title caused enormous controversy in Cuba with a flurry of responses and counterresponses. In what follows, I use the Zurbano incident to discuss Cuba's racial contract as it relates to ideas of nationality, as well as the universalist influences of Rousseau and socialist thought on thinking about race in Cuba. In analyzing these philosophical underpinnings, I will engage Zurbano's responses to his op-ed and consider the ramifications of race in terms of citizenship, civil society, and identity. The chapter discusses the historical perspective, but also comments on the degree of debate in contemporary Cuba (especially since 2008), as well as how recent economic reforms affect race generally and the relation among philosophical notions of equality under Cuba's economic model.

Zurbano's original piece in Spanish was titled "El país que viene: ¿y mi Cuba negra?" (The Country to Come: and My Black Cuba?) The title resonates with Cuba's distinctive commitment to social equality and is rich with transformative possibilities for Cuba's future: Zurbano envisions true equality for its black population while locating his critique within an active, ongoing Cuban revolutionary process in which justice must be worked for and cannot be taken for granted. This understanding of a future to be constructed is significant because the whole essay/editorial builds on the unfinished nature of the Cuban revolution, particularly in light of new economic changes that the country is living through, unleashing new social realities, some good, some troubling.

The final title for the piece was "For Blacks in Cuba, the Revolution Hasn't Begun." This about-face in the title is not only appallingly false but flies in the face of the historical record. But more important than *The New York Times's* ineptitude are the issues of race that Zurbano raises for the "coming" Cuba and the debate the article has unleashed on the island.

Zurbano's original Spanish text offers a politics and poetics of historical change in the making of a future yet to be determined, which is intricately woven throughout the text and worth discussing in detail. The first paragraph of the original Spanish speaks about the recent economic changes: "The results of these gestures which are not only economic, will bring about true change and permit Cuba to exit History and enter, once and for all, into the Present. The Future (the country to come) approaches swiftly, desperately, and in that race dreams and utopias shared until recently by Cubans fall by the wayside." Zurbano is not suggesting that Cuba will avoid history, but a certain static, utopian vision of History (with a capital "H") that seems entirely tethered to the past and unable to move forward. His use of the Present, then, is to highlight the notion that Cuba has some catching up to do before it can go fully forward into the future.

His reference to the future recalls Zizek's distinction of *futur* and *avenir* in French, both of which translate as "future" in English. *Futur*, he claims, is a "future as the continuation of the present as the full actualization of tendencies already in existence; while *avenir* points towards a radical break, a discontinuity with the present—*avenir* is what is to come (*a venir*), not just what will be" (Zizek 2012, 134). In the original title, *el país que viene* is an example of *avenir*, that interruption or disruption of the automatic drift to the fixed point of the future. It is the notion of *avenir* that ends the piece, when he says "The country as yet to come has not arrived, but aside from dreaming

ALAN WEST-DURÁN

it, I go out each morning searching for it." This leap into the unknown is what underlines the whole piece and is entirely missing from what *The New York Times* printed.

In addition to these political and historical mistranslations, the editors initially inserted text ostensibly to clarify historical or contemporary information unfamiliar to U.S. readers but clearly emphasizing a particular editorial vision and reporting bias. These included irrelevant references to Fidel and Raúl Castro. Again, Zurbano is looking at the future *(avenir)* where Cuban society is building something different (youth, blacks, women). *The Times* and most of the rest of Western reporting has a tradition of explaining everything about Cuba through the lens of Raúl (or Fidel). Zurbano's piece moves beyond that narrow lens and thus at his request *The New York Times* removed several of their insertions.

The reaction in Cuba, much of which has come out in *La Jiribilla,* suggests that society is debating issues of race. Since they have only what came out in *The New York Times* they do not know the original Spanish text, nor do they know what was truly lost in translation, especially with the title. The title has elicited the most contentious response from commentators in Cuba, but interestingly few have engaged the real issues brought up by the piece: why has racism persisted after 54 years of revolution, why are black and brown Cubans still on the low end of the societal totem pole, why are they still largely living in poorer housing, why are they such a large percentage of the prison population, why are they largely absent from the Central Committee of the Communist Party (or the Politburo), why are they cast in stereotyped roles in the media and vastly underrepresented as anchors, newscasters, and TV reporters?

Some of these issues have been discussed and raised by different groups, from La Cofradía de la Negritud, ARAC (African Descendants from Latin America and the Caribbean), the Partido Arco Progresista (a social democratic party considered dissident), and working groups within the UNEAC (Unión Nacional de Escritores y Artistas de Cuba), National Union of Writers and Artists of Cuba] and the Cuban Communist Party. Despite these efforts, the groups are not large, their efforts are not given wide play in the media (especially on television), and the work done by these groups is watched closely by the government, ever conscious that they not divert their attention so much by racial matters that they lose sight of the socialist goals of the revolution. Several books have been published on the matter, recently by Esteban Morales (2007, 2010), Nuñez González et al. (2011), Zuleica Romay Guerra (2012), Gisela Arandia Covarrubias (2012), and Rolando Rodríguez (2010), along with essays in more specialized journals by the likes of Tomás Fernández Robaina, Zurbano, and others. The literature on race by both local and international scholars is growing. Within the last few years there have been a proliferation of blogs (on and off) the island dealing with racial concerns. Cubans are dedicated bloggers, but the issue here is the readership, which still tends to be heavily concentrated outside the island, for political and economic reasons. Cuban television also ran a documentary series in 2013 of 50 half-hour programs on race, slavery, and discrimination. Overall, the debate on the island suggests that in spite of some "updating" of the system in terms of economics and increased social debate about racism, this debate has yet to lead to any major policy changes.

Zurbano's critics tend to be supporters of the revolutionary view on race and mostly on the island, although some cubanos abroad have criticized his views for being either too timid (i.e., too supportive of the revolution), or too left wing. These critics have also brought up insightful critiques of the piece, not surprising since it is impossible to deal with the full dimensions of Cuban racial realities in 1,200 words. Some have questioned how Zurbano is defining blackness, or issues of racial discrimination brought up by figures in Cuban polls or research, the economic realities of the Special Period (which hit all Cubans hard, not just blacks), the continued presence of black professionals in Cuba, the country's increasingly lively debate about race (even if it is not on the nightly news), or differing strategies about how to advance the plight of their black brethren. What is significant for a volume concerned with reforms in Cuba is that Zurbano's article suggests that Cuban society still faces important issues: blacks and their sense of citizenship, the combatting of racial inequality, the kind of society Cuba wants to be in the coming years, how the recent economic changes have class and racial dimensions, and how a new Cuba will embrace racial, cultural, religious, and sexual diversity.

CUBA'S RACIAL CONTRACT

In understanding Cuba's racial realties of the twenty-first century, it is germane to look at the historical formation of what Charles Mills calls the racial contract. Cuba's, like many other societies of the Americas, was deeply inflected by its history of slavery, attempts at whitening, and also coercive and noncoercive methods of exclusion. Mills, in his oft-cited work *The Racial Contract*, speaks to an invisibility of race within Western political theory and philosophy. Referring to the former he says: "Western political theory is not a contract between everybody ('we the people'), but between people who count, the people who really are people ('we the white people'). So it is a Racial Contract" (Mills 1997, 3). Mills makes his argument on three claims:

ALAN WEST-DURÁN

existential (white supremacy has existed locally and globally for centuries); conceptual (white supremacy constitutes a political system); methodological (white supremacy can be theorized as a "contract" between whites, hence it is a Racial Contract)[1] (Mills 1997, 7). Both the written and unwritten aspects of this contract have deep political, philosophical, social, and legal consequences for nonwhite populations.

A good example of some elements of Cuba's racial contract can be seen in Tomás Gutiérrez Alea's film *The Last Supper* (1976), set in the 1790s on a sugar plantation, as the island is poised to take over Haiti's role as the major sugar producer of the Caribbean. The plot evolves during Holy Week and the master of the plantation, who considers himself to be a good Christian, decides he will host a banquet on Maundy Thursday for 12 of his slaves, including a runaway who has been recently recaptured, Sebastián.

During the banquet, fueled by considerable amounts of wine, both master and different slaves speak (Antonio, Bangoché, Anselmo, Pascual), often with great eloquence. The master, perhaps out of guilt, maybe because he is too drunk, promises to give them Holy Friday off. He lectures them about St. Francis of Asisi, asking them to emulate the saint's life of humility, poverty, and willingness to endure suffering. The slaves listen somewhat attentively, but are not entirely convinced. As the master dozes off to sleep, Sebastián tells a Yoruba story about Olofi, who made the world, including the Truth and the Lie. "The Truth was beautiful and strong, the Lie ugly and skinny. To compensate Olofi gave the Lie a machete to defend itself. One day the Truth and the Lie met and fought, since they were enemies; when the Truth lets his guard drop the Lie cuts off his head. Not being able to see, the Truth searches for its head and blunders, grabbing instead the head of the Lie and places it where his own had been." At this point Sebastián takes the head of a pig from the banquet table, places it before his own like a mask (a man with a pig's head) and says: "And from then on he goes about the world, deceiving all the people, the body of the Truth, with the head of the Lie."[2]

The next day the slaves are forced to work, despite the words of their master. Some of them rebel and set fire to the plantation and attempt to run away, killing the overseer and his wife (inadvertently). Except for one, all the runaways are rounded up and killed. A chilling scene, one that shows the Racial Contract at its cruelest, takes place in the church. The bodies of the overseer and his wife are laid out, about to be mourned and buried. To their right are two more bodies, those of slaves. The master is furious and asks what they are doing there. The priest says "In death and before God we are all. . . ." The master then silences him and sardonically finishes the sentence: "Equal?" In this one scene we see all the moral, political, and legal dimensions of the racial contract. This is biopolitics at its leanest and meanest. In addition, we see how this contract also races space, in establishing certain areas where nonwhites are excluded. To a degree, this scene mirrors the banquet scene, where slaves have been invited but only on this special occasion, since normally the master's dining room would be completely off limits. Sebastián's Olofi tale is prophetic: the master has the body of the Truth, with the head of the Lie. Such is the Racial Contract, which has the body of the truth (the mutual contract between equals) and the head of the lie (a contract for those who "really count").

Cuba's racial contract was part of its colonial legacy as well and many have pointed out some its traits, arguing that they have carried over into the republican era and beyond: 1) rigid power hierarchies, 2) subordination to authority, 3) paternalism, 4) patriarchy, and 5) a spirit of plunder. All of these relate to the island's racial realities and to the "coloniality of power," but also have consequences for politics, democratic debate, human relations (from the social to the intimate), and workplace policy.

Cuba's racial contract is embedded in a practice of biopolitics (Foucault, Agamben) and immunity-community (Esposito). The history of biopolitics is rooted in the nineteenth-century legacy of sovereign power becoming a discourse based on racist-biological notions. The scientific discourse of evolutionism laid out a conceptual grid of superior to inferior races and a compulsion for purity that was not only racial but much wider in scope: to purify society (of criminals, the insane, the "deviant," the sick, political dissidents, etc.) of all elements that threaten disorder. This discourse helped decide who lived and who died. In terms of the latter death does not mean physical extinction, but exclusion, expulsion, social or political death.[3] Cuba has exhibited all of these different types of "death," from the murderous rampage of 1912 to the subtler (but still damaging) offenses of jokes and slurs.

This evolutionist eugenics articulates a logic of immunity. At first glance, immunity means you are exempt from a social obligation; in a sense, one is removed from a community. But as Esposito states, the two are intimately entwined. Immunity in the biomedical sense is meant to protect life; in the social sense it is meant to protect a community. One way to protect a community is to physically dispel all that is "undesirable" or "threatening." But in most cases, that can be costly or counterproductive; the better alternative is to absorb and disarm, that is, immunize. Danger "must be thwarted, but not by keeping it a distance from one's border; rather, it is included inside them. The dialectical figure that thus emerges is that of exclusionary inclusion or exclusion by inclusion. The body defeats a poison not by expelling it outside the organism, but by making it somehow part of the body" (Esposito 2011,

ALAN WEST-DURÁN

8). In Cuba's case this danger was the fear of the racial other (nonwhites becoming a majority of Cubans, a threat to the social order; Cuba turning into another Haiti, etc.) In the Cuban racial contract and its biopolitical discourse, the exclusion of race is expressed in an inclusion within society. Not surprisingly, Brazilian scholar on race Edward Telles has used the term "inclusionary discrimination" (Sawyer 2006, 35). At times the exclusion meant "social death" (slavery), or exclusion through whitening (Spanish emigration 1880–1910), "inclusion" using Caribbean labor (Haitians, Jamaicans, and others), or inclusion through race mixing ("bettering the race" or eventually making it disappear). Through work practices and social restrictions exclusion was practiced rampantly until 1959. Of course, the most blatant example of exclusion (but meant to ensure inclusion) was La Guerra de 1912, where thousands were slaughtered. But all of these were a means of immunization meant to preserve a community and fashion a racialized notion of citizenship.

CUBA'S RACIAL CONTRACT IN THE TWENTY-FIRST CENTURY

Both Zurbano and his critics are faced with dilemmas that blacks in Cuba were faced with before 1959: *regeneración* or bicultural nationalism (but not separatism).[4] The revolutionary government did away with black organizations post-1959—clubs like Club Atenas and many others that were not only social clubs but institutions that sought to advance the social, economic, and political plight of their brethren. *Regeneración*, or uplift, took on a different value under a revolutionary regime. Black advancement meant becoming a revolutionary; *el hombre negro* had to give way to *el hombre nuevo*. The new government desegregated beaches, workplaces, clubs, schools, and hotels; these gains were significant and these measures were meant to dismantle and eradicate discrimination. These steps taken in the early 1960s were comprehensive and successful, undeniably catapulting many Cubans of color into the professional ranks or positions of authority (doctors, scientists, teachers, engineers, middle-level managers, party leaders, military officers, etc.)

However, the powerfully resistant structure of white privilege remained intact in certain ways. Invoking Mills, we could say that certain elements of the racial contract (ideological, moral, the norms of universalism) have not been seriously amended or altered. Despite the rhetoric of the leadership, the top circle of the July 26 movement—with the exception of Juan Almeida—was predominantly white and middle-class, and in contemporary Cuba the higher you ascend in the political hierarchy, the whiter it is. This is a conundrum for Cubans living in Cuba—black, brown, white, or other—and who are critical voices within the revolutionary process because they must account for something that should have either disappeared or should be on the verge of doing so. For those outside Cuba and not supportive of the revolution the task is somewhat easier: they can chalk it up to one of the many unfulfilled promises of the revolution, the evils of communism, or the willful ignorance of the revolutionary leadership.

My focus, thus, will be on Cuba's ever-changing post-2008 climate of economic, social, and cultural reform and how it related to racial matters. My reason for doing so is twofold: to avoid conflating racism with the current government (which does not mean that racism is not embedded in some of their practices) and to conceptualize the persistence of racism under socialism.

The latter point is important because the traditional view of racism in a postrevolutionary society is that is one of the many "isms" of capitalism, along with classism, sexism, ageism, and homophobia. Marxists (and other revolutionaries) were well aware that racism existed before the advent of capitalism, but they were equally cognizant that colonialism and imperialism were both linked to notions of cultural and racial superiority, i.e., that racism took on a renewed relevance in European empire building and the subjugation/exploitation of non-European peoples. In this regard modernity, race and the rise of the nation-state are linked to capitalist expansion, under the rubric of colonialism and imperialism.

After more than 50 years of revolution Cuban society has had to face the collapse of its major economic and political partner, the USSR, and despite generous help from Venezuela, Cuba has had to introduce market reforms that previously would have been unthinkable to the leadership. Cuba has had to become part of the globalized economy (for better and worse) with tourism playing a key role in its attempt at economic recovery. No scholar of Cuban reality can overlook the increasing levels of inequality on the island, although compared to most Latin American countries Cuba is still quite egalitarian.[5]

However, this increasing inequality has a racial dimension that is inescapable. Scholars attribute it to several factors: inaccessibility to work that pays in CUC (Cuban convertible currency or foreign equivalents), lack of family abroad who can send remittances, long-term employment patterns, nepotism, absence of proper social networks that facilitate access to certain types of jobs, lack of educational achievement, and, of course, entrenched racial attitudes about who is suited or given types of work. To complicate matters for both scholars and policy makers, Cuba does not compile data on health disparities, education, crime, employment, and crime by race.

The standard Marxist approach to racism under capitalism is to subsume it under class exploitation, arguing that in a society with class and racial di-

ALAN WEST-DURÁN

visions black workers are doubly exploited (as workers and blacks), enabling capitalists to bribe white workers and keep them divided as workers. But what happens in a socialist economy where the means of production are meant to be in the hands of the workers (or at least the state)? Either you have to admit that there are classes and exploitation under socialism (highly controversial if not politically suspect in Cuba) or find an alternative explanation that relies on societal norms, the subsistence of historical patterns, personal or collective psychology, cultural traits, scientific or anthropological analysis, or religious doctrine. As Cuba "updates" its model, which includes greater market mechanisms, it will also be forced to wrestle with these notions.

PATRIA, NACIÓN, RACE

Cuba's racial contract goes back to its creation as a colony and its definitions of *patria* and *nación*, which are not synonymous (Rojas 2008, 17) Patria is often grounded in "the mystique of a particular landscape" (Schama in Rojas 2008, 15), with an ethnic and religious identity that does not always lead to the building of a state or nation, the latter being a much broader concept. In either case, patriotic or nationalist sentiment in the nineteenth century was defined by leaving out its black and brown populations as true citizens. Only with the advent of the Ten Years' War (1868–1878) does the idea of nation begin to take hold among the *criollo* elites, leading up to the founding of the republic. Despite their nationalist credentials (Varela, Luz, Saco, and others), Cuban elites still upheld a kind of patrician morality as well as a belief in racial distinction. Black and mixed-raced Cubans were not seen as fully part of the nation. But they were cognizant of the island's need to embrace modernity and in their view *nación* and *patria* were for whites. Nation and modernity were constructed on racial subordination (and Cuba was no exception), succinctly summarized in the words of one historian: "Race and nation were born and raised together; they are the Siamese twins of modernity" (Nicholson 2001, 7).

Cuba has distinctive strands to its nationalisms, which in some cases retained the notion of patria within its discursive practices. Rojas talks about civic, ethnic, and cultural nationalism. The civic type would be represented by the likes of Fernando Ortiz and Ramiro Guerra; one could also identify liberal (Mañach, Ortiz), conservative (Lamar Schweyer) and Marxist (Roa, Marinello) nationalists. Ethnic nationalism could be based on ideas of *hispanismo* (Lamar Schweyer in the 1920s), *mestizaje* (Guillén, 1930s), or racial pride (Betancourt in the 1940s and 1950s), not to mention a transcultural nationalism (Ortiz 1940). Cultural nationalism was defended by many, but perhaps acquired a unique expression in the Orígenes group (1944–1956) led by Lezama and Vitier (although it overlaps with *hispanismo*, was cosmo-politan in its aesthetics, and laced with a catholicism at times expansive and inclusive, at others insular and more conservative).

Zurbano, while sympathetic to Ortiz, is aware that his vision of racial har-mony seems romantic in that the ultimate stage of Cuban transculturation is one where race disappears: "I don't assume Fernando Ortiz's romantic idea that for Cuba to be integrated the final stage would be of racial indifferenti-ation. The use and manipulation of the work by this prestigious scholar go hand in hand; in the efforts of some experts on racial matters there is a lot more brazenness than scientific rigor" (Zurbano 2014, 57–58). Zurbano is critical of Ortiz's color-blindness (although aware that the final stage has yet to appear) and how scholars have used Ortiz to deny the presence of racism in Cuba; but, like Martí, Ortiz is often used to evoke Cuba as a racial democ-racy (see Ortiz 1995/1940 and 1975/1946).

Martí and Ortiz were used, post-1959, to argue that Cuba had achieved an enviable degree of racial integration, not surprising given the social, political, and intellectual prestige of these two figures in the Cuban social imaginary. Overlaid with the increasing socialist ethos of the ruling ideology, the only obstacles to discrimination to be removed were seen as public ones: full ac-cess to clubs, schools, workplaces, and beaches. Figures who emphasized Cu-ba's African heritage or made specific demands along racial lines were either marginalized (like Walterio Carbonell) or left the country (Betancourt, Car-los Moore). The official position was that the race problem had been settled by 1962. Interest in Afro-Cuban culture and life did not vanish, but was chan-neled in two directions: one toward ethnography, the other towards history (with a focus on slavery), but in neither case was the emphasis on current Afro-Cuban realities. This would not change until the late 1980s and into the 1990s, with the advent of the Special Period.

The complexities of Cuban nationalism, however, should not obscure the nature of the underlying racial contract, with its overt or tacit recognition of whiteness as the norm. (The exception to the nationalists mentioned pre-viously would be Guillén and Betancourt.) Whether from a perspective of *hispanismo*, color-blindness, liberal-universalist notions of citizenship, or a culturalist Catholicism, all of them either shun blackness or make it disap-pear into a wider notion of *cubanía*. Interestingly, the group that most at-tacked racism and discrimination in republican Cuba were the communists (the Partido Socialista Popular).

Cuba's greatest blindness to racial disparities resides in one of its greatest strengths: José Martí. Martí is Cuba's greatest ideologue for a race-blind so-ciety. All recite his "*Ser cubano es más que ser blanco, más que ser negro, más que ser mulato*" ("To be Cuban means more than being white, more than being black, more than being mulatto") as a phrase that defines their *cubanía*. However, many, overlook that Martí expressed that as an ideal for society, not a reality for the Cuba he was living in at the time. He was appealing to the nationalism of Cubans and trying to unite them in their cause for overthrowing the yoke of Spanish colonialism, not writing a sociological analysis of Cuban race relations.

However, since as Cubans we have made Martí our "imaginary monarch" (Rojas 2008), we have lost some of our historical perspective when we deal with Martí. For many it seems enough to quote him and with that you can take a moral high ground without having to give much thought about the persistence of racism in Cuba (or among Cubans outside of the island). If we must quote Martí it must be as a starting point (at best), not as a conclusion. As Esteban Morales reminds us, more than the words of Martí, it seems that Saco's thoughts about whitening hold more sway (Morales 2013/2006 172–73) in the education and thought of Cubans. Morales has also argued that Cuba's educational system is thoroughly Eurocentric and minimizes the Afro-Cuban contributions to the country's history, religions, and culture. Writer and ethnographer Miguel Barnet concurs, but so far the country has not revamped its history books or teaching syllabi to reflect that desired inclusiveness.

NATIONALISM, TRANSPARENCY, COLOR-BLINDNESS

Cuban revolutionary thought, and particularly post-1959, owes much to the Enlightenment tradition of universalist thought. In this regard, the Bolshevik Revolution both deepened and radicalized this thought, but by no means overturned its universalist aspirations. These aims were considered to be progressive, promote social egalitarianism (the creation of a new man), foster a transparent order of political institutions always open to the scrutiny of the citizen (and the state), all for the purpose of building a new order (socialism, and eventually communism). All these aims are at the core of the Cuban revolutionary experience and thought post-1959.

However, in certain respects, Cuban radical thought owes much to Rousseau and the need for the creation of a civil religion and the notion of general will. Rousseau's thought tried to reconcile self-love and freedom with collective responsibility, balancing individual passions and the general will, obedience, and freedom, political autonomy with social equality. It is a tall order, one that has bedeviled political thought for centuries, and has not been satisfactorily resolved in any society.

Rousseau's critique of our human alienation in society is unequivocal:

"We no longer live in our own place, we live outside of it. . . . Man is beginning to be at war with himself" (in Wolin 2004/1960, 330). Sheldon Wolin sums up the material, political, psychological, and spiritual dimensions of this dysfunction according to Rousseau:

> Civilized man, in contrast, had fabricated endless complications to existence. As a creature whom society had rendered rational and endowed with imagination, he uses what he has acquired to make his condition miserable. He is cursed by the ability to imagine new needs, to extend without limit the horizon of his possibilities, to turn reason into cunning and place it at the service if desired. He has destroyed the balance between needs and desires: what he needs he does not desire, what he desires he does not need. Living in close proximity to others multiplies his wants; he is forced into making comparisons between what he has and what others have. Existence is turned into a running sore of discontent. Now man must compete with others for the objects of desire; he must adopt stratagems of dissimulation, hypocrisy, and insincerity. "To be and to seem become two totally different things." (Wolin 2004/1960, 331)

Despite his critique of society, Rousseau does not argue for an uncritical and idealistic return to nature; on the contrary, he makes the case for a civil religion that creates a general will (*volonté générale*) from the sovereignty of the people, superseding the individual passions and egotisms that can divide a society. Rousseau even sees this general will as an impersonal force, that of law. It is not difficult to read into Rousseau's idea of general will other impersonal forces that have been used to organize societies: history, necessity, laws of nature, the master race, World Spirit, or society, allowing an unmediated access to reality that leads us to true freedom (Wolin 2004/1960, 334).

Rousseau's general will is not only impersonal but universalistic. As Dick Howard points out: "Because the *volonté générale* is political, it leaves no place for particularity and has no room for difference" (Howard 2010, 252). Rousseau had a troubled relationship with Otherness; at both a moral and existential level he wanted it to disappear (Starobinski 1988/1971, xxiii).

Because deceptive appearances so troubled him, Rousseau was obsessed by transparency, the ability to see (and see through) others: "If I could change my nature and become a living eye, I would do so willingly . . . while not concerned about being seen, I need to see [my fellow man]" (Rousseau in Starobinski 1988/1971, xxi, from *La Nouvelle Héloïse*). The transparency was needed to avoid the "scandal of deceit," the "appearances that condemn him."

Rousseau's idea of the general will is built on this notion of transparency, where the inner and outer aspects of a human being are in perfect harmony: "How sweet it would be to live among us, if the outward countenance were always the image of the heart's dispositions." (Starobinski 1988/1971, 3, from *The Discourse on the Science and the Arts*). Some have referred to the emotional aspects of Rousseau's thought and its relationship to politics as a "dictatorship of the heart" (Han 2013/2012, 82). These characteristics of Rousseau's thought permeate Cuban political discourse from Varela and Martí to Mañach and Marinello, and include Fidel's celebrated speech "History Will Absolve Me."

What do these notions of the "living eye," deception and appearance, transparency, and the dictatorship of the heart have to do with the revolutionary and now reforming Cuba? Rousseau's notion of the general will has deep resonances with the use of the word *pueblo* in revolutionary Cuba. Post-1959, it has taken on the meaning somewhat akin to Rousseau's "general will," where pueblo means *campesinos*, workers, students, professionals, scientists, artists, teachers, and health workers. Only recently has *pueblo* started to recognize issues related to gender (outside the framework of the Cuban Women's Federation, FMC), sexual preference, and race.

Rousseau's transparency implies the absence of color, in the literal sense that something transparent can be purely traversed visually or otherwise, without opacity or obstruction. This transparency has its socialist-communist equivalent in that a classless society other -isms (racism, sexism, ageism, etc.) cease to exist under a crystalline dome of equality. In this we must distinguish capitalist versus communist transparency. Byung-Chul Han (2013/2012) focuses on the notion of transparency under cognitive capitalism, where information, commodity fetishism, and the circulation of capital form a coercive triangular relationship that is ultimately violent: "El imperativo de la transparencia hace sospechoso todo lo que no se somete a la visibilidad. En eso consiste su violencia" (Han 2013/2012, 31). If Han's definition holds true, both capitalist and communist submission to visibility are violent. This allows us to see racism, then, as a double instantiation of violence: one of visibility (whiteness as norm) and the other of invisibility or erasure (blackness as otherness).

As he discusses the body under the regime of capitalist transparency, Han says that the body is exposed, exploited, and then consumed (Han 2013/2012, 30). Under communism we might argue that the body is exposed (as the true embodiment of work, socialist labor) and idealized (if not also exploited in the fulfillment of five-year plans), then dissolved into the collective glory of the masses. If the capitalist version represents commodity fetishism, the communist version represents the fetishism of the people (or of the party).[6]

Han speaks to the leveling aspects of commodity production and argues that capitalism imposes a kind of brutal equivalence that abolishes singularity and uniqueness: "The transparent society is a hell of sameness (equality)" ("La sociedad de la transparencia es un infierno de lo igual") (Han 2013/2012, 12). Does the sameness of capitalism (the commodity) have an analogous sameness under communism? Is it the sameness of nationalism or that of classlessness? The sameness, predicated on the notion of visibility, is one where difference is seen as outside the norm, refractory, and in the highly ideological climate of communism can be seen as a deviation, one that elicit all sorts of accusations (counterrevolutionary, unpatriotic, divisive, Trotskyite, Titoist, revisionist, rightist, infantile leftist, etc.) Boris Groys argues that under communism deviation is not actually forbidden but instead unthinkable because in a utopian society "all members are equally enlightened" (Groys 2009/2006, 77). It is this unthinkability, so widespread and deep-rooted, which contributes to color-blindness under socialism.

This philosophy, however, confronts the reality that Cuban society has not been colorblind. Zurbano warns us about what he calls neoracism, which thrives under color-blind ideology, and it exhibits a colonial logic that still persists in Cuban society (Zurbano 2014, 22, 39) He claims that contemporary Cuban society is one that avoids complexity, is socially and intellectually authoritarian, and is obsessed with unanimity, all traits that render it difficult to deal with the opacities of race. The revolution sought to decolonize Cuban institutions, the media, and civil society of its domination, racial othering, and exclusion, but the official rhetoric and restrictions on internal debate never reached the utopian ideal. Now, with some new openness to market strategies that could further exacerbate inequalities, the society will face a growing breach between the ideal and the reality.

Rousseau's transparency also applies to language. If the general will means a political discourse that does away with appearances and deception, then its locution must also be diaphanous, unambiguous. Rousseau was inimical to theater, describing it as artificial, as a place of "disfiguration, seduction, false appearances" (Han 2013/2012, 84) and chides it for its lack of transparency. Our notion of the "theatricality of politics" would be abhorrent to him, both a travesty of the general will and an insult to moral rectitude. Here is where modern party-state socialism parts ways with Rousseau despite its aim of having its citizens be visible to the state and the party; its discourse and practices are theatrical to the core. This theatricality appears more absurd as official rhetoric becomes more unglued from lived social realities in the current changing environment.

Régis Debray claims that ceremony is the typical commodity of actually existing socialism and that the overabundance of ceremony compensates for the lack (or shortages) of goods (Debray 1983/1981, 9). He provides an extensive (if not exhausting) list of ceremonies that propel the life of state socialist societies: "In the heartlands of 'real socialism,' collective life expresses itself and exhausts itself in the repetitive enthusiasm of endless popular processions, military parades, corteges, anniversaries, inaugurations, closures, festivals, congresses, tributes, funerals, visits (artists, athletes, foreign dignitaries), meetings, galas, exhibitions, receptions, speeches, oath-taking ceremonies, presentations of medals, flags, trophies, diplomas, pennants, and so on . . . The ornamental becomes the basic fabric, decorum becomes the substance of the drama" (Debray 1983/1981, 9, 10).

It is not only the theater or performativity of these events, but the substance of this ceremonial proliferation that allows us to peek into this "hell of sameness" and see that these ceremonies are both an exercise of state power (from above, if you will) and the participation of the masses (from below). Some will object and say that what Debray describes is merely a top-down process (*verticalismo en cubano*) but that's too simplistic a view on power in Cuba. There is a give and take where the state provides a degree of security (employment, health, education, stable political climate, low crime) and the individual reciprocates (does his military service, takes part in the ceremonies, and abstains from high politics).

And it is precisely this abstention from politics that makes racism under socialism a difficult task. As Alana Lentin says, racism is an inherently political topic because it deals with the nature of power, both in its inclusions and exclusions (Lentin 2008, xiii). She also states that it is the "nation state that is the main political vehicle for racism" (Lentin 2008). Discussing issues of power in Cuba, racially inflected or otherwise, is a perilous task, which is why in official discourse two different explanations on racism seem to circulate with more frequency. The first is seeing racism as an individual pathology, "arising from either delusions, akin to those associated with madness or ignorance" (Lentin 2008, xi). This argument is also used in the United States as well, and here we see the universalist aspects of liberalism and socialism coincide. This explanation tends to leave aside the historical context of slavery, exclusion, and oppression within societies that have racialized inequality.

The second is what Lentin calls "repackaging racism as discrimination" (Lentin 2008, 147), where racism is often compared to other types of discrimination (physical ability, gender, sexual preference). Again, this ignores its complex relationship to issues of nationalism, colonialism, slavery, and immigration, and again tends to equate racism with matters of prejudice. This repackaging as discrimination is succinctly stated by Fernando Rojas, Cuba's vice minister of culture, in a film titled *Raza* (2008), directed by Eric Corvalán Pellé. When asked about racism in Cuba he says it does not exist, but that there is racial discrimination. Rojas, with the best of intentions, while trying to address the existence of racial disparities in contemporary Cuba, winds up evading the question of whether there are institutional and societal barriers to racial equality in Cuba. What Rojas's statement reveals is that "unthinkable" aspect of deviation with regard to race, as articulated by Groys. But equally, it reflects what Sawyer refers to as "inclusionary discrimination" (which he borrows from Brazilian scholar Edward Telles), in arguing that both racial mixture and exclusionary practices can coexist and even thrive (Sawyer 2006, 35).

The multicultural paradigms of the United States or Europe are regarded rather suspiciously by Cuba, and to a degree, they coincide with right-wing critics who argue that multiculturalism weakens national unity and identity. Cuba is a country that is obsessed with national unity, a theme that goes back to the failures of the independence movement of the Ten Years' War. Here the totalizing fantasies of the right and left might overlap and perhaps the words of Adorno might serve as a reminder: "An emancipated society, on the other hand, would not be a unitary state, but the realization of universality in the reconciliation of differences. Politics that are still seriously concerned with such a society ought not, therefore, propound the abstract equality of men even as an idea. Instead, they should point to the bad equality today, the identity of those with interests in films and weapons, and conceive the better state in which people could be different without fear" (Adorno 1974/1951, 103). Adorno's definition of emancipation echoes his dictum of "The whole is the false" (Adorno 1974/1951, 50). Socialist systems have traditionally been built on the notion of a "beautiful totality," the realm of freedom beyond necessity. Yet they have not been able to adequately resolve "the incompatibility of the human needs for freedom and for security, for individualism and for belonging" (Ignatieff, as cited in Taguieff 2001/1987, 304). In Cuba, security and belonging have won the upper hand.

How will the recent attempts at updating the economic system affect racial tensions and disparities in Cuba? First, the fact that Raúl Castro is dedicated to slashing state employment will affect black and brown Cubans more, comparatively speaking. Cuba does not have unemployment insurance. In another chapter of this book Carmelo Mesa-Lago discusses Cuba's social se-

ALAN WEST-DURÁN

curity system, which at one point was a "model" for Latin America but has run into trouble due in large part to the collapse of the USSR. Social assistance, while still significant compared to hemispheric standards, has greatly diminished post-1989. As poverty rates have tripled in Havana from 1988 to 2002, the poor population's social assistance has decreased by 50 percent, especially from 2009 to 2013 (see chapter 10). Cuba's pension system is inadequate, since most retirees receive around 250 Cuban pesos (roughly $10) per month. Compounding this problem is the island's aging population: in 1970 9 percent of the population was 60 years or above; by 2025 it is predicted to be 26 percent. This means that there are fewer economically active persons per pensioner, adding further strain to the social security system.

Even Cuba's health system, also considered exemplary for a developing country, has suffered. Immunization of the population has declined, many hospitals have closed, there are scarcities of medicine, some infectious diseases are on the rise, and the infrastructure of potable water and sewerage needs dramatic improvement. Even though there has been an increase in Cuban doctors, one-third of them are working abroad in countries such as Venezuela, Brazil, and Angola, earning billions of dollars in foreign currency for Cuba. These health indicators also affect Afro-Cubans disproportionately, although Cuba does not collect health data along racial categories.

As part of the economic changes the Cuban rationing system has been overhauled and fewer items are available through the ration booklet. To many observers the rationing system was a reflection of the inefficiencies of the Cuban economic system, but it was also a commitment by the government to ensure that Cubans were guaranteed a certain amount of food monthly at vastly subsidized rates. That this egalitarian commitment is being eroded also reflects the precarious nature of many poor communities, where black and brown Cubans predominate. Add to this the dual currency (Cuban pesos and CUC), which allows some Cubans to earn wages in a more sustainable way, but again, these jobs are limited to tourism and the health and biotechnology sector, areas vastly underrepresented by non-white Cubans. Venezuela's economic troubles are only compounding Cuba's fragile economic recovery. The island's gross fixed-capital formation, below 10 percent, needs to be around 25 percent for true economic growth to thrive. Without that type of growth the ability for the economy to become more racially inclusive is curtailed.

As Cuba's economy changes to accommodate individual businesses, this could mean more black-owned *negocios*, but given the current racial disparities, it is likely to exacerbate inequalities between whites and blacks since the latter lack the same access to remittances. As for addressing racial disparities, the government will have to face more autonomy and greater power for black organizations to present their needs (and have them dealt with), and at the same time there will be a demand for new legislation (and the will to enforce it) that will make the state a key player and enforcer of racial equality. This will be a delicate balancing act for the Cuban state, but crucial in maintaining its legitimacy through this ever-changing period of reforms.

CONCLUDING COMMENTS

This view on difference and totality has relevance to socialist views on citizenship and its relationship to race, an understudied area in the scholarship of socialism. In the case of Cuba the definition of citizenship has narrowed since 1959, focusing on binaries like revolutionary vs. counterrevolutionary, patriots vs. *vendepatrias* [traitors], defenders of progressive change vs. reactionaries, those who have left vs. those who have remained. This narrowing makes it very difficult to discuss race within Cuban society and those who do are often labeled as divisive, as tearing Cuba down, accused of ideological confusion that is "useful to the enemy."

Zurbano is critical of these narrow attitudes and practices, coming down hard on a certain kind of Marxist-inspired communism, but he insists that antiracism work is "anti-capitalist, anti-hegemonic"; it is "democratizing, decolonizing, anti-fascist, and anti-imperialist" (Zurbano 2014, 55, 58). In addition, he argues that "Socialism is the last opportunity that Cuban blacks have to emancipate themselves on their own" (Zurbano 2014, 57). His suspicion of how capitalism reinforces social inequality and racism is coherent with how he defines antiracist activism. In his defense of socialism he implies that it be more inclusive in practice, distancing itself from the state socialisms of the twentieth century, especially when he argues for a more vigorous civil society, greater openness in the press, and a less monolithic political system.

When Zurbano brings up the issue of civil society we have to qualify what that means. Many analysts of Cuba, drawing on the experiences of Eastern Europe and the USSR, understand Cuban civil society as a collection of forces that are not only nonstate but against the state. For them, civil society is a bulwark of democracy against the encroachment of the party-state. Zurbano, and others like Rafael Hernández do not see civil society as being against the state. The latter, drawing on Gramsci in trying to develop a socialist theory of civil society, does not see the state and civil society as antithetical but as profoundly interrelated and mutually beneficial to each other in a socialist society. (Under theoretical communism, presumably, that would change since the state is supposed to "wither away.") Zurbano's call for greater autonomy in civil society for blacks to organize and present their political and economic demands does not have the goal of withdrawing from the state sphere (or wanting to overthrow it), but of making the state accountable to its principles of racial equality. The history of state socialism in the twentieth century indicates that this is a difficult balancing act. As Ehrenberg says: "Liberalism developed a theory of civil society because it wanted to democratize the state. Marxism developed a theory of the state because it wanted to democratize civil society. The twists and turns of contemporary history would bring them face to face in Eastern Europe" (in Edwards 2011, 23). This is a conundrum faced by Cuba, too.

In a critical piece published in *La Jiribilla* (April 15, 2013, reprinted in *The Afro-Hispanic Review*, pp. 195–99) Zurbano refers to a left conservatism inside and outside of Cuba that misreads (and misjudges) the role of blacks in the Cuban revolution. He further criticizes *La Jiribilla* for publishing an onslaught of attacks on him without letting him respond (for a week), and by then most of the damage was done. More importantly, he insists, there is no "Caso Zurbano," a not so veiled reference to the Caso Padilla, which happened some forty-two years earlier, with disastrous consequences for Cuba, domestically and internationally. Zurbano is right in stating as such: he was not imprisoned, he has since travelled out of Cuba and returned, he is published on the island, he continues to voice concerns about racism openly and publicly. More important is that what is at stake is not Zurbano's views versus the Cuban state, but the fate of black Cubans in the social realities of Cuba. His situation, then, is different from Walterio Carbonell's (1920–2008) who was marginalized for his work and thought for decades, and yet the events surrounding the article and his demotion at Casa de las Américas, are a reminder that when black intellectuals speak about race in Cuba, there can be a price to pay for being outspoken on this issue. Over time, however, this price seems to have diminished and increasingly black Cubans are expressing their misgivings and the issue is no longer as taboo as it was. Cuban visual artists like René Peña, Alexis Esquivel, Juan Roberto Diago, Manuel Arenas, and Armando Mariño are questioning their society's racial paradigms and contract. Recently, Cuban rapper Alexey from Obsesión posted a rap on Facebook calling for the tearing down of the statue of José Miguel Gómez on the the Avenida de los Presidentes. Gómez is the former President of Cuba and was responsible for the slaughter of at least 4,000 black and brown Cubans in 1912. Voicing this demand so publicly would have been unthinkable a decade ago.

Despite Zurbano's persuasiveness on matters of race and discrimination, the historical record shows that capitalism, socialism, communism, European social democracy, state capitalism (whether of the Singapore or Chinese variety) have not been able to eliminate racism (or sexism for that matter). This should not be cause for despair, but a sobering reminder that not all change occurs at the same rate and that some social ills require more multifaceted approaches (legal, political, law enforcement, education, psychology, job equity, media), and that there are no magic bullets in dealing with racism.

One area that is significant in the discussion of racism is that of citizenship, something that seems almost self-evident but is not. Roberto Alejandro reminds us that citizenship is an extremely complex set of languages, practices, politics, symbols, meanings, and identities.

> Citizenship, then, should be viewed as a space of memories and struggles where collective identities are played out. It should also be viewed as a space where citizens can decode languages and practices. As a space of memories, citizenship requires symbols (like the Constitution, the flag); signs (like the tradition of rights); rites (like national celebrations); myths (like the invention of a "national unity"); and even instances of forgetfulness (who celebrated, for instance the centennial of the American Civil War?) This perspective allows us to see citizenship not as a juridical category or a collection of civic attitudes, but as a hermeneutic horizon, a practice, and even a textual reality. By hermeneutic horizon I mean a worldview nurtured by traditions, institutions, and practices with open boundaries for reflection. By practice I mean a way of life that assumes social, but not necessarily shared norms and pursues certain but not necessarily common, goals with a shared historical context. By textual reality I mean a web of principles and practices addressed to a plurality of readers. To say that citizenship is a practice is not to say that citizens have a uniform understanding of meanings . . . or that they share a uniform culture. They share a historical context; that is, they share the boundaries within which meanings are challenged or accepted or enacted, and in which different cultures strive to define the identity of both groups and individuals. Moreover, citizenship as a practice has to do with the discourses and symbols that establish the collective identity of a community. (Alejandro 1993, p. 37)

For Cuba, then, national unity need not imply uniformity, symbols need to transcend geographical borders, narratives have to include the victors and the vanquished, rites must include those who have been forgotten, myths must incorporate that rebellious mosaic of black and brown Cubans who have made the Cuban nation what it is. When Cubans create a society where they do not have a uniform understanding of citizenship or culture—a direction to which the economic and political reforms discussed elsewhere in this volume may contribute—then perhaps Zurbano's dream of walking into the street and seeing the country to come will materialize and his *Cuba negra* will be *cubano-afreecano*.[6]

NOTES

1. Mills offers ten theses on the racial contract (RC). I include the first seven: 1) The RC is political, moral, and epistemological; 2) the RC is a historical actuality; 3) the RC is an exploitation contract; 4) the RC norms (and races) space 5) the RC norms (and races) the individual; 6) The RC underwrites the modern social contract; and 7) the RC has to be enforced through violence and ideological conditioning (Mills, see table of contents).

2. This cautionary tale should be kept in mind as we look at what has transpired between *The New York Times* and Zurbano. The head of the article (the title) turns out to be the head of the Lie, even if the body (the text) is the Truth. But in viewing what happened in the translation process we also see that a pig's head wound up on top of a thinking, perceptive body. As we look closer at what has transpired we can begin to join the rightful Head with the truthful Body.

3. See Foucault in Timothy Campbell and Adam Sitze, eds., *Biopolitics: A Reader* (Durham: Duke University Press, 2013), 74–81. Foucault further argues that socialism has the same racist logic that distinguished capitalism by using the same techniques of power and exclusion. Socialism might not practice what he calls "ethnic racism," but in its desire to purify society (of deviants, political opponents, antisocial elements) ends up reproducing the "racist logic" of biopolitics. For reasons of space, I cannot discuss the strengths or weaknesses of this argument.

4. For more on the responses and commentary on Zurbano see AfroCubaWeb (online). Another valuable resource is *The Afro-Hispanic Review* 33, no. 1 (Spring 2014), pt. I, which contains over 200 pages of analysis on the Caso Zurbano. Both AfroCubaWeb and *The Afro-Hispanic Review* also contain the original piece by Zurbano (in Spanish), plus an English translation of the original (without changes made by *The New York Times*).

5. See *The New York Times* article on inequality (and capitalism) in Cuba by Randall Archibold (February 24, 2015).

6. I take the last word from Omar Sosa's album "Afreecanos."

BIBLIOGRAPHY

Adorno, T. W. *Minima Moralia*. London: Verso, 1974/1951.

Alejandro, Roberto. *Hermeneutics, Citizenship and the Public Sphere*. Albany: SUNY Press, 1993.

Debray, Regis. *Critique of Political Reason*. New York: Verso, 1983/1981.

Edwards, Michael, ed. *The Oxford Handbook of Civil Society*, Oxford, 2011.

Esposito, Roberto. *Immunitas: The Protection and Negation of Life*. Malden: Polity Press, 2011.

Groys, Boris. *The Communist Postscript*. New York: Verso, 2009/2006.

Han, Byun-Chul. *La sociedad de la transparencia*. Barcelona: Herder Editorial, 2013/2012.

Howard, Dick. *The Primacy of the Political: A History of Political Thought from the Greeks to the French and American Revolutions*. New York: Columbia University Press, 2010.

Lentin, Alana. *Racism A Beginner's Guide*. Oxford: Oneworld Publications, 2008.

Mills, Charles W. *The Racial Contract*. New York: Cornell University Press, 1997.

Morales Domínguez, Esteban. *Race in Cuba, Essays on the Revolution and Racial Inequality*. New York: Monthly Review Press, 2013/2006.

Nicholson, Philip Yale. *Who Do We Think We Are? Race and Nation in the Modern World*. Armonk: M. E. Sharpe, 2001.

Ortiz, Fernando. *El engaño de las razas*. Havana: Ciencias Sociales, 1975/1946.

Ortiz, Fernando. *Cuban Counterpoint: Tobacco and Sugar*. Durham: Duke University Press,
1995/1940.

Porter, Dennis. *Rousseau's Legacy Emergence and Eclipse of the Writer in France*. New York: Oxford University Press, 1995.

Rojas, Rafael. *Motivos de Anteo: Patria y nación en la historia intelectual de Cuba*. Madrid: Colibrí Publishers, 2008.

Sawyer, Mark Q. *Racial Politics in Post-Revolutionary Cuba*. Cambridge University Press, 2006.

Starobinski, Jean. *Jean-Jacques Rousseau Transparency and Obstruction*. Chicago: Chicago University Press, 1988/1971.

Taguieff, Pierre-André. *The Force of Prejudice on Racism and Its Doubles*. Minneapolis: Minnesota University Press, 2001/1987.

Wolin, Sheldon. *Politics and Vision*. Princeton: Princeton University Press, 2004/1960.

Zizek, Slavoj. *The Year of Dreaming Dangerously*. New York: Verso, 2012.

Zurbano, Roberto. "Soy un negro más: Zurbano par lui-même." in *The Afro-Hispanic Review* 33, no. 1 (Spring 2014): 13–61.

ANA BELÉN MARTÍN SEVILLANO

12

FROM DOMESTIC TO STATIST VIOLENCE

DEBATE AND REPRESENTATION IN THE CUBAN CULTURAL FIELD

> *Aprendí de un buen amigo*
> *a pegarle a mi mujer,*
> *a llevar los pantalones,*
> *como es la tradición.*
> —Silvio Rodríguez, "Cierta historia de amor."
> *Mujeres* (1978)

In February 2013, the conviction and imprisonment of Ángel Santiesteban following criminal charges of violence against his ex-wife set off a heated debate in different cultural Cuban media. As a writer, Santiesteban has participated actively in the Cuban literary scene over the past two decades, publishing several works of fiction and winning important national awards, such as the prize of the Unión Nacional de Escritores y Artistas de Cuba (UNEAC) [National Union of Writers and Artists of Cuba] in 1995, the Alejo Carpentier prize in 2001, and the Casa de las Américas prize in 2006, all in the short-story category. However, in 2008 he launched the blog "Los hijos que nadie quiso" [The Children Nobody Wanted], in which he expressed his discontent with the Cuban government.[1] During the trial, Santiesteban and his lawyer, Amelia Rodríguez Cala, argued that the charges were false, and repeatedly pointed out serious irregularities in the due process. When the guilty verdict came out, a number of Cuban writers in the diaspora, such as Amir Valle in Berlin or Enrique del Risco in New York, launched a campaign and circulated a petition to bring international attention to what they thought had been a legal farce that had used sensitive charges of domestic violence to conceal political reasons.

The activity in the transnational social networks was quickly contested from within Cuba with a letter written by eight feminist intellectuals who stated that Cuban Justice was indeed just, since in their knowledge Santiesteban was guilty of domestic violence.[2] Two days later, Antonio José Ponte, one of the most important figures of the Cuban cultural field in exile, published a brief article in which he deplored the absurdity of this letter, the purpose of which was, in his opinion, to reject any criticism of the Cuban judicial system. Santiesteban was able to respond to the accusatory letter from his cell, questioning the authors, who despite their general concern for gender-based violence had failed to denounce the state's violence against the Damas de Blanco [Ladies in White], a group of activists that periodically protest in the streets against the government.[3] At the same time, international support was somehow weakened by the fact that for many, it was impossible to know whether Santiesteban was innocent, even if they suspected political reasons behind the official charges against him.[4] The Santiesteban affair soon became a tragic soap opera when another well-known Cuban writer, José Miguel Sánchez, publicly accused him of being guilty, surprisingly retracting his claim a month later.[5] In the summer of 2014 Santiesteban's son claimed in different Cuban media outside the island that he had been forced by the State Security to testify against his father during the trial.[6] Around the same time, Santiesteban escaped from prison. He then spent two weeks in Havana until he surrendered to the authorities and was returned to his cell, where he remained until he was released in July 2015.

It is noteworthy that some of the women who wrote the accusatory letter have played an important role in bringing awareness about issues related to gender inequalities in Cuba. That would be the case of Danae Diéguez, a professor at the Instituto Superior de Arte [National Art School], the coordinator of the group *Cultura y género* [Culture and Gender] at UNEAC in 2011 and 2012. The group held a monthly debate, "Mirar desde la sospecha" [Looking Critically], that addressed issues related to gender representation in Cuban media and cultural production. In many ways, this group picked up the agenda of *Magín*, a women's association created in 1994, which was quickly banned (Fernandes 2005, 439–45; López Vigil 1998). But Santiesteban had a point when he criticized the silence of Diéguez and her colleagues on the state's violence toward dissident women; condemning certain types

ANA BELÉN MARTÍN SEVILLANO

of violence and not others implies a problematic moral ground, since violence operates on many levels and in many possible instances. Regardless of the intention of its authors, the letter was defending a system that accused an individual of domestic violence but failed to indict the authorities that sank the tugboat 13 de Marzo, killing women and children (Inter-American Commission 330–91), or a police force that has repeatedly beaten women who were peacefully protesting against the government. Santiesteban was therefore pointing to statist violence as an augmented, mirroring reflection of the domestic gender-based violence of which he had been accused. Following Santiesteban's argument, violence, like a Mobius strip, would proceed as a single continuous moving phenomenon that challenges the political practices that attempt to establish boundaries within it. In this chapter I follow the narrow edge between statist and domestic violence, analyzing how it has been considered in the cultural field through the Cuban telenovela[7] *Bajo el mismo sol*, broadcast in 2011 with a considerable impact on Cuban society.

REVOLUTIONARY AND DOMESTIC VIOLENCE

The Marxist political thought that fueled the Cuban revolution conceived revolutionary violence as a necessary, ethical method to liberate the nation from the neocolonial capitalist system embodied by the dictatorship of Fulgencio Batista. Contemporary political philosophy (Fanon 1963, Sartre 1963) has considered that this emancipatory violence was crucial to eradicate statist violence. Morally, Castro's revolutionary violence positioned itself at the other end of the oppressive violence that Batista had implemented. Once in power, Castro nourished the idea of his regime's inherent emancipatory nature, which entailed the use of violence, presenting it as a legitimate resource to eliminate any political threats (Guerra 2012, 170–88), and often exercising it as a warning performance for Cuban society (Rojas 2007). The threat of a U.S. military invasion after the failed attempt of Bay of Pigs in 1961, and the long-lasting embargo, gave the Cuban government a convincing reason for establishing a permanent state of exception, in which violence was required to preserve the country's freedom and sovereignty. In this situation, people are produced not as individuals but as "bare life" or *homo sacer*, in Agamben's terms, dispossessed of all rights (Agamben 1998).

However, the long repression of dissident opinions and actions has turned the emancipatory violence of the Cuban revolution into the very same oppressive violence that it originally fought. The Cuban single-party state, together with its legal system, is underpinned by the use of different forms of violence: from physical punishment to displacement or dispossession. The most representative figures of the Cuban opposition—Damas de Blanco, Oswaldo Payá, Estado de SATS, Yoani Sánchez or Guillermo Fariñas, among others—have repeatedly reported aggressions from the Cuban security and police forces. Laura Pollán's and Oswaldo Payá's families maintain that the Cuban government was behind the sudden death of both opposition leaders, in 2011 and 2012, respectively. Significantly, these dissident voices share a common stance: the rejection of violence as a political instrument and an active but peaceful opposition to the Cuban state's violence. In this sense, it seems that Cuban society is articulating a broader and more complex analysis of violence, and of the connections between its various expressions. Cuban intellectuals, academics, and artists are formulating the existing connections between subjective or individual violence and objective violence, whether symbolic or systemic (Zizek 2008, 9–14). Thus, acts of factual (subjective) violence, such as domestic physical aggressions, are not exclusively the expression of a singular individual conflict, but a visible manifestation of a system that has normalized violence through different (symbolic) cultural narratives and (systemic) institutions.

As part of the socialist project, the revolution initially implemented a substantial array of policies that endorsed women's emancipation and their active participation in the new society. Still, women remained underrepresented in the social sphere, excluded from high-profile positions (Shayne 2004, 136–45; Smith and Padula 1996, 45–49). This "emancipation from above" changed many socioeconomic practices but left others untouched, particularly in the private realm (Molineux 1990, 25–28). In fact, the revolution enacted a masculine sociopolitical and cultural project that was based on traditional virile values, such as strength and authority. Furthermore, the institutions in charge of representing women, most notably the Federación de Mujeres Cubanas (FMC, Federation of Cuban Women), have not—until recently—supported a gender-based discourse to address the structural practices of gender inequality that have persisted in Cuba (Molineux 1990, 32–33), many of which intensified after the end of Soviet economic support in the early 1990s.

It is quite telling that domestic violence as a concept is absent in Cuban law, and therefore there are no legal procedures to address it (Gazmuri Núñez 2007; Hamilton 2012, 201–09). International observers pointed out in the early 2000s the apparent lack of social consciousness about this problem (Coomaraswamy 2000, 4–5; Perkovich and Saini 2002). The Cuban Commission of Human Rights and National Reconciliation and the Cuban Chapter of the Latin American Federation of Rural Women explicitly denounced the pervasiveness of this social problem, which is rarely reported (U.S. De-

ANA BELÉN MARTÍN SEVILLANO

partment of State). However, different Cuban institutions are focusing on domestic gender-based violence, considering it on theoretical grounds and also setting up educational campaigns and events. In 2004 the Grupo Nacional de Trabajo para la Prevención y la Atención de la Violencia Familiar (National Working Group to Prevent and Assist Domestic Violence) was created within the Federación de Mujeres Cubanas. (One of its most prominent members, the sociologist Clotilde Proveyer, pointed out the persistence of gender inequalities and sexist views in Cuban society despite the many socioeconomic reforms that the revolution implemented. Likewise, at the Centro de Investigaciones Psicológicas y Sociológicas (CIPS, Psychology and Sociology Research Center), the most important research hub on gender and family issues, specialists are carefully considering the many angles of domestic violence, highlighting the relationship between the structural and systemic characteristics of Cuban society and the occurrence of domestic violence (Valdés et al. 2011), a link also considered in the unpublished studies of the FMC (Coomaraswamy 2000, 8). As with other sensitive social issues such as homophobia or racism, many of the changes materialized in Cuba regarding gender inequalities, and in particular domestic violence, have not followed a top-down agenda but have arisen from below, often prompted by cultural production, intellectual work, and the emerging activism in civil society. Once the concern was clearly voiced by certain groups of society, government programs targeting these issues have been designed. While some of these social practices, such as civil activism, might clash with censorship and government control, others, like visual media funded by the state, might negotiate social demands without clearly opposing the hegemonic political discourse, as we will illustrate shortly in our analysis of the telenovela *Bajo el mismo sol*.

GENDER-BASED VIOLENCE AND CULTURAL PRODUCTION

Gender-based domestic violence has been a key aspect in a number of Cuban fictional works, such as *Máscaras* (1997) by Leonardo Padura, *Río Quibú* (2008) by Ronaldo Menéndez, *Cien botellas en una pared* (2002) by Ena Lucía Portela or *Todos se van* (2006) by Wendy Guerra. In these novels the domestic aggression is clearly placed in the context of a violent society, and specifically in connection with statist violence (Martín Sevillano 2014). However, and given the nonexistence of a Cuban publishing market, the impact of these novels remained limited, without effect on the general public. There have been other cultural attempts to promote a nonviolent social environment and to raise consciousness about gender-based violence, such as the campaign led by the musician Rochy Ameneiro in 2011, "Todas contracorriente," which presumably had a larger impact since it involved a series of concerts, videoclips, and workshops that addressed teenagers across the country (Hernández 2013).

When Cuban television broadcast the second season of *Bajo el mismo sol,* the debate on domestic violence finally reached the vast majority of the Cuban population. This telenovela, produced in Cuba in 2011, consisted of three seasons—"Casa de cristal," "Soledad," and "Desarraigo"—that approached a range of conflicts affecting the Cuban people, from housing problems to lack of basic goods. It also considered internalized social beliefs and behaviors that entail prejudices or actual discrimination practices. Based on a radio script written by Freddy Domínguez, the first and last seasons were directed by Jorge Alonso Padilla and the second by Ernesto Fiallo.

As in many other Latin American countries, telenovelas enjoy wide popularity in Cuba and run in prime-time slots. The public Cuban TV only airs one daily episode, after dinner, when families gather around the television. Telenovelas are a common topic of discussion at different social sites, such as the bus stop, the *bodega* or the workplace. While the genre originated in Cuba in the 1950s (Martínez 2009) and enjoyed wide popularity for decades, the particular characteristics of the revolution's cultural and political project put an end to most melodramatic productions.

The revival of the genre in the country took place during the late 1980s and the 1990s, when the national broadcaster started to import Brazilian series such as *A escrava Isaura, Dona Beija, Roque Santeiro,* or *Vale tudo,* which had a remarkable impact on the Cuban population. A telling and often-cited example of this impact is the word *paladar,* which in standard Spanish means "palate." In Cuba the term was used in that sense until the early 1990s, when the Brazilian series *Vale tudo* was aired in the country; its main character, Raquel, was a food street vendor in Rio who moved her business into her own house, naming it "Paladar," and successfully expanded it to a chain of restaurants. Cubans started to apply the name "Paladar" to new entrepreneurial ventures opening in private houses that could not be considered restaurants in the strictest sense, given their limited space and menu choices (Henken 344–45). Furthermore, *paladares* were initially invisible, since they were illegally operated, known only to trustworthy locals who would bring tourists for a small commission. In 1995, the Cuban government legalized *paladares* in what seemed an attempt to control their growing activity rather than to promote economic efficiency. Once legalized, *paladares* were forced to operate under certain restrictions, which were often circumvented (Ritter and Henken 2015, 245–73). The case of the *paladares* suggests that not all reforms that the Cuban government has implemented in the past two decades

ANA BELÉN MARTÍN SEVILLANO

have followed a top-down program designed to attain economic efficacy and productivity. In some cases, the reforms have been driven from below by new practices and behaviors that did not emerge from an official program, but quite the opposite—they were the result of state failure. As was the case in other socialist states such as Vietnam, China, Poland, or Hungary, some of the initial economic changes in Cuba were driven by bottom-up social agents who established a "local market" in which basic and low-level commercial and service activities took place. However, state control has prevented the emergence of a more sophisticated private sector that could further develop economic transformation (Font and Jancsics 2015, 151–60).

Today, *paladar* is still used in Cuba to designate a small restaurant. The sway of these early telenovelas was such that Lopez argues that in post-Soviet Cuba the "Brazilian *telenovela* . . . functioned as a funky Caribbean glasnost; as a symbolic (and practical) 'opening up' of the nation toward the popular mass culture of the Latin American continent" (Lopez 2015, 264). Ever since, Cuban television has aired numerous telenovelas from different Latin American networks, but the audience has traditionally favored Brazilian series, in which melodramatic devices usually are kept under control in order to present a historically contextualized plot and a realistic depiction of characters and conflicts (Lopez 2015, 261; Martín-Barbero 1995, 279). Not surprisingly, contemporary Cuban telenovelas also present nationally contextualized scripts, filled with characters that viewers can easily identify or relate to. This allows different social actors to interpret or appropriate discourses and conducts. On the one hand, the depiction of common individuals bestows social recognition for many viewers, who feel that the hardships they endure in their daily lives receive credit in the public arena; on the other hand, the telenovela characters provide a set of identities, from values and behaviors to looks, that the audience might find inspirational. Telenovelas echo and shape social opinions, beliefs, and practices (Martín-Barbero 1987a: 243–45; 1987b), operating within the hegemonic logic and reproducing either popular or institutional discourses. This seems to be particularly obvious in the context of Cuba, where all mass media are owned by the state.

However, not all telenovelas are the same, and the formulaic depiction of characters and the usual set of conflicts are sometimes challenged by daring critical scripts that address controversial conflicts and practices, stimulating social transformation. In the past two decades many Latin American productions have dealt with sensitive social issues, like homophobia, that were rarely mentioned in TV shows in the past. By considering and resignifying specific social conflicts, telenovelas become a space for negotiation, a "mediation" (Martín-Barbero 1987a: 245–46) in which social change can be instigated. However, this social and educational scope of the Latin American telenovela is hardly new, since it has been present in many successful productions since the 1960s (Guerra, Rios, and Forbus 2011, 151–53). Thus, in Cuba we can find productions that might present obvious dogmatic elements while still considering social needs, which could be understood by the audience as criticism of sociopolitical practices and policies. It is this ambiguity and complexity, as well as the extent of their social impact, which makes telenovelas a valuable social and cultural site.

VIOLENCE AND CUBAN TELENOVELAS

In contrast to its Latin American counterparts, the Cuban telenovela is usually a modest production constrained by a limited budget; it employs local actors, makes use of simple sets, and implements a number of editing strategies to save costs. It is never conceived as a marketable product outside the island, and it is regularly aired together with a foreign, often Brazilian, telenovela in alternating days. Cubans usually favor foreign productions, and in general they seem to have a poor opinion of the national telenovela industry, but occasionally some local telenovelas have sparkled important social debates. That is the case of *La cara oculta de la luna*, aired in 2006, which brought to a wider audience issues related to the widespread social and institutional prejudices against male homosexuality. The debate about Cuban homophobia had been previously considered in less accessible Cuban cultural media (literature, cinema), as well as in the political field through the Centro Nacional de Educación Sexual (CENESEX, National Center for Sex Education). *La cara oculta de la luna* presented the issue to a general audience with familiar syntax: the melodramatic structure. As in the case of "Soledad," the author of the script was Freddy Domínguez.

Indeed, national series have the potential to address issues that are of particular interest to Cuban society, presenting in a recognizable, simple, and individualized fashion complex sociopolitical issues, and thus facilitating the viewer's identification and recognition. One of the traits that made of *Bajo el mismo sol* a controversial telenovela was its depiction of a variety of feminine characters and conflicts, visually representing the specific struggles that emerge out of gender roles and attributions. Out of the three seasons, "Soledad" seems to have had the strongest impact on the audience.[8] Despite the noticeable visual austerity and the somewhat confusing structure, the production found a smooth balance between the usual melodramatic devices and the depiction of Cuban reality (Armas Fonseca 2012, González Rojas 2012, Nórido 2011). There was no interest in portraying sexy, exotic, or wealthy individuals, as is often the case in Latin American telenovelas, quite

ANA BELÉN MARTÍN SEVILLANO

the opposite—most of the characters dressed and behaved like average Cuban people do in daily situations.

In "Soledad" there were several narrative lines that followed specific characters and conflicts. At their center appeared to be the troubled relationship between a married couple: Saúl and Odalys. Saúl—Julio César Ramírez—inflicted constant psychological and physical abuse on his wife, Odalys—Tamara Castellanos. The construction of these two characters and the plot that delves into their relationship was based on specialized literature on domestic violence. Their behavior replicated the "cycle of abuse" described in 1979 by Leonore Walker, who explained for the first time how victims of domestic violence are trapped in a repetitive pattern of events that usually follow a sequence of abuse, reconciliation, calm, tension building, and abuse. Their relationship complied with traditional patterns of gender inequality; at the same time, racial inequality was subtly hinted at as Odalys was Afro-Cuban and Saúl was white.

Within the first five episodes of the series, Saúl displayed the range of abusive behavior: verbal, physical, and sexual. His outbursts normally took place when his wife did not comply with his wishes, and occasionally when he was drunk, both normal traits of abusers. "Soledad" did not use any scenic or script subterfuge in order to avoid presenting the abuse in the screen; this took place in front of a perplexed audience, unaccustomed to witnessing the repetitive scenes of harm and mistreatment that take place in the life of abused women. Thus, this telenovela made public what is usually considered a private affair, openly revealing its dishonest and criminal nature.

As battered women do, Odalys tried to satisfy and even anticipate all her husband's needs to avoid further conflict (Goodman et al. 2003). She could not bring herself to trust her problems to anybody, even when requested by Leslie—Mariela Bejerano—her neighbor and friend. Leslie represented the counterpart of Odalys; an independent and active hairdresser who worked for the state and simultaneously had her own business. One of the reasons that made "Soledad" a successful national product was that the characters faced the same challenges that Cubans encounter daily, which stimulates empathy, and offers recognition to many individuals in the audience. As most Cuban people do, most characters in the telenovela suffered from a persistently shaky economy, in which average official salaries do not always provide basic goods (Monreal 2016). In the series, Odalys strives to make ends meet given that her husband's salary, in Cuban *pesos* (CUP), but it is insufficient to run her household. Leslie, however, has access to convertible pesos (CUC) through her private business; equivalent to the American dollar, convertible pesos not only have a higher buying power than their national counterpart, they also buy otherwise unattainable produce and merchandise. Through the pair Odalys-Leslie, "Soledad" subtly presents the inherent unfairness of the dual-currency system, since it benefits those individuals who receive remittance, work in the tourist industry, or are self-employed. In 2002, only one-third of the Cuban population had continuous access to dollars (Eckstein 2008, 186), a fact that breaks the socialist dogma by establishing a social divide and generating inequality. Leslie usually dons less modest outfits than Odalys, the furniture in her house looks modern for the Cuban standard, and she can afford to go out quite often; furthermore, Odalys borrows money from her in order to feed her family. Ultimately, Leslie portrays an empowered personality while Odalys is abused whenever she does not follow her husband's commands. Not surprisingly, when Odalys finds the determination to regain control over her life, her first initiative is to open, with Leslie's help, an in-house business as a manicurist. Since the new economic reforms were launched under Raúl Castro's rule, self-employment has increased substantially, a social reality that "Soledad" considers on several occasions. The telenovela suggests that women's agency and emancipation might be strongly linked to work and, in particular, to self-employment, promoting a new social and economic model.

It was Leslie who, at the request of Odalys's daughter, intervened to stop Saúl during one of his outbursts. At that point Leslie was in the company of a boyfriend, with whom she was starting a relationship. He conveyed to her his opinion on this matter, voicing the traditional and common belief that domestic violence is a private affair, and that if women put up with it, it might be for a reason. Leslie, surprised and offended by his views, asked him to leave the apartment. When, shortly after, a local policeman visited Leslie for an unrelated issue, she asked how she could help a friend who was the victim of domestic violence. The interaction between Leslie and the police officer had an obvious educational tone, but at the same time it was relevant since it offered valuable information and, by being included in a production broadcast at prime time, it reached a wide percentage of Cuban women who might have been suffering, or at risk of suffering, domestic violence. Leslie clearly mentioned the center that helps battered women in Cuba: *Casa de orientación a la mujer y la familia*, which is part of the FMC. Not long after her conversation with the policeman, Leslie held at her home a meeting of the FMC—commonly known as *círculo de la federación*—in which women in the community, including Odalys and her daughter, discussed the complexity of violence and its social consequences. The appearance of the law enforcement officer in the telenovela conveyed to women in the audience that domestic abuse is a crime, and as such it needs to be reported to the authorities.

ANA BELÉN MARTÍN SEVILLANO

The overall educational tone of the scene seems to reveal a genuine official concern about the issue. Furthermore, specifically citing the institution that helps battered women conveys that Cuban agencies in charge of women's rights have determined the need to campaign against domestic violence. Indeed, the FMC considers that this crime is highly underreported, accounting for only 2 percent of the cases assisted in their centers (Díaz et al. 2006: 102).

The lack of determination and the submissive behavior that Odalys displayed through a significant number of episodes bewildered and dismayed not only some of her fellow characters but also the audience. Only when she was viciously beaten in the last episode was her husband finally reported and arrested. Contrary to what is often the pattern in telenovelas, the victim in "Soledad" does not experience individual transformation through the episodes, despite some willingness to do so; Odalys embodies the feelings of fear, guilt, isolation, depression, and low self-esteem that abuse produces, which also explains the inability of battered and abused women to leave their violent partners (Anderson et al. 2003). Indeed, Danae Diéguez pointed out that one of the main achievements of *Bajo el mismo sol* was the way it had presented how the "cycle of abuse" works (Grogg 2011).

The traditional asymmetric distribution of power in heterosexual couples is the primary set in which the androcentric logic operates, irradiating the rest of social and political institutions (Bourdieu 1998: 7–11). Saúl abuses his wife whenever he feels she is not following his wishes and commands, and so does the Cuban state with those who oppose its policies and practices. Significantly, Saúl and Odalys, together with their daughter, are the only traditional family that appears in the telenovela. Most of the female characters live by themselves or are single mothers. They are usually self-confident women who are quick to contest any invasion of their personal freedom, for which they suffer from loneliness and prejudice. This social depiction responds to a fact in Cuban society: the steady increase of female-headed households, which in 1995 accounted for 36 percent (Safa 2005: 324). The wide range of social policies that the revolution implemented indeed had a positive effect on women's personal agency and freedom. However, the dominant patriarchal ideology remained fairly untouched. Thus, the social depiction presented in "Soledad" conveys that traditional patriarchal structures have become dysfunctional and hostile for those women with a certain level of agency and gender consciousness. The representation of this specific issue in one of the most important forms of national entertainment suggests that it is a real concern for the Cuban government. Traditionally, female-headed households are associated with lower income and poverty, and the steady increase of this family structure could further destabilize Cuban society (Safa 2010: 62–67).

Certainly, the telenovela's endorsement of work and self-employment for women seems related to the fact that female-headed households are usually vulnerable and stricken by poverty. Telenovelas circulate representations that the audience recognizes, legitimizing and crediting common experiences and behaviors, such as those of the many Cuban women who routinely confront a challenging social and economic situation. Likewise, they display exemplary behaviors and practices that the audience, as was the case with *Vale tudo*, might replicate.

Parallel to the story of Saúl and Odalys, "Soledad" presented different subplots that pivoted around the connection between statist or systemic violence and domestic abuse. That is the case of the storyline that followed the character of Tania—Ketty de la Iglesia—one of the three female characters featured in the first season of *Bajo el mismo sol*. The connection between power and violence becomes more complex through the experience of this woman, who constantly suffered from disempowerment, rejection, and discrimination because she was an ex-convict—the central narrative in the first season of the telenovela. In "Soledad," as a secondary character, she revealed that she had been a victim of domestic violence, and had been sent to prison for responding with violence to that of her partner. Indeed, research shows that a high percentage of Cuban women prisoners have previously been victims of abuse (Navarrete Calderón 2006; Hernández 2003), and that violence against women is linked to conditions of social inequality (Álvarez Villar & González Márquez 2010).

Tania suffered violence from multiple sources: her husband, the state, and society—as a system of beliefs and practices. These three spheres share the same logic of power, which operates on the naturalized assumption of gender inequality. Tania's husband physically punished her for rejecting his domination. At another level, the state ratifies the husband's behavior by condemning and punishing Tania through its judicial and disciplinary systems. Finally, society, as a structure organized by the same androcentric principles, reminded Tania of her wrongdoing by refusing to grant her any meaningful social role. In this sense, "Soledad" presented a criticism that is rare in Cuban cultural production, that of state and systemic violence. Subtly but consistently, the telenovela renders a set of situations in which violence dominates, finely linking the effects of different kinds of violence on individuals. It would certainly be premature to state that the Cuban government allows open criticism toward its repressive practices or that the production of TV shows like "Soledad" reveals a substantial change in the traditional authoritarian policies that control cultural production in Cuba. However, the subtle

ANA BELÉN MARTÍN SEVILLANO

connection between private and statist violence in this telenovela is present-ed, and submerged, in a set of violent situations that reveal the nature of the national debate about the uses and consequences of violence as an accepted social practice. Telenovelas, as *mediations*, acknowledge social anxieties, but they also rearticulate and fit them into the hegemonic logic. Audience con-cerns about institutional violence were somehow addressed by presenting a critique, even if subtle, of the judicial and disciplinary systems in Cuba. The mere representation of these deficiencies conveyed that the government is aware of them, implicitly suggesting a possible change or a correction of the situation. Thus, "Soledad" might have revealed a new official view on violence, a view that considers it as a systemic and structural problem that needs to be readdressed through a vertical program of reform able to deal with both individual and institutional practices of violence.

One situation that expands the reflection on violence in "Soledad" is the depiction of a young woman who is married to a wealthy Spaniard many decades her senior. Through her words and actions it becomes clear that she married him for his economic status, but was not satisfied with this rela-tionship. When the husband found out that his attractive wife had a young Cuban lover, he brutally beat her. Surprisingly, she refused to press charges against him for fear of losing her social and economic status. Once again, violence emerges from a situation of inequality between the two partners, in which one depends economically on the other. The woman's acceptance of a humiliating and dangerous relationship stemmed from her fear of returning to her earlier life, when she did not have access to dollars and could not afford the life she enjoys now. This subplot referred to a controversial and prolific debate in Cuban society: the actual condition of the *jineteras*. A sui generis variation of prostitution, *jineterismo* appeared when Cuba opened its doors to international tourism in the early 1990s. Frequently *jineteras* are attractive young women who might offer sexual services to foreigners in ex-change for money, food, or clothing, but whose goal is usually to establish lasting relationships that can in the long run improve their lives and that of their families (Alcázar Campos 2010). The view "Soledad" offers seems to agree with the official one, which considers prostitution the result of moral corruption. The character of the *jinetera* in "Soledad" enjoys a luxurious life and does not contribute to society in a productive way. She leads a lonely existence in Havana, estranged from a family that does not approve the way she lives. Still, most women in Cuba do not engage in prostitution to indulge themselves, but to escape hunger and scarcity. For Cubans who do not re-ceive dollars through remittances or through their direct involvement in the tourist industry, this activity is one of the few ways they have to participate in the dollar-based economy, which provides access to essential commodities such as food, clothing, or medicines (Berg 2004, 48–51).

Tourism is an important source of revenue for the Cuban government, and Cuba in particular is a prime destination for international sexual tourists (Trumbull 2001, 358–59). The state-operated tourist industry has continuously marketed a sexualized image of the Cuban women in a clear attempt to attract male foreigners to the island. However, *jineterismo* is considered offensive for the socialist moral *credo*. Furthermore, it signals that the revolution has failed in what once was a major achievement: the eradication of prostitution in the country (Trumbull 2001, 363). Thus, the Cuban state seems to be stuck in a clear contradiction, which might explain the somehow ambivalent and erratic policies that have been implemented in order to control prostitution.

STATIST VIOLENCE

"Soledad" expands the prevalent argument of violence moving away from the depiction of physical abuse in domestic spaces in order to focus on pure statist violence. Through the character of Lázaro—Emar Xor Oña—the production evokes a controversial event in the recent history of the country: the Mariel exodus. Making use once again of the dual pattern that characterizes melodramatic structures, Saúl, Odalys's husband, is counterbalanced by his friend Lázaro, who shows himself to have a well-adjusted and kind personality. Lázaro lives with his elderly mother, for whom he devotedly cares, and his adult son, with whom he has a tense relationship. As it is often the case in Cuba, members of three generations live together in a limited living space due to the persistent housing problem in the country.

As the plot evolves, the audience finds out that the tension between father and son lies in the fact that, years ago, Lázaro had left the country for the United States, abandoning his family. During the final episodes, and as Lázaro becomes involved in a romantic relationship with Leslie, he recounts the experience of terror he endured while imprisoned in the United States. Despite the absence of details, the audience quickly understands that Lázaro left the country through the Mariel boatlift in 1980, when more than 125,000 Cubans fled to the United States. Some of them were Cuban prisoners who had been purposely sent to the United States by the Cuban authorities. On their arrival, a few thousand were considered "excludable," which meant that American immigration laws would not be applicable to them since, technically, they had yet not entered the country. This "excludable" status made it possible for the authorities to send them back to Cuba without a legal hear-

ANA BELÉN MARTÍN SEVILLANO

ing (Erickson 1988, 271–72). Shull argues that, compared to the initial white upper-middle class of Cuban exiles, the Mariel boatlift brought for the first time a racially diverse group, which affected the kind of decisions made by American authorities (244–45). It might not be irrelevant to mention here that Lázaro and his family are Afro-Cuban, an ethnic group that is overrepresented in the lower classes of Cuban society. Many of the Mariel migrants were detained for years: in 1987, more than 2,000 of them rebelled against the authorities in the Oakdale and Atlanta Federal Prisons after learning they would be soon deported (Hamm 145–47). Back in Cuba, the term *excluíble* had become a synonym of "criminal" and counterrevolutionary.

Even though Lázaro explains that he had not committed any crime and that his trip to the United States was the result of his lack of maturity, Leslie finds unacceptable that he was an *"excluíble."* Lázaro seems unable to overcome the violence he was subjected to during his migration experience, and he still suffers from post-traumatic stress syndrome. A double victim of statist violence, subjected to the political game between Cuba and the United States, Lázaro suffered for years in the American criminal justice system. Once he is back in Cuba, he is subjected to social exclusion and discrimination, an issue that is repeatedly considered in *Bajo el mismo sol*.

DISCURSIVE VIOLENCE

Finally, the telenovela offers a comprehensive view of the daunting reach of violence by considering its discursive dimension. Aggression and hostility simmer in many of the dialogues among characters, revealing the permanent state of anxiety in which they live. One example of discursive violence would be the rapport between Odalys's sister Tatiana—Mirtha Lilia Pedro—and her son Rudy—Abdel Castro. As a working-class single mother, she strives to make ends meet, offering a clear representation of the difficulties that female-headed household can experience. After countless hours working in a restaurant, Tatiana returns home only to find chores and problems that need to be addressed. Out of exhaustion and desperation she inflicts, even if unconsciously, continuous verbal abuse on her beloved child, who in turn disengages from family and school duties. It is quite shocking that Tatiana is usually unaware of her verbal aggressions, which paradoxically are prompted by her wish to protect her son. In the series, there are a significant number of characters that seem to have internalized a belligerent form of speech in daily situations. This discursive violence appears constantly through the production, such as in the interactions that take place in the *agro* [fruit market] or in the *bodega,* showing how it has become a communicative pattern.

CONCLUSION

In "Soledad," Cubans found a critical representation of many crucial social issues: from migration to economic inequality or food shortages. The telenovela also approached important historic episodes, such as the Operación Peter Pan or the Mariel exodus, that left tragic scars in people's lives and memories. Officially produced and broadcast, the telenovela was framed within the hegemonic logic of the revolution, but it incorporated social demands and anxieties. The different characters in the series voiced many of the difficulties, worries, and discontents that Cubans experience on a daily basis. Still, the telenovela somehow dogmatically questioned the behavior of those who do not follow the official codes or who opt for leaving the country. This particular discourse was clearly presented by the character of Simón— Raúl Pomares—a lonely old man whose family fled the country, and whose thoughts were often inserted as a voice-over. It is precisely this interplay of different voices and experiences that made the series a mediation site. As such, the telenovela was able to acknowledge structural and systemic failures before the people who suffer from them. The representation of important social concerns not only bestows recognition on the individuals in the audience, it also conveys official awareness, implicitly signaling an eventual reform. Despite the sometimes overly obvious moral undertone, "Soledad" clearly presented the complexity of a society that has endured severe difficulties.

Acknowledging systemic and structural problems in a prime-time TV show suggests that the government is prepared to consider its own errors, at least to some extent. The new economic direction that the government of Raúl Castro has been pursuing would not be feasible without political changes. As was the case in other socialist countries, social and political stability are essential in the transition to a market economy; it indeed requires a certain degree of social compromise and democratization (Fischer and Gelb 1991, 94, 104).

The debate on violence arises from the perceived need to move toward a more inclusive, respectful, and consensual society. Like some other instances of the Cuban cultural field, "Soledad" expresses the subtle connection between individual and statist violence, between gender domination and political repression. As Santiesteban pointed out, the violence that the *Damas de Blanco* have endured for protesting against the government is closely related to the violence he allegedly inflicted on his wife. The cultural and intellectual debate on violence in contemporary Cuba focuses on the profound ethical dilemma posed by political and statist violence. Through the lens of domes-

ANA BELÉN MARTÍN SEVILLANO

tic violence, cultural production might ultimately be considering the illegitimate use that the Cuban government has made of violence. By producing and broadcasting a telenovela that considers these issues in front of a vast audience, the Cuban state might be suggesting that the reforms under way in the country would eventually address systemic practices of violence.

NOTES

1. Elisa Tabakman, who managed Santiesteban's blog while he was imprisoned, compiled and edited a collection of his posts in the volume *Isla interior*.

2. This letter was posted on "La isla desconocida," a blog by Enrique Ubieta, on March 8, 2013. It was titled "8 de marzo: tod@s contra la violencia (a propósito de la sentencia contra el escritor Ángel Santiesteban)" and had been previously read at the UNEAC. The authors were Sandra Álvarez, Marilyn Bobes, Luisa Campuzano, Zaida Capote Cruz, Danae Diéguez, Laidi Fernández de Juan, Lirians Gordillo Piña, and Helen Hernández Hormilla.

3. Santiesteban's letter was published on the electronic news site Café Fuerte.

4. Elisa Tabakman compiled a dossier, *Elogio de la decencia*, with the notes, articles, and letters written by different authors in support of Santiesteban at the time of his trial.

5. The letters of this writer were published in the blog *La llaga* on March 14 and April 15, 2013. http://www.eforyatocha.com/category/la-llaga/.

6. *Diario de Cuba*, July 16, 2014.

7. While this genre bears similarities to the American soap opera, and it was born around the same time, they are not equivalent.

8. In 2014 Ernesto Fiallo presented in Cubavisión *La otra esquina*, a production that bears many resemblances with "Soledad."

BIBLIOGRAPHY

Agamben, G. *Homo sacer: Sovereign Power and Bare Life*. Stanford: Stanford University Press, 1998.

Alcázar Campos, A. "Jineterismo": ¿turismo sexual o uso táctico del sexo?" *Revista de Antropología Social* 19 (2010): 307–36.

Álvarez Villar, D., and Y. González Márquez. "El perfil criminológico de la delincuencia femenina en los delitos de homicidio y asesinato." Ámbito *jurídico* 78 (2010). www.ambito-juridico.com.br.

Anderson, M. A., P. M. Gillig, M. Sitaker, K. McCloskey, K. Malloy, and N. Grigsby, N. "'Why Doesn't She Just Leave?': A Descriptive Study of Victim Reported Impediments to Her Safety." *Journal of Family Violence* 18, no. 3 (2003): 151–55.

Armas Fonseca, P. "Bajo el mismo sol: un necesario reflejo de parte de la realidad." *Cuba Debate*, February 23, 2012. http://www.cubadebate.cu/opinion/2012/02/23/bajo-el-mismo-sol-un-necesario-reflejo-de-parte-de-la-realidad/#.VEGZ6RZCjx4.

Berg, M. L. "Tourism and the Revolutionary New Man: The Specter of Jineterismo in Late 'Special Period' Cuba." *Focaal—European Journal of Anthropology* 43 (2004): 46–56.

Bourdieu, P. *La domination masculine*. Paris: Éditions du Seuil, 1998.

Coomaraswamy, R. *Integration of the Human Rights of Women and the Gender Perspective: Violence against Women. Report on the Mission to Cuba*. Geneva: Economic and Social Council of the United Nations, 2000.

Díaz, M., et al. *Violencia intrafamiliar en Cuba. Aproximaciones a su caracterización y recomendaciones a la política social*. Informe de investigación. Havana: Centro de Investigaciones Psicológicas y Sociológicas, 2006.

Díaz, M., et al. *Violencia familiar en Cuba. Estudios, realidades y desafíos sociales*. Havana: Acuario, 2011.

Eckstein, S. "Dollarization and its Discontents in the Post-Soviet Era." *A Contemporary Cuba Reader: Reinventing the Revolution*. Edited by P. Brenner et al., 179–92. Lanham: Rowman & Littlefield Publishers, 2008.

Erickson, P. "The Saga of Indefinitely Detained Mariel Cubans: Garcia Mir v. Meese." *Loyola of Los Angeles International and Comparative Law Review* 10, no. 271 (1988): 271–98.

Fanon, F. *The Wretched of the Earth*. New York: Grove Press, 1963.

Fernandes, S. "Transnationalism and Feminist Activism in Cuba: The Case of Magín." *Politics & Gender* 1, no. 3 (2005): 431–52.

Fisher, S., and A. Gelb. "The Process of Socialist Economic Transformation." *Journal of Economic Perspectives* 5, no. 4 (Fall 1991): 91–105.

Font, M., and D. Jancsics. "From Planning to Market: A Framework for Cuba." *Bulletin of Latin American Research* 35, no. 2 (2015): 147–64.

Gazmuri Núñez, P. "Un acercamiento al tratamiento legal de la violencia intrafamiliar en Cuba." Buenos Aires: Consejo Latinoamericano de Ciencias Sociales, 2007. http://bibliotecavirtual.clacso.org.ar/Cuba/cips/20120827022903/gazmuri.pdf.

González Rojas, A. "Íntima cartografía de la contemporaneidad cubana." *El caimán barbudo* March 21, 2012. http://www.caimanbarbudo.cu/audiovisuales/2012/03/intima-cartografia-cubana/.

Goodman, L., M. A. Dutton, K. Weinfurt, and S. Cook, S. "The Intimate Partner Violence Strategies Index: Development and Application." *Violence Against Women* 9, no. 2 (2003): 163–86.

Grogg, P. "Televisión-Cuba: La violencia contra la mujer sale del closet." *Inter Press Service* November 24, 2011.

ANA BELÉN MARTÍN SEVILLANO

Guerra, L. *Visions of Power in Cuba. Revolution, Redemption, and Resistance, 1959–1971.* Chapel Hill: University of North Carolina Press, 2012.

Guerra, P., D. Rios, and R. Forbus. "Fuego en la Sangre Fires Risky Behaviors." *Soap Operas and Telenovelas in the Digital Age.* Edited by D. Rios and M. Castañeda, 147–64. New York: Peter Lang, 2011.

Hamm, M. S. "The Abandoned Ones: A History of the Oakdale and Atlanta Prison Riots." *Crimes by the Capitalist State. An Introduction to State Criminality.* Edited by Gregg Bark, 145–80. Albany: State University of New York Press, 1991.

Hamilton, C. *Sexual Revolutions in Cuba: Passion, Politics and Memory.* Chapel Hill: University of North Carolina Press, 2012.

Henken, T. "'Vale todo' (Anything Goes): Cuba's Paladares." *Cuba in Transition* 12, 344–53. ASCE: 2002.

Hernández, I. "Mujeres de víctimas a victimarias: Una aproximación desde la sociología y el trabajo social." Ph.D. diss., Universidad de La Habana. Havana, 2003.

Hernández, H. "Enfrentar la violencia de género desde las artes." *La Jiribilla* 615, February 16, 2013.

Inter-American Commission on Human Rights, "Report 47/96. Case 11.436. Victims of the Tugboat '13 de marzo' vs. Cuba." *Inter-American Yearbook on Human Rights,* 331–91. The Hague: Kluwer Law International, 1998. http://www.cidh.org/annualrep/96eng/Cuba11436.htm.

Lopez, A. M. "Our Welcomed Guests. Telenovelas in Latin America." In *To be Continued . . . Soap Operas around the World.* Edited by Robert C. Allen, 256–75. London: Routledge, 1995.

López Vigil, M. "Cubanas: trazos para un perfil, voces para una historia." *Envío* 200. http://www.envio.org.ni/archivo.es/1998.

Martín-Barbero, J. *De los medios a las mediaciones.* Mexico: G. Gili, 1987a.

Martín-Barbero, J. "La telenovela en Colombia: televisión, melodrama y vida cotidiana." *Diálogos de la comunicación* 17 (1987b). http://dialogosfelafacs.net/wp-content/uploads/2012/01/17-revista-dialogos-la-telenovela-en-colombia.pdf

Martín-Barbero, J. "Memory and Form in the Latin American Soap Opera." In *To be continued . . . Soap Operas around the World.* Edited by Robert C. Allen, 276–84. London: Routledge, 1995.

Martín Sevillano, A.B. "Violencia de género en la nueva narrativa cubana: deseo femenino y masculinidad hegemónica," *Hispanic Review* 82.2 (2014): 175-197.

Martínez, I. "Romancing the Globe." *Foreign Policy* 151 (2009): 48–56.

Molineux, Maxine. "The 'Woman Question' in the Age of Perestroika." *New Left Review* 183 (1990): 23–49.

Monreal, Pedro. "El salario en Cuba: los falsos paradigmas y la terca realidad." *Cuba posible,* November 1, 2016. http://www.cubaposible.net.

Navarrete Calderón, C. "Violencia doméstica y delictiva. Investigación criminológica y protección jurídica y social de la mujer en Cuba." 2006. Paper presented at the Congreso internacional del derecho internacional de los derechos humanos, Instituto de investigación jurídica, UNAM.

Nórido, Y. "Telenovela cubana: de Soledad a Desarraigo." *CubaSí,* December 19, 2011. http://www.cubasi.cu/cubasi-noticias-cuba-mundo-ultima-hora/item/2852-telenovela-cubana-de-soledad-a-desarraigo.

Perkovich, R., and R. Saini. "Women's Rights in Cuba: 'Más o menos.'" *Emory International Law Review* 16 (2002): 399–444.

Ponte, A. J. "Ángel Santiesteban: juicio después del juicio." *Diario de Cuba*, March 10, 2013. www.diariodecuba.com.

Proveyer, C. *Identidad femenina y violencia doméstica, una aproximación desde la Sociología.* Ph.D. diss., Universidad de La Habana. Havana, 2000.

Ritter, A., and T. Henken. *Entrepreneurial Cuba. The Changing Policy Landscape.* Boulder: FirstForumPress, 2015.

Rojas, R. "Anatomía del entusiasmo. La Revolución como espectáculo de ideas." *América Latina Hoy* 47 (2007): 39–53.

Santiesteban, Á. *Isla interior.* Elisa Tabakman, comp. Berlin: Otro Lunes, 2013. http://otrolunes.com/26/files/2013/02/isla-interior-angel-santiesteban-prats.pdf.

Safa, H. "The Matrifocal Family and Patriarchal Ideology in Cuba and the Caribbean." *Journal of Latin American Anthropology* 10, no. 2 (2005): 314–38.

Safa, H. "Female-Headed Households and Poverty in Latin America. A Comparison of Cuba, Puerto Rico, and the Dominican Republic." In E. Maier and N. Lebon, eds., *Women's Activism in Latin American and the Caribbean,* 60–75. New Brunswick: Rutgers University Press, 2010.

Sartre, J.-P. "Preface." *The Wretched of the Earth*, by Franz Fanon, 7–31. New York: Grove Press, 1963.

Shayne, J. D. *The Revolution Question: Feminism in El Salvador, Chile, and Cuba.* New Brunswick: Rutgers University Press, 2004.

Smith, L., and A. Padula. *Sex and Revolution: Women in Socialist Cuba.* New York: Oxford University Press, 1996.

Shull, K. "'Nobody Wants These People': Reagan's Immigration Crisis and the Containment of Foreign Bodies." *Body/Nation: The Global Realms of U.S. Body Politics in the Twentieth Century.* Edited by Emily S. Rosenberg and Shanon Fitzpatrick, 241–63. Chapel Hill: Duke University Press, 2014.

Tabakman, E. comp. *Elogio de la decencia.* Edited by Amir Valle. Berlin, 2013. http://amirvalle.com/a-titulo-personal/files/2013/03/elogio-de-la-decencia-dossier-de-apoyo-intelectual-al-escritor-angel-santiesteban.pdf.

Trumbull, C. "Prostitution and Sex Tourism in Cuba." *Cuba in Transition*, ASCE [Association for the Study of the Cuban Economy] (2001): 356–71.

U.S. Department of State. *2009 Human Rights Report: Cuba.* www.state.gov/j/drl/rls /hrrpt/2009/wha/136108.htm.

Valdés, Y., et al. *Violencia de género en las familias. Encrucijadas para el cambio.* Havana: CIPS & Acuario, 2011.

Walker, L. *The Battered Woman.* New York: Harper and Row, 1979.

Zizek, S. *Violence: Six Sideways Reflections.* New York: Picador, 2008.

TANYA SAUNDERS

13

SOMOS MUCHO MÁS
(WE ARE MUCH MORE)

AN ANALYSIS OF CUBAN
HIP-HOP ARTIVISM AND
ARTS-BASED PUBLIC SPHERES

At the writing of this chapter, the United States is in the process of ending the 60-year embargo of Cuba. During this period, sociological research about Cuban society and processes of social change has certainly been affected by decades of U.S. foreign policy toward Cuba. Also affecting analyses of social life during the pre–December 17, 2015 (when Obama announced the thawing of U.S.–Cuba relations) era, are hegemonic notions of what constitutes political participation and democratic practice. Hegemonic notions of political participation, which are based on the European experience of democratization, are premised upon the existence of economic liberties (i.e., neoliberalism), and the ability of citizens to form independent organizations that are able to influence as well as freely check and challenge the power of the state.

As I (2015), and numerous cultural studies and Latin American studies scholars have argued, hegemonic notions of what constitutes legitimate political participation, that is, the narrow definition of what constitutes democratic praxis and political activism, has resulted in distorting or rendering invisible the large field of political activism occurring within the hemisphere. Much of this activism is occurring within the cultural sphere. For a region that is undergoing a process of decolonization, the cultural sphere—the sphere that is central in the (re)negotiation of episteme and ontology—has become a crucial site of political contestation. This is also the case in Cuba, where hegemonic notions of democratic praxis, in addition to the United States's Cuba policy, which classified Cuba as a state sponsor of terrorism, has prevented nuanced, contextualized research concerning Cuban society— one that locates Cuba within the Americas and understood within its own historical trajectory, instead of a part of the former Soviet bloc. In academic literature Cuba has been largely framed as a totalitarian state in which there was absolutely no dissent or critique. Or, in an attempt to challenge the ideological hegemony of Western capitalism, Cuba has been presented as a socialist, socialist feminist, and/or racial paradise. Nuanced analysis of the internal contradictions of Cuba as a country that is also a heterogeneous multicultural society (home to Chinese, Jamaican, and Haitian immigrants as well as indigenous populations) was virtually nonexistent until recently.

This moment of change in the United States's ideological approach to Cuba through its foreign policy is one of infinite possibilities. For the purpose of this essay, I would like to implicitly address one of these possibilities: how will the social sciences approach analyzing social life and political agency on the island during this postembargo period? Part of the goal here is to challenge hegemonic notions of what constitutes political praxis in Cuba, in order to avoid reproducing research that does not reflect the political agency of politicized actors on the island, even with the presence of a repressive state. If Cuba is not analyzed within its own historical trajectory and cultural context and in relation to its location within the Caribbean and Latin America, then work in this area, in the social sciences in particular, will be limited in its explanatory power to predict and to understand the processes that will eventually lead to the emergence of a *Cuban* democracy.

In this chapter, I focus on the work of Somos Mucho Más as a case study of a larger phenomenon: the emergent sphere of association and grassroots activism of a new generation of politicized actors who are undertaking their activism through the arts, e.g., artivism. The collective's work centers on empowering artists with an eye toward supporting women artists, throughout the island. La Fina (Yamay Mejías Hernández) and La Cimarrona Sin Cadenas (Lourdes de Armas Suárez) compose the leadership of the grassroots arts collective. Focusing on the grassroots artivism of Somos Mucho Más is particularly instructive because the group exists in a context where, according to hegemonic notions of democratic praxis, its existence is an impossibility. Additionally, the organizers' intersectional approach in their artivism highlights the work undertaken by a new generation of independent women artivists who are emerging in the wake of the feminist debates that occurred during the previous fifteen years of the Cuban underground hip-hop movement (Saunders 2015).

The emergence of this movement in Cuba's politicized cultural sphere in the mid-1990s, a politicized space established by the artivism of the previous generation of Cuban artivists, resulted in a racialized critique of heteronormativity, emergent material inequality, gender inequality, and their intersections, and the coloniality of Cuban culture (Saunders 2015). The organizers of Somos Mucho Más emerged as artivists within the Cuban underground hip-hop movement.

It may not be intuitively obvious why groups such as Somos Mucho Más, and other artivist groups and collectives such as Grupo Omni Zona Franca and Obsesión, are examples of what Martín Sevillano (2010) refers to as an emergent civil society via Cuban artists' artivism. The artivism of Somos Mucho Más is not usually incompatible with state discourse, and the organizers of the organization have not been targeted for arrest by the state—as has happened with the leadership of Grupo Omni Zona Franca. However, while some groups (often referred to as dissidents), make a direct challenge to the state, others undertake what some may interpret as indirect political interventions in Cuban society. However, when considering that the political investment of Cuban artivists is to make ideological interventions into how people understand their social reality and inspire people to work to change it, one could easily argue that their artivism is much more direct in that it is focused on "the masses" instead of only, or primarily, the state. Cuban underground hip-hop artivists are also directly invested in addressing the ideological void that is a result of the 1990s economic crisis, and the country's current process of liberalization and regional reintegration.

I will first give some context in which to theoretically situate this artist-run, independent arts collective. I then discuss the collective's goals, and how and why they are undertaking their artivism to work for social change across the island. I end with a discussion of the Somos Mucho Más 2014 Artwoman Festival.

Somos Mucho Más's tenuous success with the Artwoman Festival highlights the other technologies of power that the state uses as it still tries to control the ideological production of people whose work does not directly challenge the state, but whose discourses have a broader impact on the state's monopoly on official revolutionary discourse, as the discourses produced by the artists often contradict official state discourse and provide an alternative vision for Cuba's population. These tactics used by the state do not reflect its more aggressive approach to dissidents who explicitly challenge the state's mandate to govern. Since the artivism of political actors on the island do not fit into hegemonic notions of political contestation and deliberation, the influence of these artivists on challenging and changing (though at a frustratingly slow pace) state policies and discourses is not often captured in social science research on Cuba. Data for this essay is drawn from a semilongitudinal study of the Cuban underground hip-hop movement, which began in 1998. For this essay I draw from the ethnographic data I have collected, as well as interviews with Cuba underground hip-hop artivists, scholars, and state officials. I will primarily center my analysis on the interview data from my interview with La Fina and La Cimarrona in Havana in 2013.

THE SOCIALIZATION OF CULTURE AND THE EMERGENCE OF CUBAN HIP-HOP ARTIVIST PRAXIS

In late 2014, media reports began to surface that USAID was trying to infiltrate the Cuban underground hip-hop movement (CUHHM) as a means of starting a youth revolution to overthrow the Cuban state. The CUHHM has garnered much attention because of the artists' public criticism of state policies, and the limitations of state policies and the day-to-day issues facing Cubans. In fact, the term "underground" refers to lyrics that challenge the hegemonic discourses that continue to make everyday life difficult for the average Cuban citizen, and that ignore or distort their needs and realities. These hegemonic discourses include Cuban state-centered, homogenizing, socialist discourses, which reduce the analysis of culturally based social inequalities such as racism, homophobia, and sexism to a focus on material inequality alone. This limited perspective restricts citizens' ability to represent social oppressions that are ideologically based, and cannot be completely resolved by redistributive policies.

Cuba's politicized musicians, who are undertaking their artivism through various artistic genres, have used the cultural sphere as a means of representing the needs of Cuba's diverse population, while challenging the state to fulfill its promise to create an egalitarian society. The ability of countercultural artistic movements to effect social change is a product of Cuba's own social and political history: the new revolutionary leaders sought to combine an economic focus with an ideological-cultural mechanism that would encourage artistic production in every aspect of cultural life and in all sectors of Cuban society. This process has been referred to as the "socialization of culture" (Moore 2007). Socializing culture as a means of encouraging social change was seen as a way to help citizens—especially those previously excluded from Cuban civil society—to make claims for social inclusion. It was also understood to be a process that could allow for the emergence of organic intellectuals, who would continue to produce innovative ideas that would ensure that Cuba's revolutionary process remained relevant and empowering.

Socially critical artists, who were empowered and excited about the new possibilities of the Cuban revolution during its early years, defined their role in the new revolutionary society as revolutionary agents of change who work at the level of ideological production. In Cuba, the empowerment of grass-roots institutions to provide artistic literacy is a key aspect of a basic education program, in addition to the public work of Cuba's politically active artists and intellectuals that has helped to create a highly politicized population. This has resulted in the creation of generations of artists who are able to articulate the relationship between culture, politics, art, and social change. In Cuba this political process, combined with larger regionally based moves toward democratization, has created a political field that differs from the one that emerged in European contexts.

In cultural studies and in Latin American studies there are multiple perspectives that center a decolonial framework in understanding political activism in the hemisphere. I will mention two here. One is that *how* populations within Latin America and the Caribbean understand politics is largely centered around two assumptions. The first assumption is that the cultural traditions of the region are centered on democratic forms of collective action: that people have the right to go out into the public square to air their grievances in various forms. The second assumption is that the state will address these concerns (Avritzer 2002).

The unfortunate aspect of common research in this area is that the process of democratization from the region is still analyzed from the perspective of a restoring political competition among elites (Avritzer 2002, 5). Instead, it would be best to approach democratization as "the result of transformations at the public level and that full democratization is the capacity to transform new practices from a societal innovation into a public form of decision-making" (Avritzer 2002, 5). This reflects what Avritzer refers to as participatory publics, which are composed of four areas: 1) the formation of mechanisms for face-to-face deliberation, free expression, and association by focusing on the problematic aspects of the dominant cultural political issues that should be addressed; 2) social movements and voluntary organizations address contentious issues by introducing alternative practices at the public level; 3) transforming informal public opinion into a forum for public deliberation and administrative decision making; and 4) the search for intuitional formats that will address the issues made contentious at the public level (Avritzer 2002, 7). This framework is in conversation with the second framework: that in the Americas, the cultural sphere has become an important site for political activism and social change.

Over the past four decades, politicized cultural actors have been some of the most active in challenging and changing social policies (Alvarez, Dagnino, and Escobar 1998). Culturally based political activism is largely centered on a politics of decolonization. A key aspect of the cultural politics of decolonization in Latin America and the Caribbean centers on antiracism and critiques of unfettered capitalism as a cultural system imposed on the non-European populations living in the Americas, while challenging the continued marginalization of non-European peoples' representations and expressions in the region. In this culturally based struggle for change, the politics of visibility and identity—claiming space and respect—are key, as well as the production of counterdiscourses and ideological frameworks (Álvarez et al. 1998; Stam and Shohat 2012).

These dynamics certainly played out in the possibilities of an alternative democratic praxis promised by Cuba's 1959 revolution, and the backlash the state received when those promises seemed like they would not be realized. Early into Cuba's revolutionary process, a debate emerged about what kind of state Cuba would be, a totalitarian one or one that supports democratic freedoms. For nearly a decade after, the Cuban state passed through a totalitarian phase. During the watershed period of the 1980s (a process that began in the late 1970s), young, revolutionary visual artists born and raised under the revolution added to the stronger, and louder, critical voices of state policy and social life.

During the 1980s there was an explosion of independent critical intellectual activity that centered on the social criticism of the problems persisting in revolutionary society (Zurbano-Torres 1996; Navarro 2002; Fernandes 2006). These artists acted out, literally at times, the revolutionary ideal of art as a revolutionary weapon of resistance. Artists and intellectuals began to locate their work within Cuban society as a means to spur social discussion about how to rectify persisting social inequalities. These artists said out aloud the many whispers circulating within the Cuban public sphere (Craven 2002; Camnitzer 2003; Navarro 2002; Alfonso 2005; Armony 2005).

Within the realm of poetry and literature, the 1980s was a decade of legitimation for subjectivities that had been previously silenced by revolutionary ideology. The ideological changes that occurred during this period broadened the utopic and ideological framework of revolutionary ideology. The effect has been the recognition and inclusion of diverse subjectivities, ideologies, themes, ideas, and ways of being into Cuba's public sphere. The changes that occurred during the 1980s affected nearly every area of cultural production, such as film (Chanan 2004); music (Fernandes 2006; Moore 2007); literature and poetry (Zurbano-Torres 1996); and visual arts such as theater, painting, and sculpture (Craven 2002; Camnitzer 2003; Fernandes 2006).

On the island, the 1990s are referred to as the Special Period. This was the decade after the fall of the Soviet Union, Cuba's primary economic partner. The Cuban state failed to guarantee many of the material-based, and merit-based, economic programs many Cubans had come to see as representing the success of socialism on the island. This struck at the very core of revolutionary identity politics: that socialism was to provide a better alternative to capitalism, in which social inequalities such as racism and sexism would be eliminated through eradicating material inequality. The removal of the economic veil of the Cuban state intensified the need to address many other social ills that the state either explicitly refused to address, or simply ignored.

These factors led to a profound identity crisis for Cuban youth. What did it mean to be a revolutionary subject? What does it mean to be a socialist, if your family is starving and, in the case of gender, sexual, and racial minorities, what does it mean to be a revolutionary when you cannot guarantee your material needs because of people's internalized racism, sexism, and heteronormativity? It was in this moment of ideological crisis that the Cuban underground hip-hop movement emerged in Cuba's politicized cultural sphere.

CUBAN UNDERGROUND HIP-HOP AS A CRITICAL ARTS SPHERE

The CUHHM reflects a story of how economically disenfranchised youth, living in a marginalized nation, found their critical public voice. As the economic downturn intensified during the 1990s as a result of U.S. foreign policy, Black Cubans began to face notable increases in public discrimination. They were the first to be cut from jobs and the least likely to be hired within the lucrative, foreign currency–driven tourist industry (de la Fuente 2001; Fernandes 2006). For the first time in decades, Black Cubans could not depend on merit pay raises and experienced sharper declines in their standard of living than their White counterparts (de la Fuente 2001; Fernandes 2006).

The U.S. underground hip-hop scene had its origins in New York City in the 1970s, in the midst of an economic collapse that demonstrated the inability of capitalism, and in the 1960s movements, to provide the socioeconomic benefits associated with the American dream. Through hip-hop, new generations of critical youth have been able to ideologically address many of the social issues undertaken by the 1960s generation, without suffering the institutional backlashes that the 1960s social movements experienced

(Kitwana 2003). Members of Cuba's 1990s hip-hop generation have much in common with their U.S. American counterparts who came of age in the 1960s and 1970s.

In the 1990s many underground hip-hop artists shared similar concerns as their U.S. Black American peers such as securing opportunities for themselves and their families, and addressing community economic issues. Cuba has never been totally isolated from the rest of the world. After the 1959 revolution, socially conscious activists, scholars, and artists continued going to the island and participating in intellectual, cultural, and political exchanges. Even U.S. American scholars and activists continued going to Cuba. For example, New Afrikan Revolutionary Nehanda Abiodun and former Black Panther leader Assata Shakur now have political asylum in Cuba. In 1999 and 2002 Harry Belafonte and Danny Glover, who have gone to Cuba numerous times since 1959, met with Fidel Castro to advocate for state support for the CUHHM.

As in other Black musical traditions, Black women have played a key role in Cuban hip-hop from the beginning. Black women have always been vocal members of the genre. Women have used hip-hop as a way to critically engage issues such as sexism and heteronormativity in the larger public sphere. In Cuba, as in any other hip-hop movement, the diverse perspectives of women should not be cordoned off as a particular kind of human experience, one in which the experiences articulated by male voices are generalized and understood to represent human experiences. Hip-hop venues in Cuba, and in many global contexts, are a site of mobilization for people often not recognized as participants in political processes, through which they work for social change.

Within hip-hop artivists' movements, hip-hop feminists have addressed the relationship between blackness, heteronormativity, and the heteropatriarchy imbedded in hegemonic, transnational socially conscious hip-hop discourses and activism. Because the male gendered and (hetero)sexualized Black body is taken as representative of human beings within public space, including within hip-hop, simply being a woman who undertakes her artivism through hip-hop makes an intervention into its linguistic and cultural imaginary a queer act (Lane 2011). As such, the emergence of feminist spaces or women-centered spaces within hip-hop communities marks an opening into Black queer spaces, and as such, opens the door for various forms of Black queer subjects who were assigned female at birth to represent themselves. It is in this way that Black lesbian feminists are also key actors in global hip-hop feminist movements. And in the case of Cuba, it is the hip-hop feminists who were the first to claim a feminist identity on a public stage in nearly 50 years, and in the case of Las Krudas Cubensi, they are understood to be the first women in Cuban history to publicly articulate a lesbian and, later, a queer identity.

In the 1990s, through the independent public artivism of the Cuban underground hip-hop movement, which included public symposia, DIY events, and consciousness raising activities concerning racism, homophobia, and gender inequality, it became clear that something political was happening in Cuba's public sphere that did not reflect the hegemonic narrative of Cuba being dominated by a totalitarian regime. Sujatha Fernandes (2006) accounts for these dynamics with the term "artistic public spheres." She defines these as "sites of interaction and discussion among ordinary citizens generated through the media of art and popular culture" (Fernandes 2006, 3). Fernandes's observation, and my own research in Cuba is certainly in conversation with the observations of Ana Belén Martín Sevillano (2010): that the emergent civil society in Cuba is a result of the space gained by artivists working within Cuba's politicized cultural sphere.

In her book *Sociedade civil y arte en Cuba: cuento y artes plásticas en el cambio del siglo (1980–2000),* Martín Sevillano theorizes about the processes during the post-1959 period, focusing on the arts-based social movements of the 1980s and 1990s that laid the basis for Cuba's emerging civil society. This is important work, as it is possible, with the economic changes now occurring and the changes in U.S.–Cuban relations, that the emergence of Cuba's civil society could be reduced to a "win" for an oppressed economic and political elite, as Avritzer (2002) argues, represented by the leadership of Cuba's self-identified dissident population. Such a situation is also likely to be hailed as the success of the return of capitalism (whatever form it takes) on the island as being the foundation of Cuba's democratic transition. Martín Sevillano (2010) writes the following about the definition of "civil society" and the work of Cuban artists and intellectuals in creating a nascent civil society:

Conscientes, como hemos dicho, de la complejidad y oscuridad del término, aquí recogemos el uso que la izquierda le ha dado en su lucha contra el autoritarismo: la sociedad civil como una red pública de vías de libre expresión y de espacios de representación. Acerándonos al tema de nuestro estudio, el carácter totalitario del régimen cubano, expresado en diferente grado y forma desde los años sesenta, abre un serio interrogante sobre la capacidad representativa de sus órganos, sobre el grado y calidad de la tolerancia institucional y sobre el reconocimiento de la libertad y el derecho de asociación y expresión. Sin embargo, hoy día, gracias a la lucha por la construcción de espacios públicos de representación protagonizada por escritores y artistas en los años ochenta, acompañada y seguida por la de otros agentes, se la logrado dar forma a un estado de emergente sociedad civil que cuenta, entre otras, con diversas asociaciones totalmente independientes del estado. (11–12)

Conscious, as we have said, of the complexity and obscurity of this term, here we use it the way that the left has in its fight against authoritarianism: civil society is like a public network of routes of free expression, and spaces of representation. Affirming the theme of our study, the totalitarian character of the Cuban regime, expressing itself in different grades and forms since the 1970s, opened a series of questions about the representative capacity of its organs. . . . Nonetheless, today, thanks to the fight for the construction of public spaces of representation led by the writers and artists in the 1980s, accompanied and followed by other agents, they have given form to the state of the emergent civil society that presupposes, among other things, diverse associations completely independent of the state. (11–12; trans. by author)

Martín Sevillano argues that in taking into consideration the definition of "civil society" used by the left, artists and writers in Cuba were able to create an emergent civil society. She goes on to say, "La obra *artística* se convierte en Cuba en una obra *política,* debido a esa sujeción del campo literario al campo de poder" (30; "*Artistic* work in Cuba converted itself into a *political* work, due to the subjecting of the literary field to the field of power"). This history of arts-based activism of the 1980s culminated in the major economic rupture of the 1990s, which resulted in the public sphere being flooded with disparate groups of political actors, with varying political agendas, who collectively worked for social change. The Cuban underground hip-hop movement, as an arts-based social movement, emerged in this heavily politicized context.

ARTISTS ENTERING INTO A MOVEMENT: A CONVERSATION WITH LA FINA AND LA CIMARRONA

Somos Mucho Más is the union of two hip-hop projects: En mi barrio (In my neighborhood) and Somos muchos más (We are much more). Somos muchos más was conceptualized on July 16, 2012, by Yamay Mejías Hernández (La Fina), with the support of Lourdes Suárez de Armas (La Cimarrona). La Cimarrona is the director of the traveling hip-hop project En mi barrio, decimos hacienda, which was created on June 19, 2009. Both are not-for-profit community-centered projects. After the woman-centered hip-hop festival MAR-GENES, which had been held in Holguín, Cuba, since 2009, was canceled for the 2014, Somos muchos más and En mi barrio united to create the Artwoman festival.

La Fina emerged as an MC around 2003, during the last few years of the old school period of the Cuban underground hip-hop movement (1995–2006) (Saunders 2015). La Cinmarrona emerged earlier, in the 1980s, as an artivist in Nueva Trova while it was in the final phase of transitioning from being known as a politicized artistic movement to an incorporated music genre. It is important to note here that Somos Mucho Más is in conversation with many other grassroots arts-based collectives. La Fina, for example, has attended numerous production workshops given by David De Omni of the group Omni Zona Franca. Omni Zona Franca is an experimental arts collective known for its grassroots arts-based activism, whose members are targeted for arrest and censorship by the Cuban government.

In my 2013 interview with La Fina and La Cimarrona, we talked about their artwork, their thoughts on their artivism, the Cuban underground hip-hop movement, and their philosophies concerning the issues facing women, what constitutes a social movement, and whether they self-identify as feminists. What is clear here is that La Fina and La Cimarrona are revolutionary artists who were formed by both the state's socialization of culture as well as the nearly forty-year political struggle of Cuba's politicized artists and intellectuals who worked to advance the ideals of the revolution, that is, people who worked to pressure the state to live up to its democratic promises and possibilities.

In talking about their first years as a part of what is now known as the old school period of Cuban underground hip-hop, La Fina and La Cimarrona talked about how Cuban hip-hop started around the same time hip-hop started in the Bronx. Similar to the way it emerged in the States, the four elements of hip-hop were not at first united into something called hip-hop. Also, the theory and the term "hip-hop" did not arrive to Cuba until a few decades after it had been coined in the United States. What did exist were pockets of people in cities throughout the country who were focused on a particular area. For example, groups of MCs stuck together and battled each other; break dancers had their own scene.

Many of La Fina's and La Cimarrona's comments echoed my other interviews with Cuban artists. However, one thing that stood out is the following:

[La Fina] Yo pienso que se veía la misma necesidad de los seres humanos que no sabían realmente de qué necesitaban esa música, de que necesitaban bailar, bailarla, ¿entiendes?

[La Cimarrona] Nobleza de pensamiento y necesidad de unirse. Necesidad de identificarnos con algo, ese algo era esta cultura o este rap que llegó, este baile que apareció . . . este grafitero que estaba ahí haciendo lo suyo, que ya nos dimos cuenta. O sea, como mismo surgen en el Bronx, nosotros también lo hicimos ciegamente, o sea, sin saber qué estaba pasando. Nosotros lo hicimos también.

[La Fina] I think that you see the same necessity of human beings that do not really know for what reason they needed that music, that they needed to dance, to dance it, understand?

[La Cimarrona] Nobility of thought, and the need to unite themselves. The need for us to identity with something, that something was this culture, or this rap, that arrived, this dance that appeared . . . this graffiti artist that was there doing his thing, that we had already noticed. Or rather, just as it started in the Bronx, we were also doing it blindly, or rather, without knowing what was happening. We were doing it too.

Here La Fina and La Cimarrona are making the connection that the elements of hip-hop resonated with people early on because they needed something with which to identify. Keep in mind that they are referring to the late 1970s through the early 1990s. One could describe participation at this point as an aficionado movement, largely an affective connection with the images and sounds coming from New York City, from an artistic movement that is Afro-descendant (both Black U.S. Americans and Caribbean) in origin. Culturally, despite the verbal language barriers, there was a connection. I then asked them about the usage of the term "movement."

[Tanya] ¿Qué significa cuando dices "movimiento"?

[La Cimarrona] Movimiento porque existen, varios rumbos. Un movimiento es cuando ya se reconoce que existe algo y te estoy diciendo que no se sabía que había un movimiento que nadie había recogido estas vivencias o se habían unido estos grupos . . .

[Tanya] Yo estoy tratando de entender parte del movimiento, en el sentido que era un movimiento social o era un movimiento como el reggaetón.

[La Fina] Un movimiento cultural, el reggaetón no es un movimiento, no, el reggaetón es un baile que gusta.

[La Cimarrona] Ahí tienes una diferencia. La diferencia está en que hay un pensamiento que lo une, que hay un . . . cómo decirte, un . . . a ver, además de un pensamiento que lo une, hay una consecuencia vívida de conducta que te está diciendo que hiciste un movimiento que está defendiendo una misma idea. Aunque ya te digo, en Río, en La Habana y en Santiago de Cuba no se conocían, no se sabían que estaban. Luego de los festivales es que se dan cuenta que hay también personas que están haciendo esto a lo largo de la isla. Ahí es donde ya vamos a hablar de movimiento. Ahí es donde ya entonces podemos decir que existió un movimiento del primer momento, aunque no lo sabíamos. Porque estaban al mismo tiempo sucediendo cosas a lo largo del país.

[Tanya] What does it mean when you say "movement?"

[La Cimarrona] Movement because there exist several paths. A movement is when you already recognize that something exists and I am saying this to you because if there had not been a movement, if no one had collected these experiences, or if they had not started those groups that . . .

[Tanya] I am trying to understand part of the movement, in the sense that it was a social movement or was a movement like reggaeton?

[La Fina] A cultural movement; reggaeton is not a movement; no, reggaeton is a dance that you enjoy. There you have a difference.

[La Cimarrona] The difference is that there is a line of thinking that unites, that has a . . . how to tell you . . . a . . . look, besides a line of thought that unites, there is a living consequence of the action that is telling you that you made a movement that is defending the same idea. But as I say, in Rio, in Havana, and in Santiago de Cuba they did not know it, they did not know that they were. Later in the festivals they realized that there have been people that are doing this all over the island. That is where we began to talk about a movement. That is where we could already say that there existed a movement from the first moment although we did not know it. Because there were things that were happening at the same time all over the country.

Here La Cimarrona and La Fina argue that the movement did not start out as a movement conscious of itself. It was much more organic in the sense that people connected with the same core issues, and with the political aesthetic that would be used to express those ideas. The reason people started calling it a movement is that at the hip-hop festivals, when people of like minds came together for the first time, they realized that they were connected to the same ideas and the same goal of changing their local communities, educating themselves and the larger society. They were focused on addressing the issues left unaddressed by the Cuban state, which began to intensify during the economic downturn: limited opportunities, racism, sexism, material inequality, censorship, issues surrounding self-esteem linked to the absence of Black people from Cuban history and in the media, respect for African religious traditions, especially in the areas of the Regla de Ocha and Ifá. La Cimarrona says the following about the emergence of the movement:

Se conoció luego que vinieron de afuera a decir que existía una cultura que de esta manera estaba no sé cuánto, entonces los raperos decían "pérate, dónde yo estoy metido." Pero cuando empiezan a descubrir y porque todo es por descubrimiento que su pensamiento y su filosofía era acertada o se acertaba a este pensamiento o a esta filosofía que venía ya creada de otro país, de Estados Unidos en este caso, nos dimos cuenta de que nosotros teníamos un movimiento. Porque tú te ponías a hablar con cada uno de los raperos y raperas de aquel momento, en distintos lugares del país, te das cuenta que todo el mundo hablaba el mismo idioma.

O sea todo el mundo defendía lo mismo, todo el mundo tenía el mismo pensamiento. Por eso te digo que existió un movimiento y nadie sabía que estaba. Hasta que alguien dijo "esto es un movimiento."

Later it was known that it came from outside, to say that there existed a culture of which this was I don't know how much, so the rappers said, "wait, what am I involved in?" But when they began to discover and because it was all about the discovery that their thought and their philosophy was the same as or close to the thought or this philosophy that came already created in another country, from the United States in this case, we realized that we had a movement. Because should you begin to talk with each one of the rappers, male and female, of that moment, in different parts of the country, you realize that the whole world was speaking the same language.

That is, the whole world defended the same thing, the whole world was having the same thought. For that reason, I'm telling you that a movement existed and nobody knows that it did. Until someone said "this is a movement."

La Cimarrona says that the artists were not conscious either that they were a part of a music culture that came from the United States, or that they were a part of a larger social movement. But when they had an opportunity to come together and to talk with each other, they realized that they were a part of something bigger. As mentioned, women are also a part of global hip-hop public spheres. Cuba would be no different.

THE WOMAN-CENTERED ARTIVISM OF SOMOS MUCHO MÁS

Magia MC was one of the first Cuban underground MCs to self-identify as a feminist in the mid- to late 1990s. She was also the first Cuban MC to go onto stage with an Afro, wearing a dashiki; the first Cuban woman MC to embrace an Afrocentric aesthetic. Las Krudas CUBENSI was a fan of Magia. Odaymara and Odalys Cuesta, sisters and MCs in Las Krudas CUBENSI, were deeply moved by Magia's aesthetic. It was something that would influence their aesthetic when they emerged as Cuban underground MCs several years later. Las Krudas CUBENSI would go on to be the first Cuban MCs to explicitly challenge heteronormativity, and take an intersectional approach to Black people's oppression through their experiences as Black lesbians. These artists were making an ideological intervention, which including making interventions into aesthetics—itself a political discourse.

La Cimarrona entered into the hip-hop movement through Nueva Trova and the politicized experimental arts scene in Cuba. La Fina rose through the ranks of the Cuban underground hip-hop movement. In the interview, she talked about how when she entered into the movement Las Krudas CUBENSI, known for their feminist discourse and wearing "men's" clothing, had already become a part of the Cuban underground hip-hop leadership—the core group of artists who had a significant influence on the political discourse of the movement as well as its aesthetics. La Fina—which means the very feminine woman—did not feel comfortable wearing pants all the time. She liked to wear high heels and dresses, but she did not try to buck the norm of that time, she did not want to be the one to stand out as going against the trend. So she would dress in jeans and sneakers, "though very feminine ones," as she said in the interview, and then come home and change her clothes. But in the end, she decided to change her style to one that she liked. She says the following about why she decided to dress in an "elegant" way:

> Pero tienen que ver con el desarrollo y la existencia de la mujer en el hip-hop cubano. Eso va a existir siempre, siempre va a haber gente que nos quiera discriminar por ser mujeres, negras, que cantamos rap. Ya esas tres cosas, ya te afectan y ya por esas tres cosas te pueden discriminar.... A ver, yo primero cambié porque cuando fui al rap me di cuenta de que las mujeres se vestían como hombres, estaban estereotipadas a la hora de vestirse. Y yo dije "bueno yo no puedo ser tampoco el punto discordante." Pero me sentía muy incómoda a la hora de rapear como que me veía muy varonil y no me gustaba eso.

> It has to do with the development and the existence of women within Cuban hip-hop. This is always going to exist, always there are going to be people who want to discriminate against us for being women, Black women, who sing rap. Already the three things, they already affect you and for these three reasons they can discriminate against you.... Look, I first changed because when I went to rap I realized that women were dressing like men, they were stereotyped the moment they dressed. And I said, "well, I cannot be a discordant point." But I felt very uncomfortable when it came time to rap because I felt very masculine and I did not like that.

In one of her popular songs "Paraiso Perdido" (Paradise Lost), based on a violent assault, La Fina insults her attacker and talks about her experience.

It was these types of these lived experiences and the way women were treated for dressing in a feminine way; she realized that nothing could protect women from gender-based violence, and it was any sign of femininity itself that was not respected. Women could never escape this position as women symbolized femininity. La Fina decided to embrace her femininity, and most importantly, the way she wanted to represent her feminine self. The first time she went out on stage in a dress she was terrified. People did not realize she was a rapper. People looked at her strangely and treated her poorly. But once on the stage, people's opinion of her quickly shifted. Over the course of her career, La Fina has been nominated for two Lucas Awards and two CUBADISCO awards, Cuba's version of the Grammies.

When asked if they identified as feminists, La Fina was at different moments a little more cautious in defining herself as a feminist. They were, however, firmly committed to women-centered activism. Both perspectives reflect the reality and the diversity of thought within the Cuban hip-hop movement. The artivists say the following:

[La Fina] En ese momento [2001–2004], yo . . . la palabra "feminista" no la conocía, siempre en ese momento defendía que era femenina, que era mujer rapera y negra. Eso era lo que yo defendía en ese momento y había muchas otras cosas que defender: la violencia de género, la discriminación, todos los problemas sociales que es por donde nosotras, casi siempre nos vamos las mujeres. Porque es lo que nos molesta, es lo que nos golpea y eso es lo que hacemos.

Pero el concepto "feminista" yo lo vine a descubrir más para acá y aún creo que me falta mucho por estudiar, acerca de la palabra "feminista" porque hay feministas según lo que he leído . . . feministas absolutas, las feministas feministas no pueden estar con un hombre. ¡¿Qué?! No . . . Es lo que dicen y yo no creo que eso sea así. Pienso que . . . no sé, mi pensamiento es que no debe ser así. Porque tú puedes ser feminista a tu manera, como yo. Yo lo soy a mí manera.

[Tanya] ¿Y tú?

[La Cimarrona] Si, yo soy feminista porque defiendo a la mujer. Defiendo su pensamiento . . . si, si, yo soy feminista.

In this excerpt of the interview, La Fina says that at first she had not heard of the word feminist. She just knew that she was interested in fighting for women's rights. She learned of the word feminist by participating within the Cuban underground hip-hop movement. La Cimarrona was more direct, yes. She is a feminist. However, then she goes on to talk about how she was watching a video where a woman was degrading herself. The woman was in a reggaeton video, and it was clear that they picked this woman because she was pretty, not because of her intelligence or other capablities. La Fina intervened and said that if the woman wanted to be in the video and play that role, she had the right to do so. Expecially if she was conscious of what she was doing and had her own reasons for doing it. They both disagreed. What is interesting here is that within some circles both would be considered feminists, even if, as in La Fina's case, she was fighting for women's rights without knowing the term. In fact, La Fina's feminist perspective (a woman's absolute autonomy to decide what she wants to do for herself without judgment or critique) certainly resonsates with emergent hip-hop feminist theory emerging within the United States—without her having access to it.

This also highlights another key aspect of Cuban artivism, that is, people creating their own theory and discourses in the absence of public discourses that articulate the forms of oppression they are experiencing, as a means of being able to conciously envision an alternative. A diversity of ideas have emerged in this ideological void. Two members of Las Krudas CUBENSI actively sought out foreigners in order to read what people were reading outside Cuba. They looked outside their context for discourses that they could selectively use and reframe for their particular context. La Cimarrona had more direct experience with the Federation of Cuban Women, Cuba's state-run women-centered/informally feminist organization. Odalys, Magia MC, La Fina, and a member of Las Krudas developed their feminist praxis in isolation of feminist theory, and when they heard the term feminist, they appropriated it for themselves as they saw fit, but for the most part they already had developed their own woman-centered philosophy.

There are some other important differences between La Fina and La Cimarrona—both generational differences and differences in location within Cuban society. La Cimarrona's adolescence was during the 1980s, when Cuba's politicized cultural sphere was emerging as a sphere of free association, organization, and political action. She was a part of a critical arts movement that moved through independent and state-run arts spaces and elite art worlds. La Fina's adolescence was during the 1990s. Her political identity as an artivist developed as a part of the Cuban underground hip-hop movement. Her artivist identity emerged almost exclusivley in Cuba's independent arts scene, one in which the critical cultural sphere, as a place to make an activist intervention, had been established and which artivists sought to protect and expand.

I asked them about Somos Mucho Más. La Fina's group Somos muchos más emerged with an explicitly feminist purpose that includes men. La Cimarrona's group was not woman-centered but was conscious to not exclude women. La Fina says the following about the project Somos muchos más, and then goes on to talk about a sexist incident that occurred at one of the concerts Somos muchos más organized:

[La Fina] Es un proyecto de mujeres, que de hecho así lo pusimos en grupo nosotras ahora mismo para que el nombre siga ascendiendo y que la gente conozca que existe que se llama Somos muchos más. Nosotros tenemos dentro de ese proyecto a hombres también, hombres que nos apoyaban y decidimos que ya no solamente iba a ser el que filmaba y del que hacía el background para el proyecto. Ellos también rapeaban. Decidieron unirse y cantar algunos temas dentro de los conciertos de nosotras. Nosotras organizábamos el guion artístico y ellos cantaban dentro, cuando les tocaba, que nosotras decidiéramos que ellos tienen que cantar en ese momento. Y ya por cantar una canción, imagínate tú que, no sé, por ejemplo abrían Las Positivas, después venían Las Cálidas, después venían La Real, después, te digo cuando nos uníamos, porque viajamos mucho a provincia, estuvimos casi todo el año de por ahí. Para que nos conocieran. Y haciendo trabajo comunitario todo el tiempo sin cobrar un medio, pagando de nuestro dinero. Todo el viaje, qué se yo, qué sé cuánto.

[La Fina] It is a women's project, and that's the way that we carry the group now so that the name continues to ascend and people know that there exists something called Somos muchos más. We have men in the project too, men who support us, and we decided that we would not only have them filiming and making backgrounds for the project. They also rapped. They decided to come together and sing some songs within our concert. We organized the artists' showcase and they sang within it. When they played, we decided that they were going to decide in that moment. And only to sing one song, so imagine that, I don't know, that Las Positivas opened, and then Las Cálidas, and then later came La Real, after I tell you when we got together, because we traveled a lot in the provinces, we were out there for almost the whole year. So that they would get to know us. And doing community work all the time without asking for any payment, paying our own money. The whole trip, for all I know, I don't know how much.

Here La Fina talks about the concerts and communty they organized. The artists mobilized their own resources in order to be able to organize independent events and community projects. This organzation is the only Cuban underground hip-hop organization dedicated exclusively to showcasing and supporting women's artists. There were arts collectives such as Omegas KILAY. However Omegas KILAY organized women's showcases during concerts and hip-hop festivals. The group also worked on production projects together. Somos muchos más was entirely dedicated to entire concerts centered on women, community empowerment projects centered on women's education, self-organized tours and self-produced artistic events planned, organized, and done by women. While the shows were entirely centered on women artists, and sometimes they would let men sing a few songs together in a short exhibition of their talent, in much the same way that male-dominated concerts did for women. They allowed some men to join the project as people who filmed, did background, and rapped. But in this particular concert, the men were not conscious of the event nor their public. La Fina goes on to say the following:

> Las positivas con su talla, cuando estamos en . . . hay un concierto de muchas mujeres cada cual da los mejores temas y los mejores temas son los que nos identifican nos defienden, . . . Veníamos fuerte, en el momento hacemos un intervalo para que entraran hombres y dentro de esos hombres entraron esas personas que son de nuestro proyecto . . . Entra Irina, nosotras apoyando a Irina . . . es un proyecto de mujeres andas con mujeres, estamos defendiendo todas en contra del machismo de la discriminación, de que no nos degraden, cómo tú vas a venir a hacer una canción casi prácticamente en un concierto casi feminista: "Las locas como las galletitas de chocolate!"

> Las Positivas with their work, when we were in [the provinces] there was a concert with a lot of women, each one gave the best performance and the best songs were those that we identified and defended . . . we came strong and in the moment we created an interlude so that the men could enter and with those men entered people who were a part of our project. . . . Irina entered, we supported Irina, . . . it is a project of women going with women, we were defending all women against machismo, against discrimination, so they don't degrade us, how are you going to come and do a song that is practically in a concert, [that was] almost feminist [and say]: "Queens like the chocolate cookies!"

La Cimarrona and La Fina go on to talk about how the men were not paying attention to their public, that they did not care about what the women were saying, and that they were so sexist that they felt comfortable disrespecting women on their own stage. Here, La Fina describes the concert as "almost" a feminist concert. Referencing the previous discussion of feminism, La Fina is not quite sure about what feminism is or how to define it. She heard that feminism could refer to women not having anything to do with men. Although her actions as an organizer are often considered an example of what feminism is, what is important to note is that the issue is not that La Fina is hesitant to define herself as a feminist because it is a stigmatized word. She does not identify with anything that she does not fully understand and is absolutely sure of what the politics entail, and whether they resonate with her own understanding of social oppression and women's liberation. She does not reject feminism as identity politics, she is just not sure of exactly what a feminist politics is—though she is enacting it.

Somos Mucho Más, which is the combination of En mi barrio and Somos muchos más, continues the intersectional approach of Somos muchos más in its feminist activism, by primarily focusing on up-and-coming women artists. The organization addresses the reality that women artists are less likely to receive the mentorship and support they need to develop as artists. What makes Somos Mucho Más different from Somos muchos más is that the latter is primarily a national organization. Somos Mucho Más has an international vision as a central part of its platform. That is, while supporting local and national artists, Somos Mucho Más also seeks to help women artists obtain access to international arts markets, as well as international women's artists, as a means of helping Cuban women artists have more options to develop their work as artists, especially since women are often left out of international hip-hop exchanges, which are dominated primarily by men. This was the idea behind the first Artwoman Festival in December 2014.

THE ARTWOMAN FESTIVAL 2014

During the winter of 2013, La Fina and La Cimarrona approached me about an idea. The women's festival in Holguín had been canceled. It was the only women's hip-hop festival in the country. Somos Mucho Más decided that they were going to organize an international arts festival as a way to give Cuban women artists international exposure, but also to try and to tap international networks as a way to obtain resources to support the women's hip-hop arts movement at home. They asked me to return to Cuba in the summer of 2014 to help them organize the festival. While I was away, they worked with feminist students and artists who had passed through Cuba and had been recruited to help with the project. The way that Somos Mucho Más was going about organizing everything reminded me of the old-school hip-hop movement. During that moment in the 1990s, an international network of artists and students supported the movement through their resources, including bringing CDs and sound equipment.

I returned to Cuba in the summer of 2014 to help organize the event. Initially some 12 women showed up to help. By the end of the month only three dedicated women remained plus myself, with sporadic contributions from other artists, feminist, queer activists and other women-centered activists. The artivists developed their call. The following is the English version translated by queer feminist, Cuban activist Logbona Olukonee:

The Cuban hip-hop projects En mi barrio and Somos muchos más will bring together all interested people from around the world to participate in the first festival of women artists, Artwoman. This will be an interdisciplinary event whose primary objective is to publicize and empower different manifestations of art and feminine discourse from a revolutionary, afro-descendant feminist perspective that prioritizes social justice. Artwoman puts forward activism through art, envisioning change through culture, and creating spaces for education and reflection in opposition to the oppressions of misogyny, racism, machismo, and all other forms of violence, advocating for equality between men and women from an intersectional position.

Artwoman has come together to work against invisibility, the domestication of silence and internalized oppression within which many women live. Their artistic expression may have been left out of the handicrafts market or rejected because of its lack of economic value within the Western patriarchal capitalist system. Their art may have been considered inferior to works created by men or by graduates of arts institutions.

Over the course of three days, we will split our time between theory and practice with the end goal of promoting the exchange of ideas and experiences.

This festival has as its goal the development, maintenance, and promotion of women's art and its diverse expressions of femaleness and culture.

This festival is noncompetitive and does not offer monetary awards.

Artists of all gender identities and expressions, both Cuban and non-Cuban residents, are welcome to participate within the following categories: performing arts; music; sculpture; audiovisual; visual art; all genres of literature; experimental art; feminist activism.

The festival will also create a space for intellectual and academic discussion of the following issues:

ART AND FEMINIST ACTIVISM

1. Art and its function political tool during social transformations (empowerment of feminist movements through art)

2. Art as seen from the perspective of women in the Third World (Postcolonial World)

3. What are the markets for art created by women? Strategies for the survival of female artists and their feminist and feminine rate. Feminist technologies? Economic autonomy. Use of digital media and methods of communication for women's art.

4. Art pacha mama nature environment feminine body

5. Art and the female body, women's health and pleasure

6. Art and sexual deviance (queer, lesbian, afro-lesbian, and sexual liberation discourses)

   Organizers will take suggestions for other discussion topics during the panels.

The call highlights the outcome of the hours of debates and meetings among the large collective that initially worked to support the event. In sum, the Artwoman Festival, ideologically, was a Black feminist festival. A festival intended to also help educate communities in Cuba about women's oppression, in which transwomen are included, as well as to create some visibility at the national level where the artivists could introduce new discourses, new language, and new ideological perspectives to the nation and, as a result, indirectly influence state policy through creating an intervention into state discourses. In essence, as Avritzer (2002) argues, and as I wrote earlier in this chapter: By focusing on the problematic aspects of the dominant culture political issues that should be addressed; social movements and voluntary organizations address contentious issues by introducing alternative practices at the public level; transforming informal public opinion into a forum for public deliberation and administrative decision making; seeking intuitional formats that will address the issues made contentious at the public level.

I went with the festival organizers to the Casa de Poesía to present the proposal. The organization showed interest. I left Cuba with the idea that the Casa de Poesía would host the event. I returned in December to find a crisis. The night that Artwoman was supposed to start, artists were arriving from different countries and there was no location for the event. A few months earlier, it became apparent that the Casa de Poesía was going to give the "socialist no," that is, the state was not going to come out and say it was against supporting such an event, but was beginning to show signs of offering excuses, or simply a setup for the event to be canceled at the last minute. The artivists implemented a cost structure into the program. The international artists would have to pay a fee to perform; that way the artivists could rent a private venue to hold the event. International artists dropped out when they saw the price tag. Others arrived and refused to pay. These established artists and leftist artists who idealized Cuba could not understand what was going on. I explained a little bit about how things worked in Cuba. The international artists were visibly frustrated. In the end La Fina was left trying to figure out what to do.

Figure 13.1. La Reyna. Photo by Tanya L. Saunders.

The result was a typical, and necessary, skill in Cuba. La Fina figured out how to make it happen. Collaborating with friends, the festival was able to secure an empty apartment that had just been painted, the apartment of a friend of a friend. There the festival held its art exhibition and visual arts installations. During the day people met there for symposia. The artivists were able to secure a last-minute performance space for the live performances. In the end, it turned out well, with at least 15 to 20 people circulating through the arts spaces and symposia during the day. The festival was small, there were about 15 artists participating in total, not as large as the organizers had hoped, but the most important thing is that it happened, and it happened without state support.

In Cuba, one of the promises of the socialization of culture was state support for grassroots events. If there are aspects of the event that do not conform to state discourse, the state will permit the event to happen but will not support it. So not all forms of state attempts at censorship have the same face: not everyone gets thrown in jail, but it becomes very difficult to organize an event or other activity—all a means of limiting the range and influence of artivists.

Figure 13.2. La Real (*left*) and La Reyna (*right*). Photo by Tanya L. Saunders.

CONCLUDING REMARKS

We see in the Cuban underground hip-hop movement the makings of a contemporary autonomous feminist movement. I would go so far as to say it *is* an autonomous feminist movement, though the terms and the format may not look the same as it does in other political contexts. Women were able to carve out a space for themselves while inserting themselves into Cuba's emergent politicized cultural sphere in order to articulate a women-centered and explicitly feminist politic.

In these concluding remarks, I include a picture of La Reyna. There is an earlier picture that I took of her when she was first emerging as an artist in 2010, which is, frustratingly, ruined. However, I caught La Reyna by accident in the 2010 photo. She was attending a women MC workshop as a part of the International Hip Hop Festival. Las Krudas CUBENSI organized the workshop as a way to mentor up-and-coming women MCs. Las Krudas requested that the space be women only. Magia MC, then president of the Cuban Agency of Rap, which organized the conference, said no. It would go against state policy, which advocated for all Cubans to remain united and not to divide themselves into separate identity groups. This is the same discourse that prevented women and Black Cubans from challenging racial and gender inequality. Since the state claimed it had solved inequality through its material-based programs, anyone who said otherwise was seen as counter-revolutionary.

What happened at the workshop? Men took advantage of an opportunity to improve their skills and dominated the space. Las Krudas spent a significant amount of time trying to manage the men, in order to offer new women MCs a rare opportunity to improve their skills.

I remember when La Reyna had her first shot at a mock battle. She held her body almost as if trying to make herself the least visible possible. She avoided eye contact and spoke softly. "Speak up!" Odaymara of Las Krudas yelled. "Men are going to say all kinds of messed up shit to you in an MC battle to try to humiliate you, so that you will never come back. And for women, they really attack you. They'll tell you your pussy stinks, they'll say anything to make you cry and hate yourself. You have to be ready." La Reyna sat back down in her seat. She never sat completely upright, and even in the picture she was hunched over, shyly looking at Las Krudas. One can imagine my surprise to arrive three years later and see her performing at one of the premier Cuban hip-hop awards, the Puño Arriba Awards. This photo shows a very different person. The way she transformed as an MC was impressive, and largely a result of the women-centered spaces created by collective action among women MCs, specifically via organizations such as Somos Mucho Más.

What does Cuba's politicized cultural sphere as the site for a nascent civil society mean for notions of civil society? What it means is that as politicized actors make ideological interventions that are affecting the development and course of Cuba as a nation, which includes influencing Cuban state policy through the Cuban underground hip-hop movement, we see a contemporary example of the emergence of an autonomous feminist movement, one in which women are fighting for, and securing, public space to be included in the ideological production that will form the basis for the new Cuba. That is, in Cuba, art serves as a propeller of social change, and women are certainly ensuring that they are influential participants.

BIBLIOGRAPHY

Alvarez, Sonia E., Evelina Dagnino, and Arturo Escobar. *Cultures of Politics/Politics of Cultures: Re-visioning Latin American Social Movements*. Boulder: Westview, 1998.

Avritzer, Leonardo. *Democracy and the Public Sphere in Latin America*. Princeton: Princeton University Press, 2002.

Camnitzer, Luis. *New Art of* Cuba. Austin University of Texas Press, 2003.

Chanan, Michael. *Cuban Cinema.* Minneapolis: University of Minnesota Press, 2004.

Craven, David. *Art and Revolution in Latin America, 1910–1990.* New Haven: Yale University Press, 2002.

de la Fuente, Alejandro. *A Nation for All: Race, Inequality, and Politics in Twentieth-Century Cuba.* Chapel Hill: University of North Carolina Press, 2001.

Fernandes, Sujatha. *Cuba Represent! Cuban Arts, State Power, and the Making of New Revolutionary Cultures.* Durham: Duke University Press, 2006.

Kitwana, Bakari. *The Hip Hop Generation: Young Blacks and the Crisis in African American Culture.* New York: Basic Civitas Books, 2003.

Lane, N. "Black Women Queering the Mic: Missy Elliott Disturbing the Boundaries of Racialized Sexuality and Gender." *Journal of Homosexuality* 58, no. 6/7 (2011): 775–92.

Martín Sevillano, Ana Belén. *Sociedad civil y arte en Cuba: cuento y artes plásticas en el cambio de siglo (1980–2000).* Editorial verbum, 2010.

Moore, Robin D. *Music and Revolution, Center for Black Music Research.* Berkeley: University of California Press, 2006.

Navarro, Desiderio. "In Medias Res Publicas: On Intellectuals and Social Criticism in the Cuban Public Sphere." *boundary 2* 29, no. 3 (2002): 16.

Saunders, Tanya L. *Cuban Underground Hip Hop: Black Thoughts, Black Activism, Black Modernity.* Austin: University of Texas Press, 2015.

Zurbano-Torres, Roberto. *Los Estados Nacientes: Literatura Cubana y Postmodernidad.* Havana: Ediciones Universales, 1996.

Zurbano-Torres, Roberto. *Poética de los Noventa: Ganancias de la Expresión.* Havana: Editiones Universales, 1994.

SCOTT MORGENSTERN AND RONALD H. LINDEN

CONCLUSION: COMPARATIVE LESSONS FOR UNDERSTANDING CUBA'S PATH

POLITICS, ECONOMICS, AND SOCIETY

CUBA AND ITS SETTINGS: MOVING TARGETS

The conference on which the book is based was held in Pittsburgh in November 2014 to consider changes to Cuban communism. Our discussions were held at a time when Raúl Castro had already implemented significant economic reforms on the island and thus the breadth and speed of the anticipated new reforms drove our debates. In the wake of the conference, however, the environment for those reforms changed in three important ways. The first of these changes was the joint U.S.–Cuban announcement in December 2014 of the intention to regularize diplomatic relations. The second was the election of Donald Trump as president of the United States on November 8, 2016. The third was the death of Fidel Castro later that same month, on November 25. All of these are very recent and we can only speculate as to the impact on Cuba, its society, and its policies. But we are not completely without guidance as we look into the future. The authors in this book consider these developments in the context of changes already occurring since roughly 2008. They do so by placing Cuba in a comparative perspective, which reminds us that reforms in governance and economic and social policy specifically, and democracy generally, are nonlinear. These and other lessons can be learned and expectations developed based both on what we know about Cuba, its people, its history, and its leaders and from what know about what has happened in other instances in which people and states move on after communism and/or authoritarianism.

In the postrevolution era, Cuba's political and economic systems have evolved, but generally the pace of change has been slow. The Communist Party, in particular, has not changed much since its formation in 1965. Similarly, while the economic reforms approved by Raúl Castro in the past decade have earned much discussion, the state has continued its centralized and extensive control of the economy. In areas of society, the population continues to be under surveillance, media is severely limited, and the hoped-for progress for women and Afro-Cubans that began with the coming to power of the Castro regime in 1959 has not been realized.

Quietly in Cuba, and more loudly outside, expectations have been voiced about the potential for bigger changes after the death of Fidel. While he ceded power in 2006 and formally retired in 2008, and his successor/brother has seemed to be more inclined to pragmatism, critics have pointed to the languid pace of reforms. As evidence, Raúl himself put out a statement at the end of December 2016 stating that the country would never move away from socialism. As a result, reforms have been limited and haphazard, and perhaps even comical, as exemplified by the new private employment law under which, as noted by Mesa-Lago and Pérez-López (2013)[1], citizens can be self-employed as clowns but not doctors or accountants. At the same time, private employment has skyrocketed, there is new international investment, Havana opened a free-trade zone, and Raúl Castro stepped away from power in April 2018.

This type of halting movement reflects the inherent tension that is present in both the leadership and in Cuban society, as a result of two different narratives on the island's history. The positive story emphasizes the gains of the revolution, which took away the privileges of the few to raise up the downtrodden. It gave the populace universal health care and brought literacy. The revolution gave Cubans honor and pride in their success at breaking the bonds held by the United States by withstanding an invasion force, assassination plots, and a decades-long embargo.

But there is also a darker narrative. It begins with the putting to death of hundreds who were on the losing side of the revolution. Castro gained opponents, both domestic and international, when he nationalized businesses to turn his country toward a communist economic model. Further, contrary to his promises, he consolidated power instead of holding elections. His foreign policy—which began with exporting revolution to other countries in the region, invited the Soviets to put missiles on the island, engaged in forays into the Congo and Bolivia, and placed large contingents of Cuban troops in Angola and Ethiopia—solidified the opposition by the U.S. government. And finally, when the long-promised economic successes failed to materialize and instead widespread and serious hardships developed in the 1990s and continued almost unabated, even supporters began to question the regime and the system.

These two narratives have generated deep divides between devoted loyalists and bitter critics. But there may also be a middle ground, for those who favor changes to improve the current difficult situation yet do not want to destroy the tangible and intangible successes of the Castro regime. The 2014 opening of U.S.–Cuban relations exposed this tension both within and outside of Cuba, with exiled opponents, for example, divided over the new opportunities to travel and the possibility of sending funds and communicating more easily with their relatives.

The new external environment provides similar mixed indicators. In June, U.S. President Donald Trump announced that he was "canceling the last administration's completely one-sided deal with Cuba" and reversed some policies of the Obama administration (e.g., looser restrictions on individual travel). The rhetoric was predictably harsh but in concrete terms the Trump administration left the most significant initiatives in place, including the newly opened embassies, commercial ties, cruise travel, and the ending of the "wet foot, dry foot" refugee policy.[2]

The investigative fields addressed by the authors in this volume—economics, politics and policy, leadership, citizens and society—are thus in a state of flux. This is not a new challenge for observers of any contemporary scene but it is especially fortuitous in this case. Our authors, while understandably guarded in their predictions, are nevertheless bold and revealing in their analyses.

THE APPROACH OF THIS VOLUME

The imperative of change in Cuba has been a constant concern since the revolution. Reforms have oscillated and their pace has generally been slow, but it picked up somewhat when Raúl Castro took over from his brother in 2008, as documented in the book by Mesa-Lago and Pérez-López (2013).[3] Our book was intended to follow and expand that analysis by considering continued political, economic, and societal reforms on the island. We wanted to do so, however, by taking advantage of the insights gained by studying the transition or reform processes in other parts of the world. In so doing, we

SCOTT MORGENSTERN AND RONALD H. LINDEN

hoped, we would be able to identify important areas of potential reform, cautions about reform options, and variables that affect policy makers' choices and the success of outcomes. Of course the comparative framework would also have to take into account Cuba's particular and somewhat volatile geopolitical situation in the world, along with its history and culture.

To help address this level of complexity, we asked that the authors reflect on the changes and challenges facing Cuba from an explicitly comparative perspective. We included, therefore, some scholars who are not Cubanologists, but instead focus their research and analysis on countries or regions that have experience with authoritarian, communist, or postcommunist regimes. The experience from other countries is useful for exploring issues that Cuba will face and alternative paths for Cuba's policy. In discussing political, economic, and societal issues, the comparisons help to highlight the many development challenges, as well as the variables (such as the economic system, financial necessities, the international environment, domestic coalitions, and the country's own historical and cultural legacies) that will affect the direction of developments in Cuba. In the last case, several authors maintain a close focus on how cultural activism in the service of social goals, e.g., against racism, is developing in the new Cuban environment.

Cuba's unique history, culture, and geography will undoubtedly impact the pace and direction of change. By exploiting the comparative framework, the chapters included in this volume provide a wide range of lessons for Cuba. The comparative method puts unique factors into perspective, and explores variables that might affect all actors—in this case people and countries—in similar ways. In this book, the method is also meant to highlight the differences and similarities among countries and across sectors (e.g., economics, society, the arts), thus explaining variation in development paths.

The book's authors are cautious in their predictions. The chapters on economics emphasize the need for change, but also note that, when faced with similar dynamics, most other countries have failed to implement extensive reforms, at least initially. In the Cuban case, while the country has economic potential, at least some of the market-oriented reforms would run counter to its revolutionary history and culture. Thus political pressures could slow economic change. The chapters on politics suggest that democracy is not inevitable, and that successful reforms in this direction may not yield the expected results. Finally, as illustrated by the discussions of racism and feminism, the Cuban system is being challenged by cultural "artivism." As in other sectors, reforms pushed or resisted from above and below will produce a new interaction between state and society.

Given that Cuba has successful models of economic and political change that it could follow, perhaps we should be surprised that the country would resist the reforms that have brought wealth to China, democratic freedoms to Latin America, and some combination of those virtues to many countries. Regime opponents suggest that the country's leaders will resist change simply in order to maintain their power. But several of the authors here add something else: that Cuba's leaders cling to the legacy and goals of the country's revolution. They argue that while initial hopes may have been utopian, the revolution and subsequent resistance to U.S. attempts to overthrow the regime generated a nationalist sentiment of independence and an antipathy toward capitalism. These have not dissipated—indeed they have been reinforced by 50 years of American hostility backed by sanctions that opponents of the Castro regime call an embargo and supporters call a blockade. It is possible that this has also helped create a distrust of other values associated with the United States, including democracy. At the same time, many support greater economic and political freedom, as verified by the large numbers who have emigrated or hope to do so, regardless of the great personal risk. Further, the degree of hardship brought about by the long economic malaise has clearly eroded support for the regime's policies.

As in other countries, that type of disquiet is often associated with greater interest in regime change. There are thus unanswered questions for both the leadership and the citizenry. For the leadership, has the death of Fidel and the imminent retirement of Raúl (who has announced that he will leave his government post in 2018 and his party post in 2021) changed views about the importance of maintaining their own power and the revolutionary legacy? For the citizenry, are they ready and willing to support a full-scale reform, with the consequent inequalities that might arise and the risk of returning to the shadow of the United States? Are they prepared for the sometimes brutal competition in business and in life and the often higher (unregulated) costs that a profit-oriented, nonstate economy brings with it? Is the social and political calculus changing as the Castro brothers pass from the scene? In other words, how much of the system was based on these revolutionary leaders themselves, and therefore will pass with them, rather than on an entrenched governing ideology that will transfer to the new generation? In the new domestic milieu, will the impetus for reform—and obstacles to it—come from the top, below, or outside? Or will it be absent altogether?

As a guide to the possible directions that Cuba's path might take, the authors in this volume have explored what has already happened in Cuba and what other states have gone through, or are still experiencing, as they have transitioned, to a greater or lesser degree, from authoritarianism and/or communism. We now review their findings.

SCOTT MORGENSTERN AND RONALD H. LINDEN

Economic Updating

To borrow from management terminology, a first set of chapters provides a "SWOT"—strengths, weaknesses, opportunities, and threats—analysis of the Cuban economy. Overall the analysts seem optimistic that inherent strengths in the system create many opportunities, but they also suggest that advances will require overcoming significant obstacles. A threat to the requisite changes, only implicit in some chapters, is that the suggested reforms would move the country far from its anticapitalist moorings, which some believe could threaten historical gains in terms of health care, education, and social equality. The first chapter in the part addresses this issue directly.

Working from analyses by Alzugaray and Morrison, Morgenstern and Pérez-López explore the compatibility of different economic development models with Cuban history and culture. In their view, a standard economic analysis is insufficient, because the model must also take account of the people's attachments to their cultural and historical legacy. During our conference Alzuguray was emphatic in arguing that going forward, Cuban policy makers will not impose a model that destroys the legacy of the "historic generation." That generation's passing—as symbolized by the death of Fidel himself and the promise by Raúl Castro to leave his government and party posts—may not mean the erosion of that legacy, because the younger generations are also imbued with a "tradition of demonization and elimination of the market." The chapter concludes that this will continue to hold back reform, limiting it to experiments while allowing exceptions. The free trade zone in Mariel, perhaps, is a first example of such experimentation. These may be short-term attempts to balance the need for opening to world markets while still maintaining the anticapitalist heritage. But at some point the scale is likely to tip, particularly if the experiments are deemed to be successful. How the rest of the country reacts to these "pockets of reform" may be the key to the longer-term policy directions of the economy.

In his discussion of South Korea and Taiwan, McGuire emphasizes a variety of factors affecting economic growth. Among the "initial conditions" that influence economic growth, McGuire includes colonial legacies, education, ethnic homogeneity, income inequality, the international context, and the size of the internal economy. Comparing Cuba today with South Korea and Taiwan a half century ago, McGuire concludes that many "initial conditions" that affect long-term economic growth are generally favorable for Cuba; among them, low initial GDP per capita, low wages, a healthy and well-educated population, a small domestic market, and weakly organized independent labor and business interests. (The Cuban Workers' Central and the business conglomerates are controlled by military leaders and others close to the Castros.) Tourism is not central to McGuire's analysis, but it too is rapidly growing. At the same time, he emphasizes that developing economic potential is not automatic. Cuba in some respects has low state capacity, which, without improvement, will continue to hinder its ability to develop and manage its natural resources, mitigate growth-inhibiting demographic trends, reduce income and race inequalities, and maintain and expand achievements in health and education. Despite these challenges, McGuire argues that Cuba "is in some ways well positioned to make rapid and shared economic progress over the next 50 years, as South Korea and Taiwan have done over the previous 50, provided that economic reforms broaden and deepen and that the United States lifts its trade embargo." But that conclusion is contingent, he argues, on the policy choices and state-building capacities of Cuban policy makers.

The third chapter in this part, by Pérez-López and Xiao, focuses on foreign direct investment and growth strategies, using China's success as a comparative frame. In their chapter, Pérez-López and Xiao identify options for and obstacles to Cuba attracting investment and promoting economic growth, drawing lessons for Cuba from China's policies to attract foreign investment. The authors suggest that Cuba has much potential, but realizing this potential will require significant and full-scale reform. The authors develop their argument by first describing specific policies that helped China build its economy, such as a joint venture law and another law that promoted foreign investment within "special economic zones." China also looked for other opportunities, such as encouraging investment by its diaspora.

Another lesson from their analysis of China is that half-measures (initially, the joint venture law restricted repatriation of profits, for example) are insufficient. This, it should be noted, echoes a presentation by Edward Malesky from the conference that focused on Vietnam.[4] The Cubans have the potential to attract investors—as they note, the diaspora is wealthy, and other factors such as personal safety and the educated workforce are a plus—but the country has not yet made the commitment to full reform or learned the lessons about the perils of half-measures. That said, the Cubans have made some important changes, most impressively by creating a "special development zone" in the port of Mariel (ZED Mariel). The statute that created the Mariel zone grants many concessions and provides incentives for investment, but the state still takes two-thirds of the workers' salaries. Also limiting investment are factors such as the "heavy-handed and lengthy approval process" for bureaucratic decisions, an overall poor investment climate (which

SCOTT MORGENSTERN AND RONALD H. LINDEN

is a function of rule of law, macroeconomic stability, transparency, and other factors), the inability of foreign companies to hire workers directly, and a general limited commitment to reforms.

The dynamics of economic growth may become moot if Cuba is unable to resolve its economic conflicts with the United States, which is a precondition for Cuba entering fully into the international economy. This will require finding common ground on the issue of compensation for property seized by the Cuban government in the early years of the revolution. This is the subject of the chapter by Travieso-Díaz. In that chapter the author uses the examples from Central and Eastern Europe and elsewhere to lay out several potential dispute settlement mechanisms to address property claims by U.S. citizens. Examples from the other countries provide a warning in that delayed settlement plans generate uncertainty that discourages investment. Experiences from other countries also highlight difficulties in the process of resolution. For example, significant Iranian assets were frozen in the United States after the 1979 Iranian revolution and the seizure of the U.S. embassy, which were then made available to satisfy arbitration awards in favor of private claimants. No such funds exist in the case of Cuba. Thus, while the comparison highlights different routes for dispute settlement, it also reminds us to take note of special circumstances that point to difficulties for resolving the claims against the Cuban government. Travieso-Díaz concludes that a likely scenario for Cuba might be very limited settlement, in which the main corporate claimants will forego compensation in favor of future opportunities.

Travieso-Díaz's work focuses primarily on the economic aspects of dispute settlement over U.S. property claims. As other chapters have highlighted, however, there is also a political dimension to this and to other reform issues. Cuba could attract new investment if it resolved the half-century-old claims disputes, but in doing so it would have to repudiate the property seizures and ideological underpinnings of the revolution. In that respect, Cuba contends that the embargo is illegal, and thus it is the United States that owes reparations. The cases of Central and Eastern Europe that Travieso-Díaz considers also involved ideological conflict, but the resolution of claims for those countries suggests that it is possible to break the impasse. Cuba's welcoming of international investment, as documented in other chapters of the volume, also provides evidence that the country is willing to soften its stances for economic necessity.

In sum, the chapters in the first part of the book emphasize that economic reforms will be conditioned by the unique Cuban context. As such, the country has great economic potential (strengths are opportunities), but realizing that potential will encounter significant obstacles (weaknesses and threats). To an important degree, the comparative analysis focuses on the opportunities. By reforming their economies China, South Korea, Taiwan, and Vietnam have taken off economically and to do this, certain key policy changes are crucial; for example, broader recognition of private property, elimination of the dual currency system, expansion of self-employment to include professionals, enterprise reform, elimination of forced agricultural procurement policies, liberalization of controls on employment in foreign-invested enterprises, to name a few. Further, Cuba has some fundamental strengths including a strong and wealthy diaspora, a geography that will aid tourism, and an educated population. Cuba is thus well situated in terms of attracting investors and tourists, and perhaps developing advanced industries such as pharmaceuticals. But it will be human decisions that will exploit—or neglect—these advantages.

These economic opportunities, of course, must be matched by political entrepreneurship. The transition in power (Fidel's death plus Raúl's retirement from his government, though not yet party posts) creates an opportunity, and while voices are carefully muted in Cuba, the long economic malaise has certainly created an internal hunger for reform, one matched in the Cuban diaspora and the U.S. government.

The weaknesses and threats are also evident in these analyses. Cuba has a poor infrastructure and the longstanding centralized governing structure prevents innovation. The economic decision-making system itself is a significant weakness, but some change (e.g., enactment of a new foreign investment law) has occurred. The comparisons in this book demonstrate that half measures are insufficient and without resolution of property rights, investment will be limited. The fast-growing tourist industry, however, suggests that investors are working around these concerns. The most important threat evident from these chapters, then, is that Cuba may not take the full-bodied reforms needed, as these would represent a repudiation of its characteristic anti-imperialist and anticapitalist ideology.

This discussion also suggests risks from different angles. First, trying to preserve Cuba's heritage might jeopardize the success of reform measures. Second, failure to move forward risks the hope for building a free society and a stronger economy. A third uncertainty, which perhaps fits between the others but may also be orthogonal, was articulated by John Beverley (in colorful language) during an intervention at the original conference. He argued that the challenge for Cuba is to avoid getting stuck as a lower-middle income country, replete with the problems of income disparities, racial inequalities, and domination by international firms. The experience of Latin America suggests that he could have added concerns regarding poor representative institutions and generally low-quality democracy.

The second part of the book focuses on politics, and includes discussions about the role of the state and its relation to the citizenry. In particular, the various chapters focus on the response of the state to citizen concerns, on political parties, democracy, corruption, and social protection systems. Implicit and explicit in the chapters is the question of whether Cuba will move toward democracy. There seems to be less optimism about reforms of politics than of economics, in part because authoritarianism was present even before the 1959 revolution and the current system has been successful in limiting (internal) dissent.

The first chapter in this part, by Dimitrov, uses official responses to citizen complaints (as published in the state newspaper *Granma*) to discuss the broad issue of socialist social contracts and accountability. Using explicit comparisons with the Soviet Union and China, Dimitrov shows that the state uses citizens' letters and government responses to create the impression that those who violate the terms of the social contract will be held accountable. This "serves the ultimate goal of signaling to citizens that the social contract is enforceable and thus secures their quiescence in exchange for the provision of goods, services, and the protection of property rights."

A key part of the political system, of course, is the Cuban Communist Party (PCC). As Backer discusses in his chapter, the party has so far resisted reforms. Comparing the shape of the Cuban Communist party to that in the Soviet Union and those under Soviet influence, as well as the parties in China and other parts of Asia, Backer explores the concept of socialist modernization, but argues that the Cubans reforms have not advanced in ways seen in other countries. He states that the Cuban Communist Party is an "outlier among Marxist-Leninist states, reflecting a rigid and antiquarian form." This lack of reform, which he notes is similar to what has happened in Vietnam, is the result of centralized control plus "ossification of leadership and the indifference of younger people to the benefits of joining the PCC." Backer points to potential changes, and suggests that the passing of Fidel will remove one serious obstacle to reform. He notes, however, that the Vietnamese have found ways to accommodate market reform while maintaining a centralized political structure.

Next, Pérez-Liñán and Mainwaring directly consider the prospects for democracy in Cuba. Their broad comparison examines the success of countries in transitioning from authoritarian rule based on their democratic histories. In short, they argue, countries that had spent more time as democracies prior to an authoritarian interlude had more success in (re)constructing democratic governments. Cuba does not do well by this measure. Cuba was under authoritarian rule for a comparatively long period before Castro, and the only proto-democratic period lasted a short time (1944–1952).

The next two chapters in this part focus on social welfare policies. Mesa-Lago's contribution provides extensive detail about the Cuban system in comparison with those of other Latin American countries, plus China and Vietnam. The comparisons are based on three broad social welfare programs: 1) social-insurance contributory pensions; 2) public health care; and 3) social assistance for vulnerable groups. After explaining the evolution of Cuban policies bearing on each of these programs, he uses official statistics to show successes and failures of each policy. As an example, he argues for the need for higher contributions, higher retirement ages, or cuts in the meager pensions in Cuba due to a growing elderly population and increasingly poor health indicators, comparing the Cuban situation with Uruguay's. He also argues that while the Cuban social security system started earlier and has been much more advanced than those of China and Vietnam, which subordinated the pursuit of social security programs to growth and fiscal capacity, the systems in those countries are now expanding while that of Cuba has been eroded due to economic pressures. He explains that "Cuba is ahead of other countries in unity-uniformity and coverage (except for social assistance and eroding in health care), social solidarity and gender equity, but behind the rest on benefit sufficiency, administration, and financial sustainability." Looking ahead, Mesa-Lago uses the comparisons to highlight areas of concern and suggestions for moving forward. He explains, for example, that Cuba needs to incorporate the uninsured into the system and consider ways to integrate the general and armed forces pension systems. A new system will also have to consider whether it will move toward a pay-as-you-go system or a mixed model. In health care, he argues that there is need to prioritize programs for water and sanitation, increase medicinal imports, and improve care for the elderly. Some of these programs could be paid for by reallocation of assets (infant mortality rates are already very good) and by charging the wealthy and foreigners for services. He expects that better relations with the United States could reduce the defense budget, and he proposes that tax reform could be structured such that parts of the revenue could be assigned to support social security.

Vázquez-D'Elía puts the Cuban system into a broad comparative frame, comparing the features of the health and pension systems with those in other parts of Latin America. He first describes the tremendous variation in the region, while also explaining some common trends, in terms of coverage, the degree of commodification, plans for special groups (segmentation), and

SCOTT MORGENSTERN AND RONALD H. LINDEN

other variables. He argues, in part, that reforms in these sectors have frequently reflected redistribution of political power. Other reforms are inevitable, based on socioeconomic changes. Cuba starts in a relatively good position in terms of coverage, and he notes that systems in most Latin American countries have been difficult to reform. Thus while Cuba is well positioned to maintain its benefit system even if the country does democratize, the transition has the potential to bring to power new actors, some of whom could favor dramatic changes. One possible outcome he notes is that the increasing presence of foreign or private companies could create separate plans for their privileged workers, thus leading to a more segmented system. He stresses, however, that improving or even maintaining the current system will require sustained economic growth.

In the final chapter in this part, Linden points to possible routes for a potential political transition in Cuba by using examples from Eastern Europe. He examines lessons about changes in postcommunist political structures and dynamics from the experiences of the Central and East European states. Like Cuba, these countries had a historical link to centralized communist rule, and thus provide a useful laboratory to study reform processes. Interestingly, these countries have not followed a consistent path, and he focuses on internal and external explanations for a country's progress toward democracy. Internally, factors such as economics and past conflict affect such progress. Externally the enticement of improved relations or membership in the European Union (EU) has been important to these countries.

What do these Eastern European cases say about Cuba? First, there is a strong contrast between the Europeans' external setting, which included the positive pull of the EU plus the negative push from Russia, versus the U.S.–Cuba dynamics. While reforms could yield benefits from the United States, they might appear as capitulation. Second, there is the question of how new domestic institutions might reflect Cuba's history and culture. As Linden asks, will new parties, for example, divide on ideological lines, or will they reflect social cleavages?

Another key finding from East Central Europe is that the process of change itself can have an effect on democratization. If a change in regime occurs more through negotiation than upheaval, for example, then the key concern is whether the opposition is able to develop enough support to have leverage in negotiations and whether that opposition is dedicated to building a strong democracy and civil society. Some new leadership could come from the exile groups, as happened in Eastern Europe. But the experiences of these countries show that few exiles are successful in winning acceptance in their country of origin. For Cuba, many of those who will seek leadership positions will face the added problem of trying to reform and democratize the country while at the same time preserving the legacy of Cuba's "fierce independence" and avoiding a perception that the country has capitulated to the United States.

Linden's final points serve as a useful conclusion to this part. He warns that the efforts and challenges of reform can produce a certain "democracy fatigue," especially when—but not only when—new political and economic systems have proven unable to resolve multiple social and economic problems. The experience of Eastern Europe reminds us that history is not linear, and reforms often do not meet expectations. Support for democracy at the elite or citizenry level cannot be taken for granted. In this region and elsewhere, the unequal advances toward—and some backsliding from-- democracy demonstrate that reversals can and might happen.

Citizens and Society

In the final part of the book, three authors focus on societal "updating" at the human level. These chapters are not comparative across countries but over time in Cuba. They analyze the complex intersection of race, identity, and culture at a time when Cuba struggles to update or reform its system, while preserving elements that favor those who control the distribution of goods—both cultural and tangible.

West-Durán uses the *New York Times* handling and editing of a column by a Cuban scholar to discuss race and nationality. He also examines how the economic reforms affect race and equality. He argues that the racial debate in Cuba is not straightforward, as there are controversies over definitions of blackness and different issues related to racial discrimination. A further difficulty for advancing these issues in Cuba is that "the multicultural paradigms of the United States or Europe are regarded rather suspiciously." The author argues that the economic reforms have put Cuban society under pressure to confront not only issues of race, but also other social issues such as religion and sexual diversity.

In her chapter, Belén Martín Sevillano uses a popular soap opera, *Bajo el Mismo Sol* (Underneath the Same Sun), to discuss the relation of the state and domestic violence. This analysis is useful for bringing to light the multifaceted challenge of changing gender roles within a governing system that long touted its commitment to gender equality. In terms of how reform is encouraged, the discussion is helpful for our understanding of how the state is trying to mold emerging societal debates through its use of television. It is particularly interesting for considering how the state itself probes reform, given that the production includes criticism of the police—a state entity.

SCOTT MORGENSTERN AND RONALD H. LINDEN

The final chapter in this part, by Saunders, uses a discussion of the underground hip-hop movement and in particular Black women artists working in this genre. This kind of mobilization of artists in pursuit of political change she and others label "artivism." Though the chapter is tightly focused on Cuba, the implications of the kind of cultural—and ultimately human—confrontations all of these authors address are wide ranging beyond contemporary socialist Cuba.

CLOCKS? CLOUDS? PLASTIC?

In their classic application of Karl Popper's scientific ontology to the study of politics, Gabriel Almond and Stephen Genco argue that political reality approximates neither the precision predictability of a clock nor the disorderly uncertainty of a cloud but a system of "plastic controls."[5] They suggest that we see political reality as made up of "ideas—human decisions, goals, purposes—in constant and intense interaction with other ideas, human behavior, and the physical world" (492). This does not mean that understanding political developments is impossible, even in a time of great change. It is, however, complicated. Metaphors such as this can perhaps serve to remind us of both the complex of factors affecting Cuba's future and our own modest ability to assess, much less predict, that future.

With so many variables and so much variance in mind, we can and should try to enhance our understanding of the Cuban present and future by drawing on the experience of other societies that have undergone similar if not identical experiences. This might help us winnow the possible questions that might apply to the analysis of the experience of people and systems as they pass from authoritarian government. We need to do so, of course, without falling victim to the teleological fallacy of assuming that this passage will lead inevitably to democracy. In point of fact, we do not know that democracy is necessarily an automatic end to an updating process.

Still, the authors of this volume offer some clues about which variables and dynamics will likely matter most during this turbulent time in Cuba's history. We expect, for example, that a country's legacy will matter in at least two senses: First, there is the "legacy of structures." What were they and what do they bequeath to the "new" system? Who were the elites and where did they come from? What was the power distribution in politics and was it static or dynamic? Crucially, we should ask about the nature of regime–society interaction. Did it legitimize or stigmatize autonomous political action? Was such action confined to the realm of marginal "low politics" or did people and organizations (e.g., trade unions) have a chance for any real impact on the "authoritative allocation of values"? Offering an accurate description of the system that is being modified or replaced should force us to address the question of what remnants of that system—political, structural, or psychological—might continue.

All things considered, making such an assessment is a relatively simple empirical task. Addressing the second aspect, "the legacy of attitudes," is trickier. This dimension embraces attitudes both of the governors and the governed. If the chapters of this volume are accurate, we need to ask if there is a broad national narrative, one that legitimizes and reinforces governing dynamics in certain directions and weakens the impetus for movement in another. In the Cuban case, the heroic, "David vs. Goliath" narrative or the commitment to socialist values that remains for many (as it did in Eastern Europe) are part of that legacy and thus stand as factors likely to affect policies and the reactions to those policies. To assume a "clean slate" in Cuba (as elsewhere) would be to build our explanations and predictions on a weak foundation.

But we also know that, significant as they are, the past six decades of communist rule in Cuba are not the only part of a legacy. There are at least two others to consider: 1) aspects that come from Cuba's precommunist period, including religious, cultural, and social/racial attitudes, and 2) attitudes that come from Cubans who did *not* spend the past 60 years in Cuba but who retain close ties and possibly significant influence over the island's future. If we assume that post-Castro future leaders in Cuba will spring fully formed, unaffected by history and be impervious to outside influence, our analyses and our expectations will certainly miss the mark.

Lifting our focus from a national society or national-level politics, we must, if we are to be respectful of the reality of Cuba, keep in mind its external environment, which has always had an oversized impact on the island. During (and because of) the Cold War, the Soviet Union's support played a central role in Cuba's politics and economics, and after that benefactor's fall, Venezuela propped up the regime and its economy. Going forward, others—perhaps China, Canada, or Brazil—will have an impact. In all scenarios, however, it would be impossible to analyze tiny Cuba's past or future without factoring in its relationship with the United States, its neighboring giant whose attitude toward Cuba has, for the past 54 years (if not since 1898) lived mostly in the narrow range from agitated to hostile.

Cuba's external and internal environments cannot be considered exactly analogous to those of other countries, but comparisons can still provide valuable, if uncertain, suggestions about future directions. For example, every country has faced both internal and the external pressures, with suggested solutions coming from across the political spectrum. Will the Cuban leaders—whoever they may be at a given time—respond by embracing capitalism as in parts of Eastern Europe, or by showing a more timid acceptance as in Vietnam or parts of Latin America? On the political end, can they respond to economic pressures for openness without a corresponding response to political pressures, à la China?

Answering such questions inevitably leads to consideration of Cuba's behemoth neighbor, and the degree to which Cuba can maintain autonomy in terms of setting its own political and economic courses. Cuba under Fidel took special pride in that autonomy, but it still needed allies (the Soviet Union, Venezuela) willing to provide significant subsidies. Submitting to U.S. wishes or a neoliberal model, then, would imply a disavowal of their revolutionary heritage. Though there are other partial examples (China, Vietnam, and Russia) there are no comparisons that reflect the special Cuban–U.S. history. And now, the model has become even more complex. Given the change of administrations in the United States and imminent change in Cuba, will the United States be willing to increase trade ties without requiring political reforms? Further, given the Trump administration's negative attitude toward foreign aid and most trade deals, what kind of pressure will it be able to assert toward Cuba? There are, of course, parallel questions from the Cuban side. How will the incoming leader, presumably Miguel Díaz-Canel, balance domestic and U.S. pressures for change against other demands to preserve cultural and historical legacies?

In the end, as several authors remind us, these multiple and often opposing pressures open several different paths for Cuba. Each difficult choice, moreover, will generate reactions, both within Cuba and from the international community. There is an endogeneity to the analysis, because the manner in which the pressures, especially domestic, can be transmitted to authorities is dependent on political opening. Further, the identity of the future Cuban authorities, and perhaps their attitudes toward the revolutionary heritage, economic models, social welfare, and international relations will depend on that opening. In sum, then, identifying economic weaknesses or pressures is insufficient for generating solid predictive models. While institutions and international structures can help define or limited choices, the reforms in Cuba will also be a function of emotions, values, attitudes, and political skills of Cuba's new leaders.

And, in case we thought this would be easy, we need to remind ourselves that the world we are trying to understand—even this small piece of it—is also changing rapidly. Reality does not hold still for our camera. All these factors, the legacy, the systems, the global power structure, and the human element are dynamic, not static. This last is perhaps most evident now, as a new U.S. government with a quite different orientation from that of its predecessor is in power and for the first time a non-Castro will be in Cuba's presidential office. For those of us determined to try to fashion a "clock" out of a "cloud," this kind of change makes the task all the more challenging, even as it renders the need for it all the more compelling.

NOTES

1. Carmelo Mesa-Lago and Jorge Pérez-López, *Cuba Under Raúl Castro: Assessing the Reforms* (Boulder: Lynne Rienner Publishers, 2013).

2. Under this policy, people (including Cubans) intercepted at sea ("wet foot") were turned back but Cubans (and not others) who reached the United States ("dry foot") were allowed to stay. See Andorra Bruno, *U.S. Policy on Cuban Migrants: In Brief* (Washington, DC: Congressional Research Service, 2016). The Trump administration also announced prohibitions against doing business with entities controlled by Cuba's military or intelligence services. See Martina Kunović, "Five Things You Need to Know about Trump's Cuba Policy—and Who It Will Hurt," *Washington Post*, June 22, 2017.

3. Mesa-Lago and Pérez-López, *Cuba Under Raúl Castro*.

4. In our conference, Malesky used the case of Vietnam to argue about the irrationality of partial reforms. Vietnam's 2000 Enterprise Law, for example, was so successful that the number of new private businesses tripled. But without adequate measures to enforce property rights and fairly adjudicate contract disputes, or reform of state-owned enterprises, the Vietnamese model, he argues, could deliver important short-term benefits but not sustained, long-term economic growth.

5. Gabriel A. Almond and Stephen J. Genco, "Clouds, Clocks, and the Study of Politics," *World Politics* 29, no. 4 (July 1977): 489–522.

CONTRIBUTORS

CARLOS ALZUGARAY TRETO is a Cuban educator and diplomat; he has been a Cuban foreign service officer with high-level posts in several countries. He has taught on Cuban foreign policy at the Instituto Superior de Relaciones Internacionales, the University of Havana, and the National Defense College in Havana, and was a Jean Monnet Fellow at the European University Institute in Florence, Italy. He has published extensively and is a frequent commentator on current political issues.

ANA BELÉN MARTÍN SEVILLANO is an assistant professor in the cultural studies program at Queen's University (Ontario, Canada); she obtained a PhD in Hispanic philology from Universidad Complutense de Madrid. Her research interests are: Caribbean cultural studies, African heritage, racialization and ethnicity in the Hispanic Caribbean, gender studies, migration and diaspora studies, and Caribbean and Latin American art and literature.

LARRY CATÁ BACKER is the W. Richard and Mary Eshelman Faculty Scholar, professor of law and international affairs at Pennsylvania State University (BA Brandeis University; MPP Harvard University Kennedy School of Government; JD Columbia University). He teaches and researches in the areas of economic globalization, international affairs, global governance, and party-state systems, including China and Cuba, as well as corporate law, corporate social responsibility, multinational corporations, international institutions, law and religion, and constitutional law. He has worked with the UN Secretary General special representative on the development of the UN Guiding Principles for Business and Human Rights. He has lectured in South America, Europe, and Asia, and organized graduate programs in Cuba. His work on Cuba includes Cuban corporations and cooperatives, Cuban regional trade policies, governance structures of the Cuban Communist Party, and the indigenization of Cuban ethnicity. He has written extensively on the theory and practice of the party-state system in

China, including on issues of Chinese constitutionalism and the role of the Chinese Communist Party. His short essays on many of these topics may be found on his blog "Law at the End of the Day."

JEROME BRANCHE is professor and chair of Latin American literature and cultural studies in the Department of Hispanic Languages and Literatures, University of Pittsburgh. His teaching and research focus on racialized modernity and the way creative writers across the Atlantic imagine and write about slavery, freedom, the nation, being, and gender. Among other positions, he has served on the executive board of the Association for the Study of the Worldwide African Diaspora (ASWAD), and as chair of the Ethnicity, Race, and Indigenous Peoples section of the Latin American Studies Association (LASA). Among his books are *Colonialism and Race in Luso-Hispanic Literature* (University of Missouri Press, 2006), and *The Poetics and Politics of Diaspora: Transatlantic Musings* (Routledge, 2014). He is editor of *Post/Colonialism and the Pursuit of Freedom in the Black Atlantic* (Routledge, 2018), and *Black Writing, Culture, and the State in Latin America* (Vanderbilt University Press, 2015), and other collections. His current book projects study the necropolitics of slavery, and race in the imaginary of empire and its aftermath.

MARTIN K. DIMITROV is associate professor of political science at Tulane University. His books include *Piracy and the State: The Politics of Intellectual Property Rights in China* (Cambridge University Press, 2009); *Why Communism Did Not Collapse: Understanding Authoritarian Regime Resilience in Asia and Europe* (Cambridge University Press, 2013); and *The Politics of Socialist Consumption* (Ciela Publishers, 2017. He has been a visiting fellow at the Aleksanteri Institute and has held residential fellowships at Harvard, Princeton, Notre Dame, the American Academy in Berlin, and the Woodrow Wilson International Center for Scholars. He is currently completing the book *Dictatorship and Information: Autocratic Regime Resilience in Communist Europe and China* and the edited volume *China-Cuba: Trajectories of Post-Revolutionary Governance*. He has conducted fieldwork in China, Taiwan, France, the Czech Republic, Germany, Russia, Bulgaria, and Cuba.

RONALD H. LINDEN (PhD Princeton) is professor of political science at the University of Pittsburgh, where he has been director of the European Studies Center, a National Resource Center and Jean Monnet European Union Centre of Excellence, and has also directed the Center for Russian and East European Studies. From 1989 to 1991 he served as director of research for Radio Free Europe in Munich, Germany with responsibility for observing and analyzing the extraordinary changes in Eastern Europe. He has been a Fulbright-Schuman Scholar, held a DAAD Research Fellowship at the American Institute for Contemporary Germany Studies in Washington, DC, has been a Transatlantic Academy Fellow at the German Marshall Fund, and received research grants from the National Council for Eurasian and East European Research and from the International Research and Exchanges Board. He has been a Fulbright Research Scholar, a research scholar and visiting scholar at the Woodrow Wilson International Center for Scholars and a senior fellow at the United States Institute of Peace. His current research explores the impact on U.S.-European relations of growing Chinese trade and investment in Europe. Among the publications and volumes that he has contributed to and edited are: *Turkey and Its Neighbors: Foreign Relations in Transition* (2012), *The Berlin Wall: 20 Years Later* (2009), and Special Issues of *Problems of Post-Communism*, on "The Meaning of 1989 and After" (2009) and on "The New Populism in Central and Southeast Europe" (2008).

SCOTT MAINWARING is the Jorge Paulo Lemann Professor for Brazil Studies at Harvard University. His latest book is *Party Systems in Latin America: Institutionalization, Decay, and Collapse* (Cambridge University Press, 2018). His book with coauthor Aníbal Pérez-Liñán, *Democracies and Dictatorships in Latin America: Emergence, Survival, and Fall* (Cambridge University Press, 2013) won the best book prize of the comparative politics section of the American Political Science Association and of the political institutions section of the Latin American Studies Association. He was elected to the American Academy of Arts and Sciences in 2010.

JAMES W. MCGUIRE, professor and chair in the Department of Government at Wesleyan University, received a BA from Swarthmore and a PhD from the University of California, Berkeley. He specializes in the comparative politics of developing countries, focusing on democracy, social welfare policies, and public health. He is the author of *Peronism without Perón: Unions, Parties, and Democracy in Argentina* (Stanford University Press, 1997) and of *Wealth, Health, and Democracy in East Asia and Latin America* (Cambridge University Press, 2010), which won the 2011 Stein Rokkan Prize for Comparative Social Science Research. His recent research has involved Latin American social policies, regime type and infant mortality, the conceptualization of democracy, growth, and inequality in Latin America and East Asia, conditional cash transfers in Ecuador, and the impact of women legislators on health outcomes. He is a winner of Wesleyan's Binswanger Prize for Excellence in Teaching.

CARMELO MESA-LAGO is Distinguished Service Professor Emeritus of Economics and Latin American Studies at the University of Pittsburgh; he has been a visiting professor/researcher in eight countries and lecturer in 39, founder/editor for 18 years of *Cuban Studies,* and author of 95 books/pamphlets and 318 articles/chapters published in seven languages in 34 countries, about half on Cuba's economy and social welfare. Most recent books: *Cuba Under Raul Castro: Assessing the Reforms* (with J. Pérez-López; Lynne Reinner, 2013), and main author of *Voices of Change in Cuba* (University of Pittsburgh Press, 2018). He has worked throughout Latin America as an ECLAC regional advisor, consultant with most international financial organizations, several U.N. branches and foreign foundations. He was president of LASA, is a member of the National Academy of Social Insurance, and has received the ILO International Prize on Decent Work (shared with Nelson Mandela), and the Alexander von Humboldt-Stiftung Senior Prize for his life work on the Cuban economy; he was selected among the 50 most influential Iberoamerican intellectuals of 2014.

SCOTT MORGENSTERN is professor of political science at the University of Pittsburgh and also serves as director of its Center for Latin American Studies. His research focuses on political parties, electoral systems, and legislatures, with a regional specialization in Latin America. His teaching focuses on these themes, plus U.S.–Latin American relations and democratic governance and strengthening. Among his publications are: *Are Politics Local? The Two Dimensions of Party Nationalization around the World* (Cambridge University Press, 2017), *Patterns of Legislative Politics: Roll Call Voting in the United States and Latin America's Southern Cone* (Cambridge University Press, 2004), *Legislative Politics in Latin America* (coeditor and contributor; Cambridge University Press, 2002), and *Pathways to Power* (coeditor and contributor, Pennsylvania State University Press, 2008). His articles have appeared in the *Journal of Politics, Comparative Political Studies; Comparative Politics, Party Politics, Electoral Studies, Review of International Political Economy,* and other journals. He was also the primary investigator on a grant from the USAID to produce documents related to their political party development programs.

KEVIN MORRISON: is an associate professor and past president of the faculty in the Graduate School of Public and International Affairs (GSPIA) at the University of Pittsburgh. He previously held positions at Cornell University and Princeton University. His teaching and research focuses on game theory and the political economy of developing countries. A specific focus of his research has been nontax revenues in developing countries, such as oil revenues, foreign aid, and intergovernmental grants. He has been a principal investigator of the Global Leadership Project. His work has been published in *Business & Politics, Comparative Political Studies, Comparative Politics, Development Policy Review, Electoral Studies, International Organization, Public Choice,* and the *World Bank Research Observer,* as well as edited volumes.

ANÍBAL PÉREZ-LIÑÁN is professor of political science at the University of Pittsburgh and a member of the Center for Latin American Studies at the University of Pittsburgh. He is editor of the *Latin American Research Review* and author of *Presidential Impeachment and the New Political Instability in Latin America* (Cambridge University Press, 2007) and, with Scott Mainwaring, *Democracies and Dictatorships in Latin America: Emergence, Survival, and Fall* (Cambridge University Press, 2004).

JORGE PÉREZ-LÓPEZ is an international economist. He was formerly executive director of the Fair Labor Association and an official with the Bureau of International Labor Affairs, U.S. Department of Labor. He is the author of *Cuba's Second Economy: From Behind the Scenes to Center Stage* (Transaction Publishers, 1995) and coauthor with Sergio Diaz-Briquets of *Conquering Nature: The Environmental Legacy of Socialism in Cuba* (University of Pittsburgh Press, 2000) and *Corruption in Cuba: Castro and Beyond* (University of Texas Press, 2006). His most recent book, coauthored with Carmelo Mesa-Lago, is *Cuba Under Raúl Castro: Assessing the Reforms* (Lynne Rienner Publishers, 2013). He received a PhD in economics from the State University of New York at Albany.

TANYA L. SAUNDERS is associate professor at the Center for Latin American Studies, University of Florida. She is interested in the ways in which the African diaspora throughout the Americas uses the arts as a central tool for social change. As a 2011–2012 Fulbright scholar to Brazil, she began work on her current project, which analyzes urban arts–based social movements and grassroots-based urban alternative education movements in Brazil. Dr. Saunders holds a PhD in sociology from the University of Michigan, Ann Arbor, and a Master's in international development policy from the Gerald R. Ford School of Public Policy. She is author of *Cuban Underground Hip Hop: Black Thoughts, Black Revolution, Black Modernity* (University of Texas Press, 2015).

MATÍAS TRAVIESO-DÍAZ retired in March 2015 as a partner in Pillsbury Winthrop Shaw Pittman LLP, an international law firm with offices in Washington, DC and other U.S. and foreign locations. He holds a PhD in electrical engineering (Ohio State University, 1971) as well as a J.D. (Columbia Law School, 1976). In addition to his numerous papers on matters relating to Cuba's transition to a free-market democratic society, His book *The Laws and Legal System of a Free-Market Cuba: A Prospectus for Business* (Quorum Books, 1996), focuses on the changes that will be required in Cuba's legal system during its free-market transition. He was also coeditor of *Perspectives on Cuban Economic Reforms* (Arizona State University Press, 1998).

JAVIER VAZQUEZ D'ELIA earned his PhD at the University of Pittsburgh. He has taught at numerous universities and is coordinating editor of *Panoramas,* the online magazine of the Center for Latin American Studies. He specializes in comparative politics and political theory, with interests in the politics of social policy reform, state formation, democratic governance, and comparative methodology.

ALAN WEST-DURÁN was born in Cuba and grew up in Puerto Rico. He is the author of two books of poems, *Dar nombres a la lluvia/Finding Voices in the Rain,* which won the Latino Literature Prize for Poetry (1996), and *El tejido de Asterión o las máscaras del logos* (2000); as well as a books of essays *Tropics of History: Cuba Imagined* (1997). West-Durán edited African *Caribbeans: A Reference Guide* (2003) and *Latino and Latina Writers* (2004), which includes over 60 full-length essays on Latino/a authors of the United States. He is editor in chief of the 2011 two-volume reference work *Cuba.* He is currently writing a history of Cuba through its culture. West-Durán's essays on Cuban music have appeared in the *Journal of Popular Music Studies, the Latin American Music Review, The Michigan Quarterly Review, Encuentro de Cultura Cubana, La Gaceta, Temas,* and *Hopscotch.* He has translated Alejo Carpentier's *La música en Cuba* (2001), Rosario Ferré's *Language Duel/Duelo de lenguaje* (2002), Nelly Richard's *Cultural Residues* (2004), and Luisa Capetillo's *Mi Opinión Sobre Los Derechos de la Mujer* (2005). Professor West-Durán teaches in the Department of Languages, Literatures and Cultures at Northeastern University, where he is the director of the LLACS (Latino/a, Latin American and Caribbean Studies) Program.

YU XIAO is a PhD candidate in political science at the University of Pittsburgh. She received her BPhil in philosophy from Peking University in 2008 and her MA in comparative politics from New York University in 2010. She is interested in comparative political economy in authoritarian regimes, with a regional focus on China and Latin America, and China–Latin America relations. In her dissertation, she studies why some authoritarian regimes implement economic decentralization policies while others pursue economic centralization policies. She analyzes this question using a game-theoretical model and compares two party-based authoritarian systems, China under CPC and Mexico under PRI. In addition, she has also published work on China–Latin America relations.

INDEX

accountability, 7, 24, 44, 136, 138–41, 144, 145, 148, 149, 152, 153, 192, 377; proxy accountability, 138, 139
acopio. See procurement
administrative measures, 22
Afro-Cuban. *See* race
Agrarian Reform Law, 11, 118
agricultural cooperatives, 12, 18, 215. *See* cooperatives
agriculture, 4, 6, 8, 10, 11, 12, 18, 20, 21, 23, 25, 31, 32, 48, 49, 50, 51, 60, 64, 65, 108, 118, 123, 213, 230, 376
Albania, 272, 273
Angola, 222, 315, 370
ANPP. *See* National Assembly of People's Power
anticorruption. *See* corruption
Argentina, 44, 57, 58, 71, 75, 216, 217, 228, 231, 235, 249, 252, 253, 259, 260, 265
Artemesia, 177
artivism, 10, 35, 343–64, 371, 381
arts, 2, 19, 343, 344, 348, 350, 351, 352, 356, 358, 359, 361, 362, 364, 371

Balkans, 274, 275, 284
Batista, Fulgencio, 7, 11, 159, 161, 165, 193, 323
bilateral investment treaties (BITs), 95–97

biopolitics, 304, 319
blacks. *See* race
blockade, 29, 30, 126, 148, 372. *See* sanctions
Bolivia, 44, 45, 51, 201, 216, 217, 228, 231, 248, 253, 255, 256, 260, 265, 370
Brazil, 9, 27, 48, 51, 57, 58, 75, 87, 157, 222, 224, 228, 231, 235, 249, 252, 253, 258, 263, 265, 305, 314, 315, 326, 327, 328, 382
Bulgaria, 15, 152, 272, 276, 277, 279, 281, 283, 284, 285
Bulgarian Communist Party, 138
bureaucracy, 62, 69, 70, 94, 104, 110, 143, 145, 161, 165, 169, 170, 177, 178, 180, 261, 264, 374

CADECA. *See* Casas de Cambio
cadres, 4, 52, 160, 165, 170, 173, 176
Canada, 27, 102, 118, 220, 382
capitalism, 8, 34, 51, 67, 93, 171, 172, 178, 179, 306, 311, 312, 316, 317, 319, 323, 343, 347, 348, 350, 362, 372, 383
Caribbean, 4, 10, 13, 78, 86, 87, 102, 301, 303, 305, 327, 343, 346, 347, 353
Carpentier, Alejo, 13, 321
Cartas a la Dirección. See letters to the editor

Casa de las Américas, 13, 299, 317, 321

Casas de Cambio, 17

cash transfers, 229, 256, 258

Castro, Fidel, 2, 7, 11, 12, 14, 15, 19, 33, 34, 35, 47, 48, 85, 146, 147, 159, 160, 161, 163, 166, 168, 169, 170, 172, 173, 212, 244, 288, 301, 311, 349, 368, 369, 372, 373, 376, 377, 383

Castro, Raúl, 1, 2, 5, 21, 25, 28, 33, 41, 42, 47, 48, 49, 51, 52, 108, 124, 135, 136, 140, 146, 147, 152, 161, 163, 164, 170, 171, 173, 174, 211, 212, 221, 227, 230, 233, 235, 238, 288, 301, 314, 330, 336, 368, 369, 370, 372, 373, 376

Catholic church, 14. *See also* church

censorship, 13, 325, 352, 354, 364

Central and Eastern Europe (CEE), 34, 117, 118, 271–91, 375. *See also individual countries*

central government, 71, 88, 91, 105, 137, 138, 218, 229, 232, 235

centrally planned economy, 88, 177, 274, 275, 280

Chile, 192, 193, 195, 197, 200, 201, 204, 216, 217, 224, 228, 233, 249, 252, 253, 257, 265

China, 8, 24, 26, 27, 34, 45, 48, 62, 63, 71, 85–95, 105–10, 119, 138, 139, 140, 152, 153, 157, 160, 161, 167–72, 175, 176, 211, 217, 218, 219, 225, 226, 229, 231–37, 245, 271, 327, 372, 374, 376, 377, 378, 382, 383

Chinese Communist Party (CCP) *or* Communist Party of China (CPC), 24, 89, 92, 95, 167, 168, 169, 170, 178; Central Committee, 89, 92

church, 278, 303

citizen complaints, 136, 138, 139, 140, 141, 148, 152, 377

citizenship, 23, 25, 246, 251, 299, 302, 305, 308, 316, 318

civil religion, 309, 310

civil society, 25, 32, 71, 163, 282, 283, 289, 299, 312, 316, 317, 325, 344, 345, 350, 351, 366, 379

claims resolution program, 119, 122

Clash of Civilizations, 277

class, 19, 59, 60, 161, 162, 167, 178, 179, 180

Cold War, 63, 273, 382

Colombia, 13, 86, 87, 192, 195, 196, 200, 216, 249, 253, 256, 257, 258, 265

colonialism, 58, 59, 60, 62, 68, 70, 73, 76, 196, 304, 306, 307, 309, 312, 314, 373

commodities, 11, 20, 21, 28, 65, 66, 311, 312, 313, 334

communism, 8, 11, 16, 62, 63, 135–41, 148, 149, 152, 153, 162, 163, 166, 168, 169, 172, 173, 179, 204, 245, 271, 272, 273, 275, 277, 278, 281–84, 288, 289, 290, 306, 309, 311, 312, 316, 317, 368, 369, 371, 372, 379

competitive regimes, 192, 193, 198, 199, 200, 201, 206

constitution, 15, 21, 90, 97, 161, 163, 167, 171, 174, 258, 284, 318

cooperatives, 9, 11, 18, 22, 23, 50, 108, 123, 219, 225, 235, 237, 263

corruption, 22, 69, 138, 176, 177, 202, 204, 333, 377; anticorruption, 139, 170, 175

Cortázar, Julio, 13

Costa Rica, 10, 87, 192, 193, 195, 196, 197, 201, 216, 217, 224, 228, 235, 236, 249, 253, 258, 265

Council for Mutual Economic Assistance (CMEA or COMECON), 14

Council of Ministers, 87, 100, 164, 224

courts, 69, 120, 139, 201, 202, 203, 204, 256

Cuban Communist Party (*Partido Comunista de Cuba*, PCC), 7, 9, 15, 21, 24, 25, 34, 48, 98, 100, 142, 146, 157–81, 202, 301, 377; Central Committee, 7, 159,

160, 162, 163, 164, 175, 301; Fifth Party
Congress, 21; First Party Congress, 15,
160, 169; Fourth Party Congress, 177;
Seventh Party Congress, 25, 26, 52, 158,
165, 173, 174; Sixth Party Congress, 9,
21, 25, 48, 50, 98, 140, 158, 162, 164, 165,
172, 173, 177, 181, 212
Cuban Workers' Central (CTC), 70, 71,
374
cult of personality, 170, 179. *See also*
personality
Cultural Revolution, 170
culture, 3, 8, 12, 13, 19, 20, 42, 45, 47, 48, 58,
59, 62, 77, 173, 203, 277, 288, 289, 299,
302, 306, 307, 308, 309, 314, 318, 321–28,
332, 336, 337, 342–55, 358, 362–66, 371,
373, 379, 380, 381, 382, 383
currency, 4, 6, 15, 17, 33, 49, 57, 64–67, 70,
72, 90, 96, 97, 107, 108, 119, 150, 151, 213,
221, 233, 237, 306, 315, 330, 348, 376.
See also pesos

Damas de Blanco, 322, 324, 336
decentralization, 15, 19, 105, 106, 108, 110,
140, 217, 235. *See also* devolution
del Risco, Enrique, 322
democracy, 3, 7, 8, 16, 24, 34, 35, 48, 139,
158, 167, 170, 173, 174, 192–206, 264,
272–91, 304, 308, 316, 317, 342, 343,
346, 347, 350, 352, 369, 371, 372, 376,
377, 379, 380, 381
democratic centralism, 162, 167
democratic praxis, 342, 343, 347
democratization, 170, 175, 176, 180, 192,
194, 195, 196, 200, 201, 204, 336, 342,
346, 379
demography, 4, 67, 68, 77, 246, 251, 262,
374; demographic dividend, 67, 68
Deng, Xiaoping, 88, 89, 90, 92, 93, 95, 106,
110, 170, 171, 172, 178

deregulation, 43
devolution, 160, 177. *See also* decentralization
diaspora, 88, 93, 94, 99, 101, 102, 109, 110,
322, 374, 376; diaspora investment, 88,
93, 94, 101, 109, 110
Díaz-Canel, Miguel, 33, 383
dictatorship, 60, 137, 138, 158, 165, 193, 197,
198, 200, 201, 204, 257, 258, 263, 279,
281, 311, 323
discursive violence, 335
disjunctures, 247, 250
domestic violence, 35, 322–26, 329, 330,
332, 380; domestic gender-based
violence, 323, 325

East Asia, 45, 55, 56, 58, 60, 63, 68, 75
Eastern Europe, 7, 8, 35, 51, 123, 140, 141,
172, 181, 264, 278, 281, 282, 284, 288,
289, 290, 316, 317, 375, 379, 380, 382,
383. *See also* Central and Eastern
Europe (CEE)
economic and social development
guidelines, 9, 21, 24, 25, 26, 48, 98, 99,
100, 162, 172, 176, 181. *See also* Cuban
Communist Party
economic crisis, 9, 17, 21, 49, 87, 108, 180,
212, 220, 226, 231, 233, 344
economic diversification, 11, 88
economic growth, 4, 8, 10, 15, 28, 34, 41,
42, 44, 55, 56, 58, 60–68, 70–73, 77, 78,
85–88, 108, 109, 110, 200, 230, 231, 233,
261, 279, 286, 315, 373, 374, 375, 379,
384
economic interests, 59, 70, 71, 78
economic model, 2, 8, 11, 22, 25, 35, 44, 46,
47, 51, 52, 164, 168, 299, 330, 369, 383
economic policy, 1, 11, 16, 21, 34, 41, 43, 45,
46, 78, 95, 165
Ecuador, 222, 248, 253, 255, 256, 260, 265

education, 3–6, 12, 17, 20, 41, 43, 48, 58, 59,
  60, 62, 68, 72, 73, 78, 98, 99, 226, 231,
  306, 309, 313, 318, 346, 360, 362, 373,
  374. *See also* literacy
educational attainment, 58, 59, 72, 73, 75,
  76, 77
elites, 203, 261, 282, 283, 284, 290, 307, 346,
  381
embargo, 20, 21, 29, 30, 32, 46, 52, 55, 64,
  72, 102, 117, 126, 157, 323, 342, 369, 372,
  374, 375. *See also* sanctions
employment, 4, 9, 17, 22, 33, 47, 48, 49, 50,
  52, 70, 91, 93, 99, 100, 106, 107, 211, 216,
  217, 250, 251, 252, 259, 262, 266, 306,
  313, 314, 330, 369, 376. *See also* self-
  employment
equality, 25, 254, 299, 300, 309, 311, 312,
  314, 316, 317, 362, 373, 380. *See also*
  gender: equality; gender: inequality;
  income inequality
equity, 91, 93, 119, 124, 234, 236, 318, 378;
  job equity, 318
Estado de SATS, 324
Ethiopia, 370
ethnic, 58, 59, 61, 62, 77, 198, 199, 225, 277,
  288, 307, 319, 335, 373
European Union (EU), 104, 272, 275,
  276, 277, 279, 280, 284, 286, 290, 379;
  exchange rates, 43, 64, 72
exile, 126, 179, 289, 322, 379
export processing zones, 19, 100
exports, 14, 15, 16, 19, 20, 27, 28, 29, 43, 48,
  55, 57, 58, 59, 63–66, 70, 71, 72, 75–78,
  90, 92, 98, 99, 100, 106, 198, 199, 200,
  203, 221, 230, 233, 255
expropriation, 97, 98, 117–21, 123, 124, 125;
  expropriation claims, 117, 118, 119, 121,
  123, 124, 125, 126

family doctors, 222
Fariñas, Guillermo, 324
farmers, 6, 12, 18, 22, 23, 50, 51, 60, 123, 212,
  213, 236
farms, 11, 12, 18, 23, 108
feminism, 360, 361, 371
feminist, 322, 343, 344, 349, 355, 356, 357,
  358, 360, 361, 362, 363, 365, 366
first secretary, 15, 161, 162, 163, 165, 166, 172,
  174, 175
fiscal discipline, 42
foreign (direct) investment, 2, 7, 14, 18, 19,
  24, 27, 34, 43, 85, 86, 87, 88–110, 177,
  263, 374, 376; foreign investment law,
  2, 7, 18, 24, 87, 98, 99, 100, 102, 103, 107,
  108, 376; foreign investors, 10, 18, 21, 24,
  64, 86, 90, 94, 95, 96, 97, 99, 102, 103,
  104, 105, 107, 109, 110, 283
future, 1, 2, 7, 8, 9, 10, 13, 21, 26, 27, 31, 34,
  47, 52, 65, 71, 72, 86, 92, 109, 119, 122,
  165, 179, 192, 193, 200, 203, 232, 244,
  246, 271, 288, 289, 291, 300, 301, 368,
  375, 381, 382, 383

García Márquez, Gabriel, 13
gender, 2, 61, 216, 225, 234, 236, 250, 311,
  314, 322, 323, 324, 325, 328, 329, 331,
  332, 336, 344, 348, 350, 357, 362, 366,
  378, 380; equality, 216, 234, 236, 378,
  380; inequality, 216, 322, 324, 325, 329,
  332, 344, 350, 366
general will, 309, 310, 311, 312
geography, 58, 75, 76, 278, 371, 376
governance, 60, 73, 106, 135, 141, 152, 157,
  161, 162, 168, 169, 172, 176, 177, 178, 180,
  273, 286, 368
Granma, 7, 135, 136, 137, 138, 141–49, 152,
  153, 221, 223, 224, 377
Guevara, Che, 9, 11, 12

health, 3–7, 14, 16, 17, 20, 27, 30, 31, 34, 41, 43, 48, 58, 59, 60, 69, 72, 73, 75, 76, 77, 99, 211, 213, 216, 217, 219–25, 227, 230, 232–37, 252, 253, 256–59, 261, 262, 263, 266, 267, 289, 306, 311, 313, 315, 363, 369, 373, 374, 378

health care, 4, 6, 7, 34, 58, 60, 69, 73, 75, 77, 211, 213, 216, 217, 219, 221, 224, 225, 227, 230, 232–37, 252, 253, 256–59, 261, 262, 263, 266, 267, 369, 373, 378

health insurance, 211

hip-hop, 344, 345, 348–59, 361, 362, 365, 366, 381

homophobia, 306, 325, 327, 328, 345, 350

homosexuality, 328

homosexuals, 13

housing, 4, 10, 23, 50, 140, 213, 231, 301, 326, 334

human capital, 55, 72, 73, 75, 78, 256

human rights, 16, 30

Hungary, 15, 119, 193, 272, 274, 276, 277, 281–85, 289, 327

identity, 25, 122, 161, 299, 307, 314, 318, 347–50, 353, 358, 361, 365, 380, 383

ideology, 8, 12, 19, 20, 45, 51, 158–63, 166–74, 177–80, 261, 262, 271, 278, 288, 305, 308, 312, 316, 319, 331, 343–48, 356, 358, 363, 366, 372, 375, 376, 379

immunization, 219, 220, 305, 315

imperialism, 171, 306

import substitution, 11, 48, 66, 70, 71, 99, 100

income inequality, 46, 55–59, 66, 67, 72, 73, 77, 373

India, 45, 87

industrial policies, 11

inequality, 217, 254, 258, 267, 312, 315, 345, 347, 348. *See also* equality; gender; income inequality; race

infant mortality, 5, 16, 34, 57, 73, 75, 220, 223, 224, 236, 378

inflation, 42, 198, 213, 216, 218

infrastructure, 3, 27, 43, 48, 60, 86, 93, 94, 100, 109, 142, 160, 220, 221, 224, 236, 246, 250, 256, 262, 315, 376

initial conditions, 55, 56, 58, 59, 72, 75–78, 373

institutionalization, 14, 160, 162, 166, 167, 169, 170, 171, 174, 180, 202, 203, 205

interest rates, 43, 44, 57

internal conflict, 278, 288

international context, 62, 76, 373

International Monetary Fund (IMF), 42, 45

Japan, 26, 58, 59, 60, 68, 70, 71, 73, 76

Jiang, Zemin, 92

joint venture, 14, 18, 21, 89, 90, 91, 95–98, 100, 107, 108, 122, 374

Kuomintang. *See* Taiwan

labor, 5, 6, 13, 22, 50, 56, 57, 63, 64, 66, 67, 70, 71, 72, 75, 76, 77, 100, 104, 106, 107, 108, 110, 140, 178, 200, 203, 212, 215, 216, 218, 219, 224, 225, 233, 235, 236, 250, 252, 266, 305, 311, 374

land, 4, 6, 10, 11, 12, 18, 22, 23, 33, 50, 51, 57, 60, 63, 66, 67, 70, 72, 78, 92, 93, 123

Latin America, 4, 7, 8, 11, 16, 34, 44–47, 51, 56, 58, 66, 69, 71, 72, 75, 76, 86, 87, 192–97, 199, 200, 203–6, 211, 212, 214, 216, 217, 219, 220, 224, 228, 230, 231, 233, 234, 235, 237, 244, 245, 247, 252, 254, 261, 262, 264, 265, 301, 306, 315, 326, 343, 346, 347, 372, 376, 378, 379, 383. *See also individual countries*

law, 11, 14, 18, 23, 24, 29, 30, 32, 35, 50, 69, 89–91, 96–100, 106, 107, 118, 119, 121, 125, 126, 167, 170, 175, 176, 177, 180, 202;

law (*cont.*), 213, 218, 284, 310, 318, 324, 330, 369, 374, 384; 1979 Law on Joint Ventures (China), 89, 90, 91; 1982 Constitution (China), 89, 90; 1982 Joint Venture Law (Cuba), 96; 1986 Provisions to Encourage Foreign Investment (China), 89, 90; 1992 Amendments to the Joint Venture Law (China), 89; 1995 Foreign Investment Law (Cuba), 98, 99; 2014 Foreign Investment Law (Cuba), 99, 107

leadership, 5, 6, 7, 10, 16, 19, 21, 25, 42, 46, 47, 49, 52, 53, 93, 94, 95, 109, 110, 136, 141, 152, 153, 163, 164, 165, 170, 174, 175, 177, 178, 179, 260, 282, 289, 305, 306, 343, 344, 350, 356, 369, 370, 372, 377, 379

legitimacy, 47, 140, 146, 157, 159, 245, 247, 273, 290, 316

Lenin, 161, 172

Leninism, 62, 158, 164, 166, 167, 168, 169, 170, 175, 176, 178, 179, 180

letters to the editor, 142; *Cartas a la Dirección*, 135, 137, 141, 143–49, 151, 152, 153

liberalization, 25, 43, 92, 95, 106, 108, 140, 344, 376

life expectancy, 16, 230

lineamientos. See economic and social development guidelines

literacy, 4, 12, 16, 73, 346, 369

local government, 92, 137, 138, 234, 235

Machado Ventura, José Ramón, 163

Maduro, Nicolás, 28

Malaysia, 27

manufacturing, 8, 49, 72, 75, 86, 198, 200

Mao, Zedong, 85, 160, 170, 172, 217

Mariel, 2, 7, 9, 27, 33, 47, 48, 96, 100, 103, 373, 374. *See also* special development zones

Mariel exodus, 334, 335, 336

market-oriented reform, 41, 43, 86, 110, 252, 264, 371

Martí, José, 161, 162, 163, 166, 172, 308, 309, 311

Marxism, 19, 158, 160, 161, 162, 166, 167, 168, 171–74, 177–81, 306, 307, 316, 317, 323

Marxism-Leninism, 158, 160, 161, 162, 166, 167, 171–74, 177, 179, 377

Mayabeque, 177

Mexico, 24, 26, 30, 57, 58, 75, 102, 201, 202, 204, 216, 249, 252, 253, 256, 257, 258, 265

migration, 23, 250, 258, 335, 336

Mikhailov, Stoian, 138

military, 16, 58, 59, 62, 63, 71, 73, 158, 160, 161, 163, 169, 171, 197, 200, 201, 233, 258, 263, 285, 305, 313, 323, 374, 384

mineral, 58, 59, 64, 65, 66, 198, 199, 200, 203

Murillo, Marino, 87, 224

nation, 3, 8, 11, 16, 24, 26, 31, 58, 86, 87, 97, 102, 110, 161, 162, 163, 166, 179, 276, 306, 307, 313, 318, 323, 327, 348, 363, 366; *nación*, 307

National Assembly of People's Power (Asamblea Nacional del Poder Popular, ANPP), 5, 15, 18, 28, 87, 97, 98, 158, 176, 177, 218

National People's Congress (NPC), 89, 90, 91

nationalism, 47, 62, 161, 162, 163, 166, 171, 172, 179, 290, 305, 307, 308, 309, 312, 314, 372

nationalization, 4, 8, 10, 11, 12, 13, 14, 30, 95, 369

natural resources. *See* resources

neocolonial, 323

New Era, 168, 178

nonstructural changes, 22

North Korea, 63

Obama, Barack, 1, 2, 28, 29, 32, 33, 52, 173, 231, 342, 370
oil, 6, 11, 14, 15, 17, 20, 26, 27, 28, 32, 65, 66, 86, 103, 212
oligarchic, 198, 283
Organization of American States, 11, 290

paladares, 49, 50, 326
Paris Club, 26
party. *See* Cuban Communist Party
Party Congress. *See* Cuban Communist Party
party-state, 140, 158, 159, 166, 174, 175, 181, 316
path dependence, 193, 200, 201, 206, 246
patria, 307
Payá, Oswaldo, 324
pay-as-you-go (PAYG), 216, 217, 218, 231, 232, 236, 378
PCC. *See* Cuban Communist Party
pension systems, 6, 34, 68, 212–19, 226, 228, 229, 231–37, 252, 253, 255–59, 262, 265, 266, 267, 315, 378
personality, 158, 159, 160, 169, 178, 330, 334
personality cult, 160, 170. *See also* cult of personality
Peru, 86, 87, 195, 216, 248, 253, 255, 256, 265
pesos: convertible (CUC), 6, 9, 67, 101, 107, 306, 315, 329; nonconvertible (CUP), 6, 67, 101, 107, 213, 329. *See also* currency
Piñera, Virgilio, 13
poetics, 300
poetry, 13, 347, 348
Poland, 15, 119, 193, 272, 274, 276, 277, 278, 281, 283–86, 289, 327
Politburo (Political Bureau), 15, 161–64, 166, 174, 175, 301
political parties, 34, 193, 201, 202, 204, 247, 281, 288, 377

political reforms, 24, 52, 59, 158, 159, 165, 175, 177, 180, 181, 318, 383
political rights, 3, 192, 194, 204, 273
politics, 1, 2, 3, 7, 11, 12, 45, 159, 162, 167, 169, 173, 179, 180, 192, 193, 201, 202, 203, 255, 282, 300, 304, 311, 312, 313, 318, 346, 347, 348, 361, 370, 371, 377, 381, 382
Pollán, Laura, 324
populism, 45, 291
postcommunist, 204, 273, 277, 278, 279, 281, 282, 283, 284, 286, 288, 289, 371, 379
postrevolutionary, 166, 169, 173, 245, 306
poverty, 44, 46, 218, 219, 226–29, 234, 237, 256, 257, 266, 303, 315, 331, 332
preservationism, 173, 175
private sector, 4, 9, 13, 22, 29, 43, 49, 50, 88, 97, 177, 181, 212, 215, 222, 258, 264, 327
privatization, 8, 33, 43, 44, 108, 118, 233, 253, 256, 257, 258, 262, 265, 273, 274, 275, 280, 283
procurement, 376
procurement system, 18; *acopio*, 18, 25
property rights, 21, 34, 43, 60, 69, 104, 106, 118, 136, 139, 376, 377, 384
public expenditure, 43
Putin, 138, 139, 282

race, 2, 3, 5, 10, 19, 20, 35, 56, 61, 77, 299–312, 314–17, 319, 329, 343, 348, 365, 374, 376, 380, 382; Afro-Cuban, 13, 25, 226, 308, 309, 315, 329, 335, 369; blacks, 5, 10, 19, 25, 61, 300, 301, 302, 305, 307, 315, 316, 317; racial contract, 299, 302–305, 307, 308, 319; racial inequality, 56, 61, 77, 374, 376; racism, 5, 19, 20, 25, 301, 302, 306, 308, 309, 311, 313, 314, 316–19, 325, 345, 348, 350, 354, 362, 371
reform. *See* market-oriented reform; political reforms

reform and opening-up policies, 88–93, 106, 109, 110

regime change, 200, 372. *See also* democracy

regime legacy, 193, 195–98, 200–204, 206

religion, 21, 196, 277, 278, 289, 302, 307, 354, 382. *See also* Catholic church; church

remittances, 5, 17, 19, 25, 29, 31, 56, 61, 67, 72, 213, 234, 306, 315, 333. *See also* diaspora

resource curse, 64, 65, 66; Dutch Disease, 64, 65

resources, 4, 11, 18, 34, 43, 58, 59, 64, 77, 78, 86, 88, 106, 107, 109, 142, 179, 212, 219, 220, 224, 226, 227, 231, 233, 236, 237, 238, 254, 261, 262, 264, 283, 359, 361; natural resources, 18, 59, 64, 66, 76, 102, 374

responsiveness, 138, 139, 148, 149, 153, 175, 179

restitution, 122; direct restitution, 122, 123

revolution, 4, 5, 7, 8, 10–16, 19, 23, 25, 26, 33, 47, 48, 49, 60, 61, 67, 69, 73, 117, 122, 142, 145–47, 153, 157, 159–61, 165–71, 174, 178–80, 193, 212, 219, 226, 230, 233, 253, 281, 282, 300, 301, 302, 305, 306, 309, 311, 312, 316, 317, 323–26, 331, 334, 336, 344–49, 352, 362, 369–72, 375, 377, 383; Bolshevik Revolution, 309

Revolutionary Offensive, 8

Rodríguez, José Mario, 13

Romania, 15, 272, 276, 277, 278, 279, 281, 283, 289

Rousseau, 299, 309, 310, 311, 312

rule of law, 69, 106, 170, 178, 180, 192, 202, 206, 273, 374

Russia, 26, 27, 71, 87, 138, 139, 271, 273, 276, 282, 285, 290, 291, 379, 383. *See also* Soviet Union

Sánchez, Yoani, 324

sanctions, 20, 30, 138, 139, 290, 372; economic, 11, 28. *See also* blockade; embargo

self-employment, 9, 17, 22, 23, 49, 50, 108, 237, 330, 332, 376; self-employed, 17, 22, 49, 50, 151, 212, 215, 218, 236, 330, 369

semidemocratic, 193, 197, 198, 202. *See also* democracy

settlement, 97, 118, 119, 120, 121, 124, 125, 375

shortages, 5, 17, 91, 136, 142, 143, 145, 149, 150, 151, 220, 313, 336

Simo, Ana María, 13

sin prisa, pero sin pausa, 25, 51

single-party systems, 85, 137, 141, 145, 152, 153, 193, 323

slavery, 302, 305, 308, 313, 314

Slovakia, 272, 276, 277, 284, 285

soap opera (*telenovela*), 325–33, 335, 336, 337

social assistance, 211, 226–30, 233, 234, 236, 237, 248–50, 253, 254, 256–59, 264, 265, 266, 315, 378

social contract, 34, 136, 139, 140, 141, 152, 153, 319, 377

social insurance, 14, 211, 212, 216, 218, 219, 224, 234, 235, 249, 256, 257, 258, 259, 266, 267

social policies, 21, 34, 245, 256, 264, 331, 347

social protection, 212, 213, 230, 236, 244–58, 261, 262, 264–67, 377

social risks, 246, 247, 250

social security, 3, 18, 100, 211, 212, 213, 217, 218, 230–38, 246, 250, 252, 256, 266, 267, 315, 378

social welfare, 6, 34, 136, 245, 264, 378, 383

socialism, 8, 10, 11, 14, 15, 16, 19, 24, 33, 34, 46, 47, 48, 87, 88, 91, 92, 93, 97, 108, 137, 140, 153, 161, 162, 165, 167, 168, 169, 170, 172, 173, 178, 180, 181, 212, 220, 230, 233, 238, 299, 301, 306–309, 311, 312, 313, 316, 317, 319, 324, 327, 330, 334, 336, 343, 345, 348, 363, 369, 377, 381, 382

socialist bloc, 14, 16, 87, 212, 220, 230, 233

socialist social contract, 137, 140, 153

society, 2, 3, 8, 25, 35, 41, 60, 66, 67, 70, 71, 137, 143, 161, 162, 163, 168, 169, 178, 179, 180, 204, 244, 246, 247, 253, 264, 266, 273, 277, 283, 289, 290, 301, 302, 304, 305, 306, 307, 309–12, 314, 316–19, 323, 324, 325, 328, 331, 332, 333, 335, 336, 342–47, 350, 354, 358, 366, 368-71, 376, 380, 381, 382

South Korea, 8, 34, 55–64, 66–78, 373, 374, 376

Southeastern Europe, 274, 276, 280

Southern Tour, 92, 95, See Deng, Xiaoping

Soviet Union (USSR), 1, 8, 14, 15, 16, 24, 26, 34, 46, 49, 51, 87, 108, 119, 138, 141, 152, 157, 160, 169, 172, 212, 220, 233, 272, 273, 274, 276, 290, 306, 315, 316, 348, 377, 382, 383

Spain, 14, 27, 48, 76, 102, 118, 119, 277

special development zones (zonas especiales de desarrollo, ZED), 2, 7, 24, 33, 48, 49, 96, 100, 103, 104, 374; ZED Mariel (ZEDM), 2, 7, 24, 96, 97, 100, 101, 103, 104, 107, 374

special economic zones (SEZs), 92–95, 99, 105, 109, 374

Special Period in Time of Peace, 6, 9, 10, 16, 19, 20, 24, 28, 45, 67, 143, 148, 212, 302, 308, 348

Stalin, Joseph, 160; Stalinism, 141, 160, 165, 169, 170, 179, 180

state capacity, 56, 58, 59, 68, 69, 71, 76, 77, 374

state-owned enterprises, 22, 33, 44, 51, 93, 108, 122, 124, 211, 212, 213, 217

statist violence, 321, 323, 325, 327, 329, 331–35, 337, 339, 341

structural reforms, 25, 108, 217, 238

sugar, 11, 14, 15, 27, 60, 65, 140, 303

Taiwan, 8, 34, 55–78, 92, 94, 373, 374, 376; Kuomintang, 61, 63, 70

tax code, 18, 23, 108

taxes, 17, 18, 23, 34, 43, 49, 60, 67, 72, 89, 92, 93, 96, 99, 100, 101, 108, 124, 164, 177, 213, 237, 250, 254, 257, 262, 268, 378

telenovela. See soap opera

tourism, 3, 4, 6, 9, 14, 15, 21, 27, 32, 50, 56, 71, 72, 104, 306, 315, 333, 376

trade, 7, 8, 10, 14, 15, 20, 21, 29, 30, 31, 32, 43, 44, 47, 49, 50, 55, 57, 64, 71, 72, 76, 88, 92, 97, 103, 106, 108, 110, 117, 126, 145, 212, 230, 231, 369, 373, 374, 383

trading partner, 20, 27

Trump, Donald, 1, 35, 52, 110, 174, 368, 370, 383, 384

trust, 138, 329

U.S. claimants, 120–25

U.S.-Cuba relations, 1, 21, 173, 342, 350, 370

Unidades Militares de Ayuda a la Producción, 13

United States, 1, 2, 3, 5, 7, 11, 19, 20, 21, 26, 28–35, 42, 45–47, 51, 52, 55, 57, 60, 61, 63, 64, 72, 73, 97, 101, 102, 107, 110, 117, 126, 139, 148, 157–59, 168, 173, 174, 181, 204, 206, 237, 244, 264, 272, 290, 301, 313, 314, 323, 324, 334, 335, 342, 343, 348, 349, 352, 353, 355, 358, 368, 369, 370, 372, 374–76, 378–80, 382–84

urban-rural gap, 219

Uruguay, 11, 13, 192, 193, 195, 197, 200, 201,
204, 214, 216, 217, 228, 231, 235, 236,
249, 252, 253, 259, 265, 378
usufruct, 22, 23, 50, 51, 236

vaccine, 31, 220
Valle, Amir, 322
Venezuela, 1, 2, 11, 20, 27, 28, 44, 45, 46, 51,
52, 53, 102, 157, 158, 192, 195, 196, 222,
230, 231, 249, 253, 258, 260, 265, 306,
315, 382, 383
Vietnam, 8, 25, 34, 46, 47, 87, 109, 119, 160,
165, 176, 180, 211, 218, 219, 225, 229,
232–37, 245, 327, 374, 376, 377, 378,
383, 384
Vietnamese Communist Party, 165
violence, 3, 10, 35, 204, 311, 319, 321–24, 329,
331–37, 357, 362
vulnerable groups, 211, 226, 378

Washington Consensus, 41–45, 53, 253,
255
welfare systems, 7, 245, 246, 250, 251, 254,
255, 258, 260, 267
women, 5, 6, 10, 25, 68, 212, 214, 215, 218,
219, 223, 224, 226, 234, 301, 322, 323,
324, 329–34, 343, 344, 349, 350, 352,
355–63, 365, 366, 369, 381. *See also*
gender
World Bank, 41, 42, 44, 45, 57, 69, 201
World Trade Organization (WTO), 88, 89

Yugoslavia, 272, 273, 278

zonas francas y parques industriales, 19. *See
also* export processing zones